The
Islamic
World

Past and Present

The Islamic World

Past and Present

VOLUME 3

John L. Esposito, *Editor in Chief*

Associate Editors

Abdulaziz Sachedina

Tamara Sonn

John O. Voll

OXFORD UNIVERSITY PRESS
2004

Oxford University Press

Oxford New York

Auckland Bangkok Buenos Aires Cape Town Chennai Dar es Salaam
Delhi Hong Kong Istanbul Karachi Kolkata Kuala Lumpur Madrid Melbourne
Mexico City Mumbai Nairobi São Paulo Shanghai Taipei Tokyo Toronto

Published by Oxford University Press, Inc.
198 Madison Avenue, New York, 10016
http://www.oup.com

Developed for Oxford University Press by Visual Education Corporation, Princeton, NJ

For Oxford
PUBLISHER: Karen Day
EDITORIAL DEVELOPMENT DIRECTOR: Timothy DeWerff
EDITOR: Meera Vaidyanathan
EDITORIAL, DESIGN, AND PRODUCTION DIRECTOR: John Sollami
PROJECT EDITOR: Erica Pirrung
INTERIOR DESIGN: Maxson Crandall
COVER DESIGN: Mary Belibasakis

For Visual Education Corporation
PROJECT DIRECTORS: Jewel Moulthrop, Darryl Kestler
EDITORS: Carol Ciaston, Lauren Hauptman, Doriann Markey
ASSOCIATE EDITOR: Sarah Miller
WRITERS: Jean M. Brainard, John Haley, Kent M. Krause, Elizabeth Shostak
COPYEDITORS: Helen Castro, Maureen Pancza
ELECTRONIC PREPARATION: Fiona Shapiro
PHOTO RESEARCH: Susan Buschhorn
MAPS: Patti Isaacs, Parrot Graphics

Library of Congress Cataloging-in-Publication Data
The Islamic world : past and present / John L. Esposito, editor in chief ;
associate editors, Abdulaziz Sachedina . . . [et al.].
    p. cm.
Includes bibliographical references and index.
    ISBN 0-19-516520-9 (Hardcover 3 vol. set: alk. paper).—ISBN 0-19-517592-1
    (vol. 1 : alk. paper).—ISBN 0-19-517593-x (vol. 2 : alk. paper).—
    ISBN 0-19-517594-8 (vol. 3 : alk. paper).
  1. Islamic countries—Encyclopedias. 2. Islam—Encyclopedias.
I. Esposito, John L. II. Sachedina, Abdulaziz Abdulhussein, 1942-
  DS35.53 .I86 2004
  909'.097671'003—dc22

                                    2003019665

Chronology of the Islamic World

Chronology of the Islamic World

1130–1269	Almohad dynasty conquers North Africa and part of Spain
1171–1250	Ayyubid dynasty rules Egypt and Syria
1187	Saladin, leader of Ayyubids, defeats crusaders at Battle of Hittin and reconquers Jerusalem
1198	Philosopher Ibn Rushd, known as Averröes, dies
1218	Mongol ruler Genghis Khan sweeps across Central Asia into Iran
1250–1517	Mamluks, former slave soldiers in the Ayyubid army, establish dynasty in Egypt; extend control to Syria and western Arabia
1258	Mongols capture and destroy Baghdad, the Abbasid capital
1273	Jalal al-Din Rumi, poet and Sufi mystic, dies
ca. 1300	Osman I founds Ottoman Empire
1334–1353	The Alhambra is built in Granada, Spain
1369–1405	Mongol leader Tamerlane (Timur Lang) seizes power and reclaims former Mongol territories
1406	Historian Ibn Khaldun dies
1453	Ottoman sultan Mehmed II captures Constantinople
1492	Spanish monarchs Ferdinand and Isabella conquer Granada, driving Muslims from Spain
1501	Shah Ismail establishes Safavid empire in Iran
1516–1517	Ottomans conquer Egypt, Syria, and Islamic holy cities of Mecca and Medina
1520	Suleyman takes over as Ottoman sultan and brings the empire to peak of power and prosperity
1526	Battle of Mohacs brings Hungary under Ottoman control
1526	Mughal ruler Babur captures Delhi and establishes Mughal Empire in India
1529	Ottomans lay siege to Vienna, Austria
1556–1605	Mughal Empire in India reaches its height under the rule of Akbar I
1571	European victory at Battle of Lepanto off the coast of Greece stops Ottoman advance
1588–1629	Shah Abbas I rules Safavid Empire of Iran
ca. 1645	Mughal Shah Jahan completes Taj Mahal at Agra, India
1658–1707	Aurangzeb expands Mughal Empire through conquests; costs of military campaigns weaken the state

Chronology of the Islamic World

1699	Ottoman Empire surrenders control of Hungary to Austria
1722	Afghan rebels capture the Safavid capital of Isfahan, bringing Safavid rule to an end
1750	Religious reformer Muhammad ibn Abd al-Wahhab joins forces with tribal chief Muhammad ibn Saud; the resulting Wahhabi movement conquers and unites tribes of Arabia
1798–1801	French armies led by Napoleon Bonaparte occupy Egypt
1803	British East India Company controls Delhi, seat of the Mughal Empire
1805	Muhammad Ali becomes Ottoman governor of Egypt and attempts to turn Egypt into a modern state
1809	Muslim reformer Usman Dan Fodio defeats Hausa rulers in Nigeria; establishes caliphate of Sokoto
1816	Dutch regain control of Indonesia from British
1821	Ottoman Empire takes control of Sudan
1830	French forces invade Algeria
1836	Ahmad ibn Idris, founder of Idrisi movement, dies
1857	Hindus and Muslims rebel against British rule in India; British depose last Mughal emperor
1869	Suez Canal opened in Egypt
1881	French troops invade and gain control of Tunisia
1882	British occupy Egypt
1885	In Sudan, forces of the Mahdi conquer Khartoum; establish Mahdist state
1898	Anglo-Egyptian invasion brings an end to Mahdist state in Sudan
1908	Young Turks overthrow sultan and restore constitutional government in Ottoman Empire
1914–1918	World War I
1919–1922	Ottoman Empire collapses
1921	Reza Khan seizes power in Iran; becomes Reza Shah Pahlavi in 1925
1922	British grant independence to Egypt but maintain control of foreign affairs
1923	Mustafa Kemal (later called Atatürk) establishes Turkish Republic
1928	Hasan al-Banna establishes Muslim Brotherhood in Egypt

1932   The territories of Abd al-Aziz ibn Saud proclaimed the Kingdom of Saudi Arabia

1935   Persia renamed Iran

1938   Political writer Muhammad Iqbal, who led campaign in the Indian subcontinent for a separate Muslim state (Pakistan), dies

1939–1945   World War II

1941   Muhammad Reza Shah Pahlavi replaces Reza Shah in Iran

1945   The Arab League formed

1947   Pakistan is founded as a homeland for Indian Muslims

1948   The Jewish state of Israel is established

1952   Officers under the leadership of Gamal Abdel Nasser seize power in Egypt

1954   National Liberation Front (FLN) formed in Algeria and begins war against French rule

1962   Algerians win independence

1964   Founding of Palestine Liberation Organization (PLO)

1965   Malcolm X assassinated

1966   Sayyid Qutb, religious thinker and militant Islamic leader of the Muslim Brotherhood, is executed by Egyptian government

1967   Israeli victory in Six-Day War between Israel and Egypt, Syria, and Jordan

1973   October (Yom Kippur/Ramadan) War between Israel and Egypt and Syria

1978   Egyptian president Anwar el-Sadat and Israeli prime minister Menachem Begin sign peace agreement known as the Camp David Accords; peace treaty follows in 1979

Coup in Afghanistan brings communist government to power; former Soviet Union occupies the country in 1979

1979   Ayatollah Ruhollah Khomeini leads coalition of groups in Iranian Revolution, which overthrows the Pahlavi government and drives the shah of Iran into exile

Iranians hold a group of Americans hostage at the United States embassy in Tehran

1980   Hizbullah founded in Lebanon

1980–1988   Iran-Iraq War

1981   Muslim extremists assassinate Egyptian president Anwar el-Sadat

Chronology of the Islamic World

1987 *Palestinians launch intifadah (uprising) in protest against Israeli occupation of the West Bank and Gaza*

1988 *Benazir Bhutto becomes prime minister of Pakistan; first female head of state elected in Muslim world*

1989 *Ayatollah Ruhollah Khomeini, head of Islamic Republic of Iran, dies*

1990–1991 *Iraq invades Kuwait, setting off the Persian Gulf War; United States and allies launch Operation Desert Storm against Iraq*

1992 *Resistance fighters (the Mujahidin) in Afghanistan defeat the country's communist government after 10 years of war and begin a battle for control of the country*

1993 *World Trade Center in New York City bombed; Shaykh Umar Abd al-Rahman charged with the attack*

1994 *Taliban fundamentalists take control in Afghanistan*

In West Bank city of Hebron, Jewish settler (Baruch Goldstein) kills worshippers at Friday prayer in Mosque of the Patriarch, provoking suicide bombings by military wing of Hamas

1997 *Election of Muhammad Khatami as president of Iran opens door to greater liberalization and contact with the West*

1998 *Increasing violence in Kosovo leads to international sanctions against the Yugoslavian (Serbian) government*

2001 *September 11: Members of al-Qaeda terrorist network hijack four American airliners and attack the World Trade Center in New York City and the Pentagon in Washington, D.C., killing about 3,000 people*

2001 *United States heads a military campaign against Afghanistan to destroy the al-Qaeda network and oust the Taliban*

2003 *Charging Iraq with failure to remove weapons of mass destruction, United States leads an invasion of the country and ends Saddam Hussein's regime*

Pakistan, which came into being as a result of the partition of British India in 1947, occupies a unique position in the Muslim world. It is the only country established specifically for Muslims. Since its creation, however, the depth and extent of the country's commitment to religion has been a subject of continuous debate.

Bordering India, China, Afghanistan, and Iran, Pakistan is about twice the size of California. Its population, the second largest in the Muslim world, is estimated at 145 million. An overwhelming majority of Pakistanis are Muslim, mostly Sunni*. Christians, Hindus*, and other groups make up a small minority in the country. Several ethnic* groups are represented in Pakistan, including Punjabi, Sindhi, Pashtun, and Baloch.

The Creation of Pakistan. For almost 300 years before the British seized control of India, the Mughal Empire dominated the subcontinent. Historians attribute much of this Muslim dynasty's resilience to a policy of religious tolerance toward non-Muslims, especially India's majority Hindu population. Under colonial rule, however, Indian Muslims lost much of their political and economic power.

As Hindu and Muslim activists struggled to end foreign imperialism*, two key organizations emerged. The Hindu-dominated Indian National Congress, founded in 1885, promoted the formation of a modern secular* nation state. Concerned that Hindu nationalists* would deprive Muslims of their rights after India gained independence, members of the Western-educated Muslim elite established the All-India Muslim League in 1906. The league advocated Muslim representation in all political institutions.

By the 1930s, some Muslims had begun to reject the idea that India's Hindus would respect Muslim minority rights in a democratic nation. Poet and philosopher Muhammad Iqbal became a leading spokesperson for a separate Muslim state in northwestern India. After many unsuccessful attempts to reach a compromise with the Indian National Congress, the Muslim League, under President Mohammad Ali Jinnah, adopted and vigorously promoted Iqbal's ideas.

The league convinced Indian Muslims that a separate state would preserve the glory of Islam in their community, which gave the movement a strong religious character. Choudhary Rahmat Ali, a student at Cambridge University in England, created the term *Pakstan* (later *Pakistan*) for the proposed state by combining letters from the names of the provinces of Punjab, Kashmir, Sind, and Balochistan. The term *pak* also means "pure" in Urdu, Pakistan's national language, so Pakistan means "the land of the pure." The slogan "What does Pakistan stand for? There is no god but Allah!" became a popular rallying cry.

In August 1947, Great Britain partitioned India into two independent states based on religious affiliation. India would remain predominantly Hindu, and Pakistan would become a Muslim state with Jinnah as its first governor-general. The new Muslim nation consisted of West Pakistan, to the northwest of India, and East Pakistan, a region to the northeast of India on the Bay of Bengal. The partition plan divided the provinces of Punjab and

* **Sunni** refers to the largest branch of the Muslim community; the name derives from sunnah, the exemplary behavior of the prophet Muhammad

* **Hindu** refers to the beliefs and practices of Hinduism, an ancient religion that originated in India

* **ethnic** relating to groups of people who share a common racial, national, tribal, religious, linguistic, or cultural background

* **imperialism** extension of power and influence over another country or region

* **secular** separate from religion in human life and society; connected to everyday life

* **nationalist** one who advocates loyalty and devotion to his or her country and its independence

1

Pakistan

Benazir Bhutto won election as Pakistan's first female prime minister in 1988 and again in 1993. During her second term in office, the country experienced severe economic problems and ethnic and religious clashes. Charges of corruption against Bhutto's government contributed to its fall in 1996.

Bengal and separated West and East Pakistan by more than 1,000 miles of Indian territory.

From the beginning, relations between India and Pakistan were turbulent. A dispute over the status of Kashmir, a mountainous region in the extreme northwest corner of the subcontinent that had a Muslim majority but a Hindu ruler, resulted in war. Most of the wealthy provinces of the subcontinent remained within the borders of India, creating future economic hardships for Pakistan. Partition caused approximately 10 million people to flee from regions where new state boundaries suddenly made them a religious minority. Many Muslims moved from Hindu India to the newly created state, becoming *muhajirs*, or "immigrants." Massacres on both sides claimed the lives of a million more people.

A Shaky Start. Pakistan faced critical economic and political problems, as well as ethnic and regional concerns. The most controversial issue for the young nation, however, was religious. Conflicting visions of the role of Islam in politics deeply divided various groups. Those who held political power regarded Islam as a moral force and as a base on which national unity and loyalty could be built, but they called for a secular state with equal rights for all, regardless of religion, ethnic group, or gender. In contrast, the *ulama**
and ultra-religious groups, represented by the Jamaat-i Islami, envisioned a much closer relationship between Islam and the state. They advocated an Islamic constitution, the introduction of traditional Islamic laws, and the restoration of traditional social and religious institutions. A large segment of the population aligned itself with the country's religious leaders. In subsequent years, many Pakistani regimes* professed a commitment to Islam in order to maintain their legitimacy and popular support.

In 1949 the efforts of the *ulama* and the Jamaat-i Islami movement led to the passage of a resolution requiring Pakistan's constitution to be based

* ***ulama*** religious scholars

* **regime** government in power

on Islamic principles. The country's first constitution, approved in 1956, was basically a collection of modern secular laws for the administration of a democratic state guided by Islamic beliefs. The document designated Pakistan an Islamic republic and required the president to be Muslim. The national parliament* would have 300 members, with equal representation for East and West Pakistan.

Factional, regional, and sectarian* issues soon threatened the country's political stability. In 1958 when Pakistan's first general election was scheduled to be held, President Iskander Mirza suddenly abolished political parties and the constitution and placed the country under martial law*. Shortly afterward, a military coup* brought General Muhammad Ayub Khan to power. He announced a new constitution that retained most of the Islamic provisions of the earlier document but did not make them compulsory. This constitution stated that "no law should be [inconsistent with] Islam" but gave the responsibility for making this determination to the legislature.

In addition to political challenges, Ayub Khan faced continued domestic and foreign concerns. Tensions between East and West Pakistan, partly rooted in the economic imbalance between the two regions, had come to the foreground. Hostilities with India intensified, and war broke out over Kashmir in 1965. As turmoil increased, Ayub Khan's attempts to pacify the political opposition failed. In 1969 he resigned from office, handing power over to General Agha Mohammad Yahya Khan.

Responding to Loss. General elections took place in 1970. Sheikh Mujib, the leader of East Pakistan's Awami League, won a majority of the seats in parliament. Sheikh Mujib's party advocated self-government for Bengal (East Pakistan). Unable to reach a compromise, Yahya Khan ordered troops to the region in March 1971, and a civil war ensued. Fleeing the violence, millions sought refuge across the border in India. In response, the Indian government sent its own forces into East Pakistan to end the fighting. In December 1971, East Pakistan realized its dream of independence and became the state of Bangladesh.

The trauma of civil war profoundly affected the Pakistani people. Islamic groups insisted that the country had lost East Pakistan because its leaders had betrayed the cause of Islam. They urged Pakistanis to return to religion as a remedy for political problems. In political disgrace, President Yahya Khan resigned in December 1971. His successor, Zulfiqar Ali Bhutto, began a policy of Islamic socialism*. The new 1973 constitution declared Islam to be the state religion. It made non-Muslims ineligible to hold the office of prime minister and mandated Islamic studies in schools. Other provisions strengthened the religious nature of Pakistani society.

Despite Bhutto's efforts, few concrete changes resulted from his reforms. He became increasingly autocratic*, and political unrest grew. In 1977 General Muhammad Zia ul-Haq seized power. When the people demanded elections and it seemed certain that Bhutto would win, General Zia had him arrested and charged with attempted murder. Bhutto was later sentenced to death and hanged.

Zia's military government defined its mission as "laying down the foundations of the Islamic system in Pakistan." He moved to conform the country's social, economic, and political structures to traditional Islamic law. Most

* **parliament** representative national body having supreme legislative power within the state

* **sectarian** refers to a religious group that adheres to distinctive beliefs

* **martial law** rules imposed by the military

* **coup** sudden, and often violent, overthrow of a ruler or government

See map in Gulf States (vol. 1).

* **socialism** economic system in which the government owns and operates the means of production and the distribution of goods

* **autocratic** characterized by unlimited authority

* *zakat* charity; one of the five Pillars of Islam

* *mujahidin* literally "warriors of God"; refers to Muslim fighters in proclaimed jihads, such as the war against the Soviet invasion of Afghanistan

In Her Father's Footsteps

Benazir Bhutto became prime minister of Pakistan at age 35—making her the youngest person in the country's history to hold that office and the first woman to lead a modern Muslim state. Born in 1953, she was educated at Harvard and Oxford Universities. She entered Pakistani politics in 1977 as adviser to her father, Prime Minister Zulfiqar Ali Bhutto. After General Muhammad Zia ul-Haq deposed and executed her father, Benazir Bhutto became the official head of the Pakistan People's Party. From 1979 to 1984, she spent much time in prison, including almost one year in solitary confinement. After living in exile in England, she returned to Pakistan to challenge Zia's military regime. Bhutto was elected prime minister in 1988 but lost power two years later. She was elected a second time in 1993. Her writings include *Daughter of Destiny* and *Foreign Policy in Perspective.*

importantly, Pakistan adopted Islamic penal law (*hudud*), which introduced such punishments as flogging, stoning, or amputation for the crimes of drinking, adultery, and theft. Other changes included compulsory *zakat**, Islamic-centered school textbooks, and the creation of the International Islamic University. Successive governments retained most of Zia's substantive measures. Although some Islamic groups criticized these reforms as inadequate, others regarded them as extreme and felt that Zia was merely manipulating the religious feelings of the masses for political gain.

External Influences. The Iranian Revolution of 1979 and the occupation of Afghanistan by the former Soviet Union significantly affected Pakistani society. The success of the revolution in Iran encouraged Pakistani Islamic groups to advocate similar changes at home. At the same time, millions of Afghans, fleeing war between the *mujahidin** and Soviet forces, took refuge in Pakistan. The Muslim resistance fighters, who were supported by the United States, used territory in Pakistan for military training. This arrangement provided Pakistan with extensive U.S. economic aid.

In August 1988, Zia and his leading generals, as well as the U.S. ambassador to Pakistan, died in a mysterious airplane crash. A new election brought Benazir Bhutto, daughter of Zulfiqar Ali Bhutto, to power in 1988. In less than two years, the military ousted her from office. Bhutto regained power in 1993, but economic and social problems had escalated. Ethnic and religious clashes intensified, and Islamic extremists attacked Christians and members of the Ahmadi Muslim sect. Although Bhutto attempted to quell the violence, charges of corruption against her government surfaced. Elections in 1997 brought Mohammed Nawaz Sharif to office.

A Nuclear Power. In May 1998, Pakistan conducted six successful nuclear weapons tests in the province of Balochistan and declared itself a nuclear power. Pakistan regarded its weapons program as a necessary defense against India, which had exploded five nuclear devices just two weeks earlier. Although India claimed that its nuclear program, begun in 1974, was not directed against any particular country, Pakistan felt directly threatened. Indeed, Zulfiqar Ali Bhutto had stated as early as 1965 that, if India succeeded in producing a nuclear bomb, Pakistanis would spare no expense to acquire one too.

After the Indian and Pakistani nuclear tests in 1998, both countries announced that they would prohibit further nuclear testing. Pakistan also offered to participate in new peace talks with India and proposed a nuclear-weapon-free zone in South Asia. Pakistan agreed to sign the Comprehensive Test Ban Treaty if India would sign it at the same time. In March 2003, however, both Pakistan and India tested nuclear-capable missiles, further increasing tensions between the neighboring countries.

Ongoing Challenges. Unable to achieve serious economic reform and charged with corruption, Mohammed Nawaz Sharif's government was short lived. In 1999 army chief of staff General Pervez Musharraf arrested Sharif and suspended the constitution. Musharraf's government faced significant challenges. Continued conflict in Kashmir, where Pakistan allegedly supported Muslims who rejected Indian rule, strained Pakistan's troubled relationship with its neighbor. India blamed Pakistani-backed Islamic militants for an assault on the Indian parliament in December 2001. In response, India ordered almost a million troops to Pakistan's border. War—and even the use of nuclear weapons—appeared possible. The crisis eased in June, when Musharraf promised to end the movement of militants* across the border into India. Sporadic violence between Muslims and Hindus continued.

* **militant** aggressively active in a cause

The international focus on al-Qaeda after the terrorist attacks of September 11, 2001, placed Pakistan in an extremely difficult position. Despite Pakistan's previous support for the Taliban regime in Afghanistan, Musharraf decided to back U.S. efforts to drive the regime from power when its connection to al-Qaeda became known. This decision, however, incited considerable opposition from segments of the Pakistani population who supported the Taliban's extreme version of Islam. Nonetheless, in 2002, Pakistanis granted Musharraf five more years in office.

Pakistan still faces serious domestic issues. The government's suppression of political parties and political activism has led to increased influence from religious movements. Religious intolerance and violence against women remain critical problems. The Human Rights Commission of Pakistan reported in March 2001 that at least 1,000 people had died in religious or ethnic violence every year since 1990. The report also stated that more than 1,000 Pakistani women died in 1999 as a result of honor killings. A woman can be killed by a male member of her family for a wide variety of offenses. Marital infidelity, divorce, and even rape can all be perceived as bringing shame and dishonor to a family. (*See also* **Afghanistan; Ahmadi; Bangladesh; India; Iqbal, Muhammad; Kashmir; Mughal Empire; Qaeda, al-; Taliban.**)

Palestine

Palestine (*Filastin* in Arabic) has great value and significance for Muslims, Christians, and Jews, and many religious groups refer to it as the Holy Land. Situated on the eastern shores of the Mediterranean, Palestine borders Lebanon and Syria to the north, the Kingdom of Jordan to the east, Egypt to the southwest, and the desert of the Negev to the south. Its population includes Jews, Christians, Muslims, and Druze*. Palestine contains sacred sites of Judaism, Christianity, and Islam, such as the Wailing Wall, the Church of the Holy Sepulcher, the Dome of the Rock, and the Haram as-Sharif (called the Noble Sanctuary by Muslims and the Temple Mount by Jews), which contains the mosque of al-Aqsa.

* **Druze** offshoot of Shi'i Islam in Lebanon and Syria

Muslims consider Palestine the most important site after Mecca and Medina. The miraculous Night Journey (*isra*) and Ascension (*miraj*) of the Prophet Muhammad is associated with Palestine. During the Night Journey, he traveled from Mecca to the Temple Mount in Jerusalem, where he ascended to heaven. Muhammad told his followers to turn toward Jerusalem while they prayed. Later, when the early Muslim community moved from Mecca to Medina, the direction of prayer was changed to Mecca.

See map in Middle East (vol. 2).

Jews and Christians also view Palestine as a holy site. Jews established a kingdom there in ancient times and believe that God promised Palestine to them as a homeland. Christians value Palestine for its associations with

Palestine

Jesus. During the Middle Ages*, they embarked on the Crusades, a series of wars to capture Palestine from the Muslims.

Despite the efforts of the Christians, Palestine has remained mostly under Muslim rule for the past 12 centuries. From 1517 to 1917, Palestine and the rest of the Middle East came under the control of the Turkish Ottoman Empire. The Ottomans divided Palestine into the *vilayet* (province) of Beirut and the *sanjak* (district) of Jerusalem. Palestine as an administrative unit came into existence at the end of World War I (1914–1918), when Great Britain and France defeated the Ottomans. Britain took over Palestine and Iraq, while the French gained control of Syria and Lebanon. The League of Nations granted Britain and France an official mandate* over these countries in 1923.

Britain, however, was soon involved in conflict with the Arabs and the Jews of Palestine. In order to gain support from the Arabs during World War I, Britain had promised the Arabs the establishment of an Arab kingdom that would unify all countries from the Persian Gulf to the Mediterranean Sea. Jewish interest groups, however, lobbied Britain for the creation of a Jewish state in Palestine. Faced with increasing anti-Semitism in Europe, Jews wanted control of the territory they considered the Promised Land. The Arabs felt betrayed and bitter when Great Britain entered into negotiations with Zionist* leaders and officially declared that it would support the establishment of a Jewish homeland in Palestine. Britain outlined its intentions in the Balfour Declaration in November 1917.

Britain's conflicting promises led the Arabs to organize against the British government. Afraid that they might lose their land to Jewish settlers from Europe, the Arabs rioted against the British colonial authorities in the 1920s and 1930s. The most important of these demonstrations occurred in 1936, when Muslims called for a general strike throughout major Palestinian towns, including Nablus, Jaffa, and Jerusalem. This uprising led to the deaths of several Arabs and Jews. The British, however, continued to allow Jews from Europe to immigrate into Palestine. Funded with international donations, the settlers built a modern infrastructure* and economy. The Palestinians felt the region slipping from their control. As a result of the increasing violence between Arabs and Jews, Great Britain dispatched a Royal Commission headed by Lord Peel in November 1936.

The Peel Commission recommended that Britain partition Palestine into Jewish and Arab states, with a British-mandated area that would include Jerusalem, Bethlehem, and Jaffa. The Arabs opposed the plan, believing that it prevented them from having their own nation. They initiated more anti-British actions, which led to the killing of a British colonial officer in 1937. In 1939 the British government met with Zionists, Palestinians, and representatives of various Arab governments to discuss the future of Palestine. The conference resulted in the drafting of the 1939 White Paper, which detailed a plan to halt Jewish immigration in five years. The British pledged to grant the Arabs their own state in ten years, and to limit the amount of land Jews could buy.

Both Arab and Jewish groups rejected these proposals. During World War II (1939–1945), the Zionists increasingly struggled with the British to allow more Jews into Palestine. They staged riots and armed conflicts with the British in order to secure a place for Holocaust* survivors. In July 1945, the Anglo-American Committee emerged to resolve the conflict. The commission recommended the creation of autonomous* Arab and Jewish provinces, with two areas—including a Jerusalem enclave—under the control of the British. In November 1947, the United Nations adopted a resolution ratifying this plan and ending the British mandate in Palestine. Israel declared its independence, and the Arab nations declared war on the new nation. With the help of overseas funding, Israel successfully defended itself. The establishment of the state of Israel, however, caused around 700,000 Arabs to flee the area and become refugees. Palestinian Arabs continue to struggle for the creation of their own state. (*See also* **Arab-Israeli Conflict; Israel; Jerusalem; Palestinian Liberation Organization.**)

* **autonomy** self-government

Palestine Liberation Organization

Following the first Arab-Israeli war in 1948, between 600,000 and one million Palestinians became refugees in the neighboring countries of Jordan, Syria, and Lebanon, as well as in the West Bank and Gaza Strip. Over the next decade, many of them organized small resistance groups and waged an underground political and military struggle against Israel. In 1964 the Arab League established the Palestine Liberation Organization (PLO) to centralize the leadership of these groups. Today the PLO is recognized as the representative of the world's estimated eight million Palestinians.

According to the PLO charter, the organization's goals included the complete elimination of Israeli authority in Palestine and the destruction of the state of Israel. During the early years of the PLO, however, Egypt and other Arab regimes strongly influenced PLO policy, reducing the power of its militant guerrilla* factions. In June 1967, Israeli forces routed the armies of Egypt, Syria, and Jordan. In the wake of this defeat, which disgraced the Arab regimes, Palestinians pressed for greater autonomy* in their struggle against Israel. Independent, radical* groups, most notably Fatah, soon gained control of the PLO. This change was signaled by the choice of Fatah leader Yasir Arafat as chairman of the Executive Committee of the PLO, the organization's guiding body, in 1969. Other major factions within the PLO included the Popular Front for the Liberation of Palestine (PFLP), the Democratic Front for the Liberation of Palestine (DFLP), and smaller groups sponsored by Arab governments such as Syria and Iraq.

* **guerrilla** unconventional warfare

* **autonomy** self-government

* **radical** favoring extreme change or reform, especially in existing political and social institutions

Although these groups agreed on the main objective of liberating Palestine from Israeli control, they had different methods for achieving this goal. Arafat and his supporters believed that Palestinians should use their limited military capabilities to fight Israel. Then, the rest of the Arabs would join the Palestinians in their war of liberation. These factions argued that Israel should be replaced by a democratic Palestinian state in which Jews, Christians, and Muslims would live side by side as equals. But the PFLP and DFLP were more radical in their methods and resorted to terrorist acts against Israeli and Western targets, such as the hijacking of civilian airplanes and the taking of hostages.

In the late 1960s, the PLO launched guerrilla attacks on Israel from its bases in Jordan. Israeli retaliation led to instability in Jordan, and in 1971,

Yasir Arafat has led the Palestine Liberation Organization since 1969. During this time, his policy toward the state of Israel has veered from military attack to acceptance of Israel's right to exist.

King Hussein's army forced Arafat and his allies to leave the country. For the next ten years, the PLO continued its assault on Israel from Lebanon. The organization became involved in the country's internal political disputes, which contributed to the outbreak of civil war. In addition to its military activities, the PLO established unions, businesses, and light industry. Israel invaded Lebanon in 1978 and in 1982, forcing the PLO into exile.

Without any bases from which to attack the Jewish state, and encouraged by the success of the *intifadah* (uprising) in the occupied territories, Yasir Arafat adopted a more practical stance during the late 1980s. He expressed the PLO's willingness to accept a smaller Palestinian state to be established in the West Bank and Gaza Strip. In addition, he stressed the importance of diplomatic and political means to achieve Palestinian statehood. The PLO also accepted two United Nations resolutions, indicating its acknowledgment of Israel's right to exist.

In 1993 the PLO and Israel signed a Declaration of Principles as a first step to resolving the conflict. According to the agreement, Israel would gradually cede control of the West Bank and Gaza Strip to the Palestinians. The result was the creation of the Palestine National Authority to administer the territories. Throughout the 1990s, however, peace talks faltered and eventually collapsed, provoking a second *intifadah* in late 2000. In recent years, Hamas, a militant Palestinian group, has emerged as a formidable challenger to PLO authority in the region. (*See also* **Arab-Israeli Conflict; Hamas; Intifadah; Israel; Jordan; Lebanon; Palestine.**)

People of the Book See *Christianity and Islam; Judaism and Islam.*

Philippines

The Republic of the Philippines consists of a group of islands located in the Pacific Ocean. Unlike other parts of Southeast Asia, this nation is predominantly Roman Catholic, the result of 300 years of Spanish colonial rule. Moros, as Philippine Muslims are called, make up 5 percent of the population. They are concentrated in the southern part of the Philippines, either on the large island of Mindanao or on one of the small islands that make up the Sulu Archipelago. The relationship between the Christian-controlled government and the Muslim community has often been contentious, and some militant groups continue an armed struggle for regional independence and the creation of an Islamic state.

North Versus South. Muslims from Brunei introduced Islam to Mindanao and the Sulu islands during the 1400s. By the mid-1500s, the Muslim community had established two sultanates* that incorporated some of the native groups in the area. The spread of Islam was interrupted by the arrival of the Spanish in 1565. They established a colony and converted most of the people in the northern part of the Philippines to Christianity. But the Spanish were unable to convert the Muslims in the south, whom they called

* **sultanate** government of a sultan, the political and military ruler of a Muslim state or dynasty

moros because they shared the faith of the Moors, the descendants of the Arab conquerors of Spain.

During 300 years of colonial rule, numerous wars erupted between the Spanish and the Moros. By the mid-1800s, the colonial government abandoned its mission to convert the Muslims and worked to gain political control of the southern islands. The destruction caused by continuous fighting and declining agricultural output, among other factors, led Moro leaders to sign a peace treaty with Spain. Eventually, the southern islands would have become part of the colony. The process halted, however, when Christian Filipino rebel forces staged a series of revolts against the foreign rulers in the late 1890s. Meanwhile, Spain was engaged in a war with the United States regarding the independence of Cuba. As part of the Treaty of Paris (1898), Spain ceded control of the Philippines to the United States. Although American officials forced the Moros to accept their political authority, they did not attempt to change religious practices or customary laws unless they violated the U.S. Constitution.

When the United States began to train Filipinos for self-government, Muslim religious leaders asked to be excluded from the proposed independent nation. They wanted to maintain their separation from Christian Filipinos and remain under American protection until they could establish a separate Muslim state. When the United States granted independence to the Philippines in 1946, however, the Moro regions were included in the new republic. This political arrangement caused considerable displeasure among the Moro population.

Islam became more important than ever to the Moros. Every year, hundreds of Philippine Muslims performed the hajj* and returned with renewed religious zeal. New mosques* and *madrasahs* (religious schools) opened in the southern islands. At the same time, large numbers of Christian Filipinos immigrated to the south and settled in traditional Muslim areas, often with the support of the government. The government had neglected the economic and educational concerns of the Moros and continued to discriminate against them, which led to armed clashes between Christian and Muslim groups. Some Moros involved in the conflict wanted only to preserve their Islamic identity and way of life. Others supported the formation of a separate Muslim nation.

Gains and Losses. In 1972 President Ferdinand Marcos declared martial law* in the Philippines and used force to disarm the Moros, an act that led to open revolt. One of the most popular groups in the resistance movement was the Moro National Liberation Front (MNLF), which called for the establishment of an independent Muslim republic.

With the support of Libya and other members of the Organization of the Islamic Conference (OIC), the MNLF escalated the war from 1973 to 1976. In 1976 the Philippine government signed an agreement giving autonomy* to the Filipino provinces with large Muslim populations. Although the government failed to carry out some provisions of the agreement, it did grant certain concessions to the Moros. For example, schools attended by Muslims were authorized to instruct their students in Arabic, and the government created a Ministry of Islamic Affairs. Scholarships for Moro students and appointments of qualified Muslims to top government positions increased.

* **hajj** pilgrimage to Mecca that Muslims are required to make once in their lifetime

* **mosque** Muslim place of worship

* **martial law** rules imposed by the military

* **autonomy** self-government

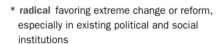

Despite these changes, some Moro groups continued to demand the withdrawal of the Muslim provinces from the Philippines. During the 1980s, the Moro Islamic Liberation Front (MILF) was established to maintain the struggle for Moro independence and the formation of an Islamic state. When the Marcos government collapsed in 1986, the army left the Muslim region to combat communist rebels, only to be replaced by other government fighters who brought a reign of destruction. The MILF eventually signed a cease-fire agreement with the government. Nevertheless, more radical* groups, such as the Abu Sayyaf, continue the armed struggle for an independent Islamic state. (*See also* **International Meetings and Organizations; Southeast Asia.**)

* **radical** favoring extreme change or reform, especially in existing political and social institutions

Philosophy

Islamic philosophy (*al-falsafah*) began around the 800s and remains a major intellectual pursuit in parts of the Muslim world. It has influenced and has been influenced by many other fields, including theology*, logic, and the sciences. Muslim philosophy grapples with such themes as free will, predestination*, the nature of God, and the relative merit of faith and good works. It focuses on the Qur'an* and hadith*, the nature of prophecy, and the role of revelation in society. Islamic philosophers believe that reason is compatible with truths passed down through scripture*.

* **theology** study of the nature and qualities of God and the understanding of His will

* **predestination** doctrine that God alone determines whether a person goes to paradise or to hell

* **Qur'an** book of the holy scriptures of Islam

* **hadith** reports of the words and deeds of Muhammad (not in the Qur'an, but accepted as guides for Muslim behavior)

* **scripture** sacred writings that contain revelations from God

Early Philosophers and Works

Early Muslim scholars discovered classical Greek philosophical works, translated them, and began to develop their own explanations of the universe. They were especially inspired by Plato and Aristotle, as well as Persian and Indian philosophers. From these thinkers, Muslims learned that the search for truth could involve logic, the natural sciences, mathematics, metaphysics*, ethics, and politics. They formed a distinctive philosophy with its roots in Islam. Several Muslim philosophers rose to fame during the Middle Ages*.

* **metaphysics** branch of philosophy that deals with that which exists beyond the senses

* **Middle Ages** period roughly between 500 and 1500

Following Aristotle. The first Muslim philosopher, Abu Ya'qub al-Kindi (died 873), is known as the "Philosopher of the Arabs." He founded the most prominent philosophic tradition in Islam—the *mashshaun*, or Peripatetic school (named after Aristotle's school), which attempted to harmonize Islamic doctrines* with elements from Aristotle's teachings. The first scholar to discuss Aristotelian thought in Arabic, al-Kindi pondered the difference between worldly and spiritual phenomena. He also confronted what he considered the central problem of a religious society: how to balance faith and reason. Al-Kindi believed that people could gain a purely human knowledge of all things through reason and study. He also stated, however, that God could provide individuals with this knowledge directly, as in the case of prophecy. God cleansed and enlightened the souls of certain humans, enabling them to spread divine teachings to others in clear, eloquent language.

An influential teacher, al-Kindi wrote an estimated 240 books on subjects ranging from astronomy to medicine and music. His major philosoph-

* **doctrine** principle, theory, or belief that is taught or presented for acceptance

ical works include *Fi al-aql* (The Intellect) and *Fi al-falsafah al-ula* (On Metaphysics). Translated into Latin, al-Kindi's works had a significant influence on European thinkers as well as on other Muslim scholars.

Provoking Opposition. Another early philosopher, the physician and scholar Abu Bakr al-Razi (died 932) inspired negative reactions from some scholars for his unorthodox* views. Al-Razi developed a theory of creation based on five eternal principles: God, Soul, matter, infinite space, and absolute time. He taught that creation occurred as the result of an unexpected and quick turn of events (*faltah*). Echoing classical Greek themes, al-Razi explained that Soul, who existed in the world of infinite space and time, ignorantly desired physical matter. Taking pity on her, God created the universe and allowed Soul to experience it so that she could understand suffering. He wanted to guide her into realizing her error, renouncing the physical world, and returning to Him. Al-Razi believed that his account relieved God of any responsibility for imperfection or sin in the universe.

* **unorthodox** contrary to accepted beliefs and practices

Al-Razi voiced some unusual beliefs that turned many scholars against him. He rejected prophecy, revelation, and divine law, stating that any reasonable human being could achieve knowledge of any subject and did not need divine guidance. Individuals could determine their own actions, know truth for themselves, and improve on the teachings of earlier authorities. Al-Razi even questioned the nature of religion, believing it to be a device that enabled evil men to hold tyranny over others and to wage war. Many Muslims expressed outrage at these ideas, and al-Razi earned the criticism of several philosophers.

Discovering Truth Through Study. The scholar Abu Nasr al-Farabi (died 950) introduced formal logic and political philosophy to the Islamic world. Al-Farabi wrote books on a variety of subjects, including mathematics, astronomy, music, and poetry. His masterpiece, *Kitab ara ahl al-madinah al-fadilah* (The Book of the Opinions of the Citizens of the Virtuous City) applies the political philosophy of Plato to Muslim society. In the text, al-Farabi discussed the ways in which humans could achieve an ideal community. He explored such issues as leadership, social order, divine law, and the fate of communities that stray from Islamic beliefs. Al-Farabi argued that philosophers alone were qualified to head a state, having discovered truth through years of study. Only philosophers could guide their subjects in correct actions and instruct them on how to fulfill moral obligations. In the event of the philosopher's death, a ruler with good judgment could take his place and implement his laws.

Al-Farabi opposed al-Razi's rejection of prophecy, stating that prophecy and philosophy are basically the same. Prophets receive the same information as philosophers, but through bursts of divine information rather than through rational thought. Al-Farabi valued philosophy above prophecy, however, claiming that it leads to a purer version of the truth. Al-Farabi's work profoundly influenced scholarship in the Muslim world, as well as in Jewish and Christian communities.

Chain of Existence. Often considered the greatest Muslim philosopher, Ibn Sina (also known by the Latin name Avicenna, died 1037) provided a detailed analysis of Peripatetic thought. His book *Kitab al-shifa* (The Book

The Mu'tazili Challenge

A group known as the Mu'tazili ("those who keep themselves apart"; also known as the party of unity and justice) influenced many Islamic philosophers, including Abu Bakr al-Razi. The Mu'tazili believed in rationalism and rejected the idea that the Qur'an had an eternal existence. They maintained that the Qur'an consists of God's speech (*kalam Allah*) but that it was created in time for a specific community. The Mu'tazili also opposed the idea of predestination, stating that humans alone were responsible for their sins. Mu'tazili theology reached its height during the 800s, when the caliph al-Mamun tried to impose it in his realm. Al-Mamun's movement failed, however, largely because of the opposition of the legal scholar Ahmad ibn Hanbal, who suffered imprisonment and flogging for his adherence to traditional views. By the 900s, the Mu'tazili movement had faded.

* **Sufi** refers to Sufism, which seeks to develop spirituality through discipline of the mind and body

of Healing) dominated Islamic scholarship for centuries. Focusing on the question of being and creation, Ibn Sina determined that life could not exist without intervention from a higher power. He distinguished between an object's essence and existence, stating that essence could not cause existence and that objects could not take on life and interact with one another by themselves. Ibn Sina argued that God bestowed a life force on all things. Moreover, God stood at the head of a great chain of being that included all the creatures in the universe, ranging from angels to dust, with each entity responsible for the existence of the one below it.

Ibn Sina also wrote on the immortality of the human soul. Created at the same time as the body, it uses the body as an instrument. It determines the individual's personality, looks, and moral character. The soul survives the death of the body and receives punishments or rewards according to its sins or good deeds. Ibn Sina's writings also deeply influenced scholars of other traditions.

Development and Opposition

Around the 1000s, Islamic philosophy underwent several significant changes. Various rulers encouraged or suppressed the development of philosophic thought in their regions, and intellectual movements emerged in different parts of the Islamic empire. Groups began to oppose one another, and philosophers debated the ideas of the early Islamic scholars.

Rise of Theologians. From the 1000s to the 1200s, the Seljuks dominated western Asia. Valuing theology over philosophy, they discouraged the teaching of science and caused a decline in philosophical thought in the region. Major theologians emerged during this period and wrote treatises against Peripatetic philosophy. The great Sufi* scholar Abu Hamid al-Ghazali (died 1111) wrote the most famous attack on the Peripatetics, along with another book explaining their views, which caused some later scholars to view him as a member of this school. In his *Tahafut al-falasifah* (Incoherence of the Philosophers), al-Ghazali criticized the Peripatetics for deviating from Islam and for wasting their time on trivial arguments. For example, he opposed their rejection of bodily resurrection and their claim that God could not have specific knowledge of aspects of His creation.

The theologian Fakhr al-Din al-Razi (died 1210) wrote a detailed criticism of Ibn Sina's work that strongly influenced the course of Islamic philosophy. Philosophers wrote furious responses to al-Razi's critique, and the scholar Nasir al-Din al-Tusi (died 1274) produced a celebrated defense that essentially revived Ibn Sina's philosophy. The debate over Ibn Sina ultimately led to a regeneration of philosophic inquiry in the Muslim world.

Islamic Philosophy in Spain. While philosophy stagnated in the Seljuk domains of Asia, it flourished in Islamic Spain. Ibn Bajjah (died 1138) was a major philosopher in the region. In *Tadbir al-mutawahhid* (The Regimen of the Solitary), he maintained that a perfect state could arise only after certain individuals had perfected themselves by uniting their intellects to an overarching Active Intellect. Ibn Bajjah also held that philosophers should lead solitary lives, shun the company of nonintellectuals, and study the sciences while pursuing contact with the Active Intellect.

One of his followers, Ibn Tufayl (died 1185), continued to explore the relationship between intuition and learning. He wrote on the interaction between inner illumination and knowledge revealed through scripture. His book *Hayy ibn Yaqzan* (Living Son of the Awake) was translated into Hebrew and Latin and became famous in Europe as *Philosophies Autodidactus.* It influenced both philosophers and literary scholars.

A physician and chief religious judge of Córdoba, Ibn Rushd (died 1198) wrote the most famous medieval* commentaries on Aristotelian philosophy. Known in the Western world as Averroës, Ibn Rushd set out to revive Peripatetic philosophy, responding to al-Ghazali's *Tahafut* with his own *Tahafut al-tahafut* (Incoherence of the Incoherence). Ibn Rushd argued that divine law exists in order to ensure the happiness of all. Individuals must accept the teachings of the Qur'an and the hadith and perform obligatory acts of worship. Each individual must also pursue knowledge according to his or her capacity. The divine law grants philosophers the right to analyze and interpret revelation as they see fit. Furthermore, it denies theologians the authority to criticize or interfere with these efforts. Considered the greatest philosopher of Muslim Spain, Ibn Rushd had a far greater influence in the West than in the eastern Islamic world.

> * **medieval** refers to the Middle Ages, a period roughly between 500 and 1500

New Philosophical Schools. Beginning in the 1100s, several Islamic schools of philosophy developed. The Iranian scholar Shihab al-Din Umar Suhrawardi (died 1191) created the School of Illumination, integrating rational and mystical* philosophy with Islamic teachings. He taught that true philosophy stemmed from *ishraq* (illumination) as well as from mental effort. Suhrawardi viewed all creatures as existing on a continuum of light and darkness. He linked light with inner purity and cited God as the perfect manifestation of this light. He stated that change occurs when lower lights experience desire for the higher lights and interact with them. Fully purified souls ascend to a world of lights after death, while darker souls inhabit a world of images that they create based on their own level of purification. Officials executed Suhrawardi in Aleppo in 1191, forcing his followers underground. A generation later, scholars revived his teachings.

> * **mysticism** belief that spiritual enlightenment and truth can be attained through various physical and spiritual disciplines

Between the 1200s and 1500s, Persia became the center of philosophical activity. The scholar Mir Damad (died 1631) founded the School of Isfahan, named after the city in which he taught. His most famous student, Mulla Sadra (died 1640) is considered the greatest of all Islamic metaphysicians*. Mulla Sadra integrated Peripatetic and mystical thought. He taught that everything other than God and divine knowledge originated both eternally and temporally. He also held that spirituality should play a significant role in political reform and that moral and ethical principles should serve as the foundation of social movements. Mulla Sadra and his followers influenced thinkers in Persia, India, and Iraq.

> * **metaphysician** one who studies metaphysics, the branch of philosophy concerned with the fundamental nature of reality

Colonialism and Contemporary Concerns. Beginning in the late 1700s, Western nations colonized most of the Islamic world. Their rule inhibited the growth of Islamic philosophy but brought European and American thought into the Muslim consciousness. Some scholars developed an interest in Western traditions. Others despised the new influences and urged a movement back to Islamic teachings.

* **ayatollah** highest-ranking legal scholar among some Shi'i Muslims

By the mid-1900s, most Islamic countries had gained their independence from the Europeans. Scholars, such as Jamal al-Din al-Afghani and Muhammad Iqbal, began a revival of Islamic philosophy, looking to earlier texts for guidance on how to create a new Muslim state. Islamic philosophy plays an especially important role in Iran. The Ayatollah* Ruhollah Khomeini taught philosophy for years before turning to politics, and he appointed a leading philosopher as head of the Council of the Islamic Revolution in 1979. Many Muslim scholars have taken a renewed interest in Islamic philosophy, and Western students show an increasing interest in Islamic works. (*See also* **Afghani, Jamal al-Din al-; Farabi, Abu Nasr al-; Ghazali, Abu Hamid al-; Ibn Rushd; Ibn Sina; Iqbal, Muhammad; Khomeini, Ruhollah al-Musavi; Mulla Sadra; Seljuk Dynasty; Theology.**)

Pilgrimage

* **Kaaba** literally "House of God"; Islamic shrine in Mecca

See color plate 1, vol. 1.

Pilgrimage—a journey to a holy site—is an important part of many religious traditions. Though Judaism and Christianity encourage voluntary pilgrimage, Islam requires it. Every able-bodied Muslim who has the financial ability to travel must go to Mecca at least once in his or her lifetime to participate in the *hajj*. This is the annual pilgrimage during the second week of Dhu al-Hijjah, the final month of the Islamic lunar calendar. Though Muslims also visit other shrines, no other pilgrimage can take the place of the *hajj*.

Hajj. The *hajj* honors the roots of the Islamic faith in God's covenant with the Prophet Abraham and his son, Ismail. Its main rituals take place at the Great Mosque in Mecca, which contains the sacred shrine of the Kaaba*. Muhammad himself set out the proper sequence of these rituals shortly before he died. Male pilgrims put on special garments, or *ihram*, consisting of two plain white sheets or towels. These simple clothes remind Muslims that they are all equal before God, regardless of race or economic class. Pilgrims do not cut their hair or nails until the *hajj* is over.

The *hajj* begins with the *tawaf*, when pilgrims circle seven times around the Kaaba. They recite prayers, run seven times between Mount Safa and Mount Marway, and visit holy places outside of Mecca, including Jabal ar-Rahmah, Muzdalifah, and Mina. Pilgrims offer animal sacrifices and participate in a stone-throwing ritual in which they symbolically attack the devil. They then return to Mecca for a farewell *tawaf*.

The *hajj*, which celebrates the reunion of the whole Muslim community, is the most powerful reminder of Islam's communal ideals. Muslims often schedule their *hajj* when they are facing an important event in their lives, such as marriage, retirement, illness, or death. Indeed, Muslims who die while performing the *hajj* are considered martyrs and are promised special rewards in the afterlife.

Ziyarah. In addition to performing the *hajj* as required, some devout Muslims also participate in other types of pilgrimage. This practice, known as *ziyarah*, includes visits to the tombs of saints. Many Arab towns have their

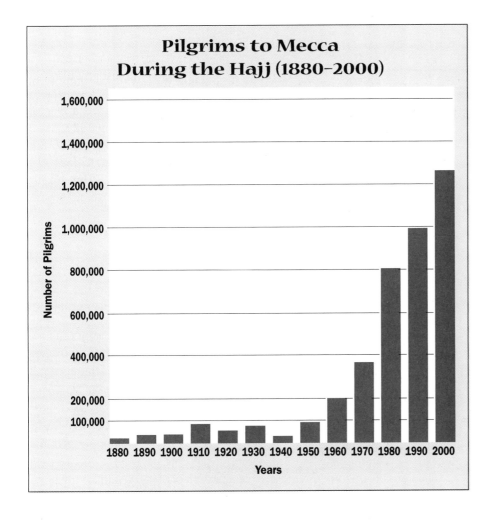

Pilgrims to Mecca During the Hajj (1880–2000)

Number of Pilgrims

1,600,000
1,400,000
1,200,000
1,000,000
800,000
600,000
400,000
200,000
100,000

1880 1890 1900 1910 1920 1930 1940 1950 1960 1970 1980 1990 2000

Years

This graph shows the number of pilgrims from outside of Saudi Arabia who have traveled to Mecca each year during the hajj. The number has increased dramatically in the last 30 years. In 2003, over 1,400,000 Muslims made the pilgrimage to Islam's most holy site.

own local saints, and area residents regularly visit their tombs. Many saints are associated with cures for specific illnesses. Muslims pray to these patron saints for blessings or cures and often slaughter an animal in sacrifice during the pilgrimage.

Shi'i* Muslims consider it very important to visit the graves of martyrs, especially the imams*, and make pilgrimages each year to *mashhads,* the gravesites of noted martyrs. Husayn ibn Ali, a grandson of the Prophet, is considered the Chief of All Martyrs. He is buried in Karbala in present-day Iraq, where believers pay their respects at his tomb. The tombs of many other imams can also be found in Iraq, with the most important being that of Ali, the Prophet's cousin and son-in-law, in Najaf. The eighth imam, Ali al-Reza, is buried in Sanabad, in northeastern Iran. Mashhad, the second-largest city in Iran and a major Shi'i center for study, sprang up around this important shrine.

Many Islamic teachers, including the fundamentalist Wahhabis of Saudi Arabia, reject the practice of *ziyarah.* They consider it against the teachings of Islam because it encourages people to pray to saints instead of to God alone. They teach that true believers should condemn *ziyarah.* (*See also* **Ali ibn Abi Talib; Hajj; Husayn ibn Ali; Kaaba; Saints and Sainthood.**)

* **Shi'i** refers to Muslims who believe that Muhammad chose Ali ibn Abi Talib and his descendants as the spiritual-political leaders of the Muslim community

* **imam** spiritual-political leader in Shi'i Islam, one who is regarded as directly descended from Muhammad; also, one who leads prayers

Pillars of Islam

Five required practices unite Muslims in a single worldwide community of believers and distinguish Islam from other religions. Known as the Pillars of Islam, these practices include: pledging one's faith; praying five times each day; setting aside a portion of one's wealth for the poor; fasting during the month of Ramadan; and making a pilgrimage to the holy city of Mecca (for every Muslim who is both physically and financially able) at least once in a lifetime. These are the basic principles of personal and collective faith, worship, and social responsibility. Both Sunni* and Shi'i* legal schools agree on the essential duties of the five pillars. Some Muslim groups consider *jihad*, or striving to accomplish God's will, to be a sixth pillar.

The profession of faith, or *shahadah* ("There is no God but Allah, and Muhammad is the messenger of God"), marks a person's entry into the Islamic community. It affirms Islam's absolute monotheism* and the acceptance of Muhammad as the messenger of God and the last and final prophet*. With the acceptance of the *shahadah*, Muslim males at the age of 15 and females at the age of 9 are required to perform the other pillars of Islam.

Prayer (*salat*) is an integral part of daily life. Islam requires Muslims to pray five times each day: at daybreak, noon, mid-afternoon, sunset, and evening. Before prayer, Muslims must perform ritual ablution, or cleansing of the mind and body. Muslims can pray alone or together, in the mosque*, outdoors, or at home. Praying with other believers is preferable, however, as it demonstrates equality and solidarity. On Fridays, Muslims perform the noon prayer communally at the mosque, if possible.

The third pillar is *zakat*, setting aside a portion of one's wealth for the poor. All Muslims who are able must give 2.5 percent of their net worth annually. Forms of wealth that may be subject to *zakat* include gold, silver, livestock, crops, currency, or other items that can be converted to cash, such as stocks and bonds. Other types of charity are recommended, but *zakat* is a formal duty.

Zakat serves both spiritual and practical functions. Those who give and those who receive *zakat* are bound together by the sharing of wealth. Fulfilling this duty challenges affluent Muslims to confront and reject the human tendency to be selfish, greedy, and excessively interested in material possessions. Because Islam discourages begging, *zakat* enables poor people to receive economic support without humiliation. Zakat also reduces the resentment the poor might harbor toward the rich.

Historically, the collection and distribution of *zakat* was often a function of the state. With the advent of colonial rule and the introduction of secular* political systems, the practice became a matter of individual choice. In recent years, some Muslim countries, including Sudan and Pakistan, have restored the state's role in *zakat* transactions. Elsewhere, Muslims may contribute to organized charities that distribute *zakat* according to Islamic principles. These organizations fund mosques, schools, libraries, and hospitals.

The fourth pillar requires Muslims to fast during Ramadan, the ninth month of Islam's lunar calendar. From sunrise to sunset, Muslims do not eat, drink, smoke, or engage in sexual relations. Fasting reminds believers of their dependence on God and it promotes spiritual self-discipline. The fast of Ramadan ends with the celebration of Eid al-Fitr.

* **Sunni** refers to the largest branch of the Muslim community; the name derives from sunnah, the exemplary behavior of the Prophet Muhammad

* **Shi'i** refers to Muslims who believe that Muhammad chose Ali ibn Abi Talib and his descendants as the spiritual-political leaders of the Muslim community

* **monotheism** belief that there is only one God

* **prophet** one who announces divinely inspired revelations

* **mosque** Muslim place of worship

See color plate 15, vol. 3.

* **secular** separate from religion in human life and society; connected to everyday life

Islam requires every adult Muslim to perform the hajj* at least once in his or her lifetime. The pilgrimage takes place during Dhu al-Hijjah, the last month of the Islamic calendar. During the hajj, Muslims perform rituals that are meant to symbolically reenact events from the life of the Prophet Abraham and his family. The hajj celebrates the reunion and the renewal of the entire Muslim community. (*See also* **Creed; Hajj; Islam: Overview; Jihad; Pilgrimage; Prayer.**)

* **hajj** pilgrimage to Mecca that Muslims are required to make once in their lifetime

Poetry

See *Arabic Language and Literature; Literature.*

Polygyny

See *Marriage.*

Prayer

Muslim tradition requires believers to pray five times each day: at dawn, noon, midafternoon, sunset, and evening. Prayer, or *salat*, is one of the Pillars of Islam. It reminds Muslims of God's constant presence as they go about their worldly business. The Qur'an* suggests that prayer itself is an acceptable mode of spirituality only if it is accompanied by good works such as giving charity.

* **Qur'an** book of the holy scriptures of Islam

Muslim prayers consist of recitations in Arabic from the Qur'an. These words glorify and praise God. Believers may pray indoors or outdoors, at home or in the mosque*, individually or in groups (but communal prayer is preferable to show the unity of the Muslim community).

* **mosque** Muslim place of worship

Origins of Salat. The explanation for the specific form of Islamic prayer is given in hadith* compiled by al-Bukhari (died 870). On the night of Muhammad's ascent to the highest heaven, the Prophet met and talked with earlier prophets, including Adam, Jesus, Abraham, and Moses. Muhammad was led to a place in heaven where he received 50 prayers, which he was to pass on to his followers. On his way back to earth, Muhammad encountered Moses, who asked how many daily prayers God had asked of the Muslims. When he heard the number, Moses said 50 was too great for the faithful to bear and suggested that Muhammad ask God to reduce the number. Muhammad went back and forth between God and Moses several times, until God reduced the number to five daily prayers, which was surely tolerable.

* **hadith** reports of the words and deeds of Muhammad (not in the Qur'an, but accepted as guides for Muslim behavior)

Salat in Practice. According to tradition, the muezzin* climbs to the top of the minaret* and calls the faithful to prayer five times daily. He chants in Arabic, "God is most great, God is most great," and invites believers to "Come [alive] to the prayer." The first call of the day, just before dawn, reminds worshippers, "Prayer is better than sleep." Nowadays, the muezzin's call is often recorded and played through loudspeakers.

* **muezzin** person who calls the faithful to prayer
* **minaret** tall, slender tower of a Muslim mosque from which the faithful are called to prayer

Muslims prepare for each daily prayer with an ablution, or cleansing. They clear their minds and hearts of any distracting thoughts and try to con-

Prayer

Counting Devotions

Since ancient times, people have used strings of beads to keep track of the prayers they offer to God. Prayer beads originated with the Hindu faith as far back as the first century B.C.E. The function of prayer beads is the same in Hinduism, Buddhism, Roman Catholicism, and Islam. They are used to count devotions. *Tasbih,* or Muslim prayer beads, consist of 99 beads. They are used to recite the 99 Beautiful Names of God.

* **hajj** pilgrimage to Mecca that Muslims are required to make once in their lifetime

* **Sufi** refers to Sufism, which seeks to develop spirituality through discipline of the mind and body

centrate on God and his blessings. Then they wash their hands, face, mouth, feet, and forehead and recite the words, "In the name of God, the Merciful, the Compassionate. I am proposing to perform ablution so that God may be pleased with me." After completing the ablution, Muslims say, "I bear witness that there is no god but Allah; He has no partner; and I bear witness that Muhammad is His servant and Messenger."

Muslims face toward the holy city of Mecca when they pray. Each act of prayer includes a series of prescribed items, including recitations, periods of remaining motionless, bowing, sitting between prostrations (touching one's forehead to the ground). Prayers begin with the declaration, "God is most Great," and end with the words, "Peace be upon you." In the mosque, the imam leads prayers. Worshippers gather in rows behind the imam, and follow his directions through the sequence of movements and recitations.

Muslim prayers must be performed on a clean surface. For this reason, people remove their shoes before entering a mosque. When prayers are performed outdoors, as they often are, the prayer rug becomes a necessity, providing a clean protective covering on the ground. Prayer rugs are small, measuring 3 feet by 5 feet. They are adorned with special motifs, such as a lamp hanging from an arch (symbolizing the presence of Allah) or a water jug (reminding the worshipper to wash before praying). Prayer rugs almost always contain a flaw to remind believers that only Allah is perfect.

Friday noontime worship has special importance. At the mosque, believers join in a communal prayer, which is followed by two sermons from the *minbar* (mosque pulpit). Special communal prayers are also offered on the festival days that follow the end of Ramadan and the completion of the *hajj**. In addition to the required daily prayers, devout Muslims also offer individual devotional prayers.

Mystical Worship. The Sufi* tradition abounds in references to prayer and its many virtues. For Sufis, *salat* is an empty ritual if it is not accompanied by devotion and humility. Supplication, which calls on God for guidance and help, is at the heart of the Sufi understanding of prayer. Sufis ask God to provide them with faith, unity, and absolute obedience to his will. They also ask for help to reject the love of worldly goods. The true Sufi is in constant contact with the divine through frequent prayer. Indeed, the main goal of Sufi worship is to transcend any barrier between God and humankind. Sufi prayer glorifies God while acknowledging human fragility and imperfection. Sufis often repeat the Qur'anic verse: "O my Lord, I have indeed wronged my soul." A Sufi meditative prayer might end by asking God to prescribe a way out of sin, anxiety, grief, anguish, and bodily temptation. Because such intense holiness can only be achieved through God's mercy, Sufis—like Muslims in general—remain hopeful of receiving God's compassion. In Islamic meditative practices, prayer is used as a means of healing and removing worry and anxiety.

See color plate 1, vol. 1.

Prayer Beads

See *Prayer*.

Prayer Rugs

See *Prayer*.

Prophets

Prophets—people believed to be divinely inspired messengers—revealed and spread the doctrines of many major religions, including Judaism, Christianity, and Islam. They urged people to forsake sin and to pursue certain courses of action in order to fulfill God's will. Muhammad, through whom Islamic beliefs and practices were revealed, viewed himself as another in the line of the Christian and Jewish prophets that included Abraham, Moses, and Jesus.

The Nature of Prophethood. Islam requires belief in Muhammad as a prophet. In the *shahadah* (profession of faith), the first Pillar of Islam, Muslims declare, "There is no god but God (Allah), and Muhammad is the messenger of God."

The Qur'an* mentions two types of prophets—*nabi* and *rasul*. Both receive divine revelations*. However, the revelations to the *nabi* contain a message for an existing community, whereas those to the *rasul* involve a major message that reforms an existing tradition or begins a new one. *Anbiya* (plural of *nabi*) typically spread knowledge through teachings and their own moral behavior. *Rusul* (plural of *rasul*) generally communicate their revelations in the form of a book of scripture. Every *rasul* is a *nabi*, but not every *nabi* is a *rasul*. According to mainstream Islamic tradition, Muhammad was the last of both.

The prophets of the major religions fulfilled many functions. They served as witnesses to the unity of God, granted people an awareness of God's call to worship, and spread God's will for individuals and societies. Prophets further warned of God's final judgment on the world. Their teachings enabled

* **Qur'an** book of the holy scriptures of Islam

* **revelation** message from God to humans transmitted through a prophet

Prophets

Islamic tradition considers Noah as one of the great prophets, along with Adam, Abraham, Moses, Jesus, and Muhammad. The account of Noah and the flood in the Qur'an is similar to that in the Bible. This illustration of Noah's Ark comes from a Turkish manuscript (1583).

people to make responsible moral decisions and to form communities based on religious principles.

Muslim scholars view prophethood as a sign of God's mercy, given in order for humans to know God's will. They believe that God chose as messengers individuals whose personalities would inspire others to accept his word and to change their lives. God elevated all messengers to the highest degree of moral and intellectual excellence. Prophets could make small mistakes, but could commit no major sins. They displayed four major traits—faithfulness to divine commands, truthfulness regarding God's word, wisdom in understanding the message, and the ability to transmit the message itself.

Prophetic messages in traditional Islamic belief also contained four common elements. First, the prophet presented a clear description of God and his attributes. Second, the message revealed the nature of the unseen spirit world, including angels, *jinn* (spirits), heaven, and hell. The revelation also explained God's will, God's purposes, and the consequences of obedience and disobedience. Finally, a prophet explained how people should structure their societies to fulfill God's law.

Muslims believe that God enabled prophets to perform miracles as evidence of the their elevated stature, indicating that they were not frauds. Islam teaches, however, that God, not the prophets, caused the miracles to occur. Through God, Jesus healed the sick and raised the dead. Moses defeated the Egyptians, demonstrating that God does not allow sinners to prosper. According to Islamic teachings, the Qur'an is Muhammad's only miracle. Islamic scholars consider its prose and poetry unmatched in eloquence. They regard it as an ongoing wonder, written in perfect Arabic, which continues to provide divine guidance to humanity.

Prophets According to Islam. Islam holds that all prophets belong to a single community and that God made a covenant* with each of them before their human creation. God sent prophets to all peoples, each messenger revealing his will in the language of the land to which he or she had been sent. Muslim scholars believe that prophets existed in societies that Muhammad knew nothing about, such as Hindus, Buddhists, Aborigines, Native Americans, and others around the world. All conveyed the same basic message, using the various methods at their disposal.

The Qur'an lists 25 prophets by name, stating that God also called on additional messengers not known to Muhammad. Muslims have debated the number of prophets sent by God. Some scholars calculate the total at 240,000. Others argue that God sent 124,000 messengers, but whichever number is used, it is meant to symbolize a quantity sufficient for all humanity. The Islamic tradition includes six great prophets: Adam, Noah, Abraham, Moses, Jesus, and Muhammad.

Like Jews and Christians, Muslims recognize Adam as the first human being. God created Adam as his steward on earth, and taught him the nature of all things. The Qur'an and the Bible provide similar accounts of Adam's temptation to sin. Islamic tradition, however, rejects the notion that Adam passed original sin down to all humanity. Muslims believe that God restored Adam and Eve to grace after they repented.

The Qur'anic account of Noah and the flood also corresponds with that found in the Bible. Ignoring the taunting of his countrymen, Noah obeyed a divine command to build an ark. God sent a flood to wipe out the unrighteous, and Noah and his family survived on the ark while the rest of humanity perished. According to the Qur'an, Noah went on to preach God's message for 950 years.

Muslims recognize Abraham as the first great prophet. They believe that Abraham was the founding father of Islam through Ismail, his son with the slave woman Hagar. At the urging of his wife Sarah, Abraham sent Ismail and Hagar into the wilderness. The two nearly died of thirst, but God saved them, saying that Ismail would become the father of a great nation. Hagar and Ismail settled in Mecca, where Abraham traveled to visit them. He and Ismail rebuilt the Kaaba* to honor God for his promise. Originally constructed by Adam, the Kaaba served as the first temple to God. After Abraham and Ismail rebuilt it, it became a symbol of their gratitude and devotion to God.

* **covenant** solemn and binding agreement

Reverence for the Prophet

Although Muslims view Muhammad as a human being and not a divine figure, they express a high degree of reverence for him. Great numbers of Muslims visit the Prophet's tomb in Medina before or after the pilgrimage to Mecca in order to receive divine blessing. Since the 1200s, many Muslims have also celebrated his birthday in a holiday called Mawlid. Descendants of Muhammad and members of his family are also shown great respect. The claim of the Moroccan and Jordanian kings to share the Prophet's lineage enhances their authority. Some early Muslims showed devotion to other prophets as well as Muhammad. They built shrines to honor Jewish and Christian messengers such as Abraham, Moses, David, Job, and Jesus.

* **Kaaba** literally "House of God"; Islamic shrine in Mecca

Muslims consider themselves the descendants of Ismail and members of the nation described by God.

Moses is the next great prophet in the Islamic tradition. He led the Hebrew slaves from Egypt and delivered the Ten Commandments to them. Islam also recognizes Jesus as a great prophet, but rejects the Christian tradition that he is the son of God. They believe that God sent Jesus to confirm the law of Moses and to foretell the arrival of a later messenger, Muhammad. The Qur'an also rejects the Christian account of Jesus dying on the cross, stating that God took Jesus directly into heaven.

Muslims accept the Jewish kings David and Solomon as prophets. They celebrate David's victory over Goliath in the face of overwhelming odds, but reject the biblical account that he sent a military leader to his death in order to marry the man's wife. They hold that a prophet of God would never commit such a sin. Muslims also acknowledge the wisdom of David's son, Solomon. The Qur'an describes his glorious kingdom and claims that he converted the Queen of Sheba to Islam.

Islam teaches that Muhammad is God's final and most perfect messenger. All of the prophets looked forward to Muhammad's coming so that he could affirm all that God had revealed to them. Muhammad did not seek to replace other religions with a new faith, claiming to serve in the monotheistic* (Judeo-Christian) tradition. However, some Jewish clans in Medina rejected him as a prophet. Even when Islam became a separate religion, Muslims believed that Muhammad did not contradict the messengers who had come before him. The Qur'an affirms the validity of the Bible, and Muslims accept Jews and Christians as People of the Book. They maintain, however, that Jewish and Christian scripture has been misinterpreted at times. The Qur'an is the only book of scripture that has not become corrupted. Muslims believe that Muhammad will play a special role on the Day of Judgment, interceding with God on behalf of believers. (*See also* **Abraham; Jesus; Muhammad; Revelation.**)

* **monotheistic** refers to the belief that there is only one God

Purification

See *Ablution.*

Qaddafi, Mu'ammar al-

1942–
Libyan ruler

* **Bedouin** nomad of the desert, especially in North Africa, Syria, and Arabia

* **nationalist** one who advocates loyalty and devotion to his or her country and its independence

* **coup** sudden, and often violent, overthrow of a ruler or government

Mu'ammar al-Qaddafi was born to a Bedouin* family in the Sirte region of the Libyan desert. Noting his intelligence, his father sent him to primary school. The first member of the family to receive an education, Qaddafi continued his studies at the University of Libya and the Military Academy of Benghazi. He opposed the weak, foreign-dominated monarchy in Libya and resented the Italian population that controlled most of the wealth in the country. Qaddafi admired the nationalist* philosophy of Egyptian president Gamal Abdel Nasser and sought to emulate him. At the academy, Qaddafi organized a Free Officers movement similar to the one created by Nasser to overthrow the Egyptian government in the 1950s. In 1969 the Libyan Free Officers led a successful military coup*, ousting King Idris I and establishing Qaddafi as leader of the new Libyan Arab Republic.

Qaddafi quickly evicted American and British military forces from Libya. He also deported most Italians and Jews and nationalized* Libya's oil assets, banks, and other businesses. He built schools, hospitals, and housing complexes throughout the country, and greatly increased the standard of living. Qaddafi established a government organized into various committees representing the legislative and executive bodies of the state. He called his system of government *jamahiriyah* (rule by the masses), but the system maintained Qaddafi's position as all-powerful leader. His basic ideas on politics and society were presented in *The Green Book*, published in the 1970s.

Qaddafi promoted Islamic values but accepted the Qur'an*—not hadith* or the sunnah*—as the only authentic source of doctrine. He rejected the power of the *ulama* and the Sufi* orders, giving himself supreme religious authority. He cracked down on extremist groups and banned gambling, alcohol, and Western music. Qaddafi also granted greater freedoms to Libyan women. In the early 21st century, most women in Libyan cities do not wear headscarves, and women comprise more than half of all university students.

Qaddafi pushed an aggressive foreign policy, calling for jihad* against imperialist* powers and Israel. He repeatedly sought to form alliances with other Arab nations. Failing at this, Qaddafi gave financial support to freedom fighters and revolutionaries in other countries, such as Native Americans and the Nation of Islam in the United States. He also backed militant groups in such countries as Nicaragua, France, Ireland, Italy, Japan, and Turkey, helping to fund the Irish Republican Army (IRA) and the Palestine Liberation Organization (PLO).

Libyan support for terrorist activities in Europe caused the United States to sever economic ties with the country in 1986. Following a 1986 attack against a nightclub in Germany frequented by Americans, which was attributed to Libyans, U.S. warplanes bombed Benghazi and Tripoli. The raids killed or wounded dozens of Libyans, including some of Qaddafi's children. In 1988 Libya refused to turn over to an international court two Libyans suspected of blowing up an American airliner over Lockerbie, Scotland. The United Nations (UN) responded by imposing sanctions against Libya in 1992.

The loss of trade and the decline in oil prices hurt the Libyan economy. Food shortages created unrest in the 1990s, enabling certain Islamic groups to challenge Qaddafi's regime. Realizing that he had to end his country's isolation, Qaddafi ended his support for terrorism and paid settlements to Great Britain and France for past attacks. Qaddafi also denounced the September 11, 2001, attacks on the World Trade Center and supported the U.S. campaign against al-Qaeda. He delivered the two Lockerbie suspects to an international court, where one was convicted and the other was acquitted. Qaddafi still, however, refuses to admit responsibility for the bombing.

Qaddafi's concessions have benefited his country. The UN lifted its sanctions against Libya in 1999, and several European nations have renewed relations with the country. The nation enjoys a higher standard of living than many other African nations and has one of the highest per capita incomes on the continent. Distribution of wealth remains more equal in Libya than in most countries, including the United States. (*See also* **Libya; Palestinian Liberation Organization; Qutb, Sayyid; Terrorism.**)

* **nationalization** process by which a government takes control of its industries

* **Qur'an** book of the holy scriptures of Islam

* **hadith** reports of the words and deeds of Muhammad (not in the Qur'an, but accepted as guides for Muslim behavior)

* **sunnah** literally "the trodden path"; Islamic customs based on the exemplary behavior of Muhammad

* **ulama** religious scholars

* **Sufi** refers to Sufism, which seeks to develop spirituality through discipline of the mind and body

* **jihad** literally "striving;" war in defense of Islam

* **imperialist** refers to an empire

Qadiani

See *Ahmadi.*

Qadiriyah

* **Sufi** refers to Sufism, which seeks to develop spirituality through discipline of the mind and body

* **theologian** person who studies the nature, qualities, and will of God

* **mysticism** belief that spiritual enlightenment and truth can be attained through various physical and spiritual disciplines

* **jihad** literally "striving"; war in defense of Islam

* *zawiyah* Sufi center that serves as a place of worship and welfare institution

* **Shi'i** refers to Muslims who believe that Muhammad chose Ali ibn Abi Talib and his descendants as the spiritual-political leaders of the Muslim community

* **Sunni** refers to the largest branch of the Muslim community; the name derives from sunnah, the exemplary behavior of the Prophet Muhammad

The Qadiri brotherhood is one of the oldest Sufi* orders, taking its name from Persian theologian* Abd al-Qadir al-Jilani (1078–1166). An expert in Hanbali law, Abd al-Qadir embraced Sufism late in life. His preaching inspired disciples from all over the Islamic world, including Christians and Jews. Abd al-Qadir's teachings reconciled mysticism* with the teachings of Islamic law. He believed Muslims should embark on a personal jihad* to conquer their desires and submit to the will of God. After Abd al-Qadir's death, his followers created legends about him, some of which earned him the wrath of his colleagues. Abd al-Qadir's followers claimed that he had crushed mountains, healed the sick, and raised the dead. Many Sufis revere him as a saint.

Abd al-Qadir did not found any particular organization or belief system. His sons organized his followers into the Qadiriyah, a Sufi order bearing his name that promoted humility, moderation, and charity. A descendent of Abd al-Qadir continues to head the central body, which governs a loose organization of regional communities. Qadiri groups develop their own prayers and *dhikrs* (ritual chants). Many practice *sama* (the use of music for meditation). The early Qadiriyah adopted Indian breathing techniques and body movements into their rituals. After the Mongol invasion of the Middle East in the 1250s, many Qadiris settled in India. The movement thrived in the region, attracting converts from prominent Muslim families.

The Qadiriyah supposedly built their first *zawiyah** near Abd al-Qadir's tomb in Baghdad soon after his death in 1166. By 1300 the order had spread to Syria, Egypt, and Yemen. The Qadiri brotherhood remained strong in Iran for three centuries. The Shi'i* Safavids, however, opposed the Sunni* teachings of the movement's founder. When they took power in 1501, they expelled most members of the Qadiriyah from Iran. The Qadiriyah reemerged in Afghanistan after the fall of the Safavids (1722). The brotherhood also expanded into Turkey, but membership decreased dramatically after Kemal Atatürk shut down Sufi brotherhoods in 1924.

According to oral tradition, Abd al-Qadir's grandsons brought the movement to Spain. Christian persecution, however, forced the Qadiriyah to flee to North Africa in the 1400s. The order gained strength in Morocco, Algeria, Tunisia, and the Sudan. By the 1800s, it had reached Nigeria, Mali, Guinea, and Senegal. Several offshoot movements formed in Africa. One group, the Jilaliyah, combines Muslim mysticism with earlier tribal beliefs and practices. They revere Abd al-Qadir as a supernatural being.

The Qadiri movement remains strong today, with a following in India, Pakistan, Turkey, and the Middle East. In addition, the Qadiri have formed communities in China, Indonesia, Central Asia, southeastern Europe, Somalia, and the East African coast. (*See also* **Law; Saints and Sainthood; Sufism; Zawiyah.**)

Qaeda, al-

The terrorist attacks in the United States on September 11, 2001, turned the spotlight on an extremist organization called al-Qaeda (Arabic for "the base") and its leader, Osama bin Laden. This group of well-trained, mostly Arab Muslims perpetrates acts of violence against the West, particularly the United States, in an attempt to rid the Middle East and other Muslim lands of Western influence. The ultimate goal of al-Qaeda is to create a central Islamic government that represents Muslims worldwide.

Volunteer Warriors. The founding of al-Qaeda has its roots in the late 1970s, a time when the former Soviet Union invaded Afghanistan. Abdullah Azzam, a Palestinian activist and member of the Muslim Brotherhood (a popular Islamic reformist organization), mobilized Muslim men to engage in jihad* and resist their communist* invaders. He toured Arab and Muslim countries, raising funds and gathering volunteers—one of whom was Osama bin Laden, a recent college graduate from Saudi Arabia. Azzam recognized bin Laden's ability to organize and inspire young people and soon became the young man's mentor. Throughout the ten-year struggle in Afghanistan, bin Laden helped recruit soldiers and financed their training. Supported by the U.S. Central Intelligence Agency, Saudi Arabia, and Pakistan, the volunteer army finally forced the Soviet Union to withdraw its troops in 1989.

* **jihad** literally "striving"; war in defense of Islam
* **communist** refers to communism, a political and economic system based on the concept of shared ownership of all property

Azzam referred to the fighters as *al-Qaeda as-Sulbah* (the solid or firm base) because they could lead the *ummah* (Muslim community) and were too strong-willed to be defeated by their enemies. Over time, the ideology* and organization of al-Qaeda evolved. Unlike a political party or militia*, al-Qaeda members pledged their allegiance to an ongoing jihad, which was generally understood by the group to mean military combat.

* **ideology** system of ideas or beliefs
* **militia** group of citizens organized for military service

After Azzam's mysterious assassination in 1989, bin Laden emerged as the undisputed leader of al-Qaeda. He regarded the withdrawal of Soviet troops from Afghanistan as evidence of God's support for the Muslim struggle against their adversaries.

Anti-American Rhetoric and Activity. Bin Laden's theology* draws heavily on the ultra-conservative* beliefs of the Wahhabi, the ruling sect* in Saudi Arabia. He preaches a blatant anti-Christian and anti-Jewish message. Bin Laden refers to Christians as "crusaders" because he believes that modern Christians are continuing the efforts of medieval crusaders to destroy Islam. He splits the world into two spheres: his world, which includes only his Muslim supporters, and the world of his enemies, which includes anyone—Muslim and non-Muslim—who disagrees with his philosophy. During the last ten years, bin Laden focused his energies on fighting the United States and destroying its influence. Bin Laden believes that Americans understand only the language of force.

* **theology** study of the nature and qualities of God and the understanding of His will
* **conservative** generally opposed to change, especially in existing political and social institutions
* **sect** religious group adhering to distinctive beliefs

After the end of the Soviet-Afghan war, bin Laden returned to his home in Saudi Arabia. In August 1990, neighboring Iraq invaded and occupied Kuwait, and Bin Laden offered to organize his followers to fight Saddam Hussein's army. The Saudi royal family rejected his offer and invited U.S. forces to the region instead. After bin Laden denounced the

* **regime** government in power

* **caliphate** office and government of the caliph, the religious and political leader of an Islamic state

Saudi government's action, he was stripped of his citizenship. Bin Laden later sought to punish the United States for what he saw as sponsorship of corrupt Muslim regimes* and for the desecration of what he often describes as the "Land of Muhammad," a reference to Saudi Arabia, the birthplace of the Prophet.

From his new location in Khartoum, the capital of Sudan, bin Laden used his considerable inheritance (estimated to be in the millions of dollars) to finance al-Qaeda activities and to win favor with the Sudanese government. His network of followers expanded in 1996 when he moved back to Afghanistan, then under the rule of the militant extremist Taliban. Al-Qaeda established terrorist training camps for volunteers. In 1998 bin Laden and Egyptian militant Ayman al-Zawahiri announced the founding of the Islamic International Front for the Combat Against the Crusaders and Jews. They endorsed the use of violence and rationalized the killing of innocent people—even if they happen to be Muslims—as an unfortunate side effect of their struggle.

The organization represented a merger between bin Laden's al-Qaeda and al-Zawahiri's Egyptian Islamic Jihad, a militant Islamic organization that was responsible for acts of violence in Egypt during the 1990s. The Islamic International Front dedicated itself to "the restoration of the caliphate*," a reference to the central Islamic government that existed until 1924, when the Turkish government abolished it.

Throughout the 1990s, al-Qaeda allegedly participated in a series of terrorist attacks. The network was suspected of involvement in two incidents in 1993—the bombing of the World Trade Center in New York City and a battle against U.S. troops serving in Mogadishu, Somalia. Al-Qaeda is also believed to be responsible for the 1998 bombings of U.S. embassies in Tanzania and Kenya and the bombing of the USS Cole in Yemen in 2000.

On September 11, 2001, terrorists hijacked four airplanes and crashed two of them into the World Trade Center in New York, one into the Pentagon in Washington, D.C., and one into a field in western Pennsylvania. The United States promptly declared a "war on terrorism," with bin Laden and al-Qaeda as its primary targets. When the Taliban refused to cooperate in efforts to bring bin Laden to justice, the United States launched a military campaign against Afghanistan. In late 2001, U.S. and allied forces succeeded in removing the Taliban from power, but bin Laden escaped.

Although the war in Afghanistan and the overthrow of the Taliban regime weakened the network, al-Qaeda remained active in its struggle against Western interests. In 2002 al-Qaeda was linked to the bombing of a French oil tanker off Yemen, firearms attacks against U.S. Marines in Kuwait, and other international incidents. In 2003 the United Nations Security Council reported that al-Qaeda was creating new training camps in Afghanistan, and the number of new recruits was increasing. As the American-led war on terrorism continued, bin Laden released audiotapes threatening more attacks on the United States. Despite his apparent but horrendous successes, bin Laden failed to inspire a mass movement among Muslims, the majority of whom condemn terrorism. (*See also* **Afghanistan; Bin Laden, Osama; Fundamentalism; Jihad; September 11, 2001; Taliban; Terrorism; United States; Wahhabi.**)

Qom

Qom, a city in central Iran located south of Tehran, is a major Shi'i* religious site and the leading center of Islamic learning in Iran. In 816 Fatimah, the sister of the eighth imam*, Ali al-Rida, died in Qom while traveling to meet her brother. Her grave, later topped with a gold dome, became the second most important Shi'i shrine in Iran.

Historically, Qom residents have developed a reputation for religious piety and resistance to government policies. Qom served as a center of opposition to the Umayyad dynasty (661–750). During the next few centuries, its citizens repeatedly rebelled against the tax demands of Sunni* governors. In the 1900s, Qom became a focal point for revolt against the government of Reza Shah Pahlavi. The state's secular* policies angered many in the city, including Ruhollah al-Musavi Khomeini, a future ayatollah*. A police crackdown on *ulama** activities led to a major uprising in 1963. After the shah's forces arrested Khomeini, three days of violent protest ensued. Qom later served as a focal point of the Iranian Revolution of 1979. The Iranian army surrendered to revolutionary forces there in 1979, and Khomeini made the city his residence.

As the home of many of Iran's religious scholars, Qom has played an important role in the administrative affairs of the Iranian republic. The city serves as a burial site of 400 Islamic saints and 10 kings. It boasts at least 20 *madrasahs**, including Iran's largest center of higher religious learning. Qom attracts legions of pilgrims and religious students each year. (*See also* **Iran; Khomeini, Ruhollah al-Musavi; Shrine.**)

* **Shi'i** refers to Muslims who believe that Muhammad chose Ali ibn Abi Talib and his descendants as the spiritual-political leaders of the Muslim community

* **imam** spiritual-political leader in Shi'i Islam, one who is regarded as directly descended from Muhammad; also, one who leads prayers

* **Sunni** refers to the largest branch of the Muslim community; the name derives from sunnah, the exemplary behavior of the Prophet Muhammad

* **secular** separate from religion in human life and society; connected to everyday life

* **ayatollah** highest-ranking legal scholar among some Shi'i Muslims

* *ulama* religious scholars

* *madrasah* religious college or university; also religious school for young students

Qur'an

For Muslims, the Qur'an is the eternal and indisputable word of God. The oldest and most sacred text of Islam, it is the cornerstone of every believer's faith and morality. But the Qur'an is also an earthly book, and its history is intimately connected to the life and history of an earthly community.

> See color plate 3, vol. 1.

The Book

The Qur'an was revealed to Muhammad over a period of about 22 years. It serves as a record of the society of his time and constitutes the most important source for tracing the historical development of Islam from its origins in Mecca to its maturity in Medina. Many of its passages reflect the conditions of the early Islamic community. Even so, for Muslims its divine message transcends time and space.

Supernatural Experience. According to Islamic tradition, Muhammad received his first divine revelation* during the month of Ramadan in 610. Seeking a solitary place to pray and meditate, Muhammad regularly withdrew to a cave on Mount Hira, a few miles north of his home in Mecca.

* **revelation** message from God to humans transmitted through a prophet

Qur'an

Islamic scholars regard the Qur'an as a literary work of unmatched eloquence, written in perfect Arabic. Few members of the early Islamic community could read or write. The introduction of the Qur'an helped transform Arabia into a literate society.

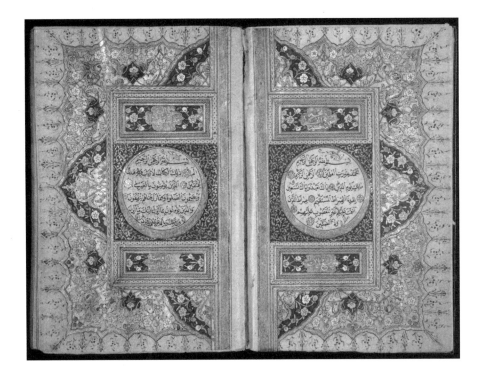

During one such retreat, a heavenly being, later identified as the angel Gabriel, appeared to him. The angel commanded him to recite and later gave him a divine revelation. Muhammad returned home frightened and confused. He feared that he was possessed by a demon. After a period of uncertainty lasting between six months and two years, during which Muhammad received no new revelations, his wife Khadija and her cousin helped convince him that the revelation was from God. Thereafter, revelations continued to come until Muhammad's death in 632. Muhammad received the divine messages verse by verse, often in response to a crisis or concern that emerged among his followers.

Most members of the early Islamic community, including Muhammad, were illiterate. The new scripture* was known as the *qur'an* (recitation) because believers learned it by listening to public readings and recitations. Many of Muhammad's followers committed the passages to memory. But the Prophet also commissioned many scribes to preserve the messages in writing. They recorded the words on a variety of available materials, including paper, stones, palm leaves, and pieces of leather.

Setting the Standard. By the time of Muhammad's death, several of his followers had memorized the entire Qur'an. Many of them, however, were killed in battle. Fearing that knowledge of the Qur'an might be lost, the leaders of the Islamic community decided to collect all the revelations, from both written and oral sources, and to compile an official version of the sacred text. Many partial collections existed. They were among the possessions of Muhammad's wives, his companions, and scribes. These collections contained variations, further demonstrating the need for a single authoritative source.

The process of gathering material was time consuming. Uthman, the third caliph*, commissioned a team of Muslim scholars to oversee it. Led by

* **scripture** sacred writings that contain revelations from God

* **caliph** religious and political leader of an Islamic state

Zayd ibn Thabit, one of Muhammad's companions, they completed their work around 650. To resolve conflicts in pronunciation among the earlier sources, the team used the dialect of the Quraysh, the tribe of the Prophet.

Although Uthman's version of the Arabic text became the official standard for the Islamic community, a large number of variations emerged, reflecting regional differences in language. Islam recognizes seven readings of the Qur'an as equally valid.

Literary Elements. The Qur'an consists of 114 chapters, or surahs, varying in length from 3 to 286 verses (*ayat*). The longest chapters, which reflect the later period of Muhammad's revelations, appear at the beginning of the book. The shortest and earliest surahs appear at the end, with the exception of the short first surah. The complete Qur'an is about the same length as the New Testament of the Bible.

The heading of each surah contains certain elements, including a title, an indication of whether the verses were revealed before or after the Hijrah (the emigration from Mecca to Medina), and the number of verses. In most cases, the name of a surah refers to a specific word in the passage, and therefore, does not reflect its contents. Examples of chapter titles include "The Dinner Table," "Jonah," "The Ant," "She Who Pleaded," and "The Disbelievers." Some titles vary by region, and in some cases, the names of chapters have been changed at different times in Islamic history. Many of the surahs vary in style or content, and the longer ones cover a range of topics.

Most Muslims consider the Qur'an to be a masterpiece of rhymed prose. It is regarded as Muhammad's only miracle, a text of such astounding beauty and wisdom that no one will ever be able to match its eloquence.

Scripture

Muslims do not consider Muhammad to be the author or editor of the Qur'an. Instead, they regard him as a prophet, chosen by God to receive and transmit a divine message. The Qur'an itself denies any earthly origins. As the word of God, the Qur'an is regarded as sacred and infallible.

Word of God. Muslims believe that the Qur'an is the eternal, literal word of God. The original version of the book is described as preserved in heaven or in the mind of God. God's direct speech, indicated by the use of the first person plural (we), appears in much of the Qur'an. In some sections of the text, Muhammad speaks to his followers. These sections are preceded by the word "say," to imply that God is relaying a message through Muhammad. Overall, the Qur'an emphasizes teaching over narrative.

Islam teaches that God revealed his will to humankind through a series of messengers, known as prophets. In particular, God spoke through Moses (in the Hebrew scriptures, the Torah) and through Jesus (in the Gospels). The Qur'an contains many references to the Torah and Gospels. Muslims believe that Jews and Christians corrupted parts of God's original message, omitting references to the coming of Muhammad, for example. Muslims believe these earlier sources contain flaws and that the Qur'an—as revealed to the Prophet Muhammad—is the only complete and unquestionable word of God.

Taking the Circumstances into Consideration

Although the Qur'an is Islam's oldest text, Muslim modernists believe that it holds the key to rejuvenating their religion. Pakistani philosopher and educator Fazlur Rahman (1919–1988) rejected literal and traditional interpretations of the Qur'an, arguing that they limited the applicability of the message to the time and place in which the revelation occurred. By understanding the spirit of the Qur'an, Rahman argued, Muslims can apply the text to modern circumstances. He believed that Muslims should study the historical context of each verse in order to find its true essence. Equipped with an understanding of their contemporary circumstances, they could apply the principles derived from the text to their own time. Rahman was convinced that an adequate understanding of Qur'anic teachings would enable believers to overcome the problems of the modern Muslim world.

See color plate 2, vol. 1.

Characteristics of Allah. The Qur'an is the primary source of Islamic belief and practice. The book stresses the existence of the one true God. The Qur'an states that God is the source of all life: "He is the First and the Last, the Outward and the Inward; And He is the Knower of every thing." Moreover, God is transcendent—humans are unable to fully comprehend his glory and essence. Muslims refer to the basic principle of the Qur'an as *tawhid*, meaning divine unity.

The Qur'an also sets forth the duties of humans. A Muslim must submit to the will of God, as revealed in the sacred text. The book describes a covenant* between God and people, in which humans assume responsibility for the earth. Those who trust in God and honor this commitment in thought, word, and deed act as God's representatives or stewards. The society made up of such faithful individuals is a witness to the truth.

Discovering Meaning. Following the death of the Prophet, the Islamic community grew rapidly, and theological* conflicts emerged among the believers. A significant doctrinal* dispute occurred during the 700s. At that time, a group of thinkers called Mu'tazili departed from the mainstream Islamic belief that the Qur'an is eternal and uncreated. In their view, God's uniqueness and unity is absolute, and therefore, nothing else besides God could exist for eternity. Consequently, the Mu'tazili taught that while the Qur'an expresses God's eternal will, he created the Qur'an itself at some point in time.

In these and other disagreements about conceptual and practical matters, Muslims looked to the Qur'an for solutions. The correct explanation and interpretation of the sacred text became the focus of a special branch of learning called *tafsir*. For centuries, Islamic scholars have devoted their careers to interpreting the book's passages. During the medieval* period, several Muslim thinkers produced noteworthy commentaries on the Qur'an.

The rise of modernism during the late 1800s brought new influences to Qur'anic studies. By that time, colonial rule had severely undermined the political and cultural authority of the Islamic state and society. Modernists noted that the early followers of Islam were willing to accommodate new ideas in their understanding of the Qur'an and its guidelines for society. As a result, during the Middle Ages, the Islamic societies had thriving centers of learning. The modern reformers advocated a revival* of this earlier flexibility as a way to restore dignity and greatness to the Muslim world. They believed that a flexible and continuous reinterpretation of the Qur'an would enable Muslims to reform various aspects of their societies, making them more suited to modern life.

Beyond the Arab World. The issue of translating the Qur'an posed a dilemma for Muslims. Although they sought to spread their faith to other lands, Islamic religious scholars insisted that rendering the words of God into another language implied a departure from the original text. The Qur'an was God's word only in Arabic. Nonetheless, non-Arab Muslims eventually created translations in their own languages. By the 1000s, a Persian edition of the Qur'an was available. The first Latin translation of the text appeared in the 1100s. Italian, German, and Dutch versions existed by the 1600s and were soon followed by the first English translation. By the 1900s, the Qur'an had been translated into nearly every major language of Europe and Asia.

* **covenant** solemn and binding agreement

* **theological** refers to the study of the nature, qualities, and will of God

* **doctrinal** refers to a principle, theory, or belief that is taught or presented for acceptance

* **medieval** refers to the Middle Ages, a period roughly between 500 and 1500

* **revival** return to traditional values or beliefs

Muslim scholars classify these works as commentaries or interpretations to distinguish them from the Arabic original. Therefore, they cannot be used for ritual purposes.

Muslim Society

The Qur'an is the means for discovering the will of God and for measuring the success of a life lived in accordance with it. As such, it shapes the individual and collective lives of Muslims in many ways.

Transforming Thought and Practice. In pre-Islamic* Arabia, few people could read or write. They passed cultural practices and traditions from one generation to another orally. The introduction of the Qur'an transformed Arabia into a literate society. The Qur'an contains numerous references to writing and reading, and it repeatedly encourages people to record the details of a loan or contract. Undoubtedly, the presence of divine communication in book form encouraged people to learn to read.

* **pre-Islamic** refers to the Arabian Peninsula or to the Arabic language before the founding of Islam in the early 600s

The Qur'an promoted the development of many disciplines in the Islamic world. The sciences of the Arabic language evolved as Muslims studied grammar, rhetoric*, and word meanings to gain an accurate understanding of the text. The Qur'an, which serves as the primary source of Islamic law, advanced the field of law beyond custom and oral tradition. References to past events inspired Arab scholars to study history, and its theological content led to the growth of religious sciences as an academic pursuit.

* **rhetoric** art of speaking and writing effectively

The Qur'an also functions as a basic source of Muslim education. Although a large majority of the world's Muslim population does not speak Arabic, in most Muslim societies young children learn the Arabic alphabet to read the Qur'an in its original language. The book also provides the first reading lessons for these young students.

Religion and Beyond. The Qur'an plays a central role in Muslim life. As the foundation of Islam, it is the final authority on all religious matters. It outlines the basic tenets of the religion and the principles of ethical behavior. Muslims also use the text in daily rituals and special observances. Each of the five daily prayers includes a recital of the opening surah and several other parts of the Qur'an. Over the course of the month of Ramadan, some Muslims recite the entire Qur'an, which is divided into 30 equal sections for this purpose.

The scripture provides guidelines for social, political, and economic activities. Its teachings on family law guide behavior in marriage, divorce, and inheritance. Muslims use the Qur'an to invoke God's blessing at a variety of social occasions. Weddings, funerals, business dinners, political meetings, and lectures often begin with a recitation from the Qur'an. In addition, the Qur'an has artistic uses. The art of Qur'anic calligraphy is among the most highly developed skills in Islamic culture. Inscriptions from the holy book appear in most mosques*.

* **mosque** Muslim place of worship

Recitation. Muslims highly value Qur'anic recitation. They believe that the act of reciting the divine word brings blessings (*barakah*). Muslims consider recitation the best way to experience the Qur'an because it captures the rhythm, sounds, and pronunciation of the original revelation. Moreover, the angel Gabriel transmitted the Qur'an to Muhammad orally.

Hearing the word of God spoken is a strong source of inspiration. Throughout the world, Muslims learn to memorize and recite the book in Arabic, its original language. Although many do not speak or understand Arabic, the practice promotes solidarity among believers worldwide.

Certain rules apply to Qur'anic recitations. The reciter should sit, facing the direction of Mecca. Using a written text is preferable to reciting from memory. The individual must proceed at an acceptable tempo. A reading of the entire Qur'an should take about three days and should not be completed in less that. Some portions of the Qur'an are read in a certain way. For example, the reciter should use a tearful voice for verses describing judgment or suffering. The reciter should stop if his or her concentration wanes. Listeners should maintain a worshipful silence. Listening practices vary, however. In some regions, audience members commonly rock back and forth, expressing intense emotions.

Islam recognizes seven principle readings of the Qur'an. (The variations in the readings are minor.) Those who complete the difficult process of mastering all of these versions earn a certificate and are held in high esteem.

The public reading of the Qur'an is a major form of performance art in the Islamic world. Crowds fill stadiums to hear musical and poetic recitations. Listeners derive great pleasure from the rich rhyming prose of the Qur'an. Muslims hire reciters for weddings, funerals, conferences, and a variety of other events. The most famous reciters can earn a comfortable living from their performances and commercial recordings.

Many countries hold Qur'an recitation contests, which attract large audiences. Both children and adults compete at local, regional, and national events. Winners receive trophies and other rewards as well as invitations to meet with high-ranking government officials. (*See also* **Allah; Islam: Overview; Law; Modernism; Muhammad; Prophets; Revelation; Theology.**)

Qutb, Sayyid

1906–1966
Writer, critic, and activist

* **nationalist** one who advocates loyalty and devotion to his or her country and its independence

* **Qur'an** book of the holy scriptures of Islam

Sayyid Qutb Ibrahim Husayn Shadhili was born in 1906 in the village of Musha in Egypt. At the time of his birth, the family was in economic decline. Owing to his father's reputation as an educated man and prominent nationalist*, the family's prestige remained intact. Qutb was a sickly child, which may have influenced his tendency toward deep spirituality. He reportedly had memorized the entire Qur'an* by age ten. After completing his primary education at a local religious school, he transferred to a government school and later attended a teacher's training college in Cairo, graduating in 1928. In 1933, Qutb received a degree in arts education from Dar al-Ulum University. He went to work at the Ministry of Education, where he served as an inspector and as a writer.

In 1948, while still working for the ministry, Qutb traveled to the United States to study Western methods of education. His two years in the United States marked a turning point in this thinking. He acknowledged the scientific and economic achievements of the country, but found American society to be racist, decadent, and pro-Israeli. Appalled by what he saw, Qutb rejected Western ideologies* as spiritually bankrupt. On returning to Egypt, he abandoned his educational career to concentrate on religious writings. Qutb joined the Muslim Brotherhood in 1953 and soon became the organization's leading thinker.

    Profoundly influenced by Islamic revivalist Sayyid Mawdudi, Qutb came to view Islam as a complete way of life. He believed that Islam provided timeless solutions to every human situation and saw no need to reinterpret the Qur'an to fit with modern realities. Instead, he urged Muslims to withdraw from mainstream society and establish a model *ummah* (community of believers) based on God's law. According to Qutb, this Islamic society would promote social justice and meet the material and spiritual needs of everyone. His writings, which have been translated into Persian, Urdu, Turkish, English, and other languages, show his uncompromising commitment to the sacred text.

    For a time, Qutb served as liaison between the Muslim Brotherhood and the Free Officers, who had overthrown the Egyptian monarchy in 1952. In 1954 Egyptian leader Gamal Abdel Nasser (one of the Free Officers) turned against the brotherhood, which had criticized him for failing to rule in accordance with Islamic law. He had several of the organization's leaders, including Qutb, arrested. Despite his poor health, Qutb was brutally tortured and spent much of his 15-year sentence in the prison hospital. While in prison, Qutb set in motion his ideas for a secret disciplined group of devoted followers. Although his original purpose for the group was self-defense, he soon came to believe that using violence against the government was justifiable. He strongly opposed the secularism* of Nasser and other leaders and believed that Muslims who accepted such rulers lived in un-Islamic ignorance. He wrote that the faithful had a duty to overthrow rulers who ignored God's law. After the assassination of a government official, reportedly by a member of the Muslim Brotherhood, Nasser had Qutb and two of his colleagues executed in 1966. Since that time, Qutb has become a martyr* to his supporters.

    One of the most influential Muslim thinkers of the 20th century, Sayyid Qutb is regarded by many as the founder of militant* Islamic politics. His writings have inspired a host of movements, including the movement to overthrow the shah in 1979 (Iran), al-Jihad (Egypt), Hamas (West Bank and Gaza), Hizbullah (Lebanon), and the Taliban (Afghanistan). Many Muslims today still embrace Qutb's revolutionary call to create a pure Islamic order. Others find in his work justification for killing people who are considered enemies of Islam.

* **ideology** system of ideas or beliefs

* **secularism** belief that religion should be separate from other aspects of human life and society, especially politics

* **martyr** one who dies for his or her religious beliefs

* **militant** aggressively active in a cause

Radio and Television

Traditionally, radio and television programming in the Islamic world has served the interests of government leaders. As the owners and operators of the communication networks, they supervised and censored the coverage of news and political analyses as well as entertainment. Moreover, Islamic values exerted a considerable influence on media outlets. As modern broad-

Radio and Television

* **infrastructure** basic facilities and institutions that a country needs in order to function

* **nationalism** feelings of loyalty and devotion to one's country and a commitment to its independence

* **mosque** Muslim place of worship

casting technologies rapidly develop and the media adopts a more global outlook, Islamic governments are responding to a changing communication climate.

On the Air. Radio broadcasting systems debuted between 1910 and 1930. At that time, creating the infrastructure* necessary to transmit signals was very expensive. Few Islamic countries were independent or able to afford such costs. During the 1930s, the governments of Egypt, Iran, and Turkey began to use radio broadcasts to provide news and information and to influence public opinion. Turkey's Mustafa Kemal Atatürk and Iran's Reza Shah Pahlavi, for example, relied heavily on radio to promote nationalism*.

As Islamic lands in Asia and Africa gained their independence during the 1950s and 1960s, their leaders established state-run broadcasting systems. Radio functioned as a symbol of national and political power and a way to promote Muslim cultural values. Moreover, broadcasts enabled politicians to maintain stability in the face of economic, political, and social change. Rulers such as President Sukarno of Indonesia and President Nasser of Egypt used radio to reinforce national policy. Iranian government leaders combined radio broadcasting with traditional methods of communication, such as the mosque* and the bazaar, to persuade citizens to nationalize the country's oil industry. Television broadcasting did not reach many parts of the Islamic world until the late 1950s and early 1960s.

Historically, several factors slowed the expansion of radio and television broadcasting in Muslim countries. Most significantly, many of these nations lacked the economic resources necessary to construct, maintain, and operate electronic communication systems. Education and training in the fields of radio and television programming and operation were limited. Linguistic diversity and incompatible broadcasting systems also prevented some countries from exchanging programs and developing a regional network.

Between the 1970s and the 1990s, the number of radio and television transmitters doubled in most Muslim countries. The number of receivers also

Founded in 1996, the Arab-language satellite television network al-Jazeera has gained a wide following. It has become a leading source of news and information about the Islamic world and provides many Arabs with the only uncensored account of developments in the region.

increased, especially in the Gulf states and Southeast Asia. Because Muslims traditionally listen to and watch broadcasts in groups, however, statistics cannot accurately reflect the actual size of the audience. Technological advances, such as the development of satellites, have dramatically affected television broadcasting in the Muslim world. All Islamic countries have access to the worldwide satellite network of the International Telecommunications Satellite Organization. Some countries, such as Egypt, maintain their own satellite broadcasting systems. With such advances in communications media, programming is no longer limited by national and international political boundaries.

Communication Challenge. In Western countries, private, independent corporations generally own and operate radio and television stations. They are usually commercial ventures designed to generate a profit for the owners. By contrast, in the Islamic world, the state typically controls the media. Radio and television programming reflects the views and policies of the establishment. Although many Muslim governments do not officially censor the media, they exercise tight control of content. For example, the Tunisian constitution guarantees freedom of the press and expression. But the government banned relays of a French channel for its critical coverage of that country's presidential elections in 1999. Algerian president Abdelaziz Bouteflika has been quoted as saying that the media should "ultimately be at the service of the state." Fearing reprisal, Algerian broadcasters tend to avoid stories about political violence.

Most Muslim nations import about one-half of their television programs, the majority of which consists of entertainment from the United States and Europe. Islamic countries justify state control of the media as a way to defend their nations from unwanted foreign influence and cultural messages. Concern about the negative influence of Western-dominated programming has led some Muslim governments to invest in locally produced cultural programs.

The growth of communications technology has made it increasingly difficult for Muslim states to control the programming that reaches their citizens. After the Persian Gulf War (1990–1991), demand for satellite dishes rose sharply in the Gulf states and North Africa. Some countries, such as Saudi Arabia and Iran, ban satellites, but such bans are difficult to enforce. Furthermore, governments have little control over the content or distribution of VCRs and videocassettes. This changing climate has led some countries, such as Algeria and Egypt, to lift restrictions on the operation of private broadcasting stations.

No Separation. Islamic principles often play a major role in determining the content and production of programs and in shaping communications regulations. Such religious influences give Muslim broadcasting a distinctive look and feel. Broadcasting typically combines civic and religious programming. In some areas, however, certain radio stations are devoted solely to the teaching of the Qur'an*.

Instead of replacing traditional forms of political and popular communication, radio and television have extended them in new ways. Mosques use both radio and television to broadcast sermons and other religious events in order to reach larger audiences. Friday prayer services, which are often a fo-

Egyptian Television Uncensored

Government ownership and censorship of the media is widespread in Muslim countries. In recent years, however, some Middle Eastern governments have purchased commercial satellites and rented access to private television stations. In late 2001, Egypt's first private television station, Dream TV, began broadcasting. Primarily focused on entertainment programming, Dream TV currently consists of two channels. Targeting the younger generation, Dream 1 features music video clips, talk shows, and the latest celebrity news. Dream 2 airs variety programs, as well as Arabic and international films. Although the station cannot financially support a news channel, several hours of prime time are dedicated to political and economic analysis, sports, and other current events. According to Hala Sirhan, vice president of Dream TV, the station is open to all types of opinions and beliefs—socialist, capitalist, and conservative.

* Qur'an book of the holy scriptures of Islam

rum for religious and political topics, are widely covered in the Islamic media. In addition, groups often gather in coffeehouses and marketplaces to observe events via radio and television.

Aside from serving citizens in their own lands, Islamic media try to reach audiences in other nations. Political developments, including the resurgence of Islam, have had a considerable influence on Islamic broadcasting. Among international broadcasters, Iran and Egypt rank third and fourth in terms of weekly program hours broadcast to the Islamic world. (*See also* **Coffee and Coffeehouses; Jazeera, al-; Newspapers and Magazines.**)

Ramadan

* **Qur'an** book of the holy scriptures of Islam

During Ramadan, the ninth month of the Islamic calendar, all adult Muslims who are physically able are required to fast from sunrise to sunset. Abstaining from food, drink, and sexual activity during this period gives Muslims a greater awareness of God's presence and helps them to recognize his blessings in their lives. Observing the fast of Ramadan is also one of the five Pillars of Islam. Ramadan is particularly sacred to Muslims because God sent the first revelation of the Qur'an* to Muhammad during that month.

The traditional Islamic (or Hijrah) calendar coincides with the phases of the moon. The month of Ramadan begins with the announcement of the first sighting of the crescent moon and concludes with the next sighting, which is usually 29 or 30 days later. If poor weather conditions conceal the moon, Ramadan ends with the completion of 30 consecutive fasts.

Fasting during Ramadan begins at sunrise, which is defined as the moment the human eye can distinguish between a black thread and a white thread, and ends at sunset. Because Muslims follow a lunar calendar, Ramadan occurs during different seasons from year to year. The period of fasting is relatively short in the winter, when daylight hours are few. By contrast, when Ramadan takes place during the summer, the fast may last as long as 20 hours.

To avoid breaking the fast, Muslims usually rise before dawn to eat a meal that must last them throughout the day. Following the example of the Prophet Muhammad, many Muslims break the fast at sunset by eating dates and drinking a glass of water. Afterward, families and friends often share a small meal, and many go to the mosque* for the evening prayer. Over the course of the month, some Muslims recite the entire Qur'an, which is arranged in 30 equal sections for this purpose.

* **mosque** Muslim place of worship

Certain groups of people are exempt from fasting during Ramadan. Among them are children, those whose health would be harmed by fasting (such as elderly or ill people), those who are traveling, and women who are nursing. Adults who are exempt from fasting must either make up the days they have missed at a later time or perform other obligations instead. For example, those who are too old or ill to fast must feed at least one poor person for every day of the fasting period that they miss during Ramadan.

The Prophet Muhammad stressed that Ramadan is not simply a time to refrain from physical pleasures. It is also a time when Muslims should redouble their efforts to avoid immoral behavior, such as lying and fighting. Muhammad reportedly said, "If someone does not stop telling lies and promoting falsehoods during the fast, then know, Allah does not want a person simply to stop eating and drinking."

Fasting is also intended to build a greater sense of community by uniting all faithful Muslims through shared traditions and practices. Modern Muslim observers note other advantages to fasting during Ramadan. These include improved physical and mental health, a greater appreciation of the suffering of others, training in patience and discipline, and purification of the soul. (*See also* **Calendar, Islamic; Fasting; Pillars of Islam.**)

Rashid Rida, Muhammad

1865–1935
Syrian reformer and writer

Muhammad Rashid Rida was an Islamic reformer who sought the establishment of a fully modernized Islamic state based on a reinterpretation of Islamic law. After his early education in a traditional school, Rida studied under Shaykh Husayn al-Jisr, a scholar who believed that the Muslim community would progress by blending religious education with the modern sciences. Al-Jisr's teachings later became the foundation for Rida's ideas about the reform of Islamic society.

As a young man, Rida was greatly influenced by the writings of Jamal al-Din al-Afghani (died 1897) and Muhammad Abduh (died 1905). They emphasized the need to reform Islam by adopting Western scientific learning and using *ijtihad* (independent reasoning) to interpret Islamic law. In 1897 Rida went to Egypt and soon became one of Abduh's leading disciples. In Cairo, he published his own magazine, *Al-manar* (The Lighthouse), which he used to spread his views.

Rida believed that European dominance and the decline of Muslim society was a result of weakness—an inability to master the sciences, to form organized political institutions, and to restrict the power of the government. He urged Muslims to acquire education and to adopt the best aspects of Western civilization, such as science and technical skill. Concerned with the unity of the Muslim community and the preservation of its identity and culture, Rida regarded the original Islamic sources as the basis of reform. He also called for the establishment of a supreme caliph* to interpret Islam for all Muslims and to offer guidance to Muslim rulers. His ideas, which had both moderate and activist features, influenced later Muslim thinkers. (*See also* **Abduh, Muhammad; Afghani, Jamal al-Din al-; Modernism.**)

* **caliph** religious and political leader of an Islamic state

Refugees

As of 2002, the Office of the United Nations High Commissioner for Refugees cared for almost 20 million people in more than 120 countries. Fleeing war, persecution, and other dangers, they had left their homes, seeking asylum and refuge elsewhere.

Refugees

For many centuries, the primary impetus for refugee movements was religious intolerance. In a Muslim context, the term *refugee* relates to the concepts of migration and flight that are central to the history of Islam. When the Prophet Muhammad and his followers fled from hostile Mecca to Medina in 622, they undertook what became known as the Hijrah. As a result, the word *hijrah*, an Arabic term for migration, came to symbolize an exodus from a land of oppression to a land of Islam.

Historically, various Muslim groups have migrated from their homelands to escape conditions under which they could not practice Islam. When Granada fell to Spanish forces in 1492, the new rulers gave the Muslims who remained in Andalusia a choice—convert to Christianity or be expelled. Many displaced Muslims settled in North Africa. After the partition of the Indian subcontinent in 1947, about 18 million Hindus* and Muslims participated in a great population transfer. Indian Muslims who moved to Pakistan identified themselves as *muhajirs*, those who perform hijrah. During the period of Soviet occupation in Afghanistan (1979–1989), about 6 million Afghans fled to Pakistan, Iran, and Central Asia. Ethnic*, political, and religious conflicts continue to affect Muslim populations worldwide. Prominent examples of Muslim refugees in recent history include Bosnian Muslims, Kurds, and Palestinians.

A Cultural Divide. By 1990 communism* in Yugoslavia had collapsed, and the separate republics of the federation began to establish themselves as independent countries. In February 1992, the republic of Bosnia and Herzegovina declared its independence, triggering a war between the region's Serbs, Muslims, and Croats. Serb forces killed thousands of Muslims and targeted them in a campaign of "ethnic cleansing"—the large-scale and forcible expulsion of Muslims and other non-Serbs from areas under Bosnian Serb control. Before the war, Muslims accounted for about 44 percent of the republic's population, or 1.9 million people. By the end of 1993, slightly more than one million remained. The others had been driven into exile, mainly to

* **Hindu** refers to the beliefs and practices of Hinduism, an ancient religion that originated in India

* **ethnic** relating to groups of people who share a common racial, national, tribal, religious, linguistic, or cultural background

* **communism** political and economic system based on the concept of shared ownership of all property

neighboring Croatia and western Europe. A 1995 peace agreement divided Bosnia into a Muslim-Croat federation and a Bosnian-Serb republic. Although hundreds of thousands of refugees have returned to their pre-war homes in recent years, many are still displaced within Bosnia, waiting to recover their homes from squatters or enduring the slow reconstruction process.

From Rebel to Refugee. The mountainous region that straddles the borders of Turkey, Iraq, Iran, Armenia, and Syria is known as Kurdistan (Land of the Kurds). The Kurds, who number about 25 million, are mostly Sunni Muslims. Traditionally a nomadic people, they began to embrace the concept of nationalism* during the early 1900s. Nevertheless, their repeated attempts to create independent states in Iran, Iraq, and Turkey have been unsuccessful.

* **nationalism** feelings of loyalty and devotion to one's country and a commitment to its independence

In Iraq, Kurdish rebellions have generated refugee crises. Fighting during the early 1970s forced about 130,000 Kurds to flee to Iran. In 1976 the Iraqi government began a concerted effort to weaken the resistance movement, destroying Kurdish villages along an 800-mile zone of the Iran-Iraq border and encouraging Arab settlement of Kurdish areas. The Kurds supported Iran during that country's almost decade-long war with Iraq in the 1980s. President Saddam Hussein retaliated with acts of brutal repression, including the use of chemical weapons. Many Kurds sought refuge in Turkey and Iran. After the Persian Gulf War (1990–1991), the Kurds mounted another uprising. Defeat by Iraqi troops resulted in the migration of two million Kurds to Iran. In an effort to create a safe haven for Kurds in Iraq, the U.S. government designated the area north of the 36th parallel a "no-fly" zone.

See map in Gulf States (vol. 1).

Seeking the Right to Return. The most intractable refugee problem facing the Middle East today is that of the Palestinians. As a result of the first Arab-Israeli war (1948), Israeli forces gained control of about 20,000 square miles of Palestinian land. The remaining portions—the West Bank and Gaza Strip—came under the control of Jordan and Egypt. Between 600,000 and 1,000,000 Arabs fled or were forced to leave their homes by the Israeli authorities. Those who left became refugees in neighboring countries, such as Jordan, Syria, and Lebanon, as well as in the West Bank and Gaza Strip.

In December 1948, the United Nations General Assembly adopted Resolution 194, which stated "that the refugees wishing to return to their homes and live at peace with their neighbors should be permitted to do so at the earliest practicable date, and that compensation should be paid for the property of those choosing not to return." Despite this resolution, the Israeli government has denied Palestinians the right to return to the country to reclaim their lands. The United Nations established the UN Relief and Works Agency for Palestinian Refugees in the Near East (UNRWA), which created camps to shelter the refugees and provided them with food, clothing, health care, education, and other services.

As of 2001, more than 3.7 million Palestinians (the refugees and their descendants) were registered with UNRWA. More than one million of them live in UN-administered camps. Almost half of the camps are located in the West Bank and Gaza Strip, territories that Israel occupied after the 1967 Arab-Israeli war. Except in Jordan, where they have been granted the rights of full citizens, Palestinians do not have the same basic rights as the rest of the population in their host countries. In Lebanon, for example, historical and economic factors prevent Palestinian refugees from obtaining work permits outside of their overcrowded and overburdened camps. They cannot build new schools or hospitals without government permission, which is difficult to obtain.

Beginning in the late 1960s, the Palestine Liberation Organization (PLO) played a very important role in providing the refugees with a sense of national identity through education and military mobilization. The PLO also created social and economic welfare agencies that employed hundreds of Palestinian men and women.

Both Arab and Israeli governments have used the issue of the Palestinian refugees as a political football. Arabs argue that the Jewish state should allow for the return and compensation of some of the Palestinian families in light of international law and UN resolutions. Israelis contend that since the creation of Israel in 1948, several Jewish families were forced out of Arab countries and that the issue is a matter of population exchange. They also assert that Arab countries are large enough to accommodate the Palestinian refugees.

The refugee issue is one of the key obstacles to the current efforts at resolving the Arab-Israeli conflict. The United Nations has called on the Israeli government to allow the Palestinian refugees the freedom to choose between rehabilitation in their host countries or repatriation to Israel. The Israelis fear that their return will change the Jewish character of the state. Recent statistics indicate that by 2030, Palestinians living inside Israel, the West Bank, and Gaza will outnumber the Jewish population of Israel. For many Palestinians, "the right of return" is now interpreted as a future Palestinian homeland in the West Bank and Gaza. (*See also* **Arab-Israeli Conflict; Bosnia; Iraq; Israel; Palestine.**)

Relics

Relics are the remains of holy persons or objects associated with those individuals. Such remains are considered sacred, and many people believe that contact with relics may result in a transference of blessing (*barakah*). Relics, such as hair or clothing from the Prophet Muhammad or other Muslim saints and martyrs, are preserved in shrines and museums throughout the Islamic world.

Muslims most often express their belief in the power of relics by making pilgrimages (*ziyarah*) to the tombs of holy persons. All Islamic schools of thought recommend that the faithful visit the tomb of the Prophet Muhammad in Medina. Shi'i* and Sufi* Muslims also journey to other sacred sites. Shi'is visit the tombs of the imams*, and Sufis travel to the graves of their saints. Sufi pilgrimages account for most of the tomb visitations in the Muslim world.

Sufis believe their great saints (*awliya*) act as spiritual guides on earth. They reside in spirit form at the site of their tomb, just as Muhammad does at his shrine in Medina. Muslims visiting a tomb or shrine sometimes ask

* **Shi'i** refers to Muslims who believe that Muhammad chose Ali ibn Abi Talib and his descendants as the spiritual-political leaders of the Muslim community

* **Sufi** refers to Sufism, which seeks to develop spirituality through discipline of the mind and body

* **imam** spiritual-political leader in Shi'i Islam, one who is regarded as directly descended from Muhammad; also, one who leads prayers

the saint to intercede with God on their behalf. Believers visit these sites for several reasons—to fulfill vows, to seek blessings or cures, to obey the command of a living ruler, to follow a spiritual request received in a dream, to show love and devotion to the saint, and even to seek miracles.

The practice of tomb visitation reflects the Islamic tradition of honoring not only the message of Islam, but also the saints and prophets who conveyed it to humankind. To Muslims, accepting Islam means showing love and devotion to the Prophet Muhammad, the members of his family, and other holy figures. Certain Muslim orders have traced the practice of tomb visitation back to the Qur'an* and hadith*.

Some scholars, however, criticize the reverence of saints and their relics. The scholar Ibn Taymiyah (1263–1328) considered saint worship a form of *shirk* (the association of others with God), the greatest sin in Islam. Many Muslim reformers agreed with this argument. In the 1800s, the Wahhabis of Arabia even tried to stop Muslims from visiting Muhammad's tomb. The Muslim Brotherhood in Egypt and the Deobandis of South Asia condemn the festivals held at the tombs of Sufi saints. Other reform groups view tomb visitation as an irrational, superstitious practice, and believe that it impedes progress among Muslims. (*See also* **Saints and Sainthood.**)

* **Qur'an** book of the holy scriptures of Islam

* **hadith** reports of the words and deeds of Muhammad (not in the Qur'an, but accepted as guides for Muslim behavior)

Religious Scholars

Unlike Christianity, Islam has no formal, ordained clergy. It does, however, recognize a wide range of religious scholars who go by various titles, including imam*, ayatollah*, mullah*, and mufti*. As a group, Islamic religious scholars are known as the *ulama*, meaning "men of knowledge." The *ulama* once played a central role in Islamic law, government, and religious life. Although their influence declined during the colonial period, they have become a significant force in the modern Islamic world.

In the early days of Islam, Muslims required no special training or status to perform religious rituals. Almost anyone familiar with a particular rite could perform it. Knowledgeable members of a mosque served as imams, leading prayers, delivering sermons, and teaching the basics of the Qur'an* and Islamic law. They also presided over weddings and funerals. In small communities, different members of the congregation still take turns fulfilling the role of imam. Large congregations, however, typically recognize one individual as the imam. This person plans community activities, administers schools or Islamic centers, visits the sick, and prepares couples for their weddings, in addition to his duties in the mosque.

The different titles given to Islamic religious scholars are generally honorary and do not represent a formal rank or office. An ayatollah, for example, is an outstanding legal scholar whom some groups of Shi'i Muslims look to as a role model or source of inspiration. Mullah refers to one who has studied religious law, teaches in a religious school, or otherwise actively supports a traditional interpretation of Islam. A mufti interprets Islamic law and issues opinions called fatwas, which guide Muslim actions in various situations. Some governments formally appoint Grand Muftis, who serve as the

* **imam** spiritual-political leader in Shi'i Islam, one who is regarded as directly descended from Muhammad; also, one who leads prayers

* **ayatollah** highest-ranking legal scholar among some Shi'i Muslims

* **mullah** Muslim cleric or learned man

* **mufti** scholar who interprets Islamic law

* **Qur'an** book of the holy scriptures of Islam

See color plate 2, vol. 1.

* **hadith** reports of the words and deeds of Muhammad (not in the Qur'an, but accepted as guides for Muslim behavior)

* **theology** study of the nature and qualities of God and the understanding of His will

* **Shi'i** refers to Muslims who believe that Muhammad chose Ali ibn Abi Talib and his descendants as the spiritual-political leaders of the Muslim community

* **secular** separate from religion in human life and society; connected to everyday life

* **shari'ah** Islamic law as established in the Qur'an and sunnah, the exemplary behavior of the Prophet Muhammad

leading clerics of the state. Scholars called *mujtahids* also work to interpret law, but use a special process—*itjihad* (independent reasoning)—to determine how best to apply the Qur'an and hadith* to current situations.

The *ulama* became a powerful force in Islamic society during the Abbasid caliphate (750–1258). The Abbasid rulers sought to legitimize their rule by identifying themselves closely with Islam and supporting the growth of the *ulama*. The first formal schools of Islamic law were established by the *ulama* shortly before the Abbasids came to power. The *ulama* eventually became a separate class, distinguishing themselves mainly by their dress. Each *alim* (religious leader) served as an expert in theology*, Islamic tradition, or law.

Until the colonial period, the *ulama* formed the educated elite in Islamic society. Their control over education and the courts enabled them to shape society, not just for their generation, but for those that came later. The *ulama* received their educations in *madrasahs*, or institutions of religious learning. In the early 1800s, however, Western colonial powers set up their own systems of government, law, and education in Muslim lands, restricting the activity of the *ulama* to religious matters. After achieving independence in the mid-1900s, many Islamic countries established schools based on Western models. These institutions produced a generation of scholars who do not belong to the traditional *ulama*. The *ulama* and these scholars often disagree on issues such as the status of women and the nature of Islamic government.

During the colonial period, the *ulama* in some Muslim countries led the resistance to Western rule. This movement reached its peak in Iran, where Ayatollah Ruhollah Khomeini led a Shi'i* revolt that overthrew the secular* government of Reza Shah Pahlavi in 1979. Since then, Iran has existed as an Islamic state, with Shi'i religious scholars in control of the government and legal system. Religious scholars also play an important role in Saudi Arabia, where *shari'ah** governs all aspects of Muslim life. (*See also* **Fatwa; Imam; Iran; Khomeini, Ruhollah al-Musavi; Madrasah; Saudi Arabia.**)

Repentance

* **Qur'an** book of the holy scriptures of Islam

* **surah** chapter of the Qur'an

The Qur'an* encourages repentance (*tawbah*) for sins, stating in surah* 25.70 that, for the person who "repents, attains to faith and does righteous deeds, God will change the evil . . . into good." The word *tawbah* means "return," and refers to the sinner's return to God after falling into sin. It can also mean God's turning to the sinner with compassion and forgiveness. Muhammad is said to have sought God's forgiveness several times a day.

In Islam, repentance is an informal act that does not involve confession to a religious leader. It requires the person to believe that he or she has committed a sin, to show remorse for the act, and to vow not to repeat it in the future. If the sin involves an offense against another person, the individual must make amends. If it offends God alone, the person has only to admit the sin, express regret, and promise to abstain from further wrongdoing.

Traditional Islamic scholars discussed sin mainly in terms of how it affected the individual, and did not relate it to society as a whole. Some modern scholars, however, tie the concept of repentance to questions of group morality and social reform. In the early 1900s, the Egyptian reformers Muhammad Abduh and Muhammad Rashid Rida argued that public admission of sin should serve as a key factor in repentance. They believed that repentance represents society's crusade against evil and that public *tawbah* could help reform the Muslim community. Mid-1900s reformers such as Sayyid Abu al-Ala Mawdudi and Sayyid Qutb took this idea a step further. They believed that society had fallen into a state of sin and could improve only with a return to Islamic law. They stated that sinners had to suffer punishment before they could repent. In contrast, the early legal scholar Muhammad al-Shafi'i (767–820) argued that repentance for a deed cancels or reduces the need for formal punishment by the law. Many modern scholars adhere to al-Shafi'i's view.

Traditional Islam accepts that an individual can achieve salvation through faith alone, as long the person atones for his or her sins. Some reformers argue that one must not only have faith, but must also perform virtuous deeds. Both views, however, oppose the Christian notion of salvation. According to Christianity, all people are born with original sin. Jesus' sacrifice on the cross served as penance for all humans, granting salvation to anyone who believes in Jesus. Many Muslims consider this a "doctrine of despair" because it suggests that individuals lack the power to attain divine forgiveness by themselves.

Some modern Islamic approaches to repentance draw from classical Sufi* thought. To Sufis, repentance does not involve admission of and forgiveness from sin, but an active process of spiritual change. Repentance serves to remind the believer of God's presence. It induces an awakening that grants the person a constant awareness of God. Sufis discourage the act of remembering a sin or feeling remorse, because such actions show that the individual has forgotten God. (*See also* **Sin; Sufism.**)

* **Sufi** refers to Sufism, which seeks to develop spirituality through discipline of the mind and body

Revelation

Islam teaches that God periodically reveals his will, providing precise information that human beings can use to guide their lives. Obedience to God's commands and prohibitions leads to rewards in the afterlife. The term *wahy*, from the Arabic verb meaning "to put in the mind," is sometimes understood as "inspiration." Revelation refers specifically to the divine inspiration God has given to select individuals, known as prophets, for the purpose of guidance. Beginning with the first human and prophet, Adam, this process of revelation continued over many generations until God's message reached its final and perfect form in his words to the Prophet Muhammad. This revelation, preserved in the Qur'an*, is the foundation of Islam.

In addition to the Qur'an, Muslims also accept the Torah*, the Psalms, and the Gospels as books of revelation. They believe that these books all contain the same basic message but are tailored for their particular time and place. The ultimate principles of revelation, however, transcend time and place and have universal meaning.

* **Qur'an** book of the holy scriptures of Islam
* **Torah** first five books of the Old Testament, constituting the holy scripture of Judaism

Throughout Islamic history, Muslims have debated the relative value of knowledge arrived at through independent reasoning and knowledge gained through revelation. Some philosophers claim that human reasoning may be sufficient to recognize the existence of God and to guide people's behavior. Human reasoning is, therefore, equal to revelation on occasion. However, it is not sufficient to determine what acts of worship God requires of human beings. In contrast, conservative* Muslims oppose the idea that knowledge of God or correct behavior can be known by human reasoning alone. In their view, humanity requires revelation for clear information about the mysteries of existence.

Islam teaches that no amount of logical analysis can reveal information about the inner dimension of divine-human exchange. Because such information is considered vital, humanity cannot arrive at ultimate truth except through divine revelation. Therefore, Muslims regard revelation as a unique and necessary area of knowledge. (*See also* **Prophets; Qur'an; Theology.**)

* **conservative** generally opposed to change, especially in existing political and social institutions

Revolution

* **Qur'an** book of the holy scriptures of Islam

* **nationalist** one who advocates loyalty and devotion to his or her country and its independence

* **fatwa** opinion issued by an Islamic legal scholar in response to a question posed by an individual or a court of law

* **imperialism** extension of power and influence over another country or region

In classical Islamic thought, the idea of revolution has a negative connotation, suggesting the overthrow of legitimate leaders of the Muslim community. Among the various terms that refer to revolution in this sense are *fitnah* (strife, dissent), *masiyah* (disobedience), and *riddah* (turning away from Islam). The Qur'an* states that "*fitnah* is worse than killing" and uses the term *masiyah* to mean rebellion against the Prophet Muhammad. During the 1800s and 1900s, Western colonial governments threatened the political and cultural interests of the *ummah* (community of believers). Nationalists* and other groups mobilized Muslims in an effort to overthrow foreign regimes. As a result, the connotation of the term began to change in the Islamic world.

Keeping the Peace. Few early Muslim writers supported the idea that revolution was ever justified. Those who advocated rebellion usually based their arguments on the immorality of the ruler, rather than on his inability to govern effectively or justly. Muslim scholar Ibn Taymiyah (1263–1328) urged Muslims to overthrow the Mongols, who had adopted Islam as their official religion but did not rule according to accepted Islamic principles. He identified them as *kafirs* (nonbelievers).

In general, Muslim jurists were reluctant to stir up resistance to corrupt rulers because they feared that doing so would create disorder in the Islamic community and threaten its existence. Jurists had to be extremely careful about issuing fatwas* regarding obedience to authority, especially if they served under unjust leaders.

Changing With the Times. After the French Revolution of the late 1700s and the beginning of the colonial era in the Muslim world, the idea of revolution generally took on more positive overtones. Several movements emerged to advocate resistance to Western imperialism*, and they spread throughout Africa, the Middle East, and Asia. Throughout the 1800s and early 1900s, local Muslim leaders, such as Colonel Ahmad Urabi of Egypt, led uprisings against colonial regimes.

Sufi* movements in North Africa, Sudan, and Egypt played a prominent role in the anticolonialist struggle. Leaders such as Muhammad al-Mahdi, a Sufi *shaykh**, took up the banner of revolt, often using the term jihad* to unite Muslims in support of the cause.

In the 20th century, Muslim activists Sayyid Abu al-Ala Mawdudi, Sayyid Qutb, Ali Shariati, and Ayatollah Ruhollah al-Musavi Khomeini protested various regimes. Mawdudi and Qutb applied Ibn Taymiyah's arguments to their own resistance movements in India, Pakistan, and Egypt. Shariati and Khomeini were Shi'i* Muslims who called on the Iranian people to resist the pro-Western government of Muhammad Reza Shah Pahlavi. Shariati encouraged Muslims to take the initiative against injustice in order to prepare the way for the Mahdi, a leader who will arrive at the end of time to deliver the Muslim community from oppression. Khomeini repeatedly used the phrase "Islamic revolution" to refer to the movement that eventually overthrew the shah in 1979 and established rule by the clergy.

Many revolutionary theorists suffered imprisonment and exile and some, such as Qutb, were executed by the state for their activities. Their ideas led to the emergence of a variety of radical* groups calling for the violent overthrow of existing regimes and the application of *shari'ah**. Such groups include al-Jihad and al-Jamaat al-Islamiyah (the Islamic Group) in Egypt, Hamas in the West Bank and Gaza Strip, and Hizbullah in Iran and Lebanon. The members of the radical movement believe that Islam is *din wa dawlah*—both religion and state. In their view, protesting against unjust political leaders is a religious duty. Failure to rebel is considered to be a way to perpetuate the oppression of Muslims. (*See also* **Hamas; Hizbullah; Ibn Taymiyah; Khomeini, Ruhollah al-Musavi; Mawdudi, Sayyid Abu al-Ala; Messianic Traditions; Qutb, Sayyid.**)

* **Sufi** refers to Sufism, which seeks to develop spirituality through discipline of the mind and body

* *shaykh* tribal elder; also, title of honor given to those who are considered especially learned and pious

* **jihad** literally "striving"; war in defense of Islam

* **Shi'i** refers to Muslims who believe that Muhammad chose Ali ibn Abi Talib and his descendants as the spiritual-political leaders of the Muslim community

* **radical** favoring extreme change or reform, especially in existing political and social institutions

* *shari'ah* Islamic law as established in the Qur'an and sunnah, the exemplary behavior of the Prophet Muhammad

Rites and Rituals

Every culture develops rites and rituals to mark significant events in the lives of its members. Birth, death, marriage, and the transition from childhood to adulthood are among the events observed with special celebrations. Rites of passage often reinforce religious principles for the individuals taking part in them and for the community members witnessing them.

Islamic rites and rituals originated in the interactions of Muslim and non-Muslim cultures in various times and places. Many Islamic practices derive from the customs of the tribes of pre-Islamic Arabia. The Prophet adapted certain Arab rites, such as pilgrimage, and connected them to Islamic teachings. As Islam spread throughout Asia and Africa, many different cultures altered certain rituals to include aspects of their own traditional ceremonies. Islamic rites among these communities often display a mixture of local and Arab influences.

Rites of passage provide members of a community with an opportunity to reflect on the meaning and purpose of life. The Qur'an* defines this purpose as *ibadah*—serving God by submitting to his will and giving thanks for his blessings. Islamic rituals thus serve as symbols of submission and thanks-

* **Qur'an** book of the holy scriptures of Islam

Rites and Rituals

Funerals are one of the major rites in the life of a Muslim. The body is laid in the grave with its face turned toward Mecca. Members of the funeral party throw handfuls of dirt into the grave to remind them of their own mortality and the meaning of death.

See color plate 12, vol. 3.

* **monotheistic** refers to the belief that there is only one God

giving, uniquely suited to each stage of life. They aim to increase spirituality and purify thoughts and intentions. The most significant Islamic rites of passage include birth rituals, circumcision, marriage, and funeral rites.

Conception and Birth. Islam views sexuality as a natural part of life subject to the same ethical rules as any other behavior. Only married couples should engage in intercourse, during which they aim for a balance between bodily pleasure and spirituality. The Qur'an advises partners to recite the following prayer during lovemaking: "In the name of Allah, O Allah, protect me and what you will bestow upon us (our offspring) from Satan." After intercourse, the partners engage in a *ghusl* (ritual bath), washing their entire body to cleanse themselves for other activities such as prayer.

After the birth of a child, adults perform a rite in which they whisper into each of the child's ears. In the right ear, an adult whispers the *adhan* (call to prayer), and in the left ear, he or she recites the *iqamah* (call to establish prayer). The child then receives a name typically taken from the prophets, their wives, or their companions. A parent may also attach the prefix *Abd* (servant) and a title of God to a name, as in the case of the name Abd al-Aziz, which means "servant of the Almighty." Seven days after birth, an adult shaves the child's head and sacrifices a goat or sheep to show happiness and gratitude to God. This sacrifice dates back to pre-Islamic Arab culture and is seen by Muslims as part of monotheistic* (Judeo-Christian) tradition, associated with the story of Abraham's willingness to sacrifice his son Ismail at God's command. The family distributes the meat of the goat or sheep among the poor, as well as among neighbors and relatives.

The Qur'an does not specifically mention circumcision (the removal of the foreskin of the penis), but most Muslims practice it. The procedure has no religious meaning in Islam, and adult converts are not required to undergo circumcision. In the early days of Islam, circumcision typically occurred between the ages of three and seven. Today, most Muslim male babies have it on the second day after birth. In rural areas, barbers perform circumcision, but parents increasingly take their children to hospitals for the procedure. Muslims participate in elaborate ceremonies in some parts of the world, including the rural areas of southern and western Asia, and parts of northern and western Africa.

Female circumcision occasionally occurs in the Muslim world. The ancient Arabs performed a ritual removing part of the clitoris, but according to hadith* Muhammad expressed reservations about the practice, and it fell out of use. Clitoridectomy, or complete removal of the external female organs, occurs in a few Muslim societies in parts of North and northeast Africa as a pre-Islamic rite. Many human rights groups and women's organizations denounce the practice and call for its abolition.

* **hadith** reports of the words and deeds of Muhammad (not in the Qur'an, but accepted as guides for Muslim behavior)

From Child to Adult. In the Islamic world, puberty represents more than just the passage from childhood to adulthood. It also enables a Muslim to take on the religious and social responsibilities of an adult. Muslims do not expect children to perform religious duties, such as daily prayer or fasting during Ramadan. These rituals, however, become obligatory once a child reaches puberty. Because all such customs require purity, children learn how to perform *wudu* (cleansing completed before daily prayers), and *ghusl* (ritual bath taken after a nocturnal ejaculation, menstruation, or sexual intercourse). Muhammad emphasized the importance of cleanliness when he stated, according to hadith, "Purification is half of faith."

Marriage also symbolizes the taking on of adult responsibilities. Through marriage, Muslims find an acceptable outlet for sexual urges and begin the process of raising a family. Muslims believe that marriage preserves social morality by helping to prevent irresponsible sexual activity. Muhammad advised those who could not afford to marry to fast, noting that abstinence from food helps to ease passion. Unlike some Christians, Muslims do not consider marriage a sacrament (sacred duty), but rather a contract between two partners. As with other rituals, a great variety of marriage ceremonies and traditions exist within the Muslim world.

Death and Burial. To Muslims, death serves as a transitional stage between life on earth and life in the next world. The Arabic word for death—*mawt*—means "cessation of breathing." Muslims traditionally bury the deceased on the day of death or as soon after death as possible. As with other rituals, the body must be given a ritual cleansing before the funeral. Persons of the same sex as the deceased wash the body and wrap it in a white shroud that covers it completely. A special funeral prayer for the dead is recited in the mosque, with the funeral bier* placed in front of the congregation. A procession of relatives, friends, and community members escorts the corpse to the grave. The body is laid in the grave with its face turned toward Mecca. Each member of the funeral procession throws three handfuls of dirt into the grave to remind them of their own mortality and of the meaning of death.

See color plate 6, vol. 3.

* **bier** stand on which a corpse or a coffin is placed before burial

Funeral practices in several Muslim lands provide insight into how indigenous* cultures have influenced Islamic rituals. For example, in Southeast Asia, members of the dead person's family distribute money to those who attend the funeral. This practice may have originated in the Buddhist concept of "merit-making" and grants the family a way to seek forgiveness for the sins of the deceased. In India, the relatives serve a communal meal on behalf of the dead person to seek God's mercy and forgiveness. They offer a

* **indigenous** refers to the original inhabitants of a place

47

similar meal every Thursday for 40 days following the death. After the meal, they recite the first chapter of the Qur'an. Some Indian Muslims read the entire Qur'an every Thursday night for the 40 days following a death. (*See also* **Ablution; Death and Funerals; Fasting; Marriage; Names and Naming.**)

Rumi

1207–1273
Sufi poet and visionary

* **mysticism** belief that spiritual enlightenment and truth can be attained through various physical and spiritual disciplines

* **Sufi** refers to Sufism, which seeks to develop spirituality through discipline of the mind and body

* **dervish** Sufi mystic; member of an order that uses music and dance to enter a trancelike state

Jalal al-Din Rumi is best known for his mystical* poetry and his influence on the Mawlawiyah, a Sufi* order founded after his death. Muslims often refer to the Mawlawiyah as the Whirling Dervishes* because of their distinctive meditative dance, a ritual based on movements Rumi performed while reading his poetry. Rumi had a profound influence on philosophy and culture in Iran, Central Asia, India, and especially Turkey.

The son of a well-known religious scholar in the city of Balkh (in Afghanistan), Rumi moved at the age of 12 with his family to escape from approaching Mongols. Rumi's family eventually settled in the city of Konya (in present-day Turkey). His father served as a legal scholar, judge, and teacher at a local *madrasah* (Islamic school), a position that Rumi took over after his father died. Rumi learned about Sufi mysticism from one his father's former pupils, Burhan al-Din al-Tirmidhi. He later traveled to Syria, where he may have met the leading Islamic thinker of the time, Ibn al-Arabi.

In 1244 Rumi met a wandering holy man and mystic named Shams-i Tabrizi. Shams made an overwhelming impression on Rumi, and the two developed a close friendship that worried Rumi's family. Bitter at Rumi's neglect, his family and disciples forced Shams to leave town. Rumi rushed after him and begged him to return, but soon after, Shams vanished entirely. Scholars have recently confirmed that Rumi's disciples and his son, Sultan Walad, conspired to murder Shams, burying him close to a well in Konya. The loss of Shams caused Rumi great grief, which he expressed in a major work of poetry. Called the *Divan-i Shams-i Tabrizi* (Collected Poetry of Shams), it displays the different stages of Rumi's love, culminating in Rumi's discovery of Shams within himself, "radiant like the moon." Rumi often read these verses while performing a whirling dance that became the hallmark of the Whirling Dervishes. Some scholars believe that he also composed his poems in a trancelike state, listening to flutes, drums, the hammering of goldsmiths, or the sound of the water mill in the countryside.

Several years later, Rumi met an illiterate goldsmith named Salah al-Din Zarkub. Once again, Rumi formed a special bond that inspired him to write poetry. Rumi's experiences with Zarkub and later with one of his disciples inspired him to write the *Masnavi*. The longest mystical poem ever written, the *Masnavi* discusses many aspects of Sufi philosophy, including religion, ethics, and metaphysics*. The poem explores the relationship between the spiritual and the secular*, focusing on relationships between human beings as well as the relationship between humans and God.

Rumi died shortly after completing the *Masnavi*. Along with his longer texts, he left several smaller works of poetry and prose. He enjoyed great

* **metaphysics** branch of philosophy that deals with that which exists beyond the senses

* **secular** separate from religion in human life and society; connected to everyday life

popularity and influence among his peers, and his son Sultan Walad later formed the Mawlawiyah out of his followers. The name of the order derives from Mawlana (Our Master), a term often applied to Rumi. Much of what we know of Rumi's life comes from Sultan Walad's writings. (*See also* **Literature; Mawlawiyah; Sufism.**)

Rushdie, Salman

1947–
Indian author

* **blasphemous** demonstrating a lack of respect toward God, a religion, or something considered sacred

* **fatwa** opinion issued by an Islamic legal scholar in response to a question posed by an individual or a court of law

* **liberal** supporting greater participation in government for individuals; not bound by tradition

* **secular** separate from religion in human life and society; connected to everyday life

Salman Rushdie is an Indian author who is perhaps best known for his 1988 novel, *The Satanic Verses.* Many Muslims felt that the book's portrayal of Islam and the Prophet Muhammad was insulting and blasphemous*. In response to its publication, Iranian leader Ayatollah Ruhollah Khomeini issued a fatwa*, sentencing Rushdie to death.

Born in Bombay, India, Rushdie was raised in a wealthy and liberal* Muslim family. He and his sisters grew up speaking both English and Urdu and were exposed to diverse cultural influences from an early age. Although Rushdie's parents were practicing Muslims, he characterizes his upbringing as absolutely secular*. He also recalls that his parents permitted discussions on any and all subjects. As a boy, Rushdie was fascinated with comic books and movies, and by age ten he had decided that he wanted to become a writer.

Rushdie attended high school in Great Britain. During his early teen years, he decided to adopt a nonreligious lifestyle. Rushdie earned a graduate degree in history from Cambridge University in 1968. By that time, his parents had moved to Pakistan. Rushdie relocated to Karachi and began working in the Pakistani television industry, but he was frustrated by the government's censorship of the media, and he returned to Great Britain. During the day, he worked as an advertising copywriter, and at night and on the weekends, he wrote fiction. In 1975 Rushdie published his first book, *Grimus.* His first major critical success was his 1981 novel *Midnight's Children*, which won the prestigious Booker McConnell Prize.

In 1988 Rushdie published *The Satanic Verses*, a novel that recounts the adventures of a character modeled on the Prophet Muhammad. Some parts of the book depict the character and his recording of the Qur'an* in an unfavorable way. Many Muslims were outraged and offended by what they regarded as a parody of the Prophet, and they organized mass demonstrations to protest the novel. On February 14, 1989, Ayatollah Khomeini proclaimed a death sentence on Rushdie and those involved in the publication of *The Satanic Verses.* He also offered a $1.5 million reward for anyone who carried out the sentence. Rushdie went into hiding the next day.

Salman Rushdie remained in hiding for several years, fearing for his life and frequently on the move. Although the strain of this experience ended his marriage, he continued to write. He published essays, short stories, and additional novels. The threats to his life have been reduced, and in the late 1990s, Rushdie moved to New York City. (*See also* **Fatwa; Khomeini, Ruhollah al-Musavi; Literature.**)

Sacrifice

Sacrifice

For Muslims, the ritual sacrifice of an animal on certain occasions serves as an outward symbol of the practice of Islam. In modern times, Muslims have also attached socioeconomic and political significance to the idea of sacrifice.

* **hajj** pilgrimage to Mecca that Muslims are required to make once in their lifetime

* **Qur'an** book of the holy scriptures of Islam

Rites and Rituals. The most important occasion of sacrifice occurs at the end of the hajj*, when pilgrims gather at the valley of Mina to commemorate the critical test of the Prophet Abraham's faith. According to the Qur'an*, God ordered Abraham to sacrifice his son (identified as Ismail in the Islamic tradition and as Isaac in Judaism) as a sign of obedience to divine will. When God saw that Abraham was prepared to obey the command, he intervened and substituted a ram. Each pilgrim offers an animal sacrifice (*qurban*)—an unblemished sheep, camel, goat, or cow—to symbolize this miraculous event. The meat is consumed by the pilgrims and shared with the needy. Although Eid al-Adha (the Feast of the Sacrifice) is one of the ceremonies that pilgrims observe on the hajj to Mecca, Muslims worldwide may also offer animal sacrifices to commemorate the event. During the hajj, Muslims may make an animal sacrifice to fulfill a vow or to atone for sin.

In many parts of the Islamic world, Muslims offer a sacrifice to celebrate the birth of a child. The tradition of *aqiqah*, the sacrifice of two animals for a male child and one animal for a female child, reportedly protects the child from potential harm in the future.

Practical and Political Functions. In addition to its ritual significance, sacrifice has always had the practical function of feeding people, especially the poor. In recent years, however, Muslims have emphasized its role in fulfilling the needs of social welfare and charity over its importance as a ritual. Technology has been a key factor in this shift. In the past, Muslims buried most of the meat of the animals slaughtered during the hajj because they could not eat it all at once and had no means of preserving it for future consumption. Today, modern technology enables the pilgrims to preserve the meat so that it can be transported over long distances to feed people in poor Muslim communities. Those who do not perform the hajj, but sacrifice animals during Eid al-Adha, also donate a portion of the food to disadvantaged groups.

* **martyrdom** act of dying for one's religious beliefs

For some, the idea of sacrifice carries political meaning. Modern Islamic movements often urge their followers to strive for martyrdom* when their religious beliefs compel them to fight for a political cause. To die in defense of Islam is viewed as the highest form of personal sacrifice. Modern commentator Muhammad Ali (1874–1951) encouraged believers to "realize that if they have sacrificed an animal over which they have control, it is their duty to lay down their own lives in the path of Allah." Social and political activist Ali Shariati (1933–1977) believed that sacrifice, expressed through the slaughter of an animal, symbolizes the struggle against the temptations of the ego. In his view, if the ego can be set free from materialism, then the possibility of a peaceful political order becomes real. (*See also* **Abraham; Charity; Dietary Rules; Eid al-Adha; Hajj; Ismail; Martyrdom; Rites and Rituals.**)

Sadr, Musa al-

As the leader of Shi'i* Muslims in Lebanon during the 1960s and 1970s, Musa al-Sadr was chiefly responsible for transforming the community into a unified political force. His mysterious disappearance in 1978 became associated with the Shi'i belief in a Hidden Imam*.

Born and educated in Iran, al-Sadr first visited Lebanon, his ancestral homeland, in 1957. During this visit, he impressed the Shi'i authorities, and they offered him the post of senior Shi'i religious leader of Tyre, a coastal city in southern Lebanon. He initially rejected the offer, but two years later, he took the position. One of his first official acts in Tyre was to establish a vocational school for training Shi'i youth. The Shi'is in Lebanon were politically weak and disadvantaged.

Ambitious, intelligent, and charismatic*, Musa al-Sadr sought to establish himself as the leader of the entire Lebanese Shi'i community. He deftly used Shi'i religious teachings, especially the martyrdom* of Husayn ibn Ali at Karbala, to motivate his many followers to political action.

In 1974 he founded an organization called Harakat al-Mahrumin (Movement of the Deprived), promising to challenge the Christian-controlled government for ignoring the rights and needs of its Shi'i citizens. The following year the movement's members formed a militia*. Although al-Sadr initially rejected violence as a way to achieve his goals, his movement became increasingly radical*. Nevertheless, al-Sadr also worked from within the Lebanese government to promote Shi'i interests, serving for six years as the head of the Supreme Islamic Shi'i Council.

After civil war broke out in Lebanon in 1975, Shi'i militia became more powerful but Musa al-Sadr continued to emphasize the importance of avoiding violence. He disappeared in 1978 on a visit to Libya. His fate remains unknown, but many suspect Libyan leader Mu'ammar al-Qaddafi was responsible for his death.

Since his disappearance, al-Sadr's followers have honored his memory. The movement he founded, now called Amal, has become the largest Shi'i organization in Lebanon and one of the most powerful. (*See also* **Lebanon; Minorities; Qaddafi, Mu'ammar al-; Shi'i Islam.**)

1928–1978?
Muslim cleric and reformer

* **Shi'i** refers to Muslims who believe that Muhammad chose Ali ibn Abi Talib and his descendants as the spiritual-political leaders of the Muslim community

* **imam** spiritual-political leader in Shi'i Islam, one who is regarded as directly descended from Muhammad; also, one who leads prayers

* **charismatic** capable of arousing enthusiasm and loyalty

* **martyrdom** act of dying for one's religious beliefs

* **militia** group of citizens organized for military service

* **radical** favoring extreme change or reform, especially in existing political and social institutions

Safavid Dynasty

The Safavid dynasty ruled Iran from 1501 to 1722. At the peak of their power, the Safavids controlled all of the territory that constitutes modern Iran, as well as parts of present-day Iraq and Central Asia. During the early years of the dynasty, the Safavids legitimized their rule by claiming to be the fulfillment of Shi'i* expectations of the messiah*. They soon changed their tactics, abandoning extremist religious beliefs for the more orthodox* Twelver Shi'ism. Facing violence and persecution, most of the predominantly Sunni* population of Iran eventually embraced Shi'ism. The legacy of the Safavids endures. Today, almost 90 percent of Iranians are Shi'i Muslims.

* **Shi'i** refers to Muslims who believe that Muhammad chose Ali ibn Abi Talib and his descendants as the spiritual-political leaders of the Muslim community

* **messiah** anticipated savior to be sent by God

* **orthodox** conforming to accepted beliefs and practices

* **Sunni** refers to the largest branch of the Muslim community; the name derives from sunnah, the exemplary behavior of the Prophet Muhammad

Safavid Dynasty

This illustration of chess players comes from a Safavid treatise on chess of the 1500s.

See color plate 8, vol. 2.

* **caliphate** office and government of the caliph, the religious and political leader of an Islamic state

* **Sufi** refers to Sufism, which seeks to develop spirituality through discipline of the mind and body

Strategic Alliances. During the mid-1200s, the Abbasid caliphate* fell to Mongol tribes, and the eastern portions of the Islamic world separated into self-governing entities. Around this time, Shaykh Safi al-Din, a religious teacher of both Sunni and Sufi* traditions, founded the Safavid movement. This mystical and military order had its center in the city of Ardabil in northwestern Iran and spread to the area southwest of the Caspian Sea.

Safi al-Din's successors allied themselves with some of the Turkish warrior tribes that settled in the eastern regions of Anatolia and across the Caucasus Mountains during the mid- to late 1300s. The tribes held extreme religious beliefs that combined elements of Christianity, pre-Islamic* religions, Muslim cults, and the Shi'i themes of devotion to Imam* Ali and his family. During the 1400s, the Safavids established a political alliance with the Qizilbash, a group that emphasized the Shi'i teaching that a messiah would soon appear and establish an ideal Islamic order on earth. The Qizilbash became convinced that the messiah would be a Safavid leader. Consequently, the Safavids abandoned Sunni Islam and adopted Shi'ism in an effort to guarantee their support.

Shifting Gears. In 1500 a 16-year-old youth named Ismail became head of the Safavid movement. He identified himself as a descendant of the imams and claimed to be the Mahdi (divinely guided one). The Qizilbash revered him as a representative of God on earth, and with their backing, he captured the Azerbaijani city of Tabriz from the Uzbeks. Shortly afterward, Ismail proclaimed himself shah (king) of Iran. Over the next decade, he and his army conquered the remaining regions of Iran and parts of Iraq.

Ismail gradually abandoned the extreme Shi'ism of his early supporters. The Safavids needed to obtain a religious consensus among the people of Iran, the majority of whom followed Sunni Islam. Ismail proclaimed the more moderate Twelver Shi'ism, or Ithna Ashari, as the state religion and began an aggressive campaign to eliminate Sunni Islam from Iran. No Shi'i ruler had ever attempted such a large-scale conversion. The country had few Shi'i groups, however, and the process was slow. Ismail hired Twelver Shi'i scholars from Syria, Lebanon, Bahrain, northeastern Arabia, and Iraq. By the late 1600s, most Iranians had accepted Shi'ism.

The shah's assault on Sunni Islam crossed the Iranian border. He fought Sunni Uzbeks in the northeast and Sunni Ottomans in the west. But his attempt to eliminate Sunni Islam outside of Iran failed. In 1514 the Ottomans defeated his army at the Battle of Chaldiran. The Safavid campaign against the Sunnis continued for many years, but subsequent defeats eventually forced them to relinquish territory and relocate their capital.

In 1524 Ismail's oldest son, Tahmasp I, assumed control of the kingdom. Iran fell into a decline during Tahmasp's reign that continued during the reigns of his successors because of their incompetence and inability to oppose repeated attacks by Turkish forces.

Reaching New Heights. Abbas I came to the throne in 1588, and under his rule, the Safavid dynasty reached its peak. Recognizing that his army was no match for the Ottomans, he made peace with them and focused his attention on the defeat of the Uzbeks. Meeting with little success, he reorganized his troops and hired someone to train them in the European style of warfare. These reforms enabled him to regain lost territory.

Under Abbas I, Iran became a great power and a center of culture. His reign is noted for an efficient, highly centralized government and a rebirth of art and learning. The construction of roads and the establishment of royal industries, such as carpet making, silk making, and ceramics, stimulated domestic and international trade. Isfahan, the new capital city, became the centerpiece of the dynasty and a model for Middle Eastern city planning. Examples of Safavid architectural achievement included parks, palaces, monuments, Islamic schools, and impressive mosques*, such as the Masjid-i Shaykh Lutfallah. Among the great Safavid painters of the period were Bihzad and Riza-i Abbari.

* **pre-Islamic** refers to the Arabian Peninsula or to the Arabic language before the founding of Islam in the early 600s

* **imam** spiritual-political leader in Shi'i Islam, one who is regarded as directly descended from Muhammad; also, one who leads prayers

Channeling Public Sentiment

Muhammad Baqir Majlisi (died 1700), perhaps one of the most influential Shi'i religious scholars of all time, significantly affected the nature of Shi'ism in Iran. As an alternative to the Sufi reverence for saints, Majlisi promoted mourning rituals to honor the death of Husayn ibn Ali, who had been killed by Sunni Muslims at Karbala. The rituals included grand processions, highly emotional songs, and crying and wailing of the crowds. The rituals became important Iranian traditions, serving as a way for the people to release their frustrations and to demand justice on behalf of the oppressed. At the same time, they directed the public's demands toward the Sunnis who had killed Husayn, rather than toward the corrupt rulers of their own state.

* **mosque** Muslim place of worship

* *ulama* religious scholars

* **madrasah** religious college or university; also religious school for young students

Abbas I continued to stress Twelver Shi'ism. He dismissed anyone in the government who still followed the extreme Shi'ism of the early dynasty. He also imported Twelver Shi'i *ulama** from Arab countries to teach in Iran. He built madrasahs* for them and provided the schools with state funding. The Shi'i *ulama* were granted control of the educational and legal system of Iran, as well as the more religious duties of the government. Although these religious scholars traditionally maintained their separation from the state, they could not refuse such a unique opportunity to spread their faith. They supported Abbas I and his government, even though they believed that they, and not the shah, were the true representatives of the Hidden Imam.

Decline and Fall. The Safavid dynasty lasted for less than a century after Abbas I died in 1629. By the end of the 1600s, the empire was in a state of decline, owing to a deterioration of trade, economic insecurity, and incompetent leadership. The capital of Isfahan was captured in an Afghan invasion in 1722. Around 1730 Shah Tahmasp II recaptured Isfahan and regained the throne. Nevertheless, he was soon overthrown by one of his military commanders. During the late 1700s, a few other members of the Safavid family claimed the title of shah, but they had no real power. (*See also* **Ali ibn Abi Talib; Iran; Ithna Ashari; Messianic Traditions; Ottoman Empire; Shi'i Islam.**)

Saints and Sainthood

* **Qur'an** book of the holy scriptures of Islam

* **monotheism** belief that there is only one God

* **Sufi** follower of Sufism, which seeks to develop spirituality through discipline of the mind and body

* **surah** chapter of the Qur'an

Originating in Christianity, the term *saint* typically describes an individual with exceptional spiritual qualities and miraculous powers. The Arabic term closest in meaning is *wali*, meaning "friend," "patron," or "helper". The word *walayah* refers to sainthood. The Qur'an* does not explicitly recognize saints or sainthood, but emphasizes that God is the *wali* of believers and that there is no *wali* but God.

Most Muslims do not believe in saints. Some view the idea of sainthood as violating the concept of monotheism*, a central tenet of Islam. Others consider saint worship a sign of ignorance and superstition. Most of those who do believe in a form of sainthood are Sufis*. Unlike Catholicism, Sufism has no specific process through which *awliya* (plural of *wali*) achieve their status. *Awliya* may be male or female, and some even achieve *walayah* during their lifetime.

Sufis point to several passages of the Qur'an to support their belief in saints. A line in surah* 10 states, "As for the friends of God, no fear shall come upon them, nor shall they grieve." Some believe that this statement indicates the existence of a special class of people selected by God for favor and divine knowledge. Other passages in the Qur'an provoke similar interpretations from those who believe in saints.

Islamic *awliya* fall into different classes. One consists of popular saints associated with simple shrines or even natural objects, such as springs or trees. Some of these *awliya* have their roots in pre-Islamic religions, which were absorbed into Muslim culture. North African Muslims revere many such figures, referring to them as *murabit*, meaning "he who watches over his soul through the night." Another class of saints consists of Sufis recognized as *awliya* during their lifetime because of their exceptional piety and good deeds. Sufis make pilgrimages* to their tombs and homes, gathering in these places to perform ceremonies and to make major decisions. They also hold birthday celebrations for these saints, sometimes taking part in songs and processions. A third class of saints consists of legendary *awliya* of the past. Sufis commemorate them in tales of their sayings, virtues, and miracles.

Saints play many roles for Sufis. Allegiance to a certain *wali* reinforces tribal alliances, and believers petition those still living to dispense advice and to help settle disputes. Sufis also travel to the tombs of saints to seek God's favor. They believe that saints can bestow *barakah* (blessing), which is transferred through the physical touch of the tomb, an artifact, or the person from whom the help is sought. Like Christians, Sufis regard some saints as specialists in certain areas. For example, they may petition a particular saint for family harmony and another for success in business.

Sunni* Muslims generally do not believe in saints, but Shi'is* frequently elevate their imams* to *walayah*. Imams fulfill many of the same roles as saints, acting as God's helpers, working miracles during their lifetime, and interceding for their followers with God. Iranian Shi'is have a kind of sainthood, visiting many local pilgrimage sites dedicated to imams and their family members. Outside of Tehran, there is a large and elaborate shrine to the Ayatollah* Khomeini that has become an important place of pilgrimage. (*See also* **Barakah; Khomeini, Ruhollah al-Musavi; Sufism.**)

* **pilgrimage** journey to a shrine or sacred place

* **Sunni** refers to the largest branch of the Muslim community; the name derives from sunnah, the exemplary behavior of the Prophet Muhammad

* **Shi'i** refers to Muslims who believe that Muhammad chose Ali ibn Abi Talib and his descendants as the spiritual-political leaders of the Muslim community

* **imam** spiritual-political leader in Shi'i Islam, one who is regarded as directly descended from Muhammad; also, one who leads prayers

* **ayatollah** highest-ranking legal scholar among some Shi'i Muslims

Saladin

1137–1193
Muslim warrior and sultan

Salah al-Din al-Ayyubi, more commonly known as Saladin, was one of the most famous warriors of the Middle Ages*. He became a hero to the Muslim people for recapturing the holy city of Jerusalem from the Christian crusaders* in 1187. He was beloved by Muslims for his humility and generosity, and he was respected by Christians for the fair and humane ways in which he treated them.

Born to a prominent Kurdish family from Armenia, Saladin began his military career as a security officer under the powerful leader Nur al-Din. With his family's influence and his own talents, Saladin quickly rose through the ranks. He distinguished himself in three successful military campaigns and soon became commander of the Syrian army in Egypt. He became vizier* of the Fatimid caliphate*, but he vanquished the unpopular Fatimids in 1171 to found the Ayyubid dynasty*. Saladin established himself as sole ruler of Egypt and replaced the Shi'i* faith of the Fatimids with Sunni* Islam.

When Nur al-Din died in 1174, Saladin returned to Syria to take control of the government. He met opposition from Nur al-Din's descendants, but he defeated them and unified the Muslim territories of Egypt, Syria, and Mesopotamia under his rule. Muslims viewed him as a firm but generous ruler who combined military force with diplomatic skill. Saladin encouraged devotion to Islam, establishing *madrasahs* (religious schools) and mosques and supporting scholarly work.

* **Middle Ages** period roughly between 500 and 1500

* **crusader** person who participated in the holy wars against the Muslims during the Middle Ages

* **vizier** Muslim minister of state

* **caliphate** office and government of the caliph, the religious and political leader of an Islamic state

* **dynasty** succession of rulers from the same family or group

* **Shi'i** refers to Muslims who believe that Muhammad chose Ali ibn Abi Talib and his descendants as the spiritual-political leaders of the Muslim community

* **Sunni** refers to the largest branch of the Muslim community; the name derives from sunnah, the exemplary behavior of the Prophet Muhammad

In 1187 Saladin turned his attention to the Christian crusaders who had invaded the Holy Land* for a second time. He declared a jihad* against them and won his first great victory that year in the Battle of Hittin in Palestine. Within a few months, Saladin and his army had conquered most of the crusaders' territory in the Middle East. His crowning achievement came when he recaptured the city of Jerusalem, which had been under Christian control for almost a century.

Shocked by the loss of Jerusalem, the Christians began the Third Crusade. This time, Saladin had less success. Although the Christians never again captured Jerusalem, repeated crusader attacks eventually weakened Saladin's army. He lost several battles to Richard I the Lionhearted, the king of England, and finally signed a truce with Richard in 1192. Saladin died soon afterward. Although he failed to fully drive the crusaders out of the Holy Land, he won lasting admiration from Muslims for his recovery of Jerusalem. He also impressed the Europeans with his intelligence, courage, and virtue. While the Christians who conquered Jerusalem massacred huge numbers of Muslims, Saladin's troops practiced restraint and behaved courteously toward their prisoners of war. (*See also* **Crusades; Fatimid Dynasty; Great Britain; Jerusalem.**)

Salafi

The term *Salafi* applies to certain Islamic reform movements, most notably one that arose in Egypt in the early 1900s. The name has its roots in the Arabic word *salaf*, meaning "ancestors." *Salaf* generally refers to Muslims who lived during—or within three generations of—the time of the Prophet Muhammad. Muslims consider such individuals to have practiced a pure form of Islam. Reformers who title themselves after the *salaf* promote a return to a society based on the Muslim values of the early community. They believe that Islam has changed for the worse since the time of Muhammad. Salafi movements strive to reform Islam by promoting the beliefs and practices of the Prophet. The modern Salafi movement continues to have a major influence on the Islamic world.

Early Development of Salafi. After Muhammad died in the early 600s, Muslims became increasingly divided as to the interpretation and application of the teachings of the Qur'an*. Some scholars, such as the Mu'tazili, favored reason in the effort to understand revelation*. They argued that Muslims had free will, the capacity to choose between good and evil, and should not blindly rely on religious edicts. Many Muslims became outraged, stating that God alone has power, that human beings are predestined*, and that obedience to the law is therefore the only route to eternal reward. This and similar controversies led to an emphasis on following the opinions of the Salaf. The first person associated with this position was the jurist Ahmad ibn Hanbal (780–855).

A member of the last generation of *salaf*, Ahmad ibn Hanbal inspired confidence from later Muslims, as well as from his own peers. He valued revelation over reason but argued that Muslims could interpret divine scripture based on their understanding of the actions of the Prophet and his companions when no precedent existed in the Qur'an or hadith*. He set strict guidelines for the use of *ijtihad* (independent reasoning) and restricted the use of *qiyas* (reasoning by analogy, or comparison based on similarities). Ibn Hanbal also promoted a return to pure Islam based directly on the Qur'an, the sunnah*, and the *ijma* (consensus) of the *salaf.*

Ahmad ibn Hanbal gained many followers, including the scholar Ibn Taymiyah (died 1328), who established a clear distinction between the changeable and unchangeable aspects of Islam. He held that the Prophet had established certain beliefs and rituals not subject to alteration. Social aspects of Islam, however, such as education and rules governing behavior, could adapt to the times. Ibn Taymiyah rejected unthinking adherence to tradition and maintained that Muslims had to balance sacred sources with their own reasoned judgment in order to understand and live according to God's law. He viewed Islam as more flexible than his predecessors, and he inspired later Salafi groups to do the same.

Salafi Movements in the Modern Age. In the 1700s, several reform movements emerged to address what many Muslims viewed as the "moral decay" of the Islamic community. The most important of these was the Wahhabi movement, founded by Muhammad ibn Abd al-Wahhab (1703–1792). Ibn Abd al-Wahhab promoted many of the ideas expressed in the teachings of Ibn Hanbal and Ibn Taymiyah. He encouraged Muslims to purge the Arabian Peninsula of what they considered un-Islamic practices and to build an Islamic society modeled on the one founded by the Prophet. The Wahhabi and other Salafi movements advocated moral and social reform and greater unity among Muslims. The Salafis, however, promoted a strict interpretation of Islam and remained rooted in the past.

The Islamic scholars Jamal al-Afghani and Muhammad Abduh established the modern Salafi movement in Egypt in the late 1800s. It shared many features of the earlier movement, advocating the restoration of Islamic beliefs and culture in society. It differed from the other groups, however, in its efforts to adapt Islam to the modern world. Al-Afghani and Abduh portrayed Islam as compatible with reason and science, and they worked to apply the scripture to modern-day conditions. They struggled to rid the community of what they considered a centuries-old mentality of *taqlid* (imitation) and *jumud* (stagnation).

Al-Afghani and Abduh focused on ridding the Islamic world of European colonial domination. Faced with the overwhelming strength of the Western powers, they searched for the causes of the apparent decline of Islam. They blamed Muslim passivity on the adoption of foreign concepts and practices, a lack of unity among Muslims, and the political despotism* that plagued some Muslim countries.

In suggesting solutions to these problems, founders of the modern Salafi movement looked to the writings of Ibn Taymiyah. Like Ibn Taymiyah, they criticized Sufis* for practicing certain rituals, such as saint worship, which they considered corrupt and damaging to Islam. They also proposed sweeping reforms in science, education, language, and law. They sought to combine traditional Islamic and Western education in order to give Muslims a more prominent role in world affairs, root out European influences from law,

* **hadith** reports of the words and deeds of Muhammad (not in the Qur'an, but accepted as guides for Muslim behavior)

* **sunnah** literally "the trodden path"; Islamic customs based on the exemplary behavior of Muhammad

American Salafi in Yemen

Following the terrorist attacks of September 11, 2001, U.S. forces attacked Islamic Taliban fighters in Afghanistan, who were believed to be protecting the terrorist leader Osama bin Laden. American soldiers captured a young American Muslim convert, John Walker Lindh, along with other Taliban fighters. They discovered that Lindh had studied with a Salafi movement in Yemen in 2000, before joining the Taliban in Afghanistan. The movement Lindh had joined favored the seclusion of Muslims from a "sinful world." Followers did not read newspapers or magazines and worked to create a society similar to that of Muhammad. Many Muslim scholars consider this sect extreme for its isolationist policies and its militant nature.

* **despotism** system of government in which the ruler has absolute power

* **Sufi** follower of Sufism, which seeks to develop spirituality through discipline of the mind and body

* **Pan-Islamic** refers to the movement to unify all Islamic peoples

grant women greater rights, and reform politics. In addition, al-Afghani and Abduh promoted Pan-Islamic* feelings. They criticized leaders who used Islam to justify their absolute rule, calling for greater representation of Muslims in government, as well as greater unity for Muslims throughout the Islamic world.

Influence of Salafi Movements. The modern Salafi movement spread from Egypt throughout the Muslim world. It influenced several other Islamic movements, including the Muslim Brotherhood. Like the modern Salafi movement, the Muslim Brotherhood promoted a return to pure Islam within modern society. More critical of the West, however, the brotherhood took a more activist approach to ending colonial domination. The Jamaat-i Islami, founded in Pakistan by Sayyid Abu al-Ala Mawdudi (1903–1979) proceeded along similar lines.

Other Salafi movements, known as the al-Salafiyun, have a greater connection with the earlier Salafi movements than with the modern one. More recent Salafi groups advocate radical programs of opposition to Western culture and Western domination. They represent an important part of the violent Muslim movements of the late 1900s. (*See also* **Abduh, Muhammad; Afghani, Jamal al-Din al-; Ibn Hanbal; Ibn Taymiyah; Mawdudi, Sayyid Abu al-Ala; Modernism; Muslim Brotherhood; Mu'tazili; Revelation; Wahhabi.**)

Sanusiyah

* **Sufi** refers to Sufism, which seeks to develop spirituality through discipline of the mind and body

The Sanusiyah is a Sufi* brotherhood that began in the early 1800s in present-day Libya and the central Sahara. Sayyid Muhammad ibn Ali al-Sanusi (1787–1859), an Algerian scholar, founded the organization. In his youth, al-Sanusi studied Islamic law and Sufism. He moved to Mecca in the 1820s, where he came under the influence of the Sufi teacher Ahmad ibn Idris. He adopted Idris's view that Muslims should follow the lifestyle of early Muslims. He disapproved of excessive rituals, such as dancing and singing, and urged his followers to look to the Prophet as a guide. He also promoted the use of *ijtihad*, or reasoned interpretation of Islamic law.

* **zawiyah** Sufi center that serves as a place of worship and a welfare institution

* **Bedouin** nomad of the desert, especially in North Africa, Syria, and Arabia

Al-Sanusi wanted not only to reform Islam, but also to spread it among non-Muslims. He established a network of Sanusi *zawiyahs** in Cyrenaica (in present-day Libya) in the mid-1800s. Each lodge served as a meeting place, a house of worship, and a place where Bedouin* traders could rest and resolve disputes. The Sanusis converted many Bedouins and gained a great deal of political influence. Several lodges arose in Arabia and Libya, including one on the Libya-Egypt border. The Sanusi brotherhood continued to spread after al-Sanusi's death, especially along key trading routes. By the late 1800s, the brotherhood had attracted a large following throughout North and Central Africa.

French forces clashed with the Sanusis in Central Africa in the late 1800s, and when the Italians invaded in the early 1900s, the Sanusi brotherhood rallied the Libyan population to fight off the Europeans. Eventually, however, the Italians overpowered the Libyans, and the country fell under Italian rule. Many members of the brotherhood were killed, and its leaders fled to Egypt.

When the United Kingdom of Libya gained its independence in 1951, al-Sanusi's grandson Idris—then the head of the Sanusi brotherhood—became king. In 1969 Colonel Mu'ammar al-Qaddafi overthrew King Idris. He later banned the Sanusi brotherhood in Libya. Only a few Sanusi lodges remain. (*See also* **Idrisi; Libya; Qaddafi, Mu'ammar al-; Sufism; Zawiyah.**)

Satan

The term *satan* comes from the Arabic word *shaytan*, meaning adversary. In Islam, *shaytan* refers to both a class of spirits and a fallen angel named Iblis. The personification* of evil and the chief of the other satans, Iblis plays the same role in Islam that Satan plays in Judaism and Christianity.

Satans as Spirits. According to the Qur'an*, God created three classes of spirits—angels, *jinn*, and satans. Made of light, angels watch over humans and relay messages from God. *Jinn* and satans are both made of fire and sometimes assume visible form. According to tradition, satans are exceptionally ugly and have hooves instead of feet. They live in dark places and ruins. Islamic tradition has never made a clear distinction between *jinn* and satans, but some commentators define satans as *jinn* who have exceptional powers and who do not believe in Islam.

Satans are not necessarily evil. According to legend, the biblical king Solomon used both *jinn* and satans to perform his work. Some inspire poets and other talented people. Others cause mischief and disease. When bad luck befalls a Muslim, a satan may be blamed. Some people wear good luck charms to ward off these spirits. Because five is a powerful magic number in Islamic folk tradition, the charms often take the shape of a hand with five fingers with an eye in the center for protection against the "evil eye" of the satan Iblis. Satans have no power during the Ramadan fast (except over those who break the fast), and they flee the room at the recitation of the Basmalah, "In the name of God, the Merciful the Compassionate." Some satans whisper into the ears of humans, trying to tempt them into wrongdoing. They have little real power, however, and can only make suggestions.

Satan as Iblis. In the Islamic tradition, Iblis is an enemy of God and humanity. He does not rule hell, as that job falls to another fallen angel named Malik. Most Muslims, however, believe God will send Iblis to hell on the Day of Judgment. In the meantime, Iblis tries to tempt Muslims into sin and lead them astray.

According to Muslim tradition, God expelled Iblis from heaven for refusing to follow his command to honor Adam. Iblis later tempted Adam in the Garden of Eden by climbing into a serpent's mouth and convincing Adam to disobey God. This action began the endless moral struggle of human beings between the forces of good and evil. The serpent lost her feathers and legs because of her part in the affair, but Iblis married her afterward. Some Muslims believe that *jinn* are children of the serpent and Iblis. Like the sa-

* **personification** representation in human form of an abstraction, such as good or evil

* **Qur'an** book of the holy scriptures of Islam

tans, Iblis whispers into the ears of humans to try to tempt them into sin, and, like the satans, he has no true control over their actions.

Some Sufis* view Iblis in a more positive light than other Muslims. They see his refusal to bow down to Adam as evidence of his firm commitment to monotheism*, a core belief of Islam. Some Sufis think that God will forgive Iblis on the Day of Judgment because of his strict allegiance to this principle.

In modern times, Muslims have identified certain unpopular rulers with Satan. For example, in the 1970s, Iranians revolted against Shah Muhammad Reza Pahlavi, referring to him as the "Great Satan." They then later transferred this title to the United States. (*See also* **Day of Judgment; Islam: Overview; Magic and Sorcery.**)

* **Sufi** refers to Sufism, which seeks to develop spirituality through discipline of the mind and body

* **monotheism** belief that there is only one God

Saudi Arabia

See map in Middle East (vol. 2).

A Middle Eastern kingdom on the Arabian Peninsula, Saudi Arabia plays a major role in Muslim affairs throughout the world. Islam originated in the region in the 600s, and Saudi Arabia continues to attract thousands of Muslim pilgrims each year. Since 1932 the House of Saud has ruled the country. These kings rely on Islam to unite Arabian society, validate their own authority, and ensure Saudi Arabia's place as the center of the Islamic world.

Overview of the Country

Around one-fifth the size of the United States, Saudi Arabia occupies 80 percent of the Arabian Peninsula. With the Persian Gulf to the east and the Red Sea to the west, the country holds a strategic position for trade and shipping. Jordan and Iraq lie to the north of Saudi Arabia, and Yemen and Oman lie to the south. Saudi Arabia also shares borders with Qatar, Bahrain, and the United Arab Emirates.

Land and People. The population of Saudi Arabia numbers around 24 million. All Saudis are Muslim, and most are Sunnis*, but the country includes a significant Shi'i* minority. About 90 percent of Saudis are Arab; the other 10 percent are Asian or African. Large numbers of foreigners have immigrated to Saudi Arabia from other Muslim countries, settling mainly in port cities. Islam plays a dominant role in Saudi Arabian life. It informs national identity, society, law, and politics. Every city and village has a mosque, and street life comes to a standstill at prayer time, when shops close and Muslims turn toward Mecca to pray.

Because Saudi Arabia has a desert climate, it relies on trade rather than agriculture as the basis of its economy. Much of the land is uninhabited, and less than 2 percent is arable*. Saudi Arabia experiences frequent sand and dust storms, as well as extremes in temperature. In the 1930s, Saudi Arabians discovered vast oil deposits in their deserts, which account for 25 percent of the world's total known petroleum reserves. Saudi Arabia ranks as the world's largest exporter of oil.

* **Sunni** refers to the largest branch of the Muslim community; the name derives from sunnah, the exemplary behavior of the Prophet Muhammad

* **Shi'i** refers to Muslims who believe that Muhammad chose Ali ibn Abi Talib and his descendants as the spiritual-political leaders of the Muslim community

* **arable** fit for growing crops

Saudi Arabia possesses about 25 percent of the world's known petroleum reserves. Its oil fields are located in the eastern part of the country along the Persian Gulf, but a pipeline carries crude oil to Yanbu on the Red Sea. Shown here is a petrochemical plant in Yanbu.

Geographical Regions. Saudi Arabia is divided into four distinct regions: al-Hasa, Hejaz, Asir, and Najd. Located near the Persian Gulf, al-Hasa is one of the kingdom's most fertile regions. It is also the location of the Saudi Arabian oil industry as well as most of Saudi Arabia's Shi'i Muslims. Hejaz borders the Red Sea and contains the holy cities of Mecca and Medina. This region has a large foreign population, especially in the port city of Jeddah, where 70 percent of the inhabitants are from outside the country.

The southwestern part of the kingdom, Asir, is a predominantly agricultural region. It shares a common border and cultural ties with Yemen. Najd is the central part of Saudi Arabia. Surrounded mostly by desert, this region includes the capital city of Riyadh, which serves as the base of the ruling Saud family.

Arabian History

Before Islam, Arabia consisted of warring tribes without a central government. In the 600s, Muhammad spread his teachings throughout Mecca and Medina. Muhammad united feuding tribes, brought the peninsula under his control, and established Islam as a world religion. Muslims began to spread Islam to other parts of the Middle East, bringing many territories under Islamic rule.

See color plate 9, vol. 2.

Arabia and the Islamic Empires. After Muhammad's death, various Islamic empires arose. From their base in Syria, the Umayyads seized control of the Middle East and established a central trade route in the Persian Gulf. When the Abbasids came to power in 750, they granted large sums of money to Mecca and Medina so that the cities could maintain themselves as the spiritual capitals of Islam.

Around the 1300s, the Mamluks took over part of Arabia, only to be conquered by the Ottomans in the 1500s. The Ottomans vied with European nations for control of the port cities in the region. While European colonialism expanded in the 1800s, Mecca provided Muslims with a sense of common heritage and ideology*. Various religious movements originated in Arabian regions, including the Wahhabis, who ultimately brought about the establishment of the modern Islamic Kingdom of Saudi Arabia.

* **ideology** system of ideas or beliefs

Wahhabi Movement and Saud Expansion. Founded by a religious reformer from Najd named Muhammad ibn Abd al-Wahhab, the Wahhabi movement began in the mid-1700s. Ibn Abd al-Wahhab rejected the veneration of saints commonly practiced by Shi'is and Sufis* and stressed the acceptance of only one God. He taught that all Muslims should receive an Islamic education so that they would behave according to the guidelines of the Qur'an* and the sunnah*. The Muslim community could then fulfill its mission of becoming the living embodiment of God's laws on earth. Ibn Abd al-Wahhab emphasized that believers should live in obedience to a just ruler, who would enforce God's laws in consultation with the ulama*.

* **Sufi** follower of Sufism, which seeks to develop spirituality through discipline of the mind and body

* **Qur'an** book of the holy scriptures of Islam

* **sunnah** literally "the trodden path"; Islamic customs based on the exemplary behavior of Muhammad

* **ulama** religious scholars

Ibn Abd al-Wahhab found a supporter in Muhammad ibn Saud, chieftain of southern Najd. Ibn Saud wanted to gain control of the Arabian Peninsula and promoted his teacher's ideas on Islamic rule. The two joined forces, and by the early 1800s, they and their successors had conquered most of the Arabian Peninsula. Egyptian armies, however, defeated the Wahhabi-Saud empire when it spread beyond the peninsula. The Wahhabis withdrew into the southern Najd region and remained there throughout the 1800s.

Saud Revival. In 1902 Abd al-Aziz ibn Saud (a descendant of Muhammad ibn Saud) captured Riyadh and began a 30-year campaign to re-unify the Arabian Peninsula. To raise an army, he sponsored missionary work in remote villages. He taught Bedouin* nomads about Islam and provided them with land, food, money, and farming supplies. In return, many joined the Ikhwan (Brotherhood), a military force that served as the backbone of Abd al-Aziz's army. Abd al-Aziz imposed strict Islamic law on Bedouin society, forbidding smoking, drinking, and music. His efforts led to a religious revival in Riyadh and other cities. Wahhabism swept through the peninsula, uniting tribes and establishing Abd al-Aziz as the leader of a vast social and political movement.

* **Bedouin** nomad of the desert, especially in North Africa, Syria, and Arabia

Kingdom of Saudi Arabia. After three decades of conquest, Abd al-Aziz had unified Saudi Arabia under his rule. He formally proclaimed the existence of the Kingdom of Saudi Arabia in 1932 and created an Islamic monarchy. The Qur'an serves as the constitution; traditional Islamic law provides the legal system; and the *ulama* serve as the judges and legal advisers. The state-funded Council of Senior Ulama grants religious approval for government policies. Religious police, known as the Committee for the Promotion of Virtue and the Prevention of Vice, monitor public behavior. They enforce rules against smoking, music, and loud laughter, as well as ensuring that shop owners close their businesses during prayer time and that women cover themselves in public. They also regulate interaction between men and women.

The Saudi king serves as chief of state and implements laws with the help of a cabinet*, the Council of Ministers, which includes many royal family members. Abd al-Aziz ruled the Kingdom of Saudi Arabia until his death in 1953. His descendants have ruled since that time. The Wahhabi influence on Saudi society remains strong, determining the ways in which people dress, behave in public, and pray.

* **cabinet** individuals appointed by a head of state to supervise departments of government and to act as official advisers

The Council of Senior Ulama plays a crucial role in sanctioning government policies. Many Muslims support the decisions of Saudi leaders when they have the backing of the religious elite. Some, however, do not always agree with the council. For example, when the *ulama* approved King Faysal's plan to promote education for women in 1960, the decision attracted fierce opposition. Muslims expressed similar outrage in 1990, when the council approved King Fahd's decision to invite American forces to Saudi Arabia to wage war against the Iraqi president Saddam Hussein.

See color plate 1, vol. 1.

In foreign policy, Saudi kings have used their power and influence to maintain Saudi Arabia as the center of the Islamic world. They support Islam and its followers around the globe, providing emergency aid and welfare to needy Muslims abroad. They build mosques and community centers in Western nations to accommodate Muslim immigrants in these countries, and they establish international organizations that promote Muslim unity. The Muslim World League and the Organization of the Islamic Conference both originated in Saudi Arabia.

Opposition to the Government. Despite its prominent place within the Muslim community, the Saudi government has had its share of rebellion from its citizens and from outsiders. During the mid-1900s, revivalist* movements sprang up throughout the Muslim world. In Iran, these led to the 1979 revolution that established the Shi'i leader Ruhollah Khomeini as head of the government. Iranians used the pilgrimage to Mecca and Medina as an opportunity to spread Khomeini's teachings. They encouraged the already discontented Saudi Shi'is to challenge their king's claim to leadership. Iranian pilgrims sometimes clashed with Saudi security forces. In 1987 more than 400 people died in a struggle between Iranian pilgrims and Saudi security officers.

* **revivalist** calling for the return to traditional values or beliefs

The 1990–1991 Gulf War stirred up dissent among Sunnis as well as Shi'is. Many had opposed the king's invitation to American forces to use Saudi Arabia as a military base. They favored a nonviolent solution to what they viewed as a regional problem, and they resented the presence of foreign soldiers, especially women in the military. The Gulf War also placed an international spotlight on certain human rights abuses in the country. A variety of Saudi groups

A King by Any Other Name

In the late 1900s, the Saudi king came under fire by Iranian Shi'is and other Muslims for being "un-Islamic." According to Iranian leader Ruhollah Khomeini, "The ruling regime in Saudi Arabia wears Muslim clothing, but it actually represents a luxurious, frivolous, shameless way of life, robbing funds from the people and squandering them, engaging in gambling, drinking parties, and orgies." In response to these and similar criticisms, the Saudi monarch tried to adopt a more conservative image. For example, he placed stricter prohibitions on alcohol, dress, and public behavior. He also implemented tighter controls on immigration. The king even changed his title from "Royal Majesty" to the traditional title of "Keeper of the Two Holy Places."

emerged to demand government reforms, such as a new constitution, a consultative council, an independent judiciary, and equality among all citizens.

In 1992 the government responded to these pressures by establishing a "Basic Law" of government and other political reforms. Human rights groups, however, considered the changes "empty reforms" that reinforced the power of the king rather than ensuring a more representative government. Declining oil prices in the 1990s also caused discontent among the Saudis, as many college-educated youth were unable to find jobs. Many joined neo-Wahhabi religious groups and demonstrated for more career opportunities, a fairer distribution of wealth, better access to health and education facilities, greater political participation, and more accountability in government. They also pushed for stricter enforcement of rules promoting Islamic values, segregating the sexes, and ensuring public modesty.

The king, however, punished those who spoke out against the government. Preachers, religious scholars, and university professors who voiced dissent were dismissed from their jobs, imprisoned, or had their passports taken away. Students who spoke out against the government were denied admission to universities. In 1990 the government punished a group of Saudi women who had demanded the right to drive cars. The head of the Council of Ministers issued a ruling that women should never drive or participate in politics.

Despite these incidents, the Saudi king maintains his control over the region and has enjoyed a relatively smooth reign. Mecca and Medina continue to attract thousands of pilgrims, and the Saudis have retained their influence on the rest of the Islamic world. In the 21st century, the most pressing issues for Saudi Arabia include overcrowding and overpopulation in cities, pollution, and fluctuating oil prices. (*See also* **Iran; Iraq; Khomeini, Ruhollah al-Musavi; Mecca; Medina; Middle East.**)

Sayyid

See *Titles, Honorific.*

Science

* **Middle Ages** period roughly between 500 and 1500

The contributions of Muslims to science have been significant, particularly during the Middle Ages*. Islamic scholars studied the works of ancient Indian, Persian, and Greek thinkers who had developed important scientific theories. Muslims advanced many fields, including astronomy, mathematics, medicine, and engineering. In modern times, however, Western science and technology have surpassed the Islamic world in scientific achievements. Muslim scholars work to find ways to make scientific progress without compromising Islamic values.

Golden Age of Science

* **patron** person of wealth and influence who supports a writer, artist, or scholar

* **caliph** religious and political leader of an Islamic state

From around 700 to 1200, Muslims led the scientific world. Many royal and wealthy Muslims served as patrons* of the sciences. The Abbasid caliph* al-Mamun, for example, constructed a research facility in Baghdad called the House of Wisdom (*Bayt al-Hikma*). Scientists congregated there and

Professor Mohammad Abdus Salam, a particle physicist from Pakistan, received the Nobel Prize for Physics in 1979. Salam, who died in 1996, also headed the Third World Academy of Sciences.

shared ideas. Influential scholars also funded scientific research, such as the Banu Musa brothers, who made their own contributions to geometry and mechanics.

Astronomy and Mathematics. The most important science in the ancient world, astronomy greatly interested Muslim scholars and led to the creation of many other branches of science. In the mid-700s, Muslims began translating and studying astronomical texts by Indian and Persian writers. The writings of Ptolemy, an ancient Greek scholar, served as the greatest influence on early Muslim astronomers. Ptolemy used geometric models to study the stars. Muslim scholars tested his theories and made their own observations. In many cases, their findings led to corrections in Ptolemy's work.

Muslim astronomers introduced new mathematical concepts, such as trigonometry, into the science of astronomy. This new field enabled them to make more accurate calculations about the stars and planets. Over the centuries, major observatories arose in cities such as Isfahan and Jaipur, attracting leading astronomers from throughout the Muslim world. The Abbasid caliph al-Mamun launched the first recorded group science project by commissioning astronomers to verify and improve upon Ptolemaic theories. Muslim astronomers also made individual contributions to the discipline. For example, Thabit ibn Qurrah (died 901) devised the first known mathematical analysis of motion. Al-Battani (died 929), who noticed after 30 years of observation variations in measurements of the sun and moon, allowed for the possibility of an annular* solar eclipse. Abd al-Rahman al-Sufi (died 986) accurately illustrated the constellations, providing their locations and sizes. Translated into Latin, his works inspired many star names.

* **annular** forming a ring

Islamic culture provided fundamental reasons for astronomical study. Muslims needed to calculate the precise times for daily prayer and to locate the proper direction in which to face during the ritual. They also depended on astronomy to determine the phases of the moon, on which they based

Ethics in Biotechnology

Developments in biotechnology—including stem-cell research, animal cloning, and in vitro fertilization (IVF), or the process of injecting a fertilized egg inside the mother's body—pose serious ethical questions. Most Muslims in the United States strongly support IVF, which they regard as a compassionate way to help infertile couples produce a child. Many Muslims also support stem-cell research, which allows testing on unused embryos from IVF. Muslim scientists, however, recommend the development of strict guidelines for the practice. Most Muslim scientific organizations express a cautious or firmly negative view of human cloning. Malaysia's highest religious council has banned cloning as "unnatural and totally against Islam." Members of the Organization of the Islamic Conference, however, have recommended further study before formulating a position on the matter.

their calendar. Other concerns, such as finding direction at night and understanding the connection between the seasons and the planets, also drove Muslims to study the heavens and to develop instruments to measure celestial movements. Astrolabes, quadrants, sextants, sundials, compass boxes, and cartographic grids allowed Muslim astronomers to make accurate calculations. The most famous Muslim observatory, established in the 1200s in Maragha, Iran, promoted the creation of such tools and tables.

Optics. Arab scholars made notable advances in optics, the science of vision. After studying the theories of Greek scholars, they transformed the field with new methods and approaches. The most important optical theorist during this period, Ibn al-Haytham (died 1040; known to Europeans as Alhazan), rejected Greeks' explanation of vision, which held that vision results from contact between the eye and an object. Ibn al-Haytham realized that the eye does not see the object itself, but receives an image that occurs when light bounces off the object to the eye. Other opticians studied burning mirrors, mirror reflections, the geometry of vision, and the makeup of the eye. Optics became a new field that far surpassed the research efforts of previous scholars.

Technology. Scholars and scientists in the Islamic world developed sophisticated technologies that greatly increased the prosperity of their societies. They used basic technological information inherited from the early Greeks to create machines for both professional needs and entertainment purposes. Most importantly, they developed methods for lifting water and irrigating farmland—crucial technology in areas where water remained a scarce resource. Engineers also built waterwheels to raise water from rivers to reservoirs; dams to regulate water flow; and networks of canals and underground channels to divert water to farmland. Such projects led to expanded agricultural production and added to the prosperity of cities throughout the Muslim empire. Water engineering contributed to quality of life as well. In the Middle Ages, 70 percent of all water used in Iran came from an elaborate system of *qanats* (underground conduits).

Muslim engineers also invented many practical machines and tools, such as water clocks, complex gears, double-acting pumps with suction pipes, crank mechanism devices, and sensitive control mechanisms. They built fountains and various machines for rich patrons. Technological advances also occurred in the production of paper and textiles, military weapons, shipbuilding, mining, and metals.

Medicine. Doctors in the Muslim world contributed greatly to the development of medicine. Physicians studied the works of Greek scholars and became familiar with the theories of Hippocrates and Galen. They also used direct observation to refine theories of disease and to develop the best methods of treatment. They adopted Galen's humoral system, which taught that four humors exist within the body—blood, phlegm, yellow bile, and black bile. According to this system, imbalances in these humors contribute to mood and physical disorders, and various medicines and foods can replenish or diminish the humors as necessary.

While the Greeks took a philosophical approach to health, Muslim physicians focused on recording case studies and finding cures for diseases. The scientist Abu Bakr al-Razi wrote extensively about illnesses and their cures. His subjects included smallpox, measles, diabetes, and hay fever. He also compiled the first overview of medical history in his book *Kitab al-Tibb al-Mansuri* (The Mansuri Book of Medicine). The great philosopher and physician Ibn Sina (died 1037) composed the most influential work on medical theories in the Middle Ages—*al-Qanun fi al-Tibb* (The Canon of Medicine).

Although Islam forbids the dissection of bodies, evidence suggests that some Muslim doctors did conduct dissections. The most striking example comes from the work of Ibn al-Nafis (died 1288), who correctly described the ways in which blood flows through the human heart. Galen and Ibn Sina had suggested that blood moves through a hole in the left and right ventricles of the heart. Ibn al-Nafis argued that no such hole exists and that blood reaches the left ventricle of the heart from the lungs. Although some scholars attribute this theory to a lucky guess, others conclude that Ibn al-Nafis must have examined the human body.

Muslim communities became famous for their hospitals, which treated all patients regardless of religion, gender, or social class. Medical institutions offered surgery and treatment for contagious diseases and mental disorders. They employed a large staff of resident physicians and often included pharmacies and medical libraries as well. Medical costs, in many cases, were covered by *waqf** endowments given by wealthy Muslims in order to help the poor.

* ***waqf*** donation of property for charitable causes

Natural Sciences. Botany and pharmacology also interested Muslim scholars. As with other sciences, Muslim scholars based their early studies on Greek texts but they expanded their work and compiled extensive new data. Botanical research provided information about the medicinal properties of plants. By the late 800s, Muslim physicians in Andalusia (in present-day Spain) had identified nearly almost all the simple uncompounded drugs. In the 1100s, Ibn al-Baytar created a dictionary of medicines and foods that included more than 2,000 entries. This book served as the most comprehensive manual of applied botany in the Middle Ages.

Alchemy, trying to turn metals into gold, also led to the creation of various medicines. Muslim alchemists developed several compounds that had therapeutic value. They also improved the process of creating drugs, and some of their methods remain in use in modern pharmacology.

Muslim Sciences in the Modern Era

After the 1300s, science in the Islamic world declined. Political instability, Mongol invasions, and lack of interest in European technology all contributed to this phenomenon. Science, however, flourished in the European world during the Industrial Revolution of the 1700s and 1800s. Technological advances allowed Europeans to dominate parts of Africa, the Middle East, and Asia, eventually establishing colonial rule in these regions. While European rule led to political and social upheaval in the Muslim world, it also introduced modern science and technology to Islamic scholars.

Introduction of Western Science. By the mid-1800s, many Muslim leaders had begun to appreciate the importance of modern science. They welcomed the introduction of new technologies such as the printing press,

* **conservative** generally opposed to change, especially in existing political and social institutions

* **ulama** religious scholars

railways, telephones, steamships, and automobiles. The Egyptian ruler Muhammad Ali made especially strong efforts to modernize his country, importing a printing press and other mechanical devices. He began major engineering and manufacturing projects and established technical schools with foreign teachers. After his death, however, more conservative* Muslim leaders shut down the schools, and the scientific momentum ground to a halt.

Other rulers also had an interest in science. However, they generally hired Europeans to develop and maintain local technology and did not take steps to train their own population. Muslims who wanted a modern scientific education studied in Europe or in the few Western-style universities that had sprung up in European-dominated areas. Medical schools in the Islamic world began to teach the discoveries of Louis Pasteur and other Western physicians. Scholars started to translate into Arabic modern scientific works, such as Darwin's *On the Origin of Species.* Many religious leaders, however, opposed modern developments, banning the printing press, public clocks, and other mechanical devices.

In the early 1900s, however, Muslim leaders began to ignore the *ulama** and to focus on promoting scientific achievement within the Islamic community. In Egypt, Turkey, Syria, and Sudan, new engineering and medical schools sprang up. In Turkey, Mustafa Kemal Atatürk launched an extensive program to modernize factories and agriculture and to promote Western-style schooling. In most areas of the Muslim world, however, industrialization lagged. Leaders continued to import technology from the West.

Rise of Scientific Learning. Most Muslim countries gained their independence from the Europeans in the mid-1900s. After suffering defeat in the Arab-Israeli war of 1948, Islamic leaders realized that they needed to provide better scientific training for their students in order to defend themselves from outsiders. More than 600 science and technology research institutions and centers now exist within the Islamic world. Governments devote the bulk of their resources to science and engineering programs, which attract top students. Turkey promotes programs in hydrology (study of water), textile production, and agriculture. Malaysia has developed programs in electronics, and Indonesia emphasizes aerospace technology. Pakistan, the only Muslim country to have nuclear weapons, conducts research in nuclear energy. Iran and Iraq have pursued petroleum and weapons research.

Schools that teach science and engineering graduate hundreds of thousands of students each year, but the quality of these institutions generally lags behind that of Western schools. Although the Muslim world accounts for 20 percent of the world's population, it contributes to only 5 percent of scientific discoveries. For the most part, Muslim countries continue to import science and technology rather than to produce it on their own. Muslim scientists living in Europe and North America, however, have achieved much greater success than their counterparts in the Middle East. For example, Mohammad Abdus Salam, a particle physicist from Pakistan, received the Nobel Prize in 1979 with Steven Weinberg and Sheldon Glashow. Abdus Salam (died in 1996) served as the founder and director of the Abdus Salam International Centre for Theoretical Physics in Trieste, Italy, and also headed the Third World Academy of Sciences.

Conflicts Between Islam and Science. Science in much of the Muslim world occupies a separate domain from religion. Most Muslim schools, for example, teach evolution, although governments have banned the study in Pakistan, Saudi Arabia, and Sudan. The majority of Muslim scientists also appear to accept such developments as Einstein's theory of relativity, quantum mechanics, chaos theory, and the big-bang theory, despite the fact that these theories challenge the traditional interpretation of the account of creation in the Qur'an*. The philosophical implications of modern science receive little commentary in most Muslim countries. Some issues, however, provoke debate. One such issue is whether the new moon must be visually sighted or whether its position can be predicted with modern astronomical techniques. Weather prediction, too, generates controversy. Traditional Islamic thinking maintains that only God can know the weather, but all Muslim countries support some form of meteorological research and provide weather information. Although traditional Islam also forbids dissection of cadavers, blood transfusions, and organ transplants, almost all Muslim societies accept these procedures.

* **Qur'an** book of the holy scriptures of Islam

A few Muslim clerics, however, have severely criticized the uses and methods of modern science. Some scholars argue that the discipline lacks values and has led to such global problems as weapons of mass destruction, environmental degradation, and unfair distributions of wealth. Others suggest that because modern science does not concern itself with God, it damages Islam itself. Those who hold these views have demanded changes in the way science is taught. The government of Pakistan, for example, has sponsored research into such topics as the temperature of hell and the chemical nature of *jinn* (spirits).

Some Muslims support the development of an Islamic science that offers an alternative to the Western approach. They claim that every scientific fact and phenomenon known today was anticipated at the time of Muhammad and that all scientific predictions have their roots in the Qur'an. Supporters of an Islamic science also reject science that advances knowledge for its own sake. In their view, God's revelation—not human reason—should serve as the ultimate guide to wisdom. Some Muslim scholars insist, for example, that the study of natural disasters must begin with an attempt to understand God's will. Some even propose introducing all scientific facts with a reference to God and removing names associated with specific laws, such as Einstein's Theory of Relativity. These thinkers, however, remain a tiny minority within the Muslim community. Scientists in the Muslim world generally conduct their work without direct reference to religion. As Abdus Salam wrote in an essay published in 1987, "There truly is no [disparity] between Islam and modern science." Abdus Salam also argued that science is universal, not specifically Western or Islamic—a view shared by many Muslim scientists.

Obstacles to Scientific Growth. The lack of significant scientific progress in Muslim countries stems from many factors. Most students of science and engineering come from higher income classes. A large number of poorer Muslims lack exposure to science and do not get a chance to make contributions in the discipline. Although women have entered scientific fields, their numbers remain relatively low. In addition, 80 percent of the world's scientific literature appears first in English, and the existing literature in Arabic, Persian, Urdu, and other languages is outdated or inadequate for teach-

* **regime** government in power

ing or research. Migration presents another challenge. Top scientists from Muslim countries increasingly take jobs outside their native countries. This "brain drain" has presented major problems in countries like Sudan, where more than 500,000 technicians and scientists have left the country since the 1960s.

Another factor discouraging scientific thought is the memorization emphasized in primary and secondary education. Graduates of such schools sometimes lack the questioning skills necessary for top-level scientific training. Universities tend to focus on teaching rather than research and have not developed strong doctoral programs or research centers. In addition, universities are chronically underfunded and overcrowded. Muslim countries spend only around 0.5 percent of their gross national product on scientific funding, compared with 2 percent or more in Western countries.

Strict regimes* also create a climate that stifles scientific advancement. They deny freedom of inquiry and dissent, conditions vital to scientific work. Scientists in countries that are governed by such regimes often cannot attend scientific conferences or keep up with new developments in their fields. Despite such challenges, however, scientists in the Muslim world agree on the most important research issues. These include the development of solar energy, desalination projects (removing excess salt from water and farmland), technologies to improve food production in dry areas, irrigation programs, and research in animal sciences. (*See also* **Ibn Sina; Mathematics; Medicine.**)

Scripture

See *Qur'an.*

Seclusion of Women

See *Women.*

Secularism

In the Islamic world, the battle between secularism—the belief that religious officials should have no direct authority in matters of public policy—and religion is more intense than ever. At one extreme are those who attempt to define Islam as a matter of personal belief alone, and at the other are those who believe that a return to traditional Islamic law and Islamic political authority is essential. In recent years, open support for secularism as a cultural value has become rare, and even dangerous, in many Muslim societies.

A Controversial Subject. The historical relationship between secularism and Islam has passed through several stages, which have varied according to the particular Muslim society under study. During the 1800s, many Muslim officials and elites were attracted to the secular educational and government systems of the West. In their view, Islamic societies could overcome European political dominance if they embraced Europe's advanced scientific and technological knowledge. During the early 1900s, a new generation of Western-educated Muslims adopted this thinking and began to criticize traditional Muslim authorities, whom they regarded as an obstacle to modernity. Muslim opponents believe that secularism is an outgrowth of Western culture and a threat to the core values of Islamic societies. After Muslim countries gained their independence during the 1950s and 1960s, many conservatives* embraced Western science and technology but continued to reject secularism, arguing that Muslim societies cannot compete with non-Muslim countries unless they preserve their own laws and principles based on Islam.

* **conservative** person generally opposed to change, especially in existing political and social institutions

Of central importance to the issue of secularism in the Islamic world is the status of women. Since the late 1800s, modernized Muslim societies have permitted greater freedom for women, including the removal of the veil, sometimes even forcing women to go unveiled. Western-oriented, well-educated Muslims have generally been more willing to support these trends. Conservatives strongly resist moves to westernize the legal status of women. In recent years, many educated Muslim women have begun to reject Western-style dress and have adopted types of covering that conform to Islamic guidelines for appropriate clothing. For some, this step represents a return to religious belief. For others, it reflects their desire to avoid criticism and harassment from men. The status and role of women in Muslim societies today is often a benchmark for evaluating the role of Islam in those cultures.

Secular State. During the 1800s, the rulers of the Ottoman Empire* instituted a state-sponsored reform movement to create secular institutions. In doing so, the government bypassed Islamic religious scholars and limited their authority to personal and family matters, such as marriage, divorce, and inheritance. These new institutions introduced Western educational methods, legal systems, and military techniques. Although this process of reform, called the Tanzimat or reorganization process, did not destroy corresponding Muslim organizations, it faced strong resistance. Nonetheless, secularists claimed that the empire would never free itself from European domination if it rejected westernization.

* **Ottoman Empire** large Turkish state existing from the early 1300s to the early 1900s

See map in Ottoman Empire (vol. 3).

After the defeat of the Ottoman Empire in the early 1900s, a new Turkish state emerged under the leadership of Mustafa Kemal Atatürk. He abolished both the political sultanate* and the religious caliphate* in Turkey. For many Muslims, the end of the religiously sanctioned office of political authority was the end of a legacy of the Prophet Muhammad. For Atatürk, it was the way to inaugurate a civil state in which Islam would be a matter of personal faith. He also replaced the Islamic calendar with the Gregorian calendar and Arabic script with Latin script, and he discouraged women from wearing the veil. These changes created a secular state but did not diminish the power of Islam among the people. When the multiparty political system came into being after World War II (1939–1945), politicians used religion to secure votes. Because this development threatened to undermine Turkey's new secularism, the military took action. Since 1960 military intervention has helped the government limit the expression of Islam within the state. Despite a strict ban on religious-based political parties, the

* **sultanate** government of a sultan, the political and military ruler of a Muslim dynasty or state
* **caliphate** office and government of the caliph, the religious and political leader of an Islamic state

Secularism

Islamist*-oriented Justice and Development Party won a parliamentary majority in 2002.

Competing for Influence. A wide range of governments exists in the Arab Muslim world. Saudi Arabia identifies itself as an Islamic state. Its rulers govern in accordance with traditional Islamic law as interpreted by the *ulama**, and they finance Islamic movements in other countries. Syria, by contrast, is avowedly secular. The government relegates religion to matters of personal faith and practice. Women have equal rights, and many wear Western clothing and work outside the home.

Since the 1930s, tensions between the secular state of Egypt and a strong religious movement have intensified. Government corruption has contributed to dissatisfaction with secular institutions and has led to a resurgence of Islamic identity. The Muslim Brotherhood, founded in 1928, promoted the restoration of Islamic law and the application of Islamic traditions, such as *zakat**, to create a more just society. Although President Gamal Abdel Nasser (ruled 1954–1970) suppressed the organization, its popularity led his successor, President Anwar el-Sadat, to permit its open operation. Today the government's apparent inability to address social and economic problems contributes to a climate that is increasingly hostile to secular institutions.

Algeria's experience under French colonial rule led the country to develop a mix of secular and Islamic elements. After gaining independence from France in 1962, Algeria adopted a socialist* government that identified Islam as its official religion. By the 1980s, the failures of the government had led to the emergence of Islamist groups calling for the establishment of an Islamic state. Since the early 1990s, the members of the Islamic movement and the secular authorities have been engaged in a violent struggle to promote their conflicting goals.

Religious Orientation. In the Islamic Republic of Iran, religious officials and Islamic law are the basis of government. Since 1500 Iran has been a Shi'i* society, and the government has strengthened its legitimacy by protecting Islam, as interpreted by Shi'i clerics. The Pahlavi dynasty* (1925–1979) represented a secular period in which state-ordered modernization ultimately ignited mass resistance, encouraged by Shi'i religious officials. The Islamic Revolution of 1979 brought together mullahs*, merchants, and many secular Iranian nationalists*, all of whom opposed the shah without necessarily expecting a religious government. Today, Iranian authorities condemn secularism and Atatürk as its Middle Eastern sponsor.

The Challenges of Diversity. The majority of the world's Muslim population lives in South and Southeast Asia, an area that stretches from Pakistan to Indonesia. This region is home to a broad range of ethnic* and religious groups, which often triggers conflict. In this environment, secular ideals have eroded. India, for example, is a democratic secular state with a sizable Muslim population. In recent years, however, India's Hindu* majority has focused on eliminating the country's Islamic past.

Indonesia, the largest Muslim country in the world, is an officially secular state. The government sponsors both Islamic and secular schools, as well as *shari'ah** and civil courts. Many Indonesian Muslims accept the idea of a secular state on the condition that the authorities do not interfere in their practice of Islam. They have protested vigorously when the state has taken steps to change traditional Islamic laws—as when the government introduced legislation to permit Muslim women to marry non-Muslim men.

In Malaysia, Islam serves as a source of national identity for the Malay population, who share the country with significant Chinese and Indian minorities. Nevertheless, the federation has a wide variety of Islamic groups. This situation has frustrated those who desire a more unified Islamic element in Malaysian society. Islamic revivalism* remains a strong influence throughout the country. (*See also* **Algeria; Atatürk, Mustafa Kemal; Clothing; Egypt; Fundamentalism; Iran; Malaysia; Modernism; Muslim Brotherhood; Ottoman Empire; Saudi Arabia; South Asia; Southeast Asia; Turkey; Women; Women and Reform.**)

* **revivalism** movement calling for the return to traditional values or beliefs

Seljuk Dynasty

A Turkic dynasty* of Central Asian origin, the Seljuks ruled much of the eastern Islamic world from 1038 to 1194. The Seljuks converted to Islam in the late 900s, probably inspired by Sufi* missionaries. Led by two brothers, Toghril Beg and Chaghri Beg, they invaded Iran and defeated the Ghaznavid sultan Mas'ud in 1040. Chaghri remained there to guard the east while Toghril marched westward, entering Baghdad in 1055 and ending the rule of the Shi'i* Buyids.

By the time of Toghril's death in 1063, the Seljuks controlled all of the area that is now Iran and Iraq, as well as parts of Central Asia. They later expanded into Syria, and one branch of the family established a sultanate* in Turkey. Seljuk rule began to weaken after 1092, when divisions developed between the eastern and western parts of the empire. The sultan of the eastern realm, Sanjar, claimed authority over the entire empire but in practice had little control. Seljuk rule in Iran ended after Sanjar's death. Nine Seljuk sultans ruled Iraq between 1118 and 1194. The last, Toghril III, died in battle against the shah*, who took over the eastern Seljuk empire. In Turkey, the Seljuk sultanate continued until its defeat by the Mongols in 1243.

The Seljuks had a loose, decentralized reign in which the government had little control over individual towns and villages. Local amirs* and members of the *ulama** governed small areas and taxed the inhabitants. Sultans expanded the empire with slave armies. They encountered resistance, however, from certain Shi'i sects, especially the Nizari. The Nizari established a network of guerrilla* groups designed to overthrow the Seljuks and to destroy Sunni Islam. The Seljuks circulated stories about the Nizari in order to crush their credibility, including one stating that they used hashish, a mind-altering drug, in order to give them the courage to fight their enemies. The word they used to describe the Nizari, *hashishin*, eventually led to the creation of the English term *assassin.* The Seljuks massacred many Nizari, but the Nizari established a small state in Alamut, in Iran, that lasted for 150 years.

Despite the attacks of the Shi'i minority, Seljuk rule marked the revival of Sunni* Islam after a period in which Shi'i Islam had dominated. It freed the Abbasid caliphate* in Baghdad from subservience to the Iranian Buyids

* **dynasty** succession of rulers from the same family or group

* **Sufi** follower of Sufism, which seeks to develop spirituality through discipline of the mind and body

* **Shi'i** refers to Muslims who believe that Muhammad chose Ali ibn Abi Talib and his descendants as the spiritual-political leaders of the Muslim community

* **sultanate** government of a sultan, the political and military ruler of a Muslim dynasty or state

* **shah** king (Persian); ruler of Iran

* **amir** military commander, governor, or prince

* *ulama* religious scholars

* **guerrilla** member of a group of fighters, outside the regular army, who engages in unconventional warfare

* **Sunni** refers to the largest branch of the Muslim community; the name derives from sunnah, the exemplary behavior of the Prophet Muhammad

* **caliphate** office and government of the caliph, the religious and political head of an Islamic state

and restored much of the caliphate's stature. Some of the most notable Sunni intellectuals, particularly the theologian* and legal scholar Abu Hamid al-Ghazali (died 1111), flourished under the Seljuks. The vizier* Nizam al-Mulk (died 1092) made the most notable contributions to Middle Eastern culture, establishing the first network of *madrasahs** in the Islamic world. This system ultimately brought about a heightened sense of Islamic unity as students traveled all over the Middle East to study with different teachers. The *ulama* gained more influence and prestige, and theology, philosophy, and the sciences flourished.

The Seljuk conquest served as the first major invasion by the Turks into the Islamic world. It marked the beginning of many centuries of Turkish political and military dominance in the Middle East, culminating in the reign of the Ottomans. Sufism also developed under Seljuk reign. The Seljuks created a lasting administrative legacy, including the establishment of governmental systems that continued into the 1800s. (*See also* **Ghazali, Abu Hamid al-; Iran; Iraq; Turkey.**)

September 11, 2001

On the morning of September 11, 2001, two passenger jets heading from Boston to Los Angeles changed course and smashed into the World Trade Center in New York City. A third plane crashed into the Pentagon, outside Washington, D.C., and a fourth crashed into a field in western Pennsylvania after its passengers attempted to subdue the hijackers who had taken control of the cockpit. By 10:28 a.m., both towers of the World Trade Center had collapsed in a roar of smoking debris. The terrorist attacks—the most deadly ever on American soil—killed more than 3,000 people and marked a major turning point in the relationship between the United States and the Muslim world.

Although no group claimed immediate responsibility for the attacks, investigators soon linked them to al-Qaeda, an Islamic extremist organization headed by Saudi Arabian militant Osama bin Laden. In 1996 bin Laden had declared a jihad* against the United States in order to force the withdrawal of American troops from Saudi Arabia, where they had been stationed to protect the Saudis from Iraqi aggression during the Gulf War (1990–1991). He later endorsed several fatwas*, stating that Muslims should kill Americans wherever they are throughout the world. Bin Laden has been charged with organizing attacks on American targets, including the bombings of two U.S. embassies in Africa in 1998, and the attack on the USS Cole, docked in Yemen, in 2000. He may also have been involved in the 1993 bombing of the World Trade Center, which killed 6 people and injured about 1,000.

But the events that became known as "9/11" jolted Americans out of a false sense of security in their own country. Until then the United States treated terrorist activities primarily as law enforcement matters. By contrast, President George W. Bush declared that the 9/11 attacks were "acts of war." He determined that the United States would fight and defeat terrorism, making no distinction between unaffiliated terrorist groups and governments that supported them.

The World Trade Center attacks on September 11, 2001, were commemorated six months later by spotlights rising from the site. The attacks led to increased awareness of Muslims and their faith in the United States.

A Range of Responses

Muslims around the world reacted to 9/11 with responses that ranged from delight to anguish. On the border between Pakistan and Afghanistan, thousands of men brandishing swords and axes declared their willingness to join in jihad against America. In other parts of the Muslim world, crowds cheered at footage of the planes flying into the Twin Towers. Palestinian leader Yasir Arafat condemned the attacks and allowed television crews to film him donating blood for the victims; other Arab leaders expressed similar views. In the United States, Sheikh Muhammad al-Gamei'a, the Egyptian-born imam of the Islamic Cultural Center and Mosque of New York City, declared that the attacks were a Jewish plot. M. A. Muqtedar Khan, a professor and board member of the Center for the Study of Islam and Democracy, called the 9/11 attacks a "horrible scar on the history of Islam and humanity."

President Bush insisted that the response to 9/11 was directed against terrorists, not against Islam itself or against law-abiding Muslims. Bin Laden and al-Qaeda became the first targets in the American war against terrorism. In late 2001, the United States led a military campaign in Afghanistan to destroy the al-Qaeda network and to oust the ruling Taliban regime that had harbored the terrorists. Surveillance of other militant groups also continued. Some groups operated in Western countries and were actively seeking nuclear, chemical, or biological weapons. Arguing that Iraq possessed such weapons and also supported terrorist groups, the United States and Great Britain led a military coalition to oust the government of Saddam Hussein in early 2003.

The American response to 9/11 inspired complex reactions throughout the world. Arab and Muslim leaders condemned the attacks as violations of Islam and insisted that the vast majority of Muslims did not support terrorism. They objected to stereotypes that portrayed Muslims as violent and denounced the growing number of hate crimes directed against American Muslims. Moreover, they condemned racial profiling measures that violated the civil rights of Muslims. Yet 9/11 also led to an increased awareness of Islam in the United States. Americans began to educate themselves about Islam and about current problems in the Middle East. Seminars, interfaith services, and media coverage addressed matters of importance to Muslims.

Despite their sympathy toward the United States immediately after 9/11, many Muslims noted that American support for Israel contributed to feelings of anger and frustration. These feelings, in turn, bred terrorism. Some criticized the American-led bombing of Afghanistan as a campaign against their faith. The invasion of Iraq in 2003 caused even more outrage across the Arab and Muslim world, and many condemned it as a new crusade to destroy Islam, a reference to the Christian campaigns against Muslims in the Middle Ages*. Opponents of the war around the world argued that it was immoral and illegal and would increase terrorism against the United States. Supporters contended that the war demonstrated America's resolve to act and that it would eventually lead suspect regimes to abandon terrorist tactics and their support for extremist groups. They also suggested that the war would inspire renewed efforts to solve the Arab-Israeli conflict and that a democratic Iraq would provide a model of stability in the Middle East.

* **Middle Ages** period roughly between 500 and 1500

Whether the American responses to 9/11 will lead to greater security or increased violence remains to be seen. What is certain, however, is that 9/11 has created a new sense of urgency about issues that have caused conflict between the Muslim world and the West. (*See also* **Bin Laden, Osama; Jihad; Qaeda, al-; Taliban; Terrorism; United States.**)

Sermon

The *khatib*, or preacher, played a significant role in the spread of Islam, especially during the years after the Prophet's death in 632. During the Umayyad period (661–750), the Friday noontime sermon, which was usually given by the caliph* or provincial ruler, became an important part of Muslim tradition. Later a special class of preachers assumed responsibility for the Friday sermon, known as a *khutbah*. This speech typically lasts 10 to 15 minutes and generally includes praise of God, blessings on Muhammad and his family, and lessons for the faithful about their spiritual and social responsibilities. The *khatib* also curses enemies of the state, praises the ruler, defends public policies, and stirs public emotion.

* **caliph** religious and political leader of an Islamic state

Popular preachers also worked to spread the faith during Islam's early years. They traveled from place to place, telling stories with religious lessons to instruct people about Islam. The Arabic word for this type of preacher, *qass*, means "storyteller." Most popular preachers lacked government approval. They delivered sermons in public places and achieved a greater degree of political freedom than official preachers. They considered it their duty to teach and support the Muslim community, and also to criticize its leadership when necessary. They also worked to convert non-Muslims to Islam. Some popular preachers even traveled with Muslim armies to spread the faith among those captured in battle.

By the end of the Middle Ages*, popular preaching began to decline. Some official preachers began to encourage political dissent. Because many Muslim governments limit freedom of expression among the population, the *khutbah* has become one of the only means of criticizing official policy. In countries such as India and Iran, preachers spoke out against colonialism and helped to lead revolts that resulted in independence. Some governments used Friday sermons to promote their own authority. For example, Egyptian and Moroccan rulers have legitimized certain programs through the *khatibs*. The *khutbah* also serves several other functions, including granting community members a forum for discussing problems, and uniting Muslims in non-Muslim lands.

* **Middle Ages** period roughly between 500 and 1500

Sexuality

Islamic law recognizes the sexual nature of human beings. Sexuality provides a balance to the spiritual, material, and intellectual spheres of life. Nevertheless, the Islamic tradition emphasizes that the only basis for sexual fulfillment is a heterosexual marriage. Premarital sex, adultery, and homosexuality are considered sinful, and therefore, punishable. As more Muslim women have participated in the workplace and other aspects of public life, issues regarding female gender roles have also come to the foreground.

Sacred Union. Sex within marriage is neither sinful nor reserved only for the purposes of procreation. Indeed, Muslims understand sexual fulfillment within marriage—for both the husband and wife—to be a fundamental part of the relationship. Marital sex serves as a means of communication between partners and as a source of comfort. The Qur'an* prohibits sex outside of marriage, however, and identifies it as a sin comparable to murder or stealing. In classical Islamic law, those convicted of this crime are subject to set punishments, either flogging or stoning.

* **Qur'an** book of the holy scriptures of Islam

To confront the sexual impulses that may arise after puberty, many Muslim societies have developed separate spheres for males and females. In general, girls and boys do not attend school together or interact in social settings. Some societies may permit young couples to date, either with a chaperone or in a group. Islam stresses the virginity* of both boys and girls before they enter into their first marriage. Brides are sometimes required to present a doctor's certificate to confirm it.

* **virginity** state of being a virgin, one who has never experienced sexual intercourse

Modern trends have begun to complicate sexual issues in many Muslim countries. Economic factors and educational pursuits have led many young people to marry at a later age, resulting in a longer period of celibacy* and greater difficulty in honoring Islamic teachings about premarital sex. In Iran, clerics and government leaders endorse temporary marriage, which is permitted under Shi'i* law, as an acceptable alternative to sexually promiscuous behavior.

* **celibacy** condition of remaining unmarried; also, abstention from sexual intercourse

* **Shi'i** refers to Muslims who believe that Muhammad chose Ali ibn Abi Talib and his descendants as the spiritual-political leaders of the Muslim community

The presence of women in the workplace has also generated tension in the Islamic world, and has resulted in the harassment of women in public. The employment of women outside the home has also triggered debate about the proper behavior of Muslim women and the potential moral dangers posed by changes in sexual norms.

Confronting Changing Sexual Behavior

Attitudes about sexual liberalization remain strongly conservative in much of the Muslim world. When a provincial health official in Indonesia, the world's most populous Muslim country, quoted the results of two studies that revealed a growing number of high school students were engaging in sexual relations, he found himself unemployed. Indonesian officials and religious leaders are hesitant to confront the changing sexual behavior of young people. Critics condemn their approach to sex education as inadequate, particularly as it relates to the spread of HIV/AIDS. The Sidikara Foundation, a nongovernmental organization in Indonesia, has responded with youth-oriented radio programs about AIDS and student discussion groups.

Education has promoted new ideas about family planning and population growth. Muslim societies accept birth control as an aid in managing family resources and as something that enables married couples to enjoy sex just for pleasure. Nevertheless, Muslims generally consider infertility to be very shameful, and many resist the use of birth control. Islam permits infertility treatments, including in vitro fertilization, but most Muslims believe that Islam forbids abortion unless the mother's life is threatened by the pregnancy.

Sensitive Topics. Homosexuality exists in the Muslim world, but virtually all Muslims believe that Islam condemns same-sex relationships. Most schools of Islamic law require punishments for homosexual activities. In Iran, Iraq, Saudi Arabia, and Sudan, the penalty is execution. Offenders in Bangladesh, Egypt, Malaysia, and Pakistan receive prison sentences ranging from 3 to 20 years.

Islam emphasizes that sexual relations must be based on mutual respect and consent and strongly condemns prostitution and rape. However, prostitution is a major social problem in many Muslim countries. Child prostitution has become a serious concern in Indonesia, and human rights groups have charged that female migrant workers in Malaysia and Saudi Arabia are subjected to sexual abuse from their employers.

The practice of female circumcision*, which occurs in parts of the Persian Gulf region and some Muslim countries of Africa, began long before Islam arrived in these regions. Intended as a means of controlling female sexuality and ensuring virginity at marriage, it limits a woman's ability to experience sexual pleasure. Many Muslims regard this practice as contrary to Islamic principles. (*See also* **Harem; Marriage.**)

* **circumcision** surgery to remove part of the external sexual organ

Shadhiliyah

* **Sufi** refers to Sufism, which seeks to develop spirituality through discipline of the mind and body

* **theology** study of the nature and qualities of God and the understanding of His will

* **Sunni** refers to the largest branch of the Muslim community; the name derives from sunnah, the exemplary behavior of the Prophet Muhammad

* **zawiyah** Sufi center that serves as a place of worship and a welfare institution

Shadhiliyah is one of the four oldest Sufi* orders (*tariqahs*) in the Muslim world. The order takes its name from the Moroccan-born scholar Abu al-Hasan Ali al-Shadhili (died 1258). He left no scholarly texts, but his teachings, collected in the book *Hikam*, helped to spread the order throughout North Africa. A modern collection of his works, *The School of Shadhiliyah*, includes a number of popular prayers, including a widely used plea for safety at sea.

Believed to be a descendant of Muhammad, Abu al-Hasan is said to have lost his sight from excessive study in his youth. He traveled around North Africa to study Islamic theology*. In Tunisia, a jealous scholar imprisoned him and had him exiled for his deviation from Sunni* Islam. Abu al-Hasan went to Alexandria, where he established a *zawiyah*. He did not, however, agree with every aspect of Sufism. Shadhilis take a practical approach to the issue of worldly comforts. In contrast with other Sufi orders, they do not regard wealth as excluding Muslims from the community of *fuqara*, "the poor in God". Abu al-Hasan stated, in fact, that he preferred the grateful rich to the patient poor. This outlook has greatly aided the Shadhiliyah in attracting contemporary followers.

The Shadhiliyah exists in many parts of the Muslim world, including 14 officially recognized branches in Egypt. It maintains a presence in Sudan, where it gained widespread popularity between the 1500s and 1800s. It also exists in sub-Saharan Africa and East Africa, and it is the majority *tariqah* of the Comoro Islands, off the coast of Mozambique.

During the Ottoman period, the Shadhiliyah gained influence in Turkey and spread into the Balkan countries of Bulgaria, Romania, the former Yugoslavia, Kosovo, and Macedonia. In the 1900s, the Fasiyah Shadhiliyah made its way to Sri Lanka, and other groups became active in China. In Yemen, the Shadhiliyah is credited with the introduction of coffee to keep the faithful awake during long prayer sessions.

In the mid-1900s, Shadhili groups in Egypt initiated reforms to counter anti-Sufi criticism and diminishing membership. The Hamidiyah gained a reputation for the careful organization and control of its public rituals. It established a rule (*qanun*) defining correct behavior for its members. Other groups have also campaigned for the reform of Sufi practices. The Ashirah Muhammadiyah introduced the 1976 Sufi Ordinance to regulate the disciplinary and financial matters of the Egyptian *tariqahs*. (*See also* **Sufism**.)

Shadow of God

The ancient Persians believed that their kings possessed divine grace and ruled by divine will. A king served as a mediator between his subjects and the gods and could thus bring good fortune to his people. After Islamic rule came to Persia, the Muslims integrated the concept of kingship into their government. Muslim caliphs* and kings called themselves *Zill Allah*, or the Shadow of God. As such, many rulers considered themselves accountable only to God and allowed no public questioning of their actions. Classical Persian texts instructed Muslims that "God has two guardians over the people; his guardians in heaven are the angels, and his guardians on earth are kings."

* **caliph** religious and political leader of an Islamic state

After the Safavid dynasty (1501–1722) came to power in Iran, Shi'i* doctrines helped to reinforce the idea of divinely guided kingship. Shi'is regarded the tribal leader Haydar (1460–1488) as the son of God and viewed his son Ismail, the founder of the Safavid dynasty, as a forerunner of the Mahdi, or Hidden Imam*. Although the Islamic doctrine of *tawhid* forbids the idea of human divinity or reincarnation, Safavid kings sometimes used Shi'i traditions to claim these attributes without significant criticism from religious leaders.

* **Shi'i** refers to Muslims who believe that Muhammad chose Ali ibn Abi Talib and his descendants as the spiritual-political leaders of the Muslim community

* **imam** spiritual-political leader in Shi'i Islam, one who is regarded as directly descended from Muhammad; also, one who leads prayers

Under Karim Khan Zand (1750–1779), however, the monarchy in Iran dropped claims to divinity. Zand instead took the title Vakili Ra'aya (Regent of the People), and acted as a tribal leader. During the Qajar dynasty (1796–1925), though, Persian rulers again took the title Shadow of God, but Qajar rulers did not claim to represent the Mahdi. Religious scholars took their place in assuming some of the authority of the imams.

During the Pahlavi dynasty (1926–1979), the monarchy became increasingly secularized*. Despite this trend, both Pahlavi monarchs used the tradition of divinely guided kingship to bolster their power. The second king, Muhammad Reza Shah, believed that the monarchy could not survive with-

* **secularize** to separate religion from other aspects of human life and society

out its traditional connotations. He also believed that the monarchy had such deep roots in Iranian culture that if he lost the throne, another king would replace him. He stated that the Iranians expected their king to be "a symbol of earthly redemption . . . because the king was the linkage with the Almighty."

The authoritarian attitudes and corruption that existed in Iranian public institutions caused the symbol of the divinely guided or appointed king to take on even more importance. The figure of the Shadow of God served as an image of divine protection, binding the nation together and giving it a sense of purpose. Even so, Ayatollah* Ruhollah al-Musavi Khomeini abolished the Iranian monarchy and deposed Muhammad Reza Shah Pahlavi in 1979. He seemed however, to continue in the tradition of the Shadow of God by proclaiming himself the religious leader of Iran who had been granted authority over the region in the absence of the Mahdi. Although he did not consider himself divinely appointed, he established a firm Islamic rule that caused some followers to refer to him as imam. (*See also* **Iran; Khomeini, Ruhollah al-Musavi.**)

* **ayatollah** highest-ranking legal scholar among some Shi'i Muslims

Shafi'i, al-

767–820
Founder of the Shafi'i school

* **Qur'an** book of the holy scriptures of Islam

* **hadith** reports of the words and deeds of Muhammad (not in the Qur'an, but accepted as guides for Muslim behavior)

* **fiqh** human efforts to understand and codify divine law

* **Sunni** refers to the largest branch of the Muslim community; the name derives from sunnah, the exemplary behavior of the Prophet Muhammad

* **precedent** prior example that serves as a model

* **sunnah** literally "the trodden path"; Islamic customs based on the exemplary behavior of Muhammad

Born in Gaza, Muhammad ibn Idris al-Shafi'i was a distant relative of Muhammad. As a child, al-Shafi'i moved to Mecca with his mother, where he studied the Qur'an* and hadith*. He lived with desert tribes noted for their eloquent poetry and later traveled to Medina to study fiqh* under the noted jurist Malik ibn Anas. After Malik's death, al-Shafi'i continued his studies in Iraq.

Al-Shafi'i became an expert on the Sunni* legal schools. Originally a member of the Maliki school, al-Shafi'i broke away, favoring precedent* over independent legal reasoning. Several jurists accepted his theories, and his teachings formed the basis for the Shafi'i school of law. Al-Shafi'i accepted only the Qur'an and sunnah* (as described in the hadith) as valid legal sources. He viewed Muhammad's words and actions as the correct interpretations of God's commands. Al-Shafi'i further insisted that each hadith had to be transmitted by a chain of devout Muslims that led directly back to Muhammad. He rejected juristic preference and personal opinion as sources of law but stated that legal scholars could use *qiyas* (reasoning based on analogy) and *ijma* (consensus, or agreement) in the absence of guidance from traditional texts. He argued that God would not allow the Muslim community to err and so any law on which everyone agreed had divine sanction.

Al-Shafi'i defined his teachings in the seven-volume work, *Al-umm*. The book covers a wide range of legal topics, including personal status, punishment, transactions, and religious customs. It also clarifies many of the differences among the other schools of law. For this reason, many Muslims consider al-Shafi'i the architect of Islamic law. The Shafi'i school gained a large following in Egypt during the Ayyubid dynasty (1171–1250) and the Mamluk dynasty (1250–1517). The school remains popular in Egypt, Palestine, Jordan, Syria, and other countries. (*See also* **Law; Malik ibn Anas; Mamluk State.**)

Shahadah

Translated as "witness" or "testimony," the *shahadah* is the profession of faith, the first of the five Pillars of Islam. To recite the *shahadah*, Muslims must utter the words, "There is no god but God (Allah), and Muhammad is the messenger of God." The Qur'an* covers the topic of witnessing, but it does not include the *shahadah* statement. The hadith* contain the actual phrase, although several early reports mention simpler statements of faith, such as, "There is no god but God."

To admit people to the faith, the early Islamic community required only that new Muslims recite the *shahadah*. Questions arose later about the status of an individual who recited the *shahadah* but did not mean it or act accordingly. Religious leaders decided that such a person would technically remain a legal member of the community and that the sincerity of a professed believer can only be judged by God. Muslim scholars also concluded that a person needed to understand fully the meaning of the *shahadah* to fulfill the requirement properly.

As the Islamic community grew, it split into several different groups. Various branches adopted more complex creeds for membership. Certain institutions, such as holy sanctuaries and Islamic universities, also required longer declarations of faith. Recitation of the basic *shahadah*, however, remains the accepted method of becoming a Muslim. A person wishing to convert needs only to repeat the statement twice in the presence of at least one other Muslim. He or she must recite the *shahadah* correctly, with full comprehension and sincerity. (*See also* **Pillars of Islam.**)

* **Qur'an** book of the holy scriptures of Islam

* **hadith** reports of the words and deeds of Muhammad (not in the Qur'an, but accepted as guides for Muslim behavior)

Shahid

See *Martyrdom.*

Shari'ah

See *Law.*

Shaykh

See *Titles, Honorific.*

Shi'i Islam

Shi'i Islam is the smaller of the two major branches of Islam. Its name derives from the term *shi'ah*, meaning "followers," "party," or "supporters." Early Shi'is called themselves *shi'at Ali*—the party of Ali ibn Abi Talib, Muhammad's cousin. Shi'i Muslims believe that Ali and his descendants are the rightful rulers and spiritual leaders of the Muslim community. While Sunni* Muslims accept the authority of Muhammad's companions, Shi'is place their faith primarily in members of the Prophet's family.

* **Sunni** refers to the largest branch of the Muslim community; the name derives from sunnah, the exemplary behavior of the prophet Muhammad

After Muhammad died, Muslims split over the question of a successor. Shi'is believed that the new leader should come from the Prophet's family. In the mid-600s, civil war divided the Muslim world, and this Safavid painting of the 1600s shows one of the battles involving a Shi'i hero.

Origins and Early Development

The Shi'i movement originated in Arabia shortly after the Prophet's death. It has its roots in the tribal divisions of the *ummah* (Muslim community). The *ummah* consisted of clans, many of which retained their old values and customs. The tribes of northern and central Arabia lacked clearly defined religious traditions. They chose new rulers according to seniority and ability. The southern faction, in contrast, had strong religious traditions relating to authority and chose leaders based on heredity and divine authority.

After Muhammad's death, the Muslim community split over who would succeed him. The majority group believed that ability should serve as the primary qualification. They held that the successor should be a forceful leader who could maintain unity among the many clans in the community. An opposing group viewed the succession issue in spiritual terms. They argued that Muhammad's family would serve as the natural leaders of the Islamic community. These Muslims cited Qur'anic* verses that spoke of God's favor passing to the Prophet's descendants and argued that members of Muhammad's line alone could become imams*.

Struggle Over the Caliphate. The Muslims who supported leadership by the Prophet's family believed that the proper successor to Muhammad was his cousin and son-in-law, Ali. The majority of Muslims, however, backed Muhammad's closest adviser and companion, Abu Bakr, and he became caliph* in 632. After Abu Bakr's death, Umar ibn al-Khattab, another close companion of the Prophet, served as caliph from 634 to 644. When Umar died, Uthman ibn Affan, a member of the Umayyad clan, succeeded him. Supporters of Ali opposed many of the new caliph's policies. Uthman also stirred opposition among Sunni Muslims by appointing his fellow

* **Qur'an** book of the holy scriptures of Islam

* **imam** spiritual-political leader in Shi'i Islam, one who is regarded as directly descended from Muhammad; also, one who leads prayers

* **caliph** religious and political leader of an Islamic state

Umayyads to influential positions. Members of the Umayyad family seized the wealth of the growing empire, caring little for the needs of the *ummah*. In 656 a mob killed Uthman, and Ali succeeded him as caliph, although he accepted the position reluctantly.

Although Ali had gained many supporters, some Muslim clans, including the powerful Umayyads, opposed him. Civil war quickly spread throughout the region. The Umayyads and several other groups rose up against Ali, and an assassin struck him down in 661. Shi'is believed the caliphate should pass to Hasan ibn Ali, the oldest son of Ali and Fatimah, Muhammad's daughter. The Umayyad chief Mu'awiyah, however, outmaneuvered Hasan and seized power for himself.

Umayyad and Abbasid Periods. The Umayyads controlled the caliphate from 661 to 750. Mu'awiyah faced strong opposition from supporters of the sons of Ali and persecuted them, but the Shi'is persevered. After Hasan died, they supported his brother, Husayn ibn Ali. After the death of Mu'awiyah, Shi'is in Kufa, Iraq, invited Husayn to their city to become caliph. The Iraqi governor, however, sent troops to stop the caravan. They massacred Husayn and many of his family members at Karbala, taking the rest as prisoners.

The tragedy at Karbala became the defining event of Shi'i Islam, infusing the movement with a newfound passion and mobilizing its members. Devotion became a key element of Shi'ism, especially in the expression of love for Muhammad's family. After Husayn's death, Shi'is revered him as a martyr*. Thousands sought vengeance against the Umayyad government. A group of 3,000 Shi'is, called the Tawwabun (Penitents), rose up against the Umayyads. These Muslims believed that their deaths on the battlefield would help them repent for their inability to help Husayn in his time of need. The Shi'i cause drew support from other Muslims who opposed Umayyad society, including members of influential families in Medina, Muslims who sought to establish a more religious state, and non-Arabs who resented Arab dominance.

As the Shi'i movement spread, a conflict over succession developed. Husayn's only surviving son, Ali Zayn al-Abidin, displayed few leadership qualities. Some Shi'is backed Ali's third son, Muhammad ibn al-Hanafiyah, as their leader. When he died in 700, Husayn's grandson, Zayd ibn Ali, gained the support of several Shi'i groups. Zayd led an armed uprising against the Umayyads, but caliphate forces crushed the revolt and killed Zayd in 740.

The Abbasids overthrew the Umayyad dynasty a decade later. Although initially allied with the Shi'is, the Abbasids suppressed the movement. Despite persecution, Shi'i Muslims maintained their traditions. Overall, the movement gained in numbers but split into three distinct branches: Zaydi, Ismaili, and Ithna Ashari.

Shi'i Buyids Gain Power. In the mid-900s, the Buyids, military adventurers from Iran, captured the Abbasid capital of Baghdad. They ruled for about a century, until the Abbasids and Seljuk Turks reestablished Sunni dominance. The Buyids supported Shi'ism. Scholars in Iran and Iraq consolidated Shi'i doctrines at this time, formulating Shi'i law and compiling collections of hadith*. Theologians* produced several major commentaries and religious works. Shi'is also established shrines and instituted worship rituals. By the end of the Buyid era, the basic principles of Shi'ism had fully emerged. All three Shi'i branches had a strong enough foundation to survive on their own.

* **martyr** one who dies for his or her religious beliefs

* **hadith** reports of the words and deeds of Muhammad (not in the Qur'an, but accepted as guides for Muslim behavior)

* **theologian** person who studies the nature, qualities, and will of God

Religious Division and Doctrine

Shi'is and Sunnis share many of the same religious beliefs. Both branches follow the Qur'an and observe the five Pillars of Islam. Shi'i Muslims, however, differ from Sunnis in certain fundamental ways. Sunnis believe that God and humans have a direct relationship. They look to their *ulama* (religious scholars) for guidance in religious doctrine, but not for intercession* with God. Shi'is, on the other hand, believe intercession to be an integral element of Islam. They maintain that the imams who succeeded Muhammad were divinely inspired and served as a link between God and the community. They also believe that an imam will return at the end of time to redeem the Shi'is and free them from oppression.

* **intercession** act of pleading for another

Shi'i Muslims developed rituals around the imams that became central to their faith. They visit shrines and tombs of imams and members of Muhammad's family to express their devotion and to celebrate these figures' birthdays or death anniversaries. Sunni Muslims shun these practices. Shi'is, in turn, have denounced the Sunni caliphates and the domination of non-Shi'is over the Muslim world. They see themselves as members of a struggling community striving to create a just society according to God's rule. Over time, different Shi'i sects* have emerged.

* **sect** religious group adhering to distinctive beliefs

Three Major Branches of Shi'ism. Disagreements over imam succession divided the Shi'is into three main branches. The Zaydi branch formed after the death of the fourth imam, Zayn al-Abidin, in 713. This faction supported Zayn's son Zayd as the fifth imam, while the majority of Shi'is favored Muhammad al-Baqir. The Zaydis further broke away from mainstream Shi'ism by rejecting the idea that the imam possesses divine powers and represents God on earth. They believed that any descendant of Ali could become imam as long as he expressed religious devotion, had an Islamic education, and could take up the sword against the enemies of Islam. This ruled out infants as well as the hidden imams later acknowledged by the other Shi'i groups. The Zaydis developed major works of Shi'i law and rejected Shi'i practices they considered extreme, such as temporary marriages.

The remaining followers of Shi'i Islam split into two groups in the 700s. The division occurred over the successor to the sixth imam, Jafar al-Sadiq. The Ismailis recognized Ismail, Jafar's dead son, as the seventh imam. Called Seveners, this group believes that Ismail is the Hidden Imam—an imam who has not died but lives in seclusion, protected by God. The Hidden Imam will return as a world ruler to establish a reign of justice. Several smaller sects, including the Druze and the Nizari, developed out of the Ismaili tradition.

Ithna Ashari, the third and largest Shi'i Muslim group, recognized Jafar al-Sadiq's son, Musa al-Kazim, as the seventh imam. Called Twelvers, the group acknowledged five more imams as Muhammad's successors. The twelfth imam, Muhammad al-Mahdi, disappeared as a child in 874. The Ithna Asharis believe that he went into hiding and will return to rule. As the divinely guided leader of the *ummah*, Muhammad al-Mahdi will restore justice and equality on earth. The Ithna Asharis refer to him as the Hidden Imam, or the Mahdi.

The Seveners and Twelvers both await a messianic* figure who will return as savior. While awaiting the Hidden Imam's return, Shi'is look to religious experts for guidance. The Twelvers developed a clerical hierarchy to

* **messianic** refers to the messiah, the anticipated savior to be sent by God

govern their community in the absence of the Mahdi. Their leaders are ayatollahs*, scholars noted for their piety and knowledge.

* **ayatollah** highest-ranking legal scholar among some Shi'i Muslims

All Shi'i Muslims view the imams as intermediaries between God and humanity. The Ithna Asharis recognize Fourteen Pure Ones. These include Muhammad, Ali, Fatimah, Hasan, Husayn, and the remaining nine imams. As the "Mother of the Imams" and a symbol of purity and virtue, Fatimah serves as a role model for women. Husayn, who sacrificed his life in battle, is an inspiration for men.

Suffering and martyrdom play a major role in the Shi'i faith. Believers revere the holy family for suffering in God's service and for enduring persecution from Sunni caliphs. They view the imams as examples of dedication and sacrifice in the face of tyranny. They believe that each imam, except the last one, died as a martyr. Some Shi'i groups regard dying for the faith as the highest honor.

Shi'ism in Practice. Shi'is and Sunnis share many of the same religious practices, including daily prayers and fasting. Shi'i Muslims, however, have developed many distinctive rituals around suffering and martyrdom. They celebrate holidays honoring the imams' birth and death dates. Many organize annual reenactments of the tragedy of Husayn's martyrdom at Karbala, engaging in recitations, street processions, and passion plays to commemorate Husayn's death. Weeping, prayer, and self-flogging all serve as part of this experience, as believers seek to atone for their own sins by identifying with Husayn's suffering. The Karbala reenactment also honors Shi'is' role as oppressed minorities fighting to restore God's justice.

Pilgrimages to the tombs and shrines of imams also serve as an important aspect of Shi'i worship. Believers journey to holy sites in order to receive blessings and intercessions. Karbala, Najaf, and Qom house some of the holiest tomb-shrines in Shi'ism. Hundreds of thousands of pilgrims visit these and other Shi'i shrines each year.

Shi'i Political Efforts

Historically, Sunni governments have dominated the Islamic world. Shi'i Islam has, nonetheless, exerted a significant political influence. In certain regions, Shi'ism has become a major force. Even when Shi'is serve as a minority, their doctrines affect the region they inhabit. In the 1900s, Shi'ism emerged as a leading voice in Islamic political activism.

Shi'i Dynasties. During the medieval period, the three major Shi'i groups built power bases in different regions. The Ithna Asharis established groups in Iran and Iraq, and Zaydi influence increased in Iraq, Yemen, and parts of Africa. The Ismailis were strongest in Syria, Egypt, India, and parts of North Africa.

The closest in outlook to the Sunnis, the Zaydis were the first Shi'is to establish an independent state. They ruled an amirate* in northern Iran from 864 to 1126. The Ismailis created the first Shi'i caliphate in the 900s, eliminating Abbasid power in Egypt. They established the Fatimid dynasty, named after Muhammad's daughter. This vast empire eventually controlled Egypt, southern Syria, and parts of North Africa. Byzantine* and Seljuk armies, however, blocked Fatimid campaigns to expand further into the Middle East.

Deep Roots

Iran has served as a Shi'i stronghold for five centuries. The last attempt to return the area to Sunni Islam occurred in the 1700s. After the fall of the Safavids in 1736, Nadir Shah Afshar gained control of Persia and established the Afsharid empire. Raised as a Shi'i, Nadir Shah professed allegiance to Sunnism in order to forge an alliance with the Sunni Ottomans. He hoped that this move would enable him to invade India without encountering Ottoman resistance. Nadir Shah banned certain Shi'i practices, such as the ritual cursing of the first three caliphs. He also persuaded the Shi'i *ulama* to give up anti-Sunni activities if the Sunni *ulama* agreed to recognize aspects of Shi'i law. However, Nadir Shah underestimated the deep roots of Shi'ism in the region. In 1747 Shi'i officers in his own army assassinated him, and his sons took control over the empire. The Afsharid empire disintegrated completely in 1796.

* **amirate** office or realm of authority of an amir

* **Byzantine** refers to the Eastern Christian Empire that was based in Constantinople

By the 1000s, internal division had weakened the dynasty. Headed by the great warrior Saladin, Sunni forces ended Fatimid rule in 1171.

Shi'is possessed little political power in the Islamic world from the 1000s until 1501, when the Safavids took control of Iran. They established Shi'ism as the official faith of their new empire, favoring the Ithna Ashari doctrine. A prominent clerical class flourished. Although Afghan invaders toppled the dynasty in 1722, Shi'ism remained firmly rooted in the region.

Less than a century after the Safavids fell, the Qajar dynasty reestablished Shi'i political rule in Iran. This dynasty's reign lasted from 1796 to 1925. The Shi'i *ulama* increased their authority during this period. In the 1800s, Russian and British encroachments weakened the dynasty's hold on the region. In 1925 military strongman Reza Shah Pahlavi ended the Qajar reign.

Modern Political Thought. In the 1900s, many Shi'is grew resentful of European colonialism and the secularization* of the Muslim world. Faced with increasing Western influence, Iranians disagreed as to how to ensure their country's progress. Although frustrated by European imperialism*, many embraced modern reforms as a means of strengthening their nation. Others favored a return to the traditional principles of Shi'ism. Religious leaders in Iran searched for a way to preserve their elevated position in Muslim society.

The Constitutional Revolution in Iran (1905–1911) revealed the growing tension between modernists and Islamic traditionalists. The proponents of secularism sought a new constitutional government based on Western models. This movement divided the religious scholars, who remained uncertain as to how the constitution would affect the religious life of the nation. Some *ulama* supported the drive, believing that it would promote national progress. Others warned that a constitutional government would override the authority of Shi'i law. Eventually, the *ulama* sided with the secular revolutionaries. By supporting the Constitutional Revolution, Shi'i clerics ensured they would occupy a prominent place in the new order. Iran adopted a new constitution. Russia and Britain, however, continued to dominate Iranian politics.

In the 1920s, Shi'i religious leaders supported a popular uprising against British dominance. Reza Shah Pahlavi's rise to power further disturbed the Shi'i clergy, as the new leader pursued a secular agenda. The state punished several outspoken Shi'i critics. Religious leaders, however, continued to speak out against the Pahlavi regime. They gained greater influence in the 1960s, when the death of Ayatollah Burujirdi, the leading teacher of the era, opened the door for increased activism. Burujirdi had had little interest in politics, and his death enabled the *ulama* to pursue a more ambitious agenda. They established Qur'anic schools and discussion groups to teach modern Shi'i political thought. Clerics and intellectuals backed the movement and spread Shi'i teachings.

Shi'i religious leaders preached opposition to the secular Pahlavi regime, now headed by Muhammad Reza Shah. The leading cleric Ayatollah Ruhollah al-Musavi Khomeini led an uprising in Qom in June 1963. Although the government crushed the revolt and deported Khomeini, the movement continued. The highly influential Iranian thinker Ali Shariati promoted an activist, radical, classless society that would oppose tyranny. He rejected the authority of the *ulama*, stating that every Muslim should think independently

* **secularize** to separate religion from other aspects of human life and society

* **imperialism** extension of power and influence over another country or region

and take charge of his destiny. Shariati identified Western imperialism, social injustice, and political repression as the great challenges of the day.

Shariati's teachings attracted many supporters in the 1970s. Meanwhile, Khomeini continued to promote opposition to the Pahlavi regime. He declared that the world had sunk into corruption during the absence of the twelfth imam. Unjust leaders, such as the shah, aggravated the situation. Khomeini preached that Shi'i jurists should seize power in Muslim states. Their knowledge of sacred law qualified them to oversee the community's daily affairs. During the Iranian Revolution of 1979, Khomeini and the Shi'i clerics came to power. Iran's new constitution embodied modern Shi'i political thought, and Khomeini established himself as the supreme religious authority of Iran.

Shi'i influence continues to grow and take hold in countries, such as Lebanon, where Shi'ism has become a strong political force. Shi'is account for about 15 percent of all Muslims, and 60 to 80 million Shi'is live in countries throughout the world. They make up a majority in Iran, Iraq, and possibly Yemen. Sizeable Shi'i populations also exist in Lebanon, Syria, India, Pakistan, and East Africa. (*See also* **Ali ibn Abi Talib; Druze; Fatimah; Husayn ibn Ali; Imam; Iran; Ismaili; Ithna Ashari; Khomeini, Ruhollah al-Musavi; Messianic Traditions; Safavid Dynasty; Zaydi.**)

Shrine

A shrine is a special building erected at a site considered to be holy. In the Muslim world shrines are often tombs of descendants of Muhammad or Muslim saints. Some are associated with natural phenomena. Many Muslims perform a series of rituals at shrines, hoping to receive a divine blessing. Shrines are particularly important to Sufi* and Shi'i* Muslims.

Shrines exist throughout the Islamic world. In North Africa, the shrines of marabouts (saints) dot the landscape. In addition to modest local shrines in rural areas, this region also has large elaborate structures devoted to key religious figures. Annual festivals are held at major shrines, attracting thousands of pilgrims. These sites have full-time caretakers, often descendants of the figure being honored there.

Shi'i Muslims have constructed shrine complexes associated with principal imams* and important religious centers. Many of these shrines, such as those in Qom (Iran) and Karbala (Iraq), are associated with religious schools. Administrators accept donations that help to support the shrines and various humanitarian causes. They also manage the finances for the maintenance of these complexes.

The most sacred shrine complex in the Muslim world is the Kaaba* and Great Mosque in Mecca (Saudi Arabia). The Dome of the Rock in Jerusalem is a major monument from the early Islamic era. Caliph* Abd al-Malik ibn Marwan built the octagonal structure as a shrine in the late 600s. According to tradition, it is the place from which the Prophet Muhammad ascended to heaven.

For many Muslims, shrines define sacred space. People involved in a conflict may seek sanctuary at a shrine. Oaths sworn at the sacred site are

* **Sufi** refers to Sufism, which seeks to develop spirituality through discipline of the mind and body

* **Shi'i** refers to Muslims who believe that Muhammad chose Ali ibn Abi Talib and his descendants as the spiritual-political leaders of the Muslim community

* **imam** spiritual-political leader in Shi'i Islam, one who is regarded as directly descended from Muhammad; also, one who leads prayers

* **Kaaba** literally "House of God"; Islamic shrine in Mecca

* **caliph** religious and political leader of an Islamic state

Shrines are an important part of Islamic tradition, especially among Shi'i and Sufi Muslims. Believers perform rituals in the hope of receiving a divine blessing. In Najaf, Iraq, Shi'i Muslims pray at the shrine of Ali ibn Abi Talib, cousin and son-in-law of Muhammad.

* **mosque** Muslim place of worship

especially binding. Some shrines are believed to possess healing powers. Visits to the shrine of Bu Ya Umar, located near Marrakesh in Morocco, are said to cure people of mental illness.

Because of their marginal status at mosques*, women pray at shrines more often than men do. They may visit a shrine after an important event in their lives, such as marriage or childbirth.

Many modern Islamic reformers criticize visits to shrines as mere superstition and a deviation from true Islam. Although some Muslims have sought to ban such visits, the practice remains popular. On certain holy days during the year, an important shrine may receive between 10,000 and 50,000 visitors. By contrast, the Wahhabis, an influential Muslim group in Saudi Arabia, reject the veneration of saints commonly practiced by Shi'is and Sufis. They have banned visits to shrines in that country, except in Mecca and Medina. (*See also* **Hajj; Kaaba; Karbala and Najaf; Muhammad; Qom; Saints and Sainthood; Saudi Arabia; Shi'i Islam; Sufism; Wahhabi.**)

Sin

* **Qur'an** book of the holy scriptures of Islam

* **sunnah** literally "the trodden path"; Islamic customs based on the exemplary behavior of Muhammad

* **hadith** reports of the words and deeds of Muhammad (not in the Qur'an, but accepted as guides for Muslim behavior)

Violating the laws and standards of a religion is commonly referred to as sin. People may sin through action or inaction, but as a rule, they are accountable only for the sins that they commit intentionally. The Qur'an* identifies two types of sin, major and minor. As the most serious offenses, major sins lead to the harshest punishments. The worst of these transgressions is claiming that God has equals. According to the Qur'an, this is the only unforgivable sin. Other major sins include murder and sex outside of marriage. The sunnah* and hadith* provide further details about major sins.

The Qur'an and sunnah offer many general warnings against sinful behavior but few details about minor sins. For Muslims, a certain action may be a sin in one context but acceptable in another situation, depending on a person's intention.

Root Cause. In the story of Adam and Eve, Satan takes the form of a serpent and persuades them to eat the forbidden fruit of a certain tree in the Garden of Eden. Unlike the Christian interpretation of the story, Muslims do not regard this act as the original sin, which resulted in the sinfulness of all human beings. Muslims believe that Adam and Eve repented of their sins and God forgave them. Instead, the Qur'an suggests that sinful behavior results when human beings willfully abuse the freedom that Allah has given to them. Sin, therefore, is an action, not a condition. Although people are not sinful by nature, they are vulnerable to temptation by Satan (Iblis). In weakness, men and women sometimes make choices that result in sinful behavior.

Islamic theologians* have addressed the subject of sin and its effect on the role and performance of prophets*. Sunni* scholars have concluded that as a human being, a prophet may make mistakes, but as a divine messenger, he is without error. Shi'i* Muslims teach that prophets as well as certain imams* are sinless.

Muhammad reportedly taught that when a person commits a sin, his or her heart is marked with a black spot. Committing sins repeatedly will eventually cover the heart with black marks. After the heart is completely covered, that person is no longer capable of good deeds.

End Result. Islam teaches that Muslims have a religious and moral duty to avoid sin. Believers should obey God's commands simply because they are based on his perfect knowledge and wisdom. Moreover, people are equipped with the ability to reason, which enables them to recognize that God's commands are just.

Muslims believe that Allah sees and knows everything. At the end of time, all human beings will appear before God to account for their actions on earth. God will weigh both their sins and good deeds and determine whether each person will be rewarded in paradise or punished in hell. The Qur'an warns that those who reject the faith will face severe consequences: "If they had everything on earth, and twice repeated, to give as ransom for the penalty of the Day of Judgment, it would never be accepted of them. . . . Their penalty will be one that endures."

The Qur'an refers to sin as it relates to the individual and to groups of people and nations. Islam teaches that a person is responsible for his or her own sin. But the Qur'an also describes the way that God punished certain groups for their immorality. In the days of Noah, Allah sent a flood to eliminate the wicked from the earth. God destroyed the people of Lot in an earthquake. The Qur'an implies that while individual sinners face their worst punishment in the afterlife, nations receive their sentences in this world.

Finding Mercy. Islam teaches that God is "quick in retribution," but he is also merciful. Muslims can eliminate their sin through repentance. If a person commits a sin, feels remorse, and makes atonement for the evil deed, God forgives the transgression. This was the pattern first set by Adam and

* **theologian** person who studies the nature, qualities, and will of God

* **prophet** one who announces divinely inspired revelations

* **Sunni** refers to the largest branch of the Muslim community; the name derives from sunnah, the exemplary behavior of the Prophet Muhammad

* **Shi'i** refers to Muslims who believe that Muhammad chose Ali ibn Abi Talib and his descendants as the spiritual-political leaders of the Muslim community

* **imam** spiritual-political leader in Shi'i Islam, one who is regarded as directly descended from Muhammad; also, one who leads prayers

The Sin of Disbelief

A key concept in Islamic tradition is *kufr* (disbelief), the direct opposite of *iman* (faith). The Qur'an mentions *kufr* hundreds of times, highlighting its offensiveness to God. *Kufr* was a serious issue to the early Islamic community. Many Arabs rejected the divine origins of Muhammad's revelations and accused him of lying. The worst form of *kufr* is *shirk*, disbelieving the uniqueness of God. The Qur'an condemns the Christian concept of the Holy Trinity (the father, the son, and the Holy Spirit) as a form of *shirk*. But it also states that all people, including Christians, who believe in God and do good works shall be saved. Modern Islamic reformers have placed great importance on the removal of *kufr* from Islamic society.

Eve. The forgiveness of sins does not require an intermediary, such as a cleric. If an individual has violated another person's rights, however, he or she must obtain forgiveness from the wronged party before God will pardon the sin.

The hadith include other teachings about removing sin. One hadith maintains that performing the hajj* restores a person to a sinless state. Another hadith states that an angel waits several hours before recording a person's sin. If the person repents during this interval, the angel does not record the sin and God will not count it on the Day of Judgment. Other hadith include Muhammad's statements that good actions and certain prayers remove sins.

Sufis* believe that Muslims can win the battle over sin by overcoming their inclination to commit evil deeds. Through repentance, they purify themselves, eventually reaching a state where the mere thought of sin disappears.

Modern Applications. Since the early days of Islam, different Muslim sects* have debated the status of political and religious leaders who are guilty of sin. One group, the Khariji, believed that a caliph* could remain in power only if he was sinless. If he erred, he lost the protection of the law and had to be overthrown or killed. Sunni Muslims rejected this belief, arguing that the importance of preserving social order outweighed the significance of the character of the ruler and that only God could judge who was worthy of punishment. Some extremist groups still follow Khariji doctrine*, calling for the overthrow of un-Islamic Muslim governments. These include Islamic Jihad, which was responsible for the assassination of Egypt's president Anwar el-Sadat. In recent decades, concerns about political freedom and social justice have led some Islamic thinkers to identify oppression as a great sin that Muslims must resist and defeat. (*See also* **Khariji; Prophets; Repentance; Satan.**)

* **hajj** pilgrimage to Mecca that Muslims are required to make once in their lifetime

* **Sufi** follower of Sufism, which seeks to develop spirituality through discipline of the mind and body

* **sect** religious group adhering to distinctive beliefs

* **caliph** religious and political leader of an Islamic state

* **doctrine** principle, theory, or belief that is taught or presented for acceptance

Slavery

The practice of slavery was widespread in the ancient world. During Muhammad's lifetime, the institution thrived in Asia, Africa, the Middle East, the Mediterranean, and some parts of Europe. Islam accepted the existence of slavery, as did Judaism and Christianity. Although most Muslim states abolished slavery by the mid-1900s, the practice still continues in pockets of the Islamic world.

Bondage According to Islamic Law. The Qur'an* recognizes the unequal relationship between master and slave, just as it does that between husband and wife. It also, however, enjoins Muslims to treat their slaves kindly, and encourages them to free their slaves as a noble deed. The Qur'an establishes guidelines to regulate and improve the living conditions of slaves.

According to the traditional Islamic law, only non-Muslims captured or imported from foreign lands could serve as slaves. The children of these slaves could also remain in slavery, although many Muslims freed them. Muslims could not enslave other Muslims or *dhimmi*—protected minorities including Jews, Christians, and others who abided by scripture—living un-

* **Qur'an** book of the holy scriptures of Islam

Abbasid dynasty rulers introduced the practice of using slaves soldiers (Mamluks) in their armies. Other Islamic states followed suit. Such soldiers could rise through the ranks to become generals, governors, and even sultans. This French engraving of 1825 shows a slave soldier of the Ottoman Empire.

der Islamic rule. The *shari'ah** further banned the enslavement of orphans and foundlings living in Muslim lands.

Islamic law recognized slaves as the legal property of their owners. A Muslim owned a slave's labor and could buy and sell slaves at will. A child born to a free man and a slave woman, however, was legally recognized as free, and a concubine* who had her master's child would gain her freedom after his death. The *shari'ah* prohibited Muslims from separating a slave mother and her child.

Islamic law included other provisions recognizing slaves as human beings. An owner could not kill or maim those that he or she held in bondage. Slaves could marry and lead prayers. If a slave committed a crime, he or she often received a reduced sentence in court because the law did not regard slaves as accountable for their actions. In some cases, masters even received punishment for a slave's wrongdoing.

* *shari'ah* Islamic law as established in the Qur'an and sunnah, the exemplary behavior of the Prophet Muhammad

* **concubine** woman who lives with a man without benefit of marriage and whose legal status is below that of a wife

Slavery

* **sultanate** government of a sultan, the political and military ruler of a Muslim dynasty or state

Slavery in Practice. Slaves in Islamic lands came from many countries. During the Abbasid dynasty (750–1258), European traders brought large numbers of Slavic captives to the Islamic world. Around the 1200s, Italian merchants supplied Muslim dynasties with slaves from Turkey, Central Asia, and Africa. Several thousand slaves reached the Ottoman Empire every year from Africa, the Caucasus, and eastern Europe. Around the 1800s, Muslim rulers began to lose control of certain trade routes and imported most of their slaves from Africa.

Abbasid leaders introduced *mamluks* (slave soldiers) into their armies. Several Muslim rulers later copied this practice, including the Delhi sultanate* in India and the Ghaznavids in Central Asia. Many slave soldiers rose through the ranks of the army to become generals, governors, and even sultans. During the Mamluk sultanate in Egypt, slave rulers governed for nearly three centuries.

The Ottomans built a formidable military force, staffed partly with slaves. They took Christian youths from villages in the Balkans, converted them to Islam, and placed them in the sultan's service. Some entered the Janissaries (elite corps), and the most promising entered palace society. If slave soldiers disobeyed their masters, they could be executed without trial. The soldiers, however, also enjoyed many privileges. They received a palace education and did not have to pay taxes. By 1500 slaves had gained enough strength to influence palace affairs and become a part of the ruling institutions.

While some slaves in the Islamic world rose to positions of power, others toiled in harsh conditions. Slaves working in agriculture or construction often faced lives of hardship, although some received payment for their work. Unbearable conditions sometimes sparked an uprising. In the 800s, a group of African slaves toiling in an Iraqi marshland rose up in a violent revolt, although authorities quickly suppressed them.

Most slaves in the Islamic world, however, worked in cities. Compared to their rural counterparts, they led relatively comfortable lives. They performed such tasks as cleaning, cooking, caring for children, and even managing financial affairs or directing armed forces. Slaves in coastal areas sometimes served as oarsmen and pearl divers.

Muslims preferred to take women and children into bondage, as they seemed more docile, and women could produce more slaves. They gave their slaves new names, provided them with an Islamic education, and taught them the ways of the household. Some even trained their slaves to be musicians and scholars. Many Muslims freed their slaves once they reached adulthood. Viewing slavery as a way of converting outsiders to Islam, they worked eagerly to bring new Muslims into the community.

Abolition of Slavery. In the 1800s, some Muslim reformers sought to eliminate slavery. They viewed the institution as outdated and morally wrong. Laws and court decisions in the mid-1800s granted greater legal equality to slaves. The British further pressured the Muslim states to end slavery, having previously abolished the practice in Europe. Britain signed a series of treaties with the Ottoman Empire to reduce the slave trade, and in 1887, the Ottomans outlawed slavery altogether.

The institution, however, persisted in some parts of the Ottoman Empire well into the 1900s. Muslims in Arabia, India, and Africa also continued to own slaves. Not until after 1950 did most of the Muslim states finally outlaw the practice. Slavery has not completely vanished from the Islamic world, however. Muslims fighting civil wars in Sudan and Somalia revived the practice in the 1980s. Combatants in these conflicts continue to enslave prisoners taken from the other side. (*See also* **Christianity and Islam; Judaism and Islam; Mamluk State; Minorities; Ottoman Empire; Somalia; Sudan.**)

Socialism and Islam

Socialism* has had a profound influence on the Islamic world. Several leading Muslim reformers combined socialist and religious ideas, although they sometimes disagreed on specific points. The combination of socialist and Islamic doctrines helped shape the development of several Muslim countries.

Principles of Socialism. Socialism calls for the public ownership and control of wealth distribution and property. Ideas relating to this concept originated in ancient Greece, in such texts as Plato's *Republic.* Modern socialism emerged in Europe in the 1700s, when intellectuals criticized the harsh social and economic conditions created by industrialization. They maintained that the new capitalist* economies brought suffering and injustice to the majority of workers while providing wealth to an elite. Socialists sought to improve conditions for workers and bring about a more equal distribution of wealth.

Scholars have applied the term *socialism* to an array of movements. No single set of beliefs, however, unites socialist thinkers. Some hold that a strong central government should control the economy. Others maintain that public boards or individual planners should guide economic affairs. Socialists further disagree on income distribution, whether to allow private ownership, and how to bring about social equality.

Rise of Socialism in the Islamic World. During the 1800s, Muslim students began to travel to Europe for a university education. Some developed an interest in socialist ideas and introduced them to the Islamic world. Most of these scholars belonged to the newly created middle class. They advocated equality among Muslims and the self-sufficiency of Muslim societies. They believed in modernization, nationalism*, and unity against colonial domination.

In the late 1800s, Jamal al-Din al-Afghani emerged as a leading Muslim reformer. He viewed socialism as a model for the Muslim community, and looked to history for examples of successful socialist societies. Al-Afghani pointed to the Bedouins* as an example of a pre-Islamic socialist group. He believed that early Muslim leaders saw the value in Bedouin ways and encouraged Bedouin traditions when they came to power in the 600s. For example, they placed high value on the welfare of all the members in the community, an important issue in socialism.

In 1913 the Egyptian scholar Salamah Musa published an essay that introduced the concept of socialism to a generation of Arab activists. Reform-

* **socialism** economic system in which the government owns and operates the means of production and the distribution of goods

* **capitalism** economic system in which businesses are privately owned and operated and where competition exists in a free-market environment

* **nationalism** feelings of loyalty and devotion to one's country and a commitment to its independence

* **Bedouin** nomad of the desert, especially in North Africa, Syria, and Arabia

* **ideology** system of ideas or beliefs

* **secular** separate from religion in human life and society; connected to everyday life

* **Qur'an** book of the holy scriptures of Islam

* **sunnah** literally "the trodden path"; Islamic customs based on the exemplary behavior of Muhammad

Reversal of Fortune

Strong opposition has occasionally forced the retreat of Islamic socialism. In Tunisia in the 1950s, the ruling Neo-Destour Party promoted socialist ideas. It implemented various state projects and farm cooperatives. Popular resistance, however, forced the government to disband the cooperatives, and the party soon lost much of its support. In post-World War II Indonesia, the Masjumi was formed as a modern Islamic socialist party. It won 20 percent of the vote in the 1955 national elections but soon drew the anger of the government for its support of rebel factions. In 1960 President Sukarno banned the party, and socialism declined as a significant force in Indonesia.

ers began to promote the ideology* as a tool for modernization. Salamah Musa helped to organize the Egyptian Socialist Party in 1920. Though short-lived, the party contributed to the rise of socialist thinking among Egyptian intellectuals.

Socialism in Egypt remained a mostly secular* movement until the 1930s. At that time, scholars began to look to religion for ideas about social reform. Founded in 1928, the Muslim Brotherhood envisioned a society based on the Qur'an* and sunnah*. Members of the brotherhood did not fully embrace socialism but promoted socialist ideals, such as community welfare and economic justice. Because of their efforts, the concept of religion became increasingly important to Islamic socialists.

By mid-century, Shaykh Khalid Muhammad Khalid emerged as Egypt's leading socialist. In his book *From Here We Start*, he argued that Islam endorsed socialism. Khalid wanted Egypt to throw off economic backwardness and British domination. He believed that the country should provide for the welfare of its citizens and viewed socialism as a necessary alternative to capitalism. Only when Egypt improved the lives of its people could the country develop economically and spiritually. Khalid believed the Qur'an mandated compassion and economic justice. He criticized the religious establishment in Egypt for endorsing what he viewed as an unequal distribution of wealth.

A contemporary of Khalid, Mustafa al-Siba'i promoted socialism in Syria. In *The Socialism of Islam*, al-Siba'i argued that a society must pursue socialism in order to prosper and mature. Only a socialist community could eliminate hunger, disease, and poverty. Al-Siba'i described Islamic socialism as promoting five natural rights: a safe and healthy life, knowledge, freedom, dignity, and ownership of property. The state would govern essential public services and redistribute property when necessary. All goods ultimately belonged to God, and humans needed to share them in a just fashion. Al-Siba'i further maintained that social groups should cooperate with one another and avoid the class warfare inherent in European socialism. In this way, he contributed to the development of a uniquely Islamic ideology. Al-Saiba'i founded the Muslim Brotherhood in Syria to promote his ideas.

Socialist Regimes. The Egyptian officer Gamal Abdel Nasser established the first Muslim socialist regime. Influenced by the ideas of Khalid and al-Siba'i, he used socialism to break the power of foreign business in Egypt and to promote economic development and equality. In 1962 he passed a law establishing the Arab Socialist Union as the only political party in Egypt. The state took control of industry, finance, parts of the economy, and certain properties formerly dominated by the British. In theory, Nasser's government merged nationalism, socialism, and Islam. In practice, Nasser ignored religion in favor of modernization. Many activists, such as Sayyid Qutb, criticized the government's secular policies. Qutb considered socialism a form of pre-Islamic ignorance. He held that Islam alone could save society.

Founded in Syria in 1943, the Ba'th Party also adopted principles of Islamic socialism. The party gained power in both Syria and Iraq in the 1960s. Ba'thist leaders promoted Arab unity, maintaining that a nation's wealth belongs to its people. They called for social reform and welfare legislation. The party nationalized industry, finance, economy, and trade. It also promoted greater educational and health care opportunities, as well as providing food and basic items at subsidized prices to the needy. Neither the Syrian leader (Hafez al-Assad) nor the Iraqi leader (Saddam Hussein) emphasized the human rights aspect of socialism, however. Both leaders concentrated primarily on maintaining power.

In 1969 Mu'ammar al-Qaddafi established a socialist regime in Libya. He sought to create a new society based on the principles of socialism and Islam. Qaddafi condemned Western governments as corrupt and tried to unite Arab societies. When his plan failed, he funded Islamic and revolutionary groups in other countries. Qaddafi nationalized the economy, redistributed wealth, and worked to improve public morality by prohibiting gambling and alcohol and closing nightclubs. He dramatically improved the quality of life in Libya, although he made many foreign enemies with his financial contributions to militant groups.

Socialism made inroads in several other Muslims countries in the latter half of the 1900s. In Algeria and Tunisia, for example, Islamic socialists joined secular nationalists in the struggle to throw off French rule. In Iran, Islamic socialism helped fuel the overthrow of Muhammad Reza Shah's government in 1979. The combination of Islamic and socialist principles continues to influence Muslim political thought. (*See also* **Afghani, Jamal al-Din al-; Communism and Islam; Egypt; Iraq; Qaddafi, Mu'ammar al-; Qutb, Sayyid; Syria.**)

Sokoto Caliphate

The Sokoto caliphate was an Islamic state in the region that is now northern Nigeria. Founded in the early 1800s by a Muslim scholar and reformer named Usuman Dan Fodio, the caliphate* included many small West African states that had never before united under one government. The caliphate lasted in one form or another until 1960, and its influence continues in Nigeria today.

Establishment of the Caliphate. The Hausa tribe of northern Nigeria adopted Islam in the 1500s. It gained an even stronger Muslim identity when members of the Fulani tribe migrated into the Hausa territory during the next two centuries. Fulani scholars and teachers spread Muslim doctrines to the rural population, which maintained many pre-Islamic practices. They attracted a large number of converts. The Fulani teacher Usuman Dan Fodio became the most prominent Muslim reformer.

Beginning in the 1770s, Usuman served as the religious and political leader of a growing Muslim community in a local Hausa state called Gobir. Much of his support came from Hausa peasants. Poor and oppressed, the peasants sought to oust the corrupt ruling class. They envisioned Usuman as the Mahdi, a legendary Muslim savior whom they expected to lead them to a better life. Usuman rejected identification with the holy figure, but he otherwise encouraged hopes of revolution.

Around 1800 the Hausa ruler of Gobir grew wary of Usuman's growing popularity and threatened Usuman's life. Usuman gathered his followers and fled. He declared a jihad* against the ruler of Gobir and the Hausa rulers who supported him. He urged the formation of a new Muslim community

* **caliphate** office and government of the caliph, the religious and political leader of an Islamic state

* **jihad** literally "striving"; war in defense of Islam

95

with its own leadership and principles. Usuman spent the next five years waging war against Hausa rulers. By 1809 he had established a new state with its capital at Sokoto. The largest political unit that had existed in West Africa for more than two centuries, the Sokoto caliphate consisted of a loose association of amirates*. Usuman's followers granted him the title of caliph* and *sarkin musulmi*, "commander of the faithful".

Usuman and His Successors. Usuman favored a regime with a simple structure that would discourage corruption. He limited the power of the central government and promoted Islamic scholars for leadership positions. Although he had established the caliphate, Usuman felt that his goals of reforming Islam had not succeeded. He decided to leave politics, dividing the caliphate into two parts. He appointed his son, Muhammad Bello, to rule one section, and his brother, Abdullahi Dan Fodio, to govern the other. Usuman kept the title of caliph but retired from active involvement in government. He spent most of his time teaching and writing. Usuman's works, dealing with community problems and the Islamic sciences, continue to enjoy a wide circulation.

Usuman died in 1817, succeeded by his son as caliph. During Muhammad's 20-year rule, he defended the caliphate from several attempts by Hausa groups to overthrow him. The British, however, became increasingly interested in Nigeria. In the mid-1800s, the caliphate signed a treaty granting the British trading privileges in Nigeria. The caliphate, however, opposed British efforts to colonize their state. Nonetheless, by 1903, British troops occupied the major cities of the Sokoto caliphate. They kept many government officials in place to run the country. The sultan of Sokoto retained a position of importance as chief ruler of northern Nigeria.

Along with many other Muslim states, Nigeria gained its independence from the British in the mid-1900s. The original amirates of the Sokoto caliphate separated into various states within the new Federation of Nigeria. The sultan of Sokoto continued to serve as the religious leader of the Nigerian Muslim community, but he no longer wielded direct political power. Many of Usuman Dan Fodio's descendants, however, assumed leadership positions in the new nation. (*See also* **Caliphate; Islamic State; Nigeria; West Africa.**)

Somalia

Virtually the entire population of this East African country, estimated between eight and ten million people, follows the Sunni* branch of Islam. Sufi* orders have greatly influenced Somalia's Islamic practices, and as in other cultures, Somalis have adopted some customs of traditional religions. Most Somalis belong to one of five clan-families. Clan-based rivalries have made it difficult for Somalis to unite as a single nation.

Strategic Location. With borders on the Gulf of Aden and the Indian Ocean, Somalia's geography has facilitated trade for many centuries. Ancient Egyptian writings describe the Land of Punt, a source of "aromatics and in-

---

* **amirate** office or realm of authority of an amir

* **caliph** religious and political leader of an Islamic state

* **Sunni** refers to the largest branch of the Muslim community; the name derives from sunnah, the exemplary behavior of the Prophet Muhammad

* **Sufi** refers to Sufism, which seeks to develop spirituality through discipline of the mind and body

cense." Between the 600s and 900s, immigrant Muslim Arabs and Persians established trading posts along the Somali coast. Several thriving Somali city-states, including Berbera, Mogadishu, and Merca, emerged. The rulers of the city-states adopted Islamic forms of administration and adapted them to the needs of this semisettled rural society. Islamic commercial laws, systems of weights and measures, and navigational tools and techniques boosted trade in the region.

European involvement in the area began in the 1500s with Portugal's interest in developing commerce in the Indian Ocean. European activity turned into imperialism* in the 1800s when the British, French, and Italians colonized various parts of Somali territory, as did the Ethiopians. In 1891 Somalia became a protectorate* administered by Great Britain and Italy. These developments led to the emergence of a radical* Islamic revivalist* movement, led by Muhammad Abd Allah Hasan. He tried to unite feuding Somali clans against foreign imperialism. Although his anticolonial message initially attracted many followers, he later lost support when he insisted that Somalis abandon a popular Sufi order and convert to his own, much stricter Sufi brotherhood. The British defeated Muhammad Abd Allah Hasan in 1920.

During World War II (1939–1945), the British conquered the Somali territories that had been under Italian control. In 1949 the United Nations granted eventual independence to Italian Somaliland and permitted Italy to administer the region for a ten-year period. The British protectorate gained its independence on June 26, 1960, and soon afterward merged with the Italian trust territory to form the Somali Republic. Between 1960 and 1969, the newly independent country was run by a national government with a parliament* and multiple political parties, which generally formed along clan lines.

Dictatorship. In 1969 General Mohamed Siyad Barre led a successful military coup* and assumed control of the government. He established a dictatorship and proclaimed scientific socialism* as the official belief system. Using Soviet methods of repression, Siyad Barre waged a war against Islam.

* **imperialism** extension of power and influence over another country or region

* **protectorate** country under the protection and control of a stronger nation

* **radical** favoring extreme change or reform, especially in existing political and social institutions

* **revivalist** calling for the return to traditional values or beliefs

* **parliament** representative national body having supreme legislative power within the state

* **coup** sudden, and often violent, overthrow of a ruler or government

* **socialism** economic system in which the government owns and operates the means of production and the distribution of goods

Turning the Tables

During the 1800s and 1900s, Islam in Somalia came under the attack of various forces, including European domination and oppressive national leaders. Several hundred years earlier, by contrast, Islam was on the offensive in East Africa. By the 1300s, the spread of Islam in what is today southern and eastern Ethiopia had begun to threaten the Christian kingdom's trade routes. During the 1500s, Ethiopian rulers invaded the Muslim state of Adal to secure a passage to the coast. In 1525 a famous Muslim religious leader named Ahmad Gran recruited Somali warriors into his army and drove the Ethiopians back. Within the next several years, Gran launched an aggressive campaign to spread Islam into Ethiopia. He was successful until the Christian kingdom received assistance from a Portuguese force. Gran was killed in battle in 1543.

* **shari'ah** Islamic law as established in the Qur'an and sunnah, the exemplary behavior of the Prophet Muhammad

* **militia** group of citizens organized for military service

In 1975 he had ten Muslim religious leaders executed for peacefully protesting new laws that violated *shari'ah**. Instead of repressing Islam, however, the regime's hostility sparked a religious revival. Many Somalis committed themselves to regular prayers and fasting and wore religious dress.

Between 1989 and 1990, Siyad Barre ordered his troops to kill hundreds of Muslim religious leaders and their followers. In response, many Somalis demanded his resignation. From bases in Ethiopia, clan-based opposition groups successfully challenged the government's forces. The regime was ousted in January 1991.

Instability and Uncertainty. Siyad Barre's fall from power resulted in chaos, civil war, and a famine that threatened more than one million people with starvation. Lacking a central government, various clan-based militias* ruled the south. This situation led the United Nations, under American leadership, to intervene in late 1992. Although the multinational operation alleviated the effects of the famine, attempts to restore order in southern Somalia failed.

Meanwhile, in May 1991, a group of clans in northwestern Somalia had declared the establishment of an independent country, called the Somaliland Republic. Although other governments do not recognize its existence, the republic remains a stable part of Somalia. In 1998 several regions in the northeast established a self-governing state called Puntland.

In August 2000, a group of Somali clans met in Djibouti and formed a transitional, parliamentary national government. Its leaders were given three years to create a new constitution and to hold elections, with the goal of creating a permanent national Somali government. By early 2003, however, the transitional government had not been able to reunite the Somaliland Republic and Puntland with the rest of Somalia. Moreover, the transitional authorities could not restrain the inter-clan fighting for control of Mogadishu and other southern regions. Although Islam continues to play a critical role in Somali culture, its role in the country's future political development remains uncertain. (*See also* **East Africa.**)

South Asia

* **dynasty** succession of rulers from the same family or group

* **sultanate** government of a sultan, the political and military ruler of a Muslim dynasty or state

The Muslims of South Asia—which includes the countries of India, Pakistan, Bangladesh, Sri Lanka, and Afghanistan—number almost 300 million. Aside from their shared religious identity, they differ significantly in social and economic circumstances, language, and in many other ways. The history of Islam in South Asia also varies greatly.

Arrival on the Subcontinent. Arab forces invaded the Indian subcontinent during the early 700s and established Muslim rule in the northwestern region of Sind. But Muslim conquest did not begin in earnest until the 1000s, when Turkish armies from Afghanistan migrated southward. By about 1200, the Turkish forces had conquered North India. In 1206 Qutb al-Din Aybeg, a general serving the Ghurid dynasty*, captured Delhi and founded the first of a series of dynasties known as the Delhi sultanates*.

The Delhi sultans acknowledged the caliph* in Baghdad as the leader of the *ummah* (Muslim community).

    In the early 1500s, a prince named Babur (about 1483–1530), who claimed descent from two great conquerors, Genghis Khan and Tamerlane, was forced to leave his Central Asian kingdom. Babur seized control of the region of northwestern India known as the Punjab and established the Mughal dynasty. By 1530 he ruled much of northern India. Over the next two centuries, the Mughal Empire dominated most of the Indian subcontinent. During the empire's peak, its power and prestige were important symbols of strength and culture throughout the Muslim world. Ultimately, the Mughal rulers were unable to prevent attacks by Afghan and Persian invaders and opposition from oppressed religious groups. Moreover, the power of the Mughal emperors weakened as they allowed Great Britain to establish trading centers in the area.

    During these years, Islam rapidly spread from the ruling class to the general population, which was largely Hindu*. The number of Muslims increased from less than half a million in 1200 to 15 million in 1600 and more than 60 million by 1900. Muslims became the majority in parts of northwestern and northeastern India and a significant minority in other parts of the subcontinent. The expansion of Islam was primarily a result of the missionary* work of Sufi* brotherhoods. They used good will, acceptance, and cooperation to convert the Indian people to Islam.

The Colonial Period. By the early 1800s, the British had established control over Delhi, the seat of the Mughal Empire. The Mughal Empire continued as a British protectorate*. Following an uprising in 1857, Great Britain abolished the Mughal dynasty and established formal political rule over India.

    Colonial rule pitted Muslims against Hindus in a new relationship as minority versus majority. Hindus had always been a majority in the country, but they had never taken advantage of their greater numbers to gain privileges over the Muslim minority. The British regarded Islam and Hinduism as two distinct cultures, and they reinforced the concept of an identity based on religion. Furthermore, because they distrusted the former rulers, they tended to favor Hindus while marginalizing Muslims. The two religious communities began to compete for opportunities and for influence in the growing nationalist* movement. The British cited the need to maintain peaceful relations between the groups as justification for colonial rule.

    Indian Muslims faced pressure from Britain's Christian missionaries, who condemned basic Islamic beliefs. The Muslim community responded to these attacks in various ways. Some groups suggested that Muslims should accommodate European values. Others rejected all Western influences, and still others joined Islam-based mass movements.

    Demands for independence from British rule grew during the late 1800s and early 1900s. Concerned that Hindu nationalists would deprive Muslims of their rights after India gained independence, members of the Western-educated Muslim elite established the All-India Muslim League in 1906. The league called for Muslim representation in all political institutions. The idea of a separate Muslim state in northwestern India was first proposed in 1930, and it became increasingly popular. Later, the name Pakistan was coined for the proposed state.

* **caliph** religious and political leader of an Islamic state

* **Hindu** refers to the beliefs and practices of Hinduism, an ancient religion that originated in India

* **missionary** person who works to convert nonbelievers to a particular faith

* **Sufi** refers to Sufism, which seeks to develop spirituality through discipline of the mind and body

* **protectorate** country under the protection and control of a stronger nation

* **nationalist** one who advocates loyalty and devotion to his or her country and its independence

See map in India (vol. 2).

Post-Independence Troubles. In August 1947, Great Britain partitioned India into two independent states based on religious affiliation. India would remain predominantly Hindu, and Pakistan would become a Muslim state. According to the terms of the partition plan, the ruler of Kashmir, a mountainous region located at the extreme northern frontier of the Indian subcontinent, could choose whether Kashmir would become part of Pakistan or India. Muslims, who accounted for almost 80 percent of the population, favored Pakistan. Nevertheless, the ruler of Kashmir agreed to join India, provoking a full-scale war. The region continues to be the subject of a heated dispute between India and Pakistan.

The formation of Pakistan also resulted in a terrible civil war. Partition caused approximately 10 million people to flee from regions where new state boundaries suddenly made them a religious minority. Massacres on both sides claimed the lives of at least a million people.

The smaller but still vital Muslim community that chose to remain in India faced formidable social and economic challenges. Most educated Muslims with professions had migrated to Pakistan. Most Indian Muslims were landless laborers, farmers, or shopkeepers, although a new middle class emerged during the 1970s and 1980s, especially in urban areas.

Today India's Muslims number more than 120 million, making them one of the largest Muslim communities in the world. As members of a religious minority in a secular* state, Indian Muslims have had to carry on the struggle to gain a voice in the government. They have also fought to protect their religious beliefs and practices, especially in matters regulated by Islamic law. Although their rights have improved over time, Indian Muslims continue to suffer from discrimination and prejudice. A growing revivalist* movement among Hindus, beginning in the 1970s, has intensified the already-difficult situation. Riots and other acts of violence continue to plague relations between India's Hindus and Muslims.

Growing Pains. Pakistan was formed from India as a Muslim homeland. It is the only modern country established in the name of Islam, and about 97 percent of Pakistanis are Muslims. In 1947 the young nation faced many difficult problems, but the most controversial issue was religious. Conflicting visions of the role of Islam in politics deeply divided various groups. Religious figures led a large segment of the population in calling for an Islamic constitution, the introduction of traditional Islamic law, and the restoration of traditional social and religious institutions. Those who held political power regarded Islam as a moral force and as a base on which national unity and loyalty could be built.

Over the decades, the struggle over the depth and extent of the country's commitment to religion led to many debates about Pakistan's constitution. The country has suffered through decades of chaotic civil rule, alternating with periods of harsh military regimes*. Pakistani governments have generally professed a commitment to Islam in order to maintain their legitimacy and popular support.

The Muslim nation established in 1947 consisted of West Pakistan, to the northwest of India, and East Pakistan, a smaller region to the northeast of India on the Bay of Bengal. The partition plan divided the provinces of Punjab and Bengal and separated West and East Pakistan by more than 1,000

* **secular** separate from religion in human life and society; connected to everyday life

* **revivalist** calling for the return to traditional values or beliefs

* **regime** government in power

miles of Indian territory. These political boundaries, combined with sharp ethnic* and linguistic differences, presented great obstacles to the creation of a stable regime and a unified national identity. During the 1960s, the people of East Pakistan, frustrated with the military, political, and economic superiority of West Pakistan, began demanding independence. In 1971 East Pakistan won its independence after a brutal war with West Pakistan. With the aid of Indian troops, East Pakistan became the independent nation of Bangladesh.

A Moderate Stance. With strong support from India and the presence of a large Hindu minority, the Bangladeshi government initially emphasized the country's national, rather than religious, identity. The constitution of 1972 was notably secular, and it banned political activity by religious groups. By the late 1970s, however, the government began to introduce Islamic principles into the country's political institutions. In the constitution of 1977, a reference to trust in God replaced the secular language of the previous document. Today the general population, estimated to be about 83 percent Muslim, holds strong Islamic sympathies, but the major political parties have adopted a moderate position between secularism and conservative Islam.

Sri Lanka. Muslims make up about 7 percent of the population of Sri Lanka, an island in the Indian Ocean, just south of India. Between the 700s and 1400s, Arab traders settled along the coasts of southern India and Sri Lanka. They adopted the Tamil language and some local customs, while preserving Islamic law and the basic doctrines of their faith. When the Portuguese seized control of Sri Lanka in the early 1500s, they persecuted the Muslims. They called the Muslims *moros* because they shared the faith of the Moors, the descendants of the Arab conquerors of Spain. The Portuguese were followed by Dutch and British colonial governments, which pursued commercial interests and generally did not engage in religious oppression. During the 1800s, the introduction of Sufi orders sparked an Islamic revival among Sri Lankan Muslims. Sri Lanka gained its independence in 1948. Growing Muslim consciousness generated interest in the Arab roots of the community, the study of Arabic as a way to understand the Qur'an*, and separate schools for Muslim children. The Sri Lankan government created a Muslim Religious and Cultural Affairs Department.

In the 1980s, ethnic tensions between Sri Lanka's Sinhalese majority and Tamil separatists plunged the country into a civil war that lasted for almost 20 years. Tens of thousands of people died in the conflict. The island's Muslims were caught in a difficult position. Although they are Tamil speakers, they generally support the Sinhalese-dominated government. As a result, the Tamils classified the Muslims as enemies and targeted them in a campaign of ethnic cleansing.

Afghanistan. Muslim Arab armies reached the region now known as Afghanistan around 700. Over the following centuries, many Muslim empires emerged in the area. Modern Afghanistan is the remnant of the Durrani empire, which was founded in the mid-1700s. Conflicts over succession as well as military and political pressures from Great Britain and Russia weakened Durrani rule. Eager to control Afghanistan in order to protect its holdings in India, Great Britain fought two Anglo-Afghan wars (1839–1842 and 1878–

* **ethnic** relating to groups of people who share a common racial, national, tribal, religious, linguistic, or culture background

Sacred Spot

From December to April, pilgrims of many faiths climb Adam's Peak, a 7,360-foot high mountain located in the hills of southwestern Sri Lanka. At the summit is a large hollow resembling the print of a human foot. Muslims claim that it belongs to Adam, who reportedly stood on the site for 1,000 years to atone for his sin in the Garden of Eden. According to Buddhists, who are the majority in Sri Lanka, Buddha left the print during one of his legendary visits to the island. Hindus maintain that the giant footprint belongs to the god Shiva, and Christians claim that it is the mark of Saint Thomas.

* **Qur'an** book of the holy scriptures of Islam

1880). However, the British failed to gain control of the country. After their second defeat, the British helped bring Amir Abd al-Rahman Khan, a descendant of the Durrani dynasty, to power in Afghanistan. The Iron Amir (commander), as he was known, became the first Afghan ruler to centralize political power in the name of Islam. Although he cooperated with the British in foreign affairs, his internal policy provided the foundation for the modern Afghan state. Abd al-Rahman Khan's descendants continued to rule Afghanistan. During their reigns, there was tension between the forces of modernization and conservative Islam.

In 1978, a coup* brought a communist* government to power. This regime met with strong resistance from most Afghans, and in 1979, the former Soviet Union invaded Afghanistan to support the unpopular government. After a decade of struggle against the *mujahidin**, the Soviets withdrew their forces. In April 1992, the mujahidin captured Kabul, a communist holdout, and declared Afghanistan an Islamic state. Nevertheless, the mujahidin failed to create a new Islamic political system, and competing groups seized control of sections of the country. The radical* Islamic group known as the Taliban eventually came to power. A U.S.-led military campaign led to the fall of the Taliban in late 2001 and the establishment of a transitional government. (*See also* **Afghanistan; Bangladesh; India; Kashmir; Minorities; Mughal Empire; Mujahidin; Pakistan; Taliban.**)

* **coup** sudden, and often violent, overthrow of a ruler or government

* **communist** refers to communism, a political and economic system based on the concept of shared ownership of all property

* *mujahidin* literally "warriors of God"; refers to Muslim fighters in proclaimed jihads, such as the war against the Soviet invasion of Afghanistan

* **radical** favoring extreme change or reform, especially in existing political and social institutions

Southeast Asia

Southeast Asia is a large region located east of India and south of China. It consists of two parts—one located on the Asian mainland, and the other an archipelago (island chain) that extends into the South China Sea. Mainland Southeast Asia includes the countries of Cambodia, Laos, Myanmar (formerly Burma), Thailand, and Vietnam. The Malay Peninsula projects from the mainland into the South China Sea. It includes the small state of Singapore and the country of Malaysia. Malaysia also occupies part of the island of Borneo, along with the tiny nation of Brunei and a section of Indonesia. The other islands of the archipelago constitute the nations of Indonesia and the Philippines.

Southeast Asians practice a wide variety of religions, including Buddhism*, Christianity, Hinduism*, and Islam. Buddhism is the most popular faith on the mainland, but Islam dominates the southern half of the Malay Peninsula and the archipelago. Isolated pockets of Islam also exist in Cambodia and northern Thailand. Muslims account for around 40 percent of the Southeast Asian population, or some 220 million people.

* **Buddhism** religion of eastern and central Asia based on the teaching of Gautama Buddha

* **Hinduism** ancient religion that originated in India

Spread of Islam in Southeast Asia

Because of its strategic location, Southeast Asia does a thriving business in trade. The people of the region have frequent contact with foreigners and are exposed to cultures from all around the world. Arab traders from the Middle East first reached Southeast Asia around 1200. They opened up a prosperous trade route and brought stories of powerful Islamic civilizations to the peo-

Some 220 million Muslims live in Southeast Asia, making up 40 percent of the population. Mosques are a common sight throughout the region. This mosque is in Brunei, a tiny Muslim nation on the island of Borneo.

ple there. Islam took on a mystique for Southeast Asian rulers. They learned the basic elements of the religion from the traders and quickly adopted it.

Islam became the dominant religion in Southeast Asian society when the ruling class made it their official faith. The rulers imposed Islam on their subjects even though Hinduism and Buddhism already had deep roots in the region. Islam spread throughout the archipelago over the next few centuries. The history of Islam in Southeast Asia falls into three major periods—the 1400s to the 1700s, the 1800s to the mid-1900s, and the period from the mid-1900s to the present day.

Role of the Early Sultans. Beginning around the 1400s, the Southeast Asian rulers who adopted Islam called themselves sultans*. Following the Persian model of leadership, they believed they were accountable only to God. They obeyed his divine will and imposed it on their subjects. The sultans were absolute rulers who would not tolerate dissent. Some claimed to have descended from Islamic rulers, tracing their family lineage back to Constantinople and Persia. The sultans incorporated traditional Islamic law into their legal codes, although they still retained many elements of traditional Southeast Asian law. Opposition occasionally arose from non-Muslims, but Islam remained the dominant faith in the region.

* **sultan** political and military ruler of a Muslim dynasty or state

Islam Under Colonial Rule. During the colonial period between 1800 and the mid-1900s, the Dutch, British, and French took control of the archipelago and most of mainland Southeast Asia. Thailand was the only Southeast Asian country never ruled by a European power. The Europeans brought Christianity to the region, and Islam declined in status. Local Muslims organized uprisings against colonial rule, but the Asians remained unable to overthrow the Europeans.

Under colonial rule, the sultanates gave way to secular* governments. Islam became divorced from the state in every colony except British Malaya, where the sultans remained religious leaders. The Europeans, however, greatly

* **secular** separate from religion in human life and society; connected to everyday life

* **mosque** Muslim place of worship

* **bureaucracy** agencies and officials that comprise a government

* **militant** aggressively active in a cause

* **hudud** punishments prescribed by the Qur'an for specific crimes

Muslims in Cambodia

About 5 percent of Cambodia's population is Muslim. At one time, Muslims accounted for at least 10 percent of the population, but more than half of them died between 1975 and 1979 at the hands of the Khmer Rouge party. In addition to massacring 1.5 million Cambodians, the Khmer Rouge tried to exterminate the Cham, a Muslim ethnic group that dominated the country. Muslims in Cambodia have recently begun working to rebuild their religion. Groups from countries such as Saudi Arabia and Indonesia fund mosques and *madrasahs* (Islamic schools), and hundreds of Cambodian Muslims study abroad in Malaysia each year. In addition, increasing numbers of young people are learning the Qur'an and the Arabic language.

restricted their activity so that they had no real power. Islam also became subject to control by the state. The Europeans passed laws regulating charity, the construction of mosques*, the publication of Islamic literature, and religious instruction. In short, Islam went from existing as the foundation of the state to serving as just one of many institutions under the control of the government.

Modern Southeast Asia. Malaysia and Indonesia have the largest Muslim populations in Southeast Asia. Neither nation, however, has modeled itself on the Islamic states of the early sultans. They instead take the form of European secular nations. They have constitutions, bureaucracies*, and national economic and social policies. Both states allow for political parties based on Islam. They have also established Islamic banks that operate according to Muslim rules on interest and profit-sharing.

Indonesia gained its independence in 1949. Today it has the largest Muslim population in the world. Almost 90 percent of Indonesia's 231 million people are Muslims. The government has incorporated Islamic codes into family law and the educational system. Islamic political parties in Indonesia, however, have had many setbacks. Groups have formed and reformed, making shifting alliances with Islamic and secular parties. Some Muslims have organized in other ways to try to change the government. In the 1950s, the militant* group Darul Islam caused considerable destruction in West Java in its attempts to overthrow the secular government. It disbanded in 1959 after negotiations with government leaders. In 1973 the government forced all Muslim political parties to unite in a single organization, the United Development Party. However, disagreements divided the party, and Muslim insurrections flared up from time to time. Some Muslim groups continued to fight for an Islamic state, and conflict increased between the Muslims and the Christians, who continued to grow in power.

Malaysia was formed when the British merged the colony of Malaya with part of the island of Borneo. The country gained its independence in 1963. About half of the population of Malaysia is Muslim, and the constitution recognizes Islam as the official religion of the country. Each of the 13 states has a Department of Religious Affairs, and the main government has a National Council for Religious Affairs. The federal government does not enforce an Islamic rule, but various states have a strong Muslim influence.

Many Malaysian political parties recognize Islam and push for Muslim reforms. The United Malay National Organization accommodates Islamic needs but does not allow religion to determine policy. In rural areas of Malaysia, however, various Islamic parties have gained power. For example, the Pan-Malayan Islamic Party promotes a strict form of Islam that does not allow women to work at night and that sanctions traditional *hudud** punishments such as cutting off the hands of thieves. Although Islamic parties control certain states within Malaysia, they have never come close to forming a national government.

Islamic Culture in Southeast Asia

The contact of Southeast Asians with a wide variety of cultures and faiths has given a unique form to Islam in the region. Many Muslims blend Islam with older religions to create distinctive rituals. Some groups, however, discourage the mixing of Islam with other practices. They call for a stricter form of Islam and engage in *da'wah* (missionary) practices to spread the religion and teach existing Muslims better ways to practice their faith.

Variations on the Faith. When the people of Southeast Asia adopted Islam, they molded it to fit in with preexisting cultures. Because the region possesses hundreds of different ethnic* groups, numerous interpretations of Islam have emerged in Southeast Asia. Traditional customs have influenced marriage practices, financial agreements, and punishments for crimes. Southeast Asians also show a great deal of tolerance for diversity of religious practice.

In Indonesia and Malaysia, most Muslims practice Sunni* Islam. Some follow strict forms of Sunnism, and others mix Islam with elements of Hinduism, nature-based religions, and Sufism*. They engage in ritual feasts, traditional medicinal practices, and spiritual ceremonies. In recent decades, however, the number of people attending Friday prayer and observing the fast during the holy month of Ramadan has increased. Muslims in Southeast Asia have also shown a greater interest in wearing traditional Islamic dress, making the pilgrimage to Mecca, and eating *halal** foods.

Language and Literature. The Muslims of Southeast Asia have made important contributions to Islamic culture, especially in the field of literature. A large number of Southeast Asians speak the Malay language, and a version of Malay serves as the official language of Indonesia. When Arabs first introduced Islam to Southeast Asia, they transmitted the teachings in the Malay language. The close association between the Malay language and Islam has lasted to the present.

Between the 1500s and 1800s, Southeast Asian Muslims produced a rich collection of writing in the Malay language. The works include histories of royal families, essays about faith, and simple guides for living. Writers also composed popular tales about the prophets* of Islam and about other figures in the Qur'an*. In addition, they translated and revised many original Arabic texts. Some of the outstanding contributions to Islamic Malay literature came from the poet Hamzah Fansuri. Best known for his writings on mysticism*, Fansuri taught that "Man is but a puppet in God's shadow play," invoking a popular form of entertainment in Southeast Asian culture. Muslims still study Fansuri's works, which remain very influential in the region. (*See also* **Brunei; Indonesia; Malaysia; Philippines.**)

* **ethnic** relating to groups of people who share a common racial, national, tribal, religious, linguistic, or cultural background

* **Sunni** refers to the largest branch of the Muslim community; the name derives from sunnah, the exemplary behavior of the Prophet Muhammad

* **Sufism** Islamic mysticism, which seeks to develop spirituality through discipline of the mind and body

* *halal* permissible; acceptable under Islamic law

* **prophet** one who announces divinely inspired revelations

* **Qur'an** book of the holy scriptures of Islam

* **mysticism** belief that spiritual enlightenment and truth can be attained through various physical and spiritual disciplines

Southern Africa

Southern Africa is a large area that includes the nations of South Africa, Mozambique, Malawi, and Zambia. Each of these countries has a relatively large Muslim minority population. Many Muslims in Southern Africa are descended from Indians or Southeast Asians brought to the region by European colonizers. Other Muslims adopted Islam after Arab traders introduced the faith to the area. The tolerant nature of traditional African religions enabled Islam to spread relatively easily throughout Southern Africa. Because local faiths do not preach the conversion of others, they never came into conflict with Islamic doctrines. Many Southern Africans adopted Islam while retaining local beliefs and rituals.

South Africa and the South Asian Influence. South Africa's 900,000 Muslims make up nearly 2 percent of the country's total population. Most Muslims are either of Indian or Malay ancestry, and less than 3 percent are purely African.

Dutch colonists arrived in South Africa in the mid-1600s. They consisted mostly of peasant farmers who settled on the Cape of Good Hope at the tip of Southern Africa. Shortly after 1800, the British seized the Cape of Good Hope from the Dutch settlers (called Boers), who went north to build new settlements. Both the Dutch and the British brought Muslims to the region from other parts of the world.

Muslims arrived in South Africa in two main groups. The first came during the 1700s, when the Boers imported prisoners and slaves from Dutch colonies in Southeast Asia to work on their farms. Most of these workers were Muslims and they settled on the Cape of Good Hope. Because many of them came from the Malay area of Southeast Asia, they became known as "Cape Malays." After slavery ended in the 1830s, the Cape Muslims maintained a peaceful relationship with their Boer neighbors. However, they did not always agree with or obey the Boer—and later English—authorities. For example, they protested against enforced smallpox vaccinations in the 1840s and promoted various Islamic causes. Nonetheless, the Cape Muslims generally prospered in Southern Africa. They became tailors and merchants and eventually gained representation in all professions.

The second group of Muslims arrived in Southern Africa between the mid-1800s and early 1900s, after the British had taken over the region. The British, like the Boers, needed cheap labor. They imported indentured servants* and other laborers from the British colony of India. Around half of these workers were Muslims. Most of them settled in the Natal province of South Africa, where the British had established huge sugar plantations. The laborers were soon followed by Muslim merchants from India, who developed trade in Natal. The Union of South Africa was established in 1910.

Muslims in both the Cape and Natal formed a number of organizations during the 1900s. Early groups, such as the Cape Malay Association, arose to negotiate with the colonial government for Muslim rights. Muslim scholars and teachers also formed organizations to serve the religious needs of Muslim communities. These groups generally had little interest in politics. Some individuals, however, fought against laws they considered discriminatory and even endured punishment and exile. South African Muslims also established many social welfare and educational organizations, including Islamic primary schools, religious schools, and colleges to meet the educational needs of Muslims. Students learned about the ideas of leading Islamic thinkers such as Sayyid Qutb and Sayyid Abu al-Ala Mawdudi.

During the late 1900s, a revivalist* movement spread throughout the Islamic world. The Muslim Youth Movement of South Africa (MYMSA) helped promote Islamic pride, bringing prominent scholars to the country to share their ideas and guide Muslim leaders. The MYMSA also led to the formation of many other Muslim organizations, such as the Islamic Medical Association, the Women's Islamic Movement, and the South African Association of

* **indentured servant** one who agrees to work for another for a certain number of years, usually in return for travel expenses, room, and board

* **revivalist** calling for the return to traditional values or beliefs

Muslim Social Scientists. Other organizations emerged to spread or reform Islam and to bring about political changes that would benefit Muslims.

In the 1990s, the policy of apartheid, or separation of races, ended in South Africa. Muslim activists played an important role in bringing about this change. A new, popularly elected government, composed mainly of black Africans, came to power once apartheid ended. Before the first election, representatives of Muslim organizations throughout South Africa met to discuss how Muslims, who were a minority, could ensure their representation in the new government. Some Muslims decided to support non-Muslim political parties. Others decided to form their own political parties, such as the Africa Muslim Party. No Muslim parties won seats in the National Assembly, but the government appointed a Muslim named Abdullah Omar as Minister of Justice, and Muslims gained several provincial and federal positions.

Mozambique, Malawi, and Zambia. Muslims made up 10 to 20 percent of the populations of Mozambique and Malawi. Zambia has a large number of Christians, but Hindus* and Muslims represent important minorities.

* **Hindu** refers to the beliefs and practices of Hinduism, an ancient religion that originated in India

Islam spread to all three countries primarily through trade with Arab Muslims. By 1000 the Arabs had established thriving trade routes along the coast of Mozambique. Trade routes also ran across Southern Africa from the coast to the interior. Both goods and ideas were transported in this trade. Islam spread from the Mozambique coast to Malawi, Zambia, and even further inland.

Mozambique existed as a Portuguese colony for hundreds of years before gaining independence in 1975. After independence, Mozambique's government discouraged the public practice of religion. Since 1979, however, the government has relaxed its policy, allowing religious groups to operate freely and to fund schools and hospitals. Most Muslims in Mozambique still live in the north, where Arab traders were most influential in the past.

Malawi was a British protectorate* that became independent in 1964. Even after adopting Islam, many people in Malawi held on to some their traditional African religious practices. Since the 1970s, an Islamic revivalist movement has swept through the country. Islamic reformers study the Arab language and Islamic law and criticize people who follow traditional religious practices. The Malawi government has established ties with many Arab states. Christians in the area worry about the building of new mosques* and the growing influence of the Middle East.

* **protectorate** country under the protection and control of a stronger nation

* **mosque** Muslim place of worship

Zambia existed as the British colony of Northern Rhodesia until 1964, when it gained independence and became the Republic of Zambia. The government proclaimed Zambia a Christian nation in 1991. Many Muslims and members of other non-Christian faiths complain of discrimination in state policies. (*See also* **Central Africa; Colonialism; East Africa; North Africa; West Africa.**)

Spain

See *Andalusia*.

Sports

See *Games and Sports*.

Stereotypes in Mass Media

Many Americans base their ideas about Islam and Muslims on images from the mass media—the movies, television shows, books, newspapers, and magazines that help shape the public's view of the world. These images, however, are often misleading. The American mass media tends to promote stereotypes of Muslims, presenting them as dangerous or simply as strange and exotic. In most cases, Muslim characters appear foreign and different from Americans.

Although most Muslims live outside the Middle East, the American media nearly always portrays Muslims as Arabs and vice versa. Non-Arab Muslims and Arabs of other faiths are all but invisible. Moreover, the media often seems to reduce the diverse cultures of the Middle East to one big desert with camels and strangely dressed men and women. Male characters tend to appear as dark-skinned and bearded, speaking with heavy accents. They often behave in a cruel or violent manner, sometimes abusing their wives and children or attacking other innocent people.

Images of Muslim women are just as extreme. Arab and Muslim women are seldom presented as complete characters. Instead, they usually appear in the background. They may be scantily clad maidens who serve a male master or submissive wives and servants wrapped in black cloth. They seldom speak or take any action on their own.

Many media sources present Muslims as violent extremists who hate Americans. Newscasts have shown angry mobs of Arabs shouting anti-American slogans. CNN ran footage of Palestinians celebrating the attacks of September 11, 2001, but Muslims mourning the incident received little airtime. Books and documentaries also often portray Islam as a violent religion, with titles such as *The Sword of Islam*, *Holy Wars*, and *Inflamed Islam*.

In many movies and television shows, Muslims appear as terrorists. Following the end of the Cold War, an extended period of hostility between the United States and the former Soviet Union, Arabs replaced Russians as the primary villains in American cinema. These Arab characters are often fanatics, willing to sacrifice their lives for a holy war. American viewers rarely see Muslims as regular people at work, on family outings, writing poetry, or helping the sick. Moreover, the American media seldom explores the true motives of those Islamic groups that do engage in violence. Newscasters may suggest that militants are jealous of American wealth or that they hate American values, rather than trying to explain the underlying causes of their anger.

Such stereotypes have had a strong impact on American attitudes toward Muslims. Many Americans view Muslims as dangerous fanatics, fundamentally different from themselves. In addition, they wrongly assume that all Muslims are Arabs and that all Arabs are Muslims. Fear and hatred of Islam have led to discrimination, as well as physical and verbal attacks, on both Muslim and non-Muslim Arabs. Some Arab-American children try to hide their ethnic* background.

In recent years, the media has made some progress toward addressing its negative images of Muslims. Films such as *The Siege* and *Robin Hood: Prince of Thieves* have presented complex and sympathetic Muslim characters. Nevertheless, negative images continue to appear at the same time. The

* **ethnic** relating to groups of people who share a common racial, national, tribal, religious, linguistic, or cultural background

mass media still has a long way to go to put an end to negative stereotypes and help Americans gain a greater understanding of Islam. (*See also* **September 11, 2001; United States.**)

Sudan

Sudan is the largest country in Africa, occupying more than 965,000 square miles. About 70 percent of Sudan's 37 million residents are Muslims. Most Sudanese Muslims live in the northern part of the nation. Other groups, located mainly in the south, practice Christianity and various tribal religions.

The Arrival of Islam. Islam first spread to Sudan from Egypt by way of the Nile River valley. Later it came from African kingdoms to the west that had adopted the religion in the 1100s. After the 1400s, Muslim influences also entered Sudan from many parts of the Muslim world. The Funj sultanate* established the first Muslim state in Sudan in 1504. Throughout the 1500s, Muslim holy men arrived from Egypt and the Middle East, bringing Islamic theology* and law into Sudan. West African pilgrims traveling to Mecca provided another source of contact with the Muslim world. By the 1800s, Islam was well established in Sudan.

The influence of Arab culture grew along with that of Islam. Today about 40 percent of the Sudanese population is Arab, and Arabic is the nation's official language. Nonetheless, ethnic groups such as the Nubians* retain their languages and traditions. To this day, African customs remain a major part of Sudanese culture.

Sufi* orders greatly advanced Sudan's conversion to Islam as well. Sufi worship practices such as drumming, chanting, and dancing blended with and enhanced the local religious customs of Sudanese tribes. Most Sufi orders promoted equality and lacked a strong central organization. Throughout Sudan's history, Sufi orders have shown little support for formal religious and political structures. As a result, tension between the popular Sufi orders and the official Islamic administration in Sudan has been ongoing.

Colonial Era. In 1821 an invading Turkish-Egyptian army took control of Sudan, making it part of the Ottoman Empire*. The Ottomans established a Turkish administration called the Turkiyah. They governed the country through Egyptians and local officials, and a Turkish-Egyptian army enforced Ottoman rule. Sudanese resented their conquerors, who imposed high taxes, forced them to serve in the army, and permitted slave raids in Sudan.

Several groups resisted Ottoman rule during the 1800s, but the most serious challenge came in 1881, when Muhammad Ahmad organized a movement called the Mahdiyah. Declaring himself the Mahdi, or "Expected One," Muhammad Ahmad proclaimed an Islamic revival* to challenge the immorality of the nation's foreign rulers. He regarded it as his divine mission to end the Turkish and Egyptian occupation.

The Mahdi and his followers, known as the Ansar, won a series of battles against the occupying army. The British, who played a major role in the government of Egypt at that time, sent General Charles Gordon to oversee

* **sultanate** government of a sultan, the political and military ruler of a Muslim dynasty or state

* **theology** study of the nature and qualities of God and the understanding of His will

* **Nubian** refers to a group of peoples who formed a powerful empire in northeastern Africa between the 500s and the 1300s

* **Sufi** refers to Sufism, which seeks to develop spirituality through discipline of the mind and body

* **Ottoman Empire** large Turkish state existing from the early 1300s to the early 1900s

* **revival** return to traditional values or beliefs

Sudan

Years of war and drought have left much of Sudan's population at or below the poverty level. Efforts to bolster the economy have focused on developing the country's substantial oil reserves. In 1999 an oil pipeline was inaugurated by Sudanese president Umar al-Bashir.

* **caliph** religious and political leader of an Islamic state

* **regime** government in power

* **nationalism** feelings of loyalty and devotion to one's country and a commitment to its independence

the withdrawal of Egyptian troops from Sudan. Gordon, however, believed that an Ansar victory in Sudan would pose a threat to the security of Egypt. He asked for, and eventually received, additional British troops to aid the Egyptian forces. In 1885 the Mahdi's forces defeated the British at Khartoum and killed Gordon. This stunning defeat marked a low point in British colonial history. For Muslims, the victory became a symbol of Islam's triumphant resistance against outside invaders.

The Mahdi died soon after his victory at Khartoum. Caliph* Abdallahi al-Ta'ishi, who succeeded him, established an Islamic government modeled after the first Muslim community at Mecca. The Mahdist state was the only successful Islamic regime* to stand against the forces of colonialism in Africa at this time. It became a symbol of glorious Muslim nationalism*. Some observers believe that the modern Islamic revival of the late 1900s had some roots in the Mahdiyah.

Culture

PLATE 1

This print of Mecca from about 1850 shows the Kaaba, the "House of God," surrounded by the arcaded walls of the Great Mosque. According to the Qur'an, Ibrahim (Abraham) and his son Ismail built the Kaaba. The mosque has been expanded, but the Kaaba remains at its center.

PLATE 2
In 1453 after a prolonged siege, Sultan Mehmed II captured the Byzantine capital of Constantinople. The conquest of the city marked the end of 1,000 years of Christian rule and the rise of the Ottoman Empire.

PLATE 3
Built in the 530s, Hagia Sophia (the church of Holy Wisdom) in Constantinople (present-day Istanbul) was a masterpiece of Byzantine architecture. Converting the church to a mosque presented a great challenge for Ottoman architects in the late 1500s. The building is now a museum.

PLATE 4

This painting shows a diplomatic event of the mid-1500s. After ruling India for ten years, the Mughal emperor Humayun was overthrown and took refuge in Iran with the Safavid Shah Tahmasp I. Humayun later regained his empire with the help of Tahmasp.

PLATE 5

The Ottoman Empire had a large and elaborate court. The Topkapi Palace in Istanbul housed the sultan, harem, staff members, schools for pages and slaves, and offices for military, civil, and religious leaders. This painting shows a reception at the court of Sultan Selim III (1789–1807).

PLATE 6

Muslim funeral rites emphasize tradition and simplicity. In South Africa, Muslims gather in front of a coffin to pray.

PLATE 7

The romantic tradition in Persian literature reached a peak with Nizami's *Khamsah*, written around 1200. The work consists of five stories, each revolving around love and adventure. This illustration of pilgrims at the Kaaba by the great Persian artist Bihzad, or one of his followers, appeared in a copy of the text produced about 300 years later.

PLATE 8

Muslims listen to a sermon in a mosque of the Nation of Islam in Chicago. In the
United States, some mosques have become centers of cultural identity for immigrants.
Others have served as outreach centers, educating Americans about Islam.

PLATE 9

Stringed instruments such as the *oud* (short-necked lute), *qanum*
(zither), tamboura (long-necked lute), and *kemence* (upright fiddle)
play a prominent role in Islamic music. This painting of the mid-
1700s shows a tamboura player.

PLATE 10

A Syrian band takes the stage at an event in Damascus in the summer of 2002. The immense embroidered mural behind the musicians contains squares with the names of Palestinian villages. Various colors indicate which villages have been destroyed (red) and which still exist (green).

PLATE 11

For the Mawlawis, members of a Sufi order also known as Whirling Dervishes, ritual dance is part of their quest for a direct spiritual experience of God. The upturned right hand symbolizes receipt of divine grace. The downturned left hand represents God's blessings being passing to humanity. Whirling Dervishes are shown in this Persian illustration of the early 1500s.

PLATE 12
The Berbers were living in North Africa when the Arabs invaded the region in the 600s. The Berbers eventually accepted Islam and became part of Islamic society. They did, however, maintain some of their customs. Here Berber women in brightly colored dress take part in a festival in Tunisia.

PLATE 13
This page on medicinal plants comes from the *Treatise of Theriac* (1217), a work based on the teachings of the Greek physician Galen. Theriac, a mixture of drugs and honey, was thought to be an antidote to poison.

PLATE 14

Muslims consider ablution, ritual washing or purification before prayer, a sign of respect for God. The process begins with a declaration that the ritual is for the purpose of purity and worship. These Muslims in India wash their faces, arms, and feet before entering the mosque to pray.

PLATE 15

Pilgrims pile onto a train after a three-day prayer session in Bangladesh. The event attracts about 2 million Muslims, making it the second largest pilgrimage after the hajj to Saudi Arabia.

The Mahdist state survived for 13 years. In 1898 the British, seeking revenge for Gordon's defeat at Khartoum, launched a powerful invasion headed by General Horatio Herbert Kitchener. Equipped with gunboats and machine guns, the British forces overwhelmed the Mahdist troops. The British massacre of Muslim defenders near the city of Omdurman marked the defeat of the Mahdiyah.

Britain took control of Sudan, ruling jointly with Egypt. The new rulers sought to control, but not crush, Islam in the colony. In order to govern through Muslim institutions, the British gained the cooperation of the heads of the largest popular Muslim organizations. They created a new structure that combined Muslim and British systems.

The court system in Sudan reflected this new duality. The criminal and civil courts followed British law, but a separate legal system followed the principles of *shari'ah**. The religious courts handled matters affecting the personal status of Sudanese Muslims, such as marriage, child support, and wills. The governor-general of Sudan appointed a member of the *ulama** as the high judge of these *shari'ah* courts. This judge, who operated under the authority of the colonial legal secretary, had the right to release Judicial Circulars that regulated the decisions and procedures of the courts. These circulars shaped the development of Islamic law in Sudan. Through them, the *ulama* maintained power as the guardians of the faith under foreign rule.

Independence. After Muhammad Ahmad's death, his family retained a substantial influence in the country. His son, Abd al-Rahman al-Mahdi emerged as the religious and political leader of the Ansar. In the 1940s, the Ansar formed the core of the nationalist Ummah Party. This group called for independence from Britain. Another nationalist group, the Unionist Party, rose up at the same time. The Unionists advocated forming a union with Egypt. These two powerful parties became bitter political rivals.

Sudan gained its independence on January 1, 1956. Its new status, however, did not bring political stability. Instead, it set off a rebellion among non-Muslims in the southern part of the country who did not want to live under a Muslim regime. This civil war continued for 16 years.

The early governments in independent Sudan were secular* regimes that tried to separate religious issues from politics. Nonetheless, several political groups focused on the role of Islam in Sudanese society. One such group was the Muslim Brotherhood, which called for an Islamic constitution in Sudan. Hasan al-Turabi, the head of the brotherhood, won support as a symbol of Islamic renewal.

In 1969 a military leader named Jafar Nimeiri seized power in Sudan, backed by communist* allies. He established a secular regime and arrested several Islamic activists, including al-Turabi. In 1972 Nimeiri signed a peace agreement with the rebels in the south, bringing a temporary halt to the civil war. In the following years, he defeated uprisings of the Ansar and other groups. At this point, the Muslim Brotherhood decided to join forces with Nimeiri. Al-Turabi and several other leading members of the brotherhood assumed positions in the government. As their ally, Nimeiri gradually turned the country towards Islamic rule. In 1983 he declared that Islamic law would govern Sudan. This move revived the rebellion in the south, where non-Muslims organized to form the Sudan People's Liberation Movement (SPLM).

* **shari'ah** Islamic law as established in the Qur'an and sunnah, the exemplary behavior of the Prophet Muhammad

* **ulama** religious scholars

* **secular** separate from religion in human life and society; connected to everyday life

* **communist** follower of communism, a political and economic system based on the concept of shared ownership of all property

Islamic Law

Islamic law in Sudan evolved considerably between 1902 and 1983. Many changes promoted women's rights in the nation. For example, judges reformed the divorce laws, making it possible for women to obtain a divorce in the courts in cases of proven harm or abuse. Judges also expanded women's rights to receive support from their husbands and to maintain custody of their children after a divorce. Rulings in the 1930s confirmed the right of fathers and other guardians to arrange marriages for women, but later rulings recognized a woman's right to withhold her consent to a marriage.

* **coup** sudden, and often violent, overthrow of a ruler or government

* **Islamist** referring to Muslim movement advocating reintegration of religion and politics; also Muslim who advocates reintegration of religion and politics

Nimeiri used *shari'ah* as a weapon to silence his political enemies. He imposed harsh punishments, known as *hudud*. Such actions sparked growing unrest, which peaked in 1985 after Nimeiri executed Mahmud Muhammad Taha, the elderly leader of a Muslim opposition group. A popular uprising overthrew Nimeiri and ushered in a democratic government.

Sadiq al-Mahdi was elected prime minister in 1986, but Sudan remained unstable under his leadership. Al-Mahdi proved unable to end the civil war or to modify the use of *shari'ah* as state law. In 1989 General Umar al-Bashir led a successful coup* and established another Islamist* regime in Sudan. Al-Turabi and the Muslim Brotherhood played a major role in the new government. Al-Bashir's harsh Islamic agenda, however, provoked opposition from moderate Muslim groups in the north and from Muslim Nubians. These groups joined forces with the SPLM to form the National Democratic Alliance (NDA). Al-Bashir, nonetheless, maintained a firm grip on the country. In 2000 the Ummah Party withdrew from the NDA and ended its opposition to his rule. Around the same time, Al-Bashir removed his ally al-Turabi from power.

Sudan faces many challenges in the 21st century. The civil war continues to bring death and destruction to the nation. Since 1983 the combination of war and persistent famine has caused more than 2 million deaths and displaced 4 million people from their homes. Sudan's agriculture-based economy remains vulnerable to drought and price declines in the world market. Much of the country's population lives at or below the poverty line, and the nation has an outstanding debt of nearly $25 billion. Moreover, Sudan has had tense relations with the outside world. International aid agencies have accused the regime of preventing food from reaching starving war victims.

Sudan has not managed to achieve political or economic stability. The nation's future depends on the government's ability to draw support from both Muslims and non-Muslims. Whether Sudan will emerge as a secular, democratic nation or as an Islamic regime remains uncertain. (*See also* **Colonialism; Egypt; Mahdiyah; Muslim Brotherhood.**)

Sufism

* **mysticism** belief that spiritual enlightenment and truth can be obtained through various physical and spiritual disciplines

* **Qur'an** book of the holy scriptures of Islam
* **sunnah** literally the "trodden path"; Islamic customs based on the exemplary behavior of Muhammad

* **doctrine** principle, theory, or belief that is taught or presented for acceptance

Sufism includes the various movements of Islamic mysticism*. Sufis pursue spirituality through the discipline of the mind and body. The Arabic term *sufi*, meaning "one who wears wool," refers to an early group of Muslims who signified their renunciation of worldly goods by wearing coarse and uncomfortable woolen garments. By the 800s, the term had come to indicate a specific group of Muslims who focused on certain teachings from the Qur'an* and sunnah*. Sufis have played a major role in spreading Islam and have contributed greatly to Muslim culture, especially in their mystical poetry.

Sufi Thought and Practice

Sufis strive above all to gain an awareness of God's presence, both in the world and in themselves. They stress contemplation over action, spiritual development over legal doctrine*, and cultivation of the soul over social interaction. They focus on God's mercy, gentleness, and beauty rather than the authority and judgment that interest Muslim legal scholars. Sufism has spread through all regions of the Muslim world and attracts both Sunni* and Shi'i* Muslims. Men and women of all social classes join mystical orders. Followers of Sufism consider it the inner core and spirit of Islam.

Development of Islamic Mysticism. Sufism emerged in the decades following Muhammad's death. It began as a reform movement led by Muslims who objected to the materialism* and wealth of the Umayyad caliphate* (661–750). Sufis also reacted against Islam's increasing emphasis on rules for behavior. Many Muslims found their society spiritually empty. They wanted to gain access to the heightened state experienced by Muhammad when he received God's revelations*.

Sufis became known as "those who always weep" and those who view the world as a "hut of sorrows." From the beginning, they emphasized discipline and self-sacrifice. They sought to introduce God into their lives by winning a struggle against laziness and personal desire. They termed this battle the "greater jihad*," as opposed to the "lesser jihad" of warfare against nonbelievers. Sufis prayed, fasted, studied the Qur'an and sunnah, and tried to prepare themselves for the Day of Judgment. In the late 700s, Rabi'ah al-Adawiyah, an Iraqi woman, added love of God as a focus of Sufism. She helped to shift the movement's primary emphasis from asceticism* to mysticism.

Sufis sought to attain complete trust in God, some condemning any thought of the future as a sign of lack of faith. They also emphasized *tawhid*, the doctrine of God's oneness. Sufism absorbed several additional ideas in the 800s. The Iraqi mystic al-Muhasibi stated that one must cleanse the soul in order to experience God. In Egypt, Dhu an-Nun stressed inner knowledge over traditional education. The Iranian scholar Abu Yazid al-Bistami introduced the concept of annihilating the self to admit the presence of God. In the early 900s, another Iranian mystic, Husayn ibn Mansur al-Hallaj, claimed that eliminating the personality could enable an individual to become one with God. Religious leaders had him executed for his extreme ideas, but al-Hallaj allegedly went to his death singing, happy at the prospect of merging with the divine.

Sufi thought continued to develop during the later medieval* period. Abu Hamid al-Ghazali (1058–1111), legal scholar and mystic, stated that only ritual and prayer could grant Muslims a knowledge of God. He claimed that Sufism, unlike theological* study, provided a direct knowledge of the divine. This endorsement from a top religious authority helped popularize the movement. The Spanish religious philosopher Ibn al-Arabi (1165–1240) furthered the spread of Sufism, stating that every person has the ability to experience God. Ibn al-Arabi believed that each human personifies* one of God's attributes and that individuals can only know the God that exists within them. Because each person has a unique relationship with God, all faiths are valid. Islam serves as one lens among many through which humans can view the divine.

Path of the Mystic. Sufi masters have devised a number of practices or paths (*tariqahs*) to develop a person's spirituality. Most paths include the

* **Sunni** refers to the largest branch of the Muslim community; the name derives from sunnah, the exemplary behavior of the prophet Muhammad

* **Shi'i** refers to Muslims who believe that Muhammad chose Ali ibn Abi Talib and his descendants as the spiritual-political leaders of the Muslim community

* **materialism** emphasis on material rather than intellectual or spiritual things

* **caliphate** office and government of the caliph, the religious and political leader of an Islamic state

* **revelation** message from God to humans transmitted through a prophet

* **jihad** literally "striving"; war in defense of Islam

* **asceticism** way of life in which a person rejects worldly pleasures to follow a spiritual path

* **medieval** refers to the Middle Ages, a period roughly between 500 and 1500

* **theology** study of the nature and qualities of God and the understanding of his will

* **personification** representation in human form of an abstraction, such as good or evil

Sufism

Sufi Muslims seek spirituality through the discipline of the mind and body. They emphasize contemplation over action and cultivation of the soul over worldly pursuits. This Mughal painting of the 1700s shows angels bringing food to a Sufi in the forest.

* **shaykh** tribal elder; also, title of honor given to those who are considered especially learned and pious

* **dervish** Sufi mystic; member of an order that uses music and dance to enter a trancelike state

* **metaphor** figure of speech in which one object or idea is directly identified with a different object or idea

following steps. After repenting for materialistic lifestyles, those who want to become Sufis seek a master who instructs them in perseverance and self-denial. Typically referred to as *shaykhs**, masters use many tactics to teach humility, including the performance of menial tasks. *Shaykhs* lead their disciples along numerous "stations," such as abstinence from certain actions, renunciation of worldly goods, and poverty. They depict the lower soul as an animal that needs taming in order to serve God. Through hard work and self-denial, disciples learn patience, gratitude, and acceptance of hardship. They ultimately gain an inner understanding of God and a feeling of universal love. Once they have attained this state, they may return to the world. There, they continue their exploration of God and serve as witnesses for other Muslims. Sufi masters typically choose one exceptional student as their successor.

Ritual prayer (*dhikr*) is an important part of the path. Sufis initiated this practice to honor the Qur'anic command to remember God. *Dhikr* involves the repetition of God's name or another religious phrase, often set to music. The Mawlawis (Whirling Dervishes*) recite prayers while performing a dance, and the Rifa'is (Howling Dervishes) inflict pain upon themselves to utter God's name more loudly. Some Sufis repeat formulas silently, while in meditation.

Medieval Sufis used metaphors* of intoxication and sobriety to describe their experiences on the path. Ecstatic in the divine presence, Sufis openly declared their union with Allah. They emphasized love and compassion and viewed God in everything, losing the ability to make distinctions. "Intoxicated" (or ecstatic) Sufis produced great works of mystical poetry. Sober Sufis viewed God as distant, majestic, and mighty—far above the concerns of humans. They emphasized law and rightful conduct. Sober Sufism appealed primarily to legal scholars and philosophers, who produced texts of Islamic doctrine. The Sufi movement generally represents a balance between these two expressions.

Influence on the Arts. Sufis had a tremendous impact on the Islamic arts. Although their devotional practices stimulated the development of music and dance, they made their most remarkable contributions in the field of literature. The hadith* "He who knows God talks much" served as the basis for an outpouring of Sufi writings. Books on Sufi etiquette informed followers on correct behavior—Shihab al-Din Umar Suhrawardi's *Adab al-muridin* (The Adept's Etiquette) served as a cornerstone. Sufis also wrote numerous commentaries on the Qur'an and hadith and published the sayings and letters of Sufi masters.

Sufis made their greatest contribution to Islamic literature in the form of poetry. Mystics composed short, musical verses expressing the yearning of the soul for the beloved, a figure that could serve as either a romantic figure or the divine spirit. They also wrote hymns praising God with lines of repetition that evoked the practice of *dhikr*. Scholars of all religions consider Jalal al-Din Rumi (1207–1273) the greatest poet in the Persian language. Inspired by his mystical union with the teacher Shams-i Tabrizi and others, he composed poems of several thousand couplets that expressed every state of spiritual attainment. Other Sufi authors explored similar themes, and Turkish mystical poets contributed greatly to Ottoman literature during the 1700s and 1800s.

Sufi Orders

Sufism took root slowly. In the early days of Islam, a small number of Sufi masters taught a handful of disciples. Over time, Sufi teachers rose in stature and attracted larger groups of followers. By the 1100s, established orders (*tariqahs*) had formed. Some lasted for only a few decades and observed a simple set of rituals. Others became permanent organizations that included different regions and took in people from all social classes.

Sufi orders served a variety of functions. In large cities such as Cairo and Istanbul, they encouraged devotion among Muslims and promoted religious teaching and trade activities. Some sponsored reform campaigns to purify Islamic faith and practice. Rural Sufi orders converted large non-Muslim populations through missionary* activities.

Types of Institutions. All Sufi orders involve regular group meetings and the recitation of prayers, poems, and selections from the Qur'an. They also include daily devotional exercises and meditative rituals. Three main types of Sufi orders developed—those based on large, inclusive traditions; those based on ancient ways; and those based on individuals. The large orders have clearly established traditions and a core body of devotional literature. The Qadiriyah, organized by Abd al-Qadir al-Jilani's followers in the late 1100s, grew rapidly, becoming the most widespread of the orders. Other inclusive groups include the Suhrawardiyah, the Rifa'iyah, the Shadhiliyah, and the Chishtiyah. Over the years, teachers added to the doctrines of their orders. The process of creating suborders continues today.

Orders based on ancient ways stem from less clearly defined traditions. Their founders drew from the prayers and writings of early Sufis but added elements to create orders with distinct identities. The Mawlawiyah is the most famous order of this type. Based on the teachings of Jalal al-Din Rumi (died

* **hadith** reports of the words and deeds of Muhammad (not in the Qur'an, but accepted as guides for Muslim behavior)

See color plate 11, vol. 3.

* **missionary** person who works to convert nonbelievers to a particular faith

1273), it continued to evolve with the teachings of later masters. Mawlawi followers, or Whirling Dervishes, incorporate dance into their meditation rituals.

Individual-based orders developed around the teachings of a master who affirmed ties to an earlier teacher but created a completely independent tradition. Founders sometimes claimed inspiration from Muhammad or other figures to validate their orders. Important individual-based orders in the modern world include the Khatmiyah and the Sanusiyah.

Shrine Culture. Certain Sufi orders revolve around shrines*. These groups began when the leaders of various orders developed reputations as saints. Followers believed that they had access to supernatural powers and that they could perform miracles such as predicting the future, being in two places at one time, and curing illness. Some even considered them divine beings. These leaders received numerous requests for blessings. After their deaths, followers believed that the leaders could still respond to such requests.

Many Sufis visit shrines to ask for blessings from a deceased saint. Some make pilgrimages to distant lands to visit shrines. Sufis petition their saints for general blessings, success in business, healing, or other favors. Some shrines attract thousands of pilgrims each year. Many Sufis perform *dhikr* and other rituals at these sites, and several orders hold annual festivals there. Across the Islamic world, Sufis gather at shrines to honor the births or deaths of saints. Many of these occasions involve lively celebrations that include feasts and processions.

Sufism in the Modern Era

The modern era brought significant changes to the Muslim world. Sufism faced opposition from reformers who sought to strengthen Islam by purging it of superstitious practices associated with some forms of Sufism. However, Sufism has remained a dynamic component of Muslim life. Over the past two centuries, Sufi orders have played a significant role in Islamic missionary work and politics.

Missionary Work. Sufism has proven to be well-suited for spreading Islam. It teaches that people of all faiths may experience God and that religions come in many different forms. Because the mystic sees God everywhere, all forms of worship are considered valid. Such tolerance enabled Sufism to take a leading role in spreading Islam in non-Muslim lands. Moreover, Sufism's decentralized structure enabled local elites to assume leadership positions in the orders. The flexibility of the faith contributed greatly to its ability to attract a large number of converts.

Sufi orders played leading roles in converting Asian and African populations to Islam in the 1700s and 1800s. Sufism further advanced the spread of Islam to Europe and America in the 1800s and 1900s. Sufi writings influenced several leading Western intellectuals, such as Ralph Waldo Emerson. Many in the West found Sufism a satisfying vehicle of religious expression and an intriguing form of mysticism. Orders in Europe and America continue to grow. For example, the Ni'matullahi order has centers in several major cities in the United States, publishes a magazine called *Sufi*, and organizes academic conferences on Sufism. The immigration of Sufis to Western countries has also contributed to a rise in popularity of mystical orders.

* **shrine** place that is considered sacred because of its history or the relics contained there

The Feminine Mystic

Sufism has generally proven more tolerant of female leadership than orthodox Islam. The mystic Rabi'ah al-Adawiyah helped shape Sufism's development in the 700s by expounding on the concept of selfless love. She frequently outwitted her male counterparts and wrote love poems that continue to inspire Sufi authors. Sufism has produced hundreds of female teachers. Many Sufi saints are women, and some have had shrines built in their honor. Sufi men, however, have expressed mixed feelings towards women. Ibn al-Arabi held that man's admiration of women serves as the most perfect vehicle for contemplating God, and Abu Hamid al-Ghazali claimed that women could either help or hinder men on their spiritual path. Al-Hujwiri, however, expressed a negative view of females, citing women as the cause of all evil.

Sufi Political Action. Sufi orders had a great political impact during the colonial era. Sufis played a leading role in resisting European dominance of the Islamic world and had some notable successes in Africa. In the 1830s and 1840s, the Qadiriyah led Algerian fighters against the French, and the Salihiyah waged a major war against the British in Somalia. In Sudan, Qurashi Sufis supported the Mahdiyah campaign against colonial rule, inflicting a crushing defeat on the British at Khartoum in 1885. The Sanusi order provided effective opposition to Italy's campaigns in Libya in the early 1900s. In Morocco, Sufis helped lead a major revolt against the French. Sufis also played roles in several independence movements in Africa after World War II (1939–1945).

Sufi orders also resisted Russian expansion in the Caucasus. Naqshbandi fighters waged a nine-year holy war against czarist troops in the late 1700s and the Qadiris later joined the Naqshbandis in anti-Russian revolts in Daghestan and Chechnya. The Naqshbandiyah opposed rulers in Central Asia as well. In China's Xinjiang province, the Naqshbandiyah waged several jihads against the Ch'ing dynasty* in the 1800s. In the 1900s, Sufi orders resisted Soviet rule in Central Asia. They rose up against the government several times between 1920 and 1942. Sufis in Central Asia helped Islam survive decades of Soviet oppression in the region. They also provided opposition to colonialism in Southeast Asia, participating in a series of anti-Dutch uprisings in Indonesia in the mid-1800s.

Sufi political influence extended beyond campaigns against European imperialism*. Sufi orders played a role in legitimizing political authority in several countries. During the the Mughal Empire (1526–1857) and the Ottoman Empire (1300–1923), Sufis had close ties to the ruling classes. In the 1800s, the head of the Mawlawi order presented each new Ottoman sultan* with the imperial sword. Although Sufism's political influence declined in the 1900s, it remains strong in Sudan and certain other areas.

Challenges for Modern Sufis. Sufism has historically faced opposition within the Muslim world. Since the 700s, critics have attacked the movement as a distortion of Islam. Orthodox* Muslims have condemned Sufis for embracing non-Islamic practices such as the venerations of saints, which they consider a form of polytheism*. They reviled Sufi masters who incorporated superstitions in their rituals and spoke out against the use of music, dancing, and other nontraditional activities.

During the period of colonization, many Muslim reformers blamed Sufism for the weakness of Muslim nations. They criticized the orders for promoting superstition, arguing that Islam needed to embrace technology and the sciences. Certain reformers hoped to eliminate mysticism in the Muslim world. The Turkish leader Mustafa Kemal Atatürk labeled Sufism a subversive movement and banned Sufi orders from his country in 1925. The former Soviet Union threatened the survival of Sufism in its Asian provinces throughout the 1900s, and Saudi Arabia continues to prohibit all Sufi activity.

However, Sufi influence in the Islamic world has not evaporated. Many Muslims prefer the personalized, intense form of worship that Sufism provides. Sufi orders continue to attract converts in non-Muslim lands, and the movement provides a spiritual identity for Muslims around the world. Millions of Muslims view Sufism as the means by which they may truly wor-

* **dynasty** succession of rulers from the same family or group

* **imperialism** extension of power and influence over another country or region

* **sultan** political and military ruler of a Muslim dynasty or state

* **orthodox** conforming to accepted beliefs and practices

* **polytheism** belief in more than one god

ship and experience God. (*See also* **Chishtiyah; Ghazali, Abu Hamid al-; Ibn al-Arabi; Mahdiyah; Mawlawiyah; Naqshbandiyah; Qadiriyah; Rumi; Saints and Sainthood; Sanusiyah; Shadhiliyah; Shrine; Tawhid; Zawiyah.**)

Suicide

* **Qur'an** book of the holy scriptures of Islam

* **hadith** reports of the words and deeds of Muhammad (not in the Qur'an, but accepted as guides for Muslim behavior)

For centuries, the topic of suicide generated little discussion among Muslims. In recent years, however, it has become a divisive issue in the Islamic world. The Qur'an* mentions suicide only once in the phrase "do not kill yourselves." Most scholars interpret the phrase as "do not kill each other," as the two are the same in Arabic. The hadith* discuss suicide in greater detail. Several reports warn a believer against the action, stating that the person who kills himself will eternally suffer by the method used to end his life. For example, an individual who dies after drinking poison will repeatedly drink poison in hell. Some scholars believe the hadith indicate the existence of a high rate of suicide in Arabia, and Muhammad's desire to end the practice. In any case, suicide is condemned in Islamic law.

Islamic Teachings. Muslims disapprove of suicide for many reasons. Islamic doctrine regards God as the sole giver of life and affirms that only He has the right to take it. Islam also teaches perseverance and the patient endurance of hardship. The religion prohibits suicide even in cases of severe pain or grave illness. A believer should not hope for death, let alone attempt to bring it about. Muhammad emphasized that God has total control over human affairs. According to a hadith, God disapproved of a man who killed himself after receiving a fatal wound in battle, stating, "My servant has attempted to preempt me; thus have I forbidden Paradise to him."

Most Muslim scholars, however, take a less strict view of suicide. They refuse to believe that the action brings eternal punishment in hell. Some hold that suicide is forgivable, similar to other sins. They conclude that a Muslim who takes his or her own life is still a believer and will receive torments in the afterlife for a limited amount of time before reaching paradise. Religious leaders typically recite funeral prayers for suicide victims, further confirming their status in the Muslim community.

Modern Muslim thinkers have devoted little attention to the topic of suicide, in part because Islamic societies have enjoyed relatively low suicide rates compared with Western nations and non-Islamic developing countries. Some scholars believe that the low suicide rate among Muslims stems from the benefits of living in traditional communities. Others, however, hold that Muslims who live in small villages underreport incidents of suicide. Some thinkers have stressed the idea that faith prevents most Muslims from taking their own lives. They view atheism* as a leading cause of suicide.

* **atheism** denial of the existence of God

Muslim Suicide Attacks. In the late 1900s, the issue of suicide took on a new relevance in the Islamic world as certain Muslim groups promoted suicide bombing and other forms of warfare that resulted in the death of the attacker. Their leaders encouraged suicidal practices by referring to them as acts of martyrdom*. Both Sunni* and Shi'i* Muslims have participated in these suicide missions.

In the early 1980s, radical* Muslim groups hit American and French military targets in Lebanon. A suicide bomber in Beirut drove a truck into American and French military barracks, killing hundreds of troops. Shi'is participated in suicide attacks during Iran's war against Iraq in the 1980s. Muslims in Southeast Asia have also taken up the practice as a protest against Western influence.

Muslim suicide bombings have attracted much attention in the 21st century. Many incidents revolve around the Arab-Israeli conflict. Palestinian suicide bombing began as a reaction to a 1994 attack in which a Jewish settler opened fire in a mosque*, killing 29 Muslims during early morning prayers. In retaliation, Hamas initiated a series of bombing campaigns, attacking civilians inside Israel and the West Bank. Suicide bombings have increased in recent years as tensions continue to rise in these areas. The most dramatic example of suicide bombing, however, occurred in the United States on September 11, 2001, when hijacked passenger jets crashed into the World Trade Center and the Pentagon, killing around 3,000 people.

The recent wave of suicide attacks has sparked much debate inside the Islamic world. Leaders and scholars remain split over the issue. Sheikh al-Sheikh, the head of Egypt's al-Azhar mosque, opposes the practice as un-Islamic, and has drawn the support of many Muslim scholars. These thinkers view suicide attacks against civilians as acts of terrorism* and a violation of God's will. They condemn suicide bombers for distorting the true message of Islam, which forbids the harming of civilians. They warn that God will punish suicide bombers in the afterlife.

Groups that promote suicide bombings also use Islamic doctrine to justify their position. Their leaders claim to be the true defenders of the faith. They view suicide attacks as part of a jihad* against injustice, foreign oppression, and lack of religious belief. The promise of a glorious afterlife has inspired some young Muslim men—and increasing numbers of women—to volunteer for suicide missions.

Muslims living under Israeli occupation are especially vigorous in their justification of suicide attacks. They view their actions as a necessary defense and last resort against an overwhelmingly powerful opponent. Palestinian resistance fighters blame Israel for creating an atmosphere of despair, economic hardship, and violence and for causing the deaths of dozens of Palestinian civilians while targeting militant leaders. Because most Israelis serve in the army, suicide bombers believe that an attack on civilians does not target the innocent.

Several prominent Muslims have openly supported suicide attacks. Leading scholars have issued fatwas* defending the practice on religious grounds. The influential Sheikh Yusuf al-Qaradawi, for example, considers suicide bombing in the case of Palestine to be an act of self-defense, maintaining that God will reward the bomber with eternity in paradise. Some other scholars agree with al-Qaradawi. In March 2003, Syria's top religious leader called for suicide bombings to stop U.S. aggression in Iraq. (*See also* **Afterlife; Arab-Israeli Conflict; Death and Funerals; Martyrdom.**)

* **martyrdom** act of dying for one's religious beliefs

* **Sunni** refers to the largest branch of the Muslim community; the name derives from sunnah, the exemplary behavior of the Prophet Muhammad

* **Shi'i** refers to Muslims who believe that Muhammad chose Ali ibn Abi Talib and his descendants as the spiritual-political leaders of the Muslim community

* **radical** favoring extreme change or reform, especially in existing political and social institutions

* **mosque** Muslim place of worship

* **terrorism** use of violence against people, property, or states as a means of intimidation for political purposes

* **jihad** literally "striving"; war in defense of Islam

* **fatwa** opinion issued by an Islamic legal scholar in response to a question posed by an individual or a court of law

Suleyman

1494–1566
Ottoman ruler

* **Ottoman Empire** large Turkish state existing from the early 1300s to the early 1900s

* **sultan** political and military ruler of a Muslim dynasty or state

* **dynasty** succession of rulers from the same family or group

* **caliph** religious and political leader of an Islamic state

* **orthodox** conforming to accepted beliefs and practices

* **mosque** Muslim place of worship

* **shari'ah** Islamic law as established in the Qur'an and sunnah, the exemplary behavior of the Prophet Muhammad

The reign of Suleyman marked the point when the Ottoman Empire* reached its peak of power and prosperity as well as the highest development of its governmental, social, and economic systems. Known as *Kanuni* (the Law-giver) within the empire and the Magnificent in Europe, Suleyman was the only son of the Ottoman sultan* Selim I. He served in the administrations of his grandfather, Bayezid II, and his father. In 1520 Suleyman succeeded Selim I as sultan.

Soon after taking power, Suleyman embarked on a campaign of military conquest in central Europe. His troops captured Belgrade in 1521. His notable victory at the Battle of Mohacs in 1526 brought Hungary under Ottoman control. Three years later, Suleyman laid siege to Vienna, but harsh weather and lack of supplies prevented him from taking the city. The Ottomans, nonetheless, remained a strong presence in central Europe. Suleyman created a force of warriors whose primary function was to carry out raids on European cities. Taking advantage of the rise of Protestantism within the Holy Roman Empire, a political body in central Europe composed of several states, he also sent financial support to Protestant countries to weaken Catholic control over the continent and to destabilize the region.

During the 1530s, Suleyman sought to expand the Ottoman Empire eastward. He took Iraq and the southern Caucasus from the Safavid dynasty*. Suleyman also established a powerful navy under the leadership of Khayr ad-Din, known in the West as Barbarossa. After defeating the Spanish and Venetian fleets in 1538, the Ottoman navy dominated the Mediterranean Sea. The empire's eastern fleet even traveled to India and Indonesia to assist Muslim rulers against European invaders.

Suleyman declared himself the supreme caliph* of Islam. He regarded Christian-dominated Europe as the principal threat to the Muslim faith and considered his invasions of the continent to be part of a holy war against the enemies of Islam. In addition to European territories, Suleyman invaded Muslim lands, justifying these conquests by claiming that their rulers had abandoned orthodox* beliefs and practices. He was thus restoring true Islam to those areas.

The sultan also sponsored ambitious construction projects. During his reign, the Ottomans built mosques*, palaces, fortresses, bridges, and aqueducts across the empire. These structures represented a triumph of Islamic architecture. Suleyman's projects helped transform Istanbul, the seat of the empire, into an impressive center of Muslim civilization.

Many Muslims regard Suleyman as the perfect ruler. He helped to establish an Ottoman code of laws separate from the *shari'ah**. Historians celebrate his reign as a period of justice and harmony. Art, music, and philosophy thrived under Suleyman, and the sultan himself was a talented poet.

Internal conflict plagued the later years of Suleyman's reign. The sultan had one of his sons executed for creating disorder in Asia Minor. A long-standing dispute between the princes Selim and Bayezid over succession to Suleyman's throne resulted in Bayezid's death. In 1566 Suleyman died while leading a military campaign in Hungary. Later sultans could not match Suleyman's ability, and the Ottoman Empire began an era of decentralized rule. (*See also* **Christianity and Islam; Istanbul; Ottoman Empire; Safavid Dynasty.**)

Sultan

The Arabic term *sultan* refers to the qualities of power, might, and authority, or to a ruler who has these attributes. The Qur'an* asserts that the source of all authority is God. The hadith* use the word *sultan* to describe worldly power or those who possess political authority.

Muslims began applying the term to individuals in the late 900s. A leader of the Ghaznavid dynasty* in Afghanistan, Mahmud (998–1030) served as the first Muslim ruler to bear the title. The Seljuks adopted the term soon after defeating the Ghaznavid sultan Mas'ud in 1040. The Abbasid caliph* conferred the title on the Seljuk leader Toghril Beg in 1051. His action affirmed Beg's power in the Islamic world.

With the creation of this new office, Muslim legal scholars began to debate the balance of authority between sultan and caliph. Certain religious and legal experts held that the caliph, as guardian of the faith, held the dominant position. Others maintained that the sultan deserved top honors as leader of the army and head of the bureaucracy*. The scholar Abu Hamid al-Ghazali (died 1111) defined the sultanate* as a bridge between religion and state. Muslim theorists concluded that an Islamic state should have a caliph to guarantee Islamic law, a sultan to preserve it, and *ulama** to interpret it. The sultan emerged as the leading political force in the Islamic world, maintaining legitimacy by upholding *shari'ah**.

Several Muslim empires adopted the office of sultan. A caliph typically gave the title to a worthy individual. Rulers of the Ottoman Empire* combined the offices of sultan and caliph to legitimize their role as Islamic leaders. Only Oman, Brunei, and Malaysia continue to use the title of sultan. In Oman, this figure has absolute power, while in Malaysia, sultans have limited authority within a parliamentary system of government. (*See also* **Amir; Caliph; Ghazali, Abu Hamid al-; Vizier.**)

* **Qur'an** book of the holy scriptures of Islam

* **hadith** reports of the words and deeds of Muhammad (not in the Qur'an, but accepted as guides for Muslim behavior)

* **dynasty** succession of rulers from the same family or group

* **caliph** religious and political leader of an Islamic state

* **bureaucracy** agencies and officials that comprise a government

* **sultanate** government of a sultan, the political and military ruler of a Muslim dynasty or state

* **ulama** religious scholars

* **shari'ah** Islamic law as established in the Qur'an and sunnah, the exemplary behavior of the Prophet Muhammad

* **Ottoman Empire** large Turkish state existing from the early 1300s to the early 1900s

Sunnah

Since pre-Islamic* times, the Arabic word *sunnah* has referred to a body of established customs and beliefs that make up a tradition. In Muslim legal and religious thought, the term became associated more specifically with the actions and sayings of the Prophet Muhammad. Inspired by God to act wisely and in accordance with his will, Muhammad provided an example that complements God's revelation* as expressed in the Qur'an*. His actions and sayings became a model for Muslim conduct as well as a primary source of Islamic law.

Because early Muslim teachings were transmitted orally, some disagreement arose about the basis of the sunnah. Scholars studied the various hadith, reports of the words and deeds of Muhammad, to develop a comprehensive, authentic source. The competing explanations and definitions of the sunnah reflected the intellectual and ideological diversity of

* **pre-Islamic** refers to the Arabian Peninsula or to the Arabic language before the founding of Islam in the early 600s

* **revelation** message from God to humans transmitted through a prophet

* **Qur'an** book of the holy scriptures of Islam

* **doctrine** principle, theory, or belief that is taught or presented for acceptance

* **Sunni** refers to the largest branch of the Muslim community; the name derives from sunnah, the exemplary behavior of the Prophet Muhammad

* **jurisprudence** science of law

* **Shi'i** refers to Muslims who believe that Muhammad chose Ali ibn Abi Talib and his descendants as the spiritual-political leaders of the Muslim community

* **imam** spiritual-political leader in Shi'i Islam, one who is regarded as directly descended from Muhammad; also, one who leads prayers

* **Sufi** refers to Sufism, which seeks to develop spirituality through discipline of the mind and body

the early Muslim community. The concept of the sunnah, however, always remained important to the quest for meaning and certainty in Islamic practice and doctrine*.

The expansion of Muslim territory and the existence of local tradition in the new lands created a need for a framework to deal with emerging legal and administrative conflicts. In this environment, Muslim scholars worked to put together the various interpretations of the sunnah. In the 800s, Sunni* jurist Muhammad al-Shafi'i (767–820) sought to establish a strict definition of the term. He believed that the sunnah complemented the Qur'an by illustrating the principles of the sacred text, and he wanted to use it as an additional basis for Islamic law. He insisted that scholars study the hadith very closely to document the authoritative sunnah.

Al-Shafi'i's definition of the sunnah created a formal, rigorous, and text-based framework for Muslim jurisprudence* and legal practice. Sunni Muslims eventually accepted the notion that the sunnah of the Prophet was best preserved through this type of framework. Shi'i* Muslims, however, continued to believe that the ideals of the Prophet could best be realized by following the teachings of the divinely guided imams*, who interpreted the sunnah.

In Sufi* writings, which reflect an emphasis on the mystical dimensions of Muslim thought and practice, the sunnah includes the Prophet's spiritual values. Sufis believe that Muhammad transmitted these values through a series of Sufi teachers. For Sufis, the sunnah provides a concrete example of how Muslims might imitate the Prophet's behavior regarding prayer and following the path toward spiritual perfection.

Since the late 1700s, when Islamic societies began to have more interaction with European powers, the nature and authority of the sunnah have come under scrutiny. New codes of behavior based on European models emerged, particularly in the areas of law, public administration, and government. Muslim reformers sought to halt this trend. Egyptian scholar Muhammad Abduh (1849–1905), for example, argued that Islam could be reconciled with progress and a scientific worldview. He advocated *ijtihad* (independent reasoning) and criticized *taqlid*, or unquestioned acceptance of tradition. Abduh did not reject the sunnah. Instead, he emphasized the difference between essential and nonessential traditions and urged Muslims to apply reason to the primary sources of Islam.

Traditionalist thinkers, by contrast, regarded the sunnah as unchanging and therefore not subject to human interpretation. Others have argued that the concept of sunnah remains valid because it serves as a tool to bring about change that benefits society.

In the later part of the 1900s, debate about the role of the sunnah took on greater significance as many Muslim countries attempted to incorporate Islamic tradition into their legal systems. This has been the case in Egypt, Iran, Libya, Pakistan, Saudi Arabia, Sudan, and elsewhere. As in the past, however, the importance of the sunnah as a source of guidance for believers transcends its public uses. The sunnah continues to influence Muslim identity and to enhance the moral lives of believers throughout the Islamic community. (*See also* **Hadith; Law; Muhammad.**)

Sunni Islam

After the death of the Prophet Muhammad in 632, strong differences arose over the method of choosing the leader of the Muslim community. These disagreements ultimately resulted in the division of Muslims into two major groups—Sunni* and Shi'i*. Sunnis, who represent about 85 percent of the world's 1.2 billion Muslims, reject the views of Shi'is and members of other Islamic sects* on the issue of religious authority after Muhammad's death.

Core Beliefs. The term *sunni* comes from the word *sunnah*, which literally means "the trodden path" and refers to Islamic customs based on the exemplary behavior of Muhammad. In addition to the sunnah, which serves as an important source of guidance for all Muslims, Sunnis rely on *ijma* (the

* **Sunni** refers to the largest branch of the Muslim community; the name derives from sunnah, the exemplary behavior of the Prophet Muhammad

* **Shi'i** refers to Muslims who believe that Muhammad chose Ali ibn Abi Talib and his descendants as the spiritual-political leaders of the Muslim community

* **sect** religious group adhering to distinctive beliefs

Abu Hamid al-Ghazali, a leading Sunni scholar who died in 1111, wrote extensively about his beliefs. His treatise *Revival of the Religious Sciences* was an attempt to integrate law, theology, ethics, and mysticism. Exquisite calligraphy adorns the copy of the treatise shown here.

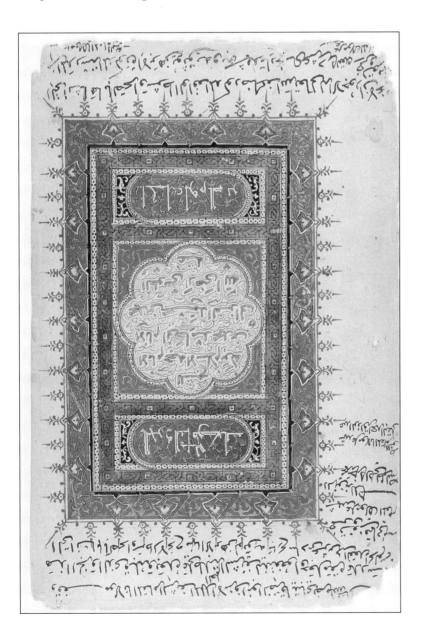

* **Qur'an** book of the holy scriptures of Islam

* **theological** refers to the study of the nature, qualities, and will of God

* **caliph** religious and political leader of an Islamic state

* **hadith** reports of the words and deeds of Muhammad (not in the Qur'an, but accepted as guides for Muslim behavior)

* **analogy** comparison based on resemblance

A Distinctly Islamic Document

In 1948 the United Nations adopted a Universal Declaration of Human Rights. In 1981 prominent Muslim thinkers issued a Universal Islamic Declaration of Human Rights. These documents identify many of the same fundamental rights and freedoms, including the right to life, the right to justice, the freedom of religion, and the freedom of speech. But the Muslim declaration articulates its standards in specifically Islamic terms. The document asserts that God is the source of all human rights and clearly states that the law on which it is based is *shari'ah*. It acknowledges the sacredness of human life as well as the sanctity of a person's body after death. According to the Universal Islamic Declaration of Human Rights, a Muslim's right to justice permits him or her to refuse to obey any command that contradicts *shari'ah*. For Muslims, the right to asylum includes sanctuary at a mosque in Mecca.

consensus, or agreement, of legal and religious scholars). The concept of consensus reflects the emphasis in Sunni Islam on community and its collective wisdom, instructed by the Qur'an* and sunnah.

Sunni Islam encompasses diverse points of view based on historical setting, location, and culture as well as the ideas of various theological* and legal schools. Nevertheless, Sunni Muslims share certain distinctive beliefs. They reject the claim of Shi'i Muslims that Muhammad designated Ali ibn Abi Talib, his son-in-law and cousin, as his successor and that only Ali's descendants have the legitimate right to lead the Islamic community. Sunnis assert that the Prophet did not name a successor. They accept the authority of the first four caliphs* after Muhammad. Known as the Rashidun, or "rightly guided," caliphs, these were accepted collectively by the Islamic community.

Early Struggles. Sunni Islam developed as a result of political and religious struggles early in the history of Islam. An army revolt in 656 resulted in the murder of Uthman ibn Affan, the third caliph. Ali ibn Abi Talib became the leader of the Islamic community, but Mu'awiyah, who ruled in Syria and was related to the slain caliph, refused to acknowledge Ali. He demanded that Uthman's killers be brought to justice. Civil war erupted. Some of Ali's troops withdrew their loyalty from him, but they also continued to oppose Mu'awiyah. This group became known as Kharijis (seceders). They rejected both Uthman and Ali as legitimate caliphs, a position that led to difficult questions about Muslim belief and law and to the development of various sects within the Islamic community.

In 661 after a Khariji murdered Ali, Mu'awiyah became caliph. His reign marked the beginning of the Ummayad caliphate. During this time, disputes arose within the Islamic community over such issues as the definition of true belief, the status of those who profess Islam but commit a major sin, and whether human beings are truly free to choose their own actions or whether an all-knowing God predetermines all actions. These became basic questions for later Sunni thinkers who sought to formulate opinions that conformed to the Qur'an and the sunnah. In 750 the Umayyad caliphate fell to the Abbasids, who were descendants of the Prophet's uncle al-Abbas. During the Abbasid caliphate (750–1258), Sunni Islam became firmly established.

Four different schools of Sunni law emerged during Abbasid rule: Hanafi, Maliki, Shafi'i, and Hanbali. In addition to the Qur'an and sunnah, which is based on the hadith*, Sunni Muslims sometimes use *qiyas* (reasoning through analogy*) and *ijma* to form laws. The four schools of law differ in their reliance on *qiyas* and *ijma*. Sunnis consider all four schools to be authentic and acceptable to God, but most Sunnis generally follow the school that is prevalent locally.

During the early years of the Abbasid caliphate, Sunnis faced two challenges: the growing influence of rationalist thought and the rise to power of the Shi'is. The rationalists used reason as the basis for the establishment of religious truth. They taught that God created the Qur'an, meaning that it was not a part of his eternal essence, although it expresses his eternal will. They also held that people have free will to choose between good and evil. These beliefs, promoted by a group known as the Mu'tazilis, alienated traditional Muslims, who maintained that the Qur'an exists eternally and that God has absolute power over all people and events.

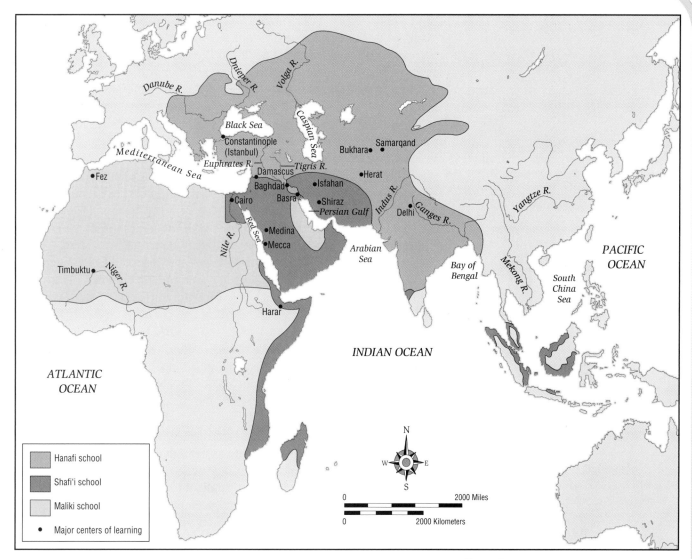

Map legend:
- Hanafi school
- Shafi'i school
- Maliki school
- • Major centers of learning

In the early 800s, the caliph al-Ma'mun embraced Mu'tazili teachings and attempted to impose them on his subjects. He and his successors persecuted dissenters, including the respected theologian* and legal scholar Ahmad Ibn Hanbal, provoking a reaction against rationalism. Within the next century, other schools of Islamic thought, which bridged the gap between a literal interpretation of the Qur'an and one based on reason, became prominent.

In the early 900s, the Shi'is gained considerable prestige and influence. The Fatimid dynasty established a caliphate in North Africa in 910 and took control of Egypt in 969, making it their base of operations. A rival Shi'i dynasty, the Buyids, became the effective rulers of Baghdad in 945. The Sunnis recaptured their power in 1055, however, when the Seljuk Turks conquered Baghdad. The Sunnis also provided military opposition to the Fatimids in Syria and nonviolent opposition through the writings of such prominent Sunni thinkers as Abu Hamid al-Ghazali (died 1111). Saladin (died 1193), who was Islam's great defender against the crusaders*, destroyed the Fatimid caliphate in 1171.

The four major Sunni schools of law—Hanafi, Maliki, Shafi'i, and Hanbali—all developed in the 700s and 800s. The map shows areas dominated by the first three schools around 1500. The Hanbali school had few followers during this period, but its influence rose again in the 1700s.

* **theologian** person who studies the nature, qualities, and will of God

* **crusader** person who participated in the holy wars against the Muslims during the Middle Ages

125

Scripture and Law. During the 1700s, reform movements emerged in Sunni Islam, as Muslim scholars looked for ways to renew Islamic thought and life to meet the demands of changing times. These movements gained momentum over the next two centuries with the colonization of Islamic countries by European powers. Islamic reformers such as Sayyid Ahmad Khan (1817–1898), Muhammad Abduh (1849–1905), and Muhammad Rashid Rida (1865–1935) published new interpretations of the Qu'ran. In the 1940s, Egyptian scholar Amin al-Khuli initiated a new approach to study of the sacred text, treating it as a literary document to be analyzed by literary methods. This approach, however, met with strong opposition from traditional Muslim authorities.

Two Algerian scholars also developed new approaches to the Qur'an. In his book *The Qur'anic Phenomena*, Malek Bennabi focuses on understanding the Qur'an as revelation* and deals with the issue of a human being—who has personal views, experience, and background—receiving a divine message. Mohammed Arkoun uses modern theories of language and symbolism to interpret the Qur'an. Arkoun's work differs considerably from the thousands of modern Sunni publications on the Qur'an because it raises new questions about the literary and historical aspects of Islam's holy book and its interpretation.

In recent years, Sunnis have placed renewed emphasis on the *sirah* literature, which deals with the biography of Muhammad. Scholars have explored the sociopolitical conditions of the Prophet's era and the historical causes for the rise of the Islamic state. The reliability of the hadith has also come under scrutiny.

Sunni scholars have also addressed concerns regarding *shari'ah**. Although the writings of medieval* jurists continue to be held in high regard, Muslim modernists have noted that their work represents a human attempt to understand divine law. As such, it should be open to review and revision. These reformers advocate a continuous reinterpretation of Islamic texts so that Muslims can develop institutions of education, law, and government suited to modern conditions.

Political Issues. The role of *shari'ah* in matters of constitutional law and the organization of the state has become a central concern for Sunni Muslims. After the Turkish government abolished the caliphate in 1924, controversy arose regarding the proper form of an Islamic government. Egyptian scholar Ali Abd al-Raziq argued that the Qur'an did not bestow special legitimacy on the caliphate and refuted the traditional belief that Islam requires a particular form of state and government. In his writings, Abd al-Raziq made an important distinction between Muhammad the prophet* and religious teacher and Muhammad the statesman, insisting that the political character of Islam is separate from its religious character.

Abd al-Raziq's ideas met with fierce resistance from traditional Muslim authorities. His book on Islam and government was banned, and some Muslim organizations rejected his teachings. The Muslim Brotherhood, founded in Egypt in 1928, claimed that Islam prescribes a religious social order that can develop only in an Islamic state. Historically, factions within the brotherhood advocated the use of violence, if necessary, to create such a state. Sayyid Abu al-Ala Mawdudi, founder of the Jamaat-i Islami party in South Asia, believed that an Islamic revolution—not necessarily of a violent

* **revelation** message from God to humans transmitted through a prophet

* **shari'ah** Islamic law as established in the Qur'an and sunnah, the exemplary behavior of the Prophet Muhammad

* **medieval** refers to the Middle Ages, a period roughly between 500 and 1500

* **prophet** one who announces divinely inspired revelations

nature—was necessary to reform existing society according to Islamic ideals. Today the various Islamic states apply *shari'ah* in widely different ways.

In modern times, Sunni Muslims have also attempted to reconcile some prominent Western ideas with Islam. During the early 1900s, the issue of nationalism* prompted intense debate. Traditionally, the leaders of the Islamic community supported the struggle for independence from colonial rule but rejected nationalism as a threat to the political unity of all Muslims.

After World War II ended in 1945, the fight against European powers resulted in the founding of new nation-states with Muslim majorities. Sunni thinkers did not object when the leaders of such states established Islamic governments. But when these leaders adopted secular* political systems, questions about the compatibility between Islam and democracy emerged. Supporters of democracy argued that the early Muslim concept of *shura*, an advisory council to the head of state, was a model of democracy. They also asserted that democracy, which insisted on the individual responsibility of its citizens, was a necessity for the development of Muslim societies. Those who supported the idea of an Islamic state argued that the democracy created under Islam is different from the Western model of democracy.

The relationship between socialism* and Islam has prompted even more discussion. In 1959 Mustafa al-Sibai, a legal scholar and head of the Syrian branch of the Muslim Brotherhood, published a book in which he argued that socialism and Islam were compatible. His model of Islamic socialism combined the principles of equality, justice, and responsibility. He claimed that Islamic socialism would eliminate poverty and enable Muslim societies to prosper. Egyptian leader Gamal Abdel Nasser and others in the Arab world embraced al-Sibai's ideas. But not all Islamic thinkers or activists agreed with the concept. Sayyid Qutb, a key figure in the Egyptian branch of the Muslim Brotherhood during Nasser's regime, condemned the idea of Islamic socialism. He believed that Islam alone provided the solution to the social, economic, national, and moral problems created by capitalism* and communism*. Sunni thinkers continue to debate whether social change should follow socialist ideals or Islamic ideals.

The Past and Present. Modern Sunni thought has increasingly concerned itself with questions of history. Muslim scholars consider the effects on the Middle East of various experiences and events. These include European imperialism*, World War I and World War II, and the subsequent nonmilitary struggle between the United States and the former Soviet Union known as the Cold War. In addition, scholars explore the impact on the Middle East of the establishment of Israel, rivalries among Muslim countries, and the rapid economic changes resulting from the discovery of oil. Some Muslim authors study the rise and fall of nations and civilizations and explore questions surrounding the future, such as whether the West or Islam will dominate the world. Others consider the place of Islam in the ongoing history of religions and take a scholarly interest in faiths other than Islam.

One of the striking features in contemporary Islamic thought is the growing call for a distinctly Islamic perspective and approach to social needs. Those who support these views regard Islam as a total way of life, encompassing both religious and worldly matters. Although the United Nations has adopted and proclaimed a Universal Declaration of Human Rights, for example, Mus-

* **nationalism** feelings of loyalty and devotion to one's country and a commitment to its independence

* **secular** separate from religion in human life and society; connected to everyday life

* **socialism** economic system in which the government owns and operates the means of production and the distribution of goods

* **capitalism** economic system in which businesses are privately owned and operated and where competition exists in a free-market environment

* **communism** political and economic system based on the concept of shared ownership of all property

* **imperialism** extension of power and influence over another country or region

* **jihad** literally "striving"; war in defense of Islam

lim leaders have proposed a separate Universal Islamic Declaration of Human Rights. This growing concern with Islam has led to an increasing concentration on subjects such as jihad*, religious tolerance, religious freedom, and the status of women. It has also contributed to a view that the Western world is an enemy of the Muslim world and a threat to Islam.

Yet other ways of thinking about Islam exist. For some Muslims, it is a domain of personal experience and of communal norms and values. For others, it is a realm of creative effort and enlightenment. Modern Sunni scholarship and literature reveals the immense variety among Muslim thinkers and the many interpretations permitted by Islam. (*See also* **Abbasid Caliphate; Ali Ibn Abi Talib; Government; Islam: Overview; Islamic State; Khariji; Law; Mu'tazili; Shi'i Islam; Socialism and Islam; Umayyad Caliphate.**)

Swahili

The term *Swahili* refers to the mixed African and Arabic culture that exists along Africa's east coast. Around the 900s, Bantu-speaking peoples from Central Africa moved into the area that is now Kenya. Arab merchants from the Persian Gulf also settled on the east African coast, hoping to profit from the trade routes there. Arabic and Bantu cultures combined to form a new culture called Swahili, from the Arabic word *sawahil*, meaning "the coast." Swahili also refers to the language spoken in this area, composed mostly of Bantu, with some Arabic elements.

As the Bantus and Arabs traveled south along the coast, a series of independent Swahili city-states arose in the present-day countries of Somalia, Kenya, Tanzania, Mozambique, and Zimbabwe. The people of these city-states established trade routes to the interior, dealing in goods such as ivory, ebony, gold, and slaves. Swahili cities became centers of international commerce, with links to places as far away as India and China. Portuguese merchants arrived in the 1500s, however, taking away much of the local trade. The Gulf state of Oman wrested eastern Africa away from Portugal in the late 1600s, and the British colonized the area in the early 1900s. East African nations gained their independence in the latter half of the century.

Swahili culture survived the collapse of its political structures and remains strong today. Merchants continue to play a leading role in East Africa's trade economy. The popularity of the Muslim faith in the region owes much to the Swahili-speaking people, who spread Islam among their inland neighbors. Swahili culture involves a stricter version of Islam than that practiced by most Africans. By 2000 the Swahili language had become increasingly important throughout East and Central Africa. (*See also* **East Africa.**)

Syria

Slightly larger than North Dakota, Syria lies in the heart of the Middle East. It shares borders with Turkey, Iraq, Jordan, and Lebanon. It also shares a small but politically significant border on the southwest with Israel. Syria's capital, Damascus, served as the political and cultural center of the first Islamic caliphate*. Although no longer the seat of Middle Eastern power, Syria still exercises substantial influence in the Muslim world.

Around 90 percent of Syrians are Arabs. Kurds, Armenians, and other ethnic* groups make up the other 10 percent. About 90 percent of the population adheres to various forms of Islam; Christians and small groups of Jews account for the remaining 10 percent.

History and Government

One of the earliest civilizations, Syria played a key role in several ancient empires. In those times, it had a prosperous trade route and carried goods such as wine, silk, and Indian spices throughout the Middle East. Christianity began in the greater Syrian region, and Christians emerged as the majority there around the 500s. However, medieval* Syria—composed of parts of present-day Turkey, Iraq, Lebanon, Israel, Jordan, and Saudi Arabia—became a fertile ground for the spread of Islam.

First Muslim Dynasty. Syria became part of the Byzantine* Empire in the 300s. It experienced Muslim invasions in 633, and by 638, the Muslims had expelled the Christian leaders of Syria and established their own rule. The first Islamic dynasty*, the Umayyads, built their capital in Damascus. Over the next century, they expanded their territory as far west as Spain and as far east as India. Many of their subjects converted to Islam, including a large number of Christians. The Umayyad caliphs grew wealthy from taxes and conquests. They used their money to improve agriculture and irrigation and to build impressive monuments such as the Dome of the Rock in Jerusalem.

In 750 the Umayyads lost power to the Abbasid dynasty, which moved the capital of the Islamic empire to Baghdad. Syria declined in importance and wealth, but its cities still enjoyed a large measure of autonomy*. The Fatimid dynasty, which supported Shi'ism*, gradually took over from the

* **caliphate** office and government of the caliph, the religious and political leader of an Islamic state

* **ethnic** relating to groups of people who share a common racial, national, tribal, religious, linguistic, or cultural background

* **medieval** refers to the Middle Ages, a period roughly between 500 and 1500

* **Byzantine** refers to the Eastern Christian Empire that was based in Constantinople

* **dynasty** succession of rulers from the same family or line

* **autonomy** self-government

* **Shi'ism** branch of Islam that believes Muhammad chose Ali ibn Abi Talib and his descendants as the spiritual-political leaders of the Muslim community

The ancient Romans left their mark on Syria, a province of the empire, with buildings such as the amphitheater shown here. In the 300s Syria became part of the Byzantine Empire. However, by 638 Muslims had gained control of the region, and Damascus emerged as the capital of the Umayyad caliphate.

Syria

* **Sunni** refers to the largest branch of the Muslim community; the name derives from sunnah, the exemplary behavior of the Prophet Muhammad

* **sultan** political and military ruler of a Muslim dynasty or state

* **Crusades** during the Middle Ages, the holy wars declared by the pope against non-Christians, mostly Muslims

* **Ottoman Empire** large Turkish state existing from the early 1300s to the early 1900s

* **coup** sudden, and often violent, overthrow of a ruler or government

 See map in Middle East (vol. 2).

Sunni* Abbasids. Unpopular among many of their subjects, the Fatimids gave way to a Sunni Turkish dynasty called the Seljuks around the 1050s. The Seljuks put an end to the autonomy of many Syrian cities by placing Syria under direct rule of the sultan*.

Crusaders and Mongols. The Seljuk empire did not maintain its strong grip for long, however, and Syria disintegrated into many small kingdoms by the 1100s. In this weakened state, it suffered an invasion by European armies during the First Crusade*. The crusaders founded a series of Christian kingdoms along the coast and conquered Jerusalem in 1099. Muslim armies under the great warrior Saladin recovered Jerusalem in 1187, but the crusader kingdoms along the coast of Syria remained intact for another century.

In the mid-1200s, the Mongol armies of Genghis Khan's successors invaded Syria and briefly occupied Damascus. By the 1260s, the Egyptian Mamluk dynasty drove the Mongols from Syria and swept the remaining crusader kingdoms from the coast. Syria became a province of an empire centered in Egypt and lost its leading role in regional affairs. In 1516 the Ottoman Turks invaded the region. Syria remained under the rule of the Ottoman Empire* until its defeat in World War I (1914–1918).

Independence and Revolt. During World War I, Amir Faysal of the Meccan Hashemite clan seized control of Damascus from the Turks. After the war, he and his supporters proclaimed an independent Kingdom of Syria with Faysal as its ruler. However, the British and French had already agreed to let France run Syria after the war, and France forced Faysal out of power in 1920. Syrians rebelled against French rule several times in the following years, but the country did not win its independence until 1946, after World War II (1939–1945) had severely weakened France.

After gaining its independence, the Syrian Arab Republic went through a period of political confusion and violence. The first government fell to a military coup* in 1949, and the army ruled the country until 1954. In 1958 Syria and Egypt merged into the short-lived United Arab Republic. This arrangement lasted until a 1961 uprising led to new Syrian leadership. By 1963 Syria had experienced nine coups. The ruling Ba'th Party outlawed other political parties that year, and Ba'th leaders have remained in power ever since.

In addition to internal problems, Syria had conflicts with some of its neighbors, especially Israel. Syria joined other Arab countries in attacking the Jewish state when it declared independence in 1948 and again during the Six-Day War of 1967. During the 1967 hostilities, Israel seized the Golan Heights, a high ground separating Israel from Syria. Although the United Nations Security Council called for Israeli withdrawal from this territory, the Israelis remain reluctant to give it up.

In 1970 Hafiz al-Assad became president of Syria, a post he held until his death 30 years later. Strongly opposed to Israel, Assad funded Palestinian terrorist* groups operating out of Lebanon. He refused to let them attack from Syria, however, and suppressed terrorist activity during the Lebanese civil war (1975–1991) in order to avoid Israeli attack. Syrian troops maintain a strong presence in Lebanon, despite the desire of many Lebanese for their removal. Bashir al-Assad, who became president after his father's death, has yet to address this issue.

Religion and Politics

Almost 75 percent of Syrian Muslims are Sunnis, with the remainder made up of four Shi'i sects*: Alawi, Ismaili, Druze, and Twelvers. The largest of these is the Alawi, considered a heretical* group by many Sunnis. The Alawi, however, have held leadership positions in the country since the 1970s. Although composed of many different religious groups, Syria retains a mostly secular* government.

Islam and Syrian Independence. Under the Ottoman Empire, Syrian *ulama** enjoyed considerable power and wealth, and they repaid the sultans by helping to maintain order in the state. In the early 1800s, for example, the *ulama* opposed an anti-Ottoman revolution backed by Arabian reformers known as Wahhabis. The close relationship between mosque* and state, however, eroded in the mid-1800s as European powers gained more influence in the empire. Concerned about the growing Christian presence in Syria, many Muslims participated in anti-Christian riots. An 1860 uprising in Damascus led to a massacre. The Ottomans blamed the violence on the *ulama* and punished scholars with imprisonment and exile. They then established a secular government largely without *ulama* participation.

Syrian Muslims challenged Ottoman authority and called for a return to an Islamic state. They founded religious institutions and schools all over the country, although various groups clashed on matters of doctrine. The French occupation of Syria after World War I crushed the hopes of these Islamic reformers. Under French rule, however, a nationalist* movement arose that united the country's many religious factions. To build support among different groups, the movement stressed issues of concern to all Syrians. Although largely secular, the movement relied on slogans and symbols that appealed to Muslims. It thus gained the backing of the *ulama*, and eventually helped bring about Syrian independence.

During the French occupation, minority groups such as the Alawi and Druze also rose in power. Under the Ottomans, Sunni elites in the cities had filled key commercial and government jobs. The French, however, extended political authority to the countryside, where the majority of the Shi'i Muslims lived. The influx of rural Shi'is into the government weakened the influence of the Sunni religious leaders. It also ensured Syria's new role as a secular state because leaders did not want to alienate sections of the population by promoting their own religious views.

Syria After Independence. Soon after independence, Syria demonstrated its commitment to secular politics. In 1949 the country abandoned the Ottoman legal code and adopted an Egyptian system that relied less heavily on traditional Islamic law. That same year, the government took control of private funds called *waqf** that financed the activities of mosques. Seizing these funds allowed the state to reward the religious leaders who supported it and punish those who did not.

The new republic, however, made some concessions to Islamic reformers. In 1953 the government reinforced Islam's influence over family life with a Law of Personal Status governing marriage, divorce, inheritance, and other matters. This code applies Islamic law to Sunnis, Alawis, and Ismailis. Druze, Christians, and Jews each have separate codes. The government made fur-

* **sect** religious group adhering to distinctive beliefs

* **heretical** characterized by a belief that is contrary to established religious doctrine

* **secular** separate from religion in human life and society; connected to everyday life

* *ulama* religious scholars

* **mosque** Muslim place of worship

* **nationalism** feelings of loyalty and devotion to one's country and a commitment to its independence

* *waqf* donation of property for charitable causes

Pan-Arab Experiment

From 1958 to 1961, Syria and Egypt merged their governments in a political experiment called the United Arab Republic (UAR). This union came about largely because of the desire of the Ba'th Party to eliminate Russian influence in Syria and to create a Pan-Arab state. Egypt's leader Gamal Abdel Nasser, however, opposed many Ba'thist ideas. Under the UAR, the Ba'th Party suffered a decline in power. Cairo became the capital of the new republic, and Egypt played the dominant role in setting policy. Many Syrians resented these developments. After the Syrian government fell in a military coup in 1961, the new leadership withdrew from the union, dissolving the UAR. Egypt, however, kept the state's name until Nasser's death in 1971.

ther concessions to Islamic reformers in the 1973 constitution, which required the head of state to be Muslim and cited Islamic law as the main source for all legislation.

Such moves, however, did not satisfy the Syrians who wanted Islam to play a larger role in public life. Many criticized the government for failing to establish Islam as the state religion. Dissatisfaction with the Ba'th party led to uprisings in the 1960s and 1970s, all of which were crushed by the government.

As President al-Assad worked to suppress his political opponents, Islamic groups such as the Muslim Brotherhood led anti-government resistance. Some factions supported armed struggle to overthrow the government. They had little influence in rural areas, however, and could gain no support among people of minority sects, who had a better life under secular rule than under Islamic rule. As a result, Islamic groups remained largely ineffective in challenging the Syrian regime.

The Ba'th party's hostility toward Islamic political groups is not reflected in its social policies, however. Although the regime assumed control over all religious schools in 1967, it allowed Islamic instruction to continue. Newspapers and television promote Syria's Muslim heritage, and the government has made no attempt to halt the distribution of religious materials. Damascus University maintains departments of Islamic law and literature. The Ba'th regime thus provides citizens the means to fulfill their religious obligations without enforcing any particular religious belief. (*See also* **Alawi; Arab-Israeli Conflict; Druze; Ismaili; Lebanon; Secularism.**)

Taliban

* **conservative** generally opposed to change, especially in existing political and social institutions

The Taliban came to power in Afghanistan in 1996 and ruled major portions of the country until they were forced out by the United States in October 2001. The group gained notoriety for providing haven to Osama bin Laden and his al-Qaeda network and for destroying ancient Buddha statues in Bamyan Province in 2000. The Taliban's strict and conservative* interpretation of Islam led to severe restrictions on women and on most cultural and entertainment activities. Although many of their policies have been attributed to Islam, they can be better understood as expressions of the ethnic Pashtun culture to which the group belonged.

Origins. The Taliban (which means "students") hailed from the poorest, most conservative and least literate Pashtun provinces in Afghanistan. The group led by Mullah Muhammad Omar, which gained the spotlight in 1994, came from Kandahar. The women in this region wore traditional garments that covered their bodies completely, except for their eyes, and the girls received no education. The Taliban believed these practices were required by the Qur'an and sought to impose them throughout the country. In their view, control over women and the exclusion of women from the public sphere was the hallmark of a truly Islamic society—as well as a symbol of manhood.

Though known as religious students, most Taliban members had little exposure to Islamic teaching and scholarship. Their education was limited to basic instruction in the Qur'an, Islamic law, and early Islamic history. As a result, they flatly rejected modern values, ideas, social structures, religious diversity, and modern political and economic theories. They did not engage in scholarly writing or debate and produced no systematic ideology*.

The Taliban have often been identified with Wahhabism, the conservative interpretation of Islam practiced in Saudi Arabia. In fact, the Taliban are Deobandis, followers of an Indo-Pakistani school of thought, but they have also been influenced by Wahhabi puritanical tendencies. The Taliban embraced and carried to an extreme the Deobandi opposition to Shi'ism, commitment to the implementation of Islamic law, and restrictions on the role of women. They discarded the Deobandi traditions of education and reform.

Taliban Rule. When the former Soviet Union withdrew from Afghanistan in 1989, the warlords (regional chieftains) who had previously fought the Soviets turned against each other and battled for control of the country. These warlords represented various ethnic groups and interpretations of Islam and were backed by different foreign countries. A short-lived coalition government between two of the warlords was followed by civil war.

The Taliban arose as a response to the rising lawlessness and ethnic conflict. They claimed that the mujahidin—those who had fought in the holy war against the Soviet invaders—had lost their right to rule by failing to obey Islamic law and by contributing to the rampant corruption and disorder in Afghanistan. By contrast, the Taliban presented themselves as purifiers and restorers of an Islamic way of life that would bring peace and prosperity to the country. The Taliban captured the Afghan capital of Kabul on September 27, 1996. Once in power, they used this claim of purifying Islam as a justification for persecuting other ethnic groups, particularly the Shi'i Tajiks.

Two of the legends surrounding the Taliban's initial appearance on the political scene center on their protection of women and the poor from rapacious warlords. Because of their willingness to physically confront those who abused the poor and defenseless, the Taliban were viewed by many as Robin Hood–like figures. The only "reward" the Taliban asked for was assistance in establishing a just Islamic system. They neither expected nor received monetary reimbursement for their deeds.

During their time in power, the Taliban did bring law and order back to Afghanistan. Their main achievement was to restore security on the roads, facilitating the transport of food and commercial goods. They also sought to disarm the general population, believing that the massive inflow of arms into Afghanistan was partially responsible for the social chaos and insecurity. In addition, their implementation of strict and conservative Islamic law, with harsh punishments such as the amputation of hands for theft, provided a structure for the legal system. The war-weary populace initially welcomed these developments.

The Taliban proved as incapable of governing as previous regimes, however. They had no effective programs for education, public health, finance, or communications. They believed that their policy of Islamic reform combined with the strict and literal implementation of traditional Islamic law would resolve all social issues and restore order and prosperity to Afghanistan.

In the early years, the Taliban ruled through a system of collective leadership based on consultation and consensus building. By 1996, however, the

* **ideology** system of ideas or beliefs

 See map in Middle East (vol. 2).

decision-making process had changed to one of secrecy, centralization of authority, and dictatorship. Mullah Omar declared himself the "Commander of the Faithful," asserted his exclusive right to interpret Islamic law and run the country, and distanced himself from both the general population and day-to-day politics. He refused to broaden the base of Taliban leadership or talk to members of the opposition.

The Taliban association with Osama bin Laden began only in December 1997. Bin Laden's influence on the Taliban can best be seen in the shift from their original goal of restoring law and order and rebuilding Afghanistan to their embrace of a Pan-Islamic* ideology that included the declaration of support for the global jihad* against the United States. (*See also* **Afghanistan; Bin Laden, Osama; Qaeda, al-; Wahhabi.**)

* **Pan-Islamic** refers to the movement to unify all Islamic peoples

* **jihad** literally "striving"; war in defense of Islam

Tamerlane

1336–1405
Mongol conqueror

* **dynasty** succession of rulers from the same family or group

Tamerlane, also known as Timur Lang (Timur the Lame), was a Mongol chieftain who conquered much of Central Asia and the Middle East in the late 1300s. Known for his brutality and destructiveness, he established a dynasty* that made many contributions to Muslim culture.

Tamerlane belonged to a tribe in Transoxania (modern Uzbekistan). He attracted a group of followers in the 1360s and set out to reconstruct the Mongol Empire as created by Genghis Khan (died 1227). After gaining control of Transoxania in 1370, Tamerlane turned his attention to neighboring regions. Ten years later, he had conquered Central Asia, leading victorious armies as far north as Moscow. During the next decade, Tamerlane became master of Persia, Iraq, Armenia, Azerbaijan, and Georgia. He also reconquered the rebellious Russians.

* **sultan** political and military ruler of a Muslim dynasty or state

* **Ottoman Empire** large Turkish state existing from the early 1300s to the early 1900s

* **artisan** skilled craftsperson

Tamerlane invaded India in 1398, defeating the sultan* of Delhi and destroying the city completely. Delhi took a century to recover. Tamerlane also attacked Egypt and the Ottoman Empire*, whose leaders had taken over some of his territories while he was fighting elsewhere. Tamerlane's army overran Syria, leaving Aleppo in ruins and moving all the artisans* in Damascus to the Mongol capital at Samarkand. His forces took Baghdad in 1401, toppling its monuments and killing tens of thousands of citizens. The following year, he stormed Anatolia, defeated the sultan, and sacked cities as far as the west coast of present-day Turkey. After signing a peace treaty with the Egyptians and Byzantines*, Tamerlane returned to Samarkand to plan an invasion of China. He set out on a campaign in 1405 but died before reaching the country.

* **Byzantine** refers to the Eastern Christian Empire that was based in Constantinople

Tamerlane owed his military success to his skillful use of mounted archers, a tactic made famous by the great Mongol conqueror Genghis Khan. He also excelled at negotiating with leaders, although he often relied on treachery, intrigue, and underhanded tactics to achieve his goals. He massacred and ruthlessly plundered in the lands he invaded, using much of the loot to enrich his capital. Samarkand became one of the world's most splendid cities, but Tamerlane rarely stayed there. Like most Mongol chieftains, he preferred to remain in camp and spent most of his time traveling with the army.

After Tamerlane's death, his sons divided his empire among themselves. Under their rule, the cities of Samarkand and Herat became centers of Muslim learning and culture. Tamerlane's son Ulugh Beg established an observatory in Samarkand, and artists in Herat developed an influential new style in which they divided paintings into several detailed scenes. In India, a descendant of Tamerlane later founded the Mughal Empire. (*See also* **Mongols; Mughal Empire.**)

Taqiyah

The act of concealing one's true religious beliefs in order to prevent death or injury to oneself or other Muslims is known as *taqiyah*. The Qur'an* permits Muslims who are subject to persecution to fulfill their religious obligations secretly in their hearts, rather than openly.

The practice of *taqiyah* is closely associated with Shi'i* Muslims, who claim that Sunnis* and those who hold political power have discriminated against them since the death of the Prophet Muhammad. Shi'is base their belief in *taqiyah* on the actions of Ali ibn Abi Talib, Muhammad's cousin and son-in-law. After the Prophet's death, some Muslims claimed that Ali was his legitimate successor. A majority, however, chose to follow Abu Bakr, who became the first caliph* after Muhammad. Instead of insisting immediately on his God-given right to lead the Muslim community, Ali temporarily accepted the rule of his opponents. He pledged his loyalty to them—even though he considered their leadership to be illegitimate—as a way to preserve his movement for the future.

Over time, pro-Shi'i movements used *taqiyah* to hide revolutionary activities. *Taqiyah* became a widely accepted practice, and in the 900s, Ibn Babawayh, a prominent Shi'i authority, declared it to be a religious obligation. Some scholars, however, voiced concerns about the danger of following a policy of deceit. They argued that *taqiyah* permits Shi'is to say anything and make any claim, and therefore, their words are not trustworthy. As a result, Shi'i scholars created rules for the use of *taqiyah*.

Today, Muslims continue to debate the appropriate application of *taqiyah*. Although jurists have identified the situations in which Muslims may practice *taqiyah*, in general, they advise against its use, whenever possible. (*See also* **Ali ibn Abi Talib; Shi'i Islam.**)

* **Qur'an** book of the holy scriptures of Islam

* **Shi'i** refers to Muslims who believe that Muhammad chose Ali ibn Abi Talib and his descendants as the spiritual-political leaders of the Muslim community

* **Sunni** refers to the largest branch of the Muslim community; the name derives from sunnah, the exemplary behavior of the Prophet Muhammad

* **caliph** religious and political leader of an Islamic state

Taqwa

A key concept of Islam, the term *taqwa* refers to piety, virtue, and a properly formed awareness or reverent fear of God. It appears in the Qur'an* more than 250 times, where it is equated with faith, justice, truthfulness, and obedience to God. The concept of *taqwa* is central to Sufi* spiritual thought and practice, but it has also acquired political significance among Muslim activists in modern times.

* **Qur'an** book of the holy scriptures of Islam

* **Sufi** refers to Sufism, which seeks to develop spirituality through discipline of the mind and body

The Indian-Pakistani scholar Sayyid Abu al-Ala Mawdudi (died 1979) identified *taqwa*, together with brotherhood and equality, as the foundation of a true Islamic society. Egyptian activist Sayyid Qutb (died 1966) regarded *taqwa* as an important aspect of Islamic political activity. For Sufis, the concept of *taqwa* implies deep spirituality and religious devotion. For Mawdudi and Qutb, the term had a more dynamic meaning, and it occupied a central place in their understanding of God's sovereignty in political matters.

Pakistani educator and modernist Fazlur Rahman (1919–1988) called *taqwa* "the most important single concept in the Qur'an." He argued that reverence for God provides human beings with insight and enables them to overcome their weaknesses. In his view, the Qur'an's central purpose is to develop this insight in Muslims, motivating them to take action and achieve progress in their societies. According to Rahman, *taqwa* involves a strong sense of moral responsibility and signifies an effort by an individual to align the public and private spheres of his or her life. (*See also* **Mawdudi, Sayyid Abu al-Ala; Modernism; Qutb, Sayyid.**)

Tawhid

The Arabic term *tawhid* means "making one" or "unifying." For Muslims, *tawhid* refers to the oneness of God. It also implies that Allah is a unity, not made up of separate parts. *Tawhid* serves as the defining concept of Islam. It establishes the religion's monotheistic* creed and asserts that God alone creates and sustains the universe.

* **monotheistic** refers to the belief that there is only one God

Classical Discussions. In the 700s, a group called the Mu'tazilis challenged the mainstream belief that the Qur'an* is eternal and a part of God. They argued that the text was created for humans within time and space. To believe otherwise compromised the concept of *tawhid* because God and the Qur'an could not be the same. The Mu'tazilis further held that God lacked features, such as hands and feet, and traits, such as will and desire. They maintained that Muslims should interpret Qur'anic references to such features as symbolic.

* **Qur'an** book of the holy scriptures of Islam

The Mu'tazili position peaked in popularity in the early 800s. The doctrine of an uncreated Qur'an, however, returned to prominence later in the century. The scholar Abu al-Hasan al-Ash'ari (died about 936) advanced a new theory, asserting that divine qualities such as speech, action, and will existed apart from God's essence and therefore did not jeopardize *tawhid*. God had created his own traits as well as the actions of humans. Muslims could never truly understand God's nature, so they must accept his revelations* without question. Ash'arism, based on the scholar's beliefs, served as the primary Sunni* doctrine until the 1800s.

* **revelation** message from God to humans transmitted through a prophet

* **Sunni** refers to the largest branch of the Muslim community; the name derives from sunnah, the exemplary behavior of the Prophet Muhammad

Muslim philosophers also discussed the principle of *tawhid*. They struggled to understand the relationship between divinity and creation and to explain how God in his oneness could have brought forth the many aspects of life. Influenced by the Greek philosophers Plato and Aristotle, these thinkers tried to determine whether the formation of the universe had changed God's nature. To resolve the issue, most made a distinction between divine essence and existence.

Sufi* thinkers viewed *tawhid* in mystical* terms. They claimed that God exists within every aspect of creation. However, humans cannot know him through reason or philosophical thought. They must pursue a path of discipline and self-denial to gain a true awareness of the divine presence. Sufis urged their followers to rid themselves of all personal desires and annihilate the self to experience a sense of oneness with God.

In the 1200s, the jurist Ibn Taymiyah shifted the *tawhid* debate from the metaphysical* to the social realm. He held that God is the sole creator, ruler, and judge of the world and that humans should submit to his will. Instead of trying to understand God, he felt people should express their faith through virtuous behavior. Individuals and organizations alike should work for the welfare of the state.

Modern Interpretations. Ibn Taymiyah's teachings inspired later thinkers to apply *tawhid* to social reform. In the 1700s, the scholar Muhammad ibn Abd al-Wahhab advanced the concept of *tawhid* as a remedy for the spiritual decline of the Islamic world. He condemned the Sufi practice of saint veneration as polytheism* and held that divine unity should serve as the basis of the state. Ibn Abd al-Wahhab taught that religious solidarity should replace tribal loyalties. His ideas eventually led to the creation of present-day Saudi Arabia with its religious monarchy.

In the 1800s, the Egyptian reformer Muhammad Abduh also discussed the concept of *tawhid*. Asserting that both reason and revelation lead to a belief in God's existence, he declared that Muslims need not concern themselves with God's nature. Instead, they should reject outdated policies and create an Islamic society that could thrive in modern times. Abduh advanced reason over tradition, stating that the Qur'an does not advocate unquestioning belief. He taught that humans have free will and that they should apply Islam to the needs of the times.

Abduh's activist interpretation of *tawhid* influenced later Muslim reformers. Sayyid Qutb, for example, viewed *tawhid* as an indication of the supremacy of Islamic law. He stated that Qur'anic revelation should serve as the basis of all governments. The Palestinian scholar Isma'il Raji al-Faruqi added that all of life should proceed according to God's will and that Muslims must establish Islamic law around the world. Having received the most perfect and complete revelation, Muslims have a universal responsibility to spread Islamic teachings.

The Iranian Shi'i* scholar Ali Shariati viewed *tawhid* as the foundation of life and held that God entrusted humans to care for all beings. He proposed social reforms based on the concept of divine unity. The Iranian Shi'i leader Ayatollah* Ruhollah al-Musavi Khomeini placed *tawhid* at the center of Islamic life. The concept shaped his political views and enabled him to revolutionize the Iranian government in 1979. (*See also* **Abduh, Muhammad; Ashari, Abu al-Hasan al-; Ibn Taymiyah; Khomeini, Ruhollah al-Musavi; Mu'tazili; Philosophy; Qutb, Sayyid; Sufism; Theology; Wahhabi.**)

* **Sufi** refers to Sufism, which seeks to develop spirituality through discipline of the mind and body

* **mysticism** belief that spiritual enlightenment and truth can be attained through various physical and spiritual disciplines

* **metaphysics** branch of philosophy that deals with that which exists beyond the senses

* **polytheism** belief in more than one god

* **Shi'i** refers to Muslims who believe that Muhammad chose Ali ibn Abi Talib and his descendants as the spiritual-political leaders of the Muslim community

* **ayatollah** highest-ranking legal scholar among some Shi'i Muslims

Taxation

* **Qur'an** book of the holy scriptures of Islam

* **hadith** reports of the words and deeds of Muhammad (not in the Qur'an, but accepted as guides for Muslim behavior)

* **caliph** religious and political leader of an Islamic state

* **Shi'i** refers to Muslims who believe that Muhammad chose Ali ibn Abi Talib and his descendants as the spiritual-political leaders of the Muslim community

* **imam** spiritual-political leader in Shi'i Islam, one who is regarded as directly descended from Muhammad; also, one who leads prayers

* **jurisprudence** science of law

Islamic governments traditionally imposed various taxes on Muslims, who considered their payment to be a religious duty. The most important of these taxes was *zakat*, a tax based on wealth. Intended to benefit the poor and needy, the funds collected for *zakat* were allocated for social and humanitarian causes. With the arrival of European rule, the Islamic system of taxation was largely abandoned. In recent years, however, some Muslim countries have restored its use.

A System of Redistribution. *Zakat*, setting aside a portion of one's wealth for the poor, is one of the five Pillars of Islam. All Muslims who can do so must give 2.5 percent of their net worth annually. Forms of wealth that may be subject to *zakat* include gold, silver, livestock, crops, currency, and other items that can be converted to cash, such as stocks and bonds.

Verses from the Qur'an* revealed to Muhammad during his early years in Mecca underscored the importance of caring for the needy. The hadith* formalized *zakat* as a religious duty for believers. Islamic officials started collecting and distributing *zakat* during the 600s. Muslim leaders took this responsibility seriously. Abu Bakr, the first caliph*, went to war against tribes that refused to pay *zakat*. Governors and appointed officials assisted the caliph in collecting the tax from distant provinces.

The payment of *zakat* is based on the Islamic belief that everything belongs to God, and human beings are merely caretakers of God's property. The word *zakat* is derived from an Arabic word associated with both growth and purification. Muslims believe that redistributing money from the rich to the poor causes community wealth to grow. Islam also teaches that *zakat* brings blessing to those paying the tax. Giving away wealth purifies the heart, enabling the individual to resist the love of wealth, which leads to sin.

Profits and Produce. Very early in the history of the Islamic community, Muslims were required to give one-fifth of the plunder from warfare to the Prophet Muhammad. The *khums* (fifth) tax, as it was known, benefited Muhammad's family and certain groups of needy people in the community. After the Prophet's death, *khums* was applied to various types of profit. The tax was particularly important to Shi'is*, who maintained the right of the Prophet's descendants to continue to receive financial support. After the disappearance of the twelfth imam* in the late 800s and the end of the line of visible imams, most Shi'is abandoned the practice of paying *khums*. During the 1200s, the Usuli school of jurisprudence* revived the tax and outlined new regulations for its distribution. One portion supported the needy among the Prophet's descendants and the other portion went to the *mujtahids*, members of the Shi'i clergy. The practice of *khums* gave the Shi'i clergy in Iran a source of income that contributed to their independence from state control.

Historically, Muslim governments collected a tax on the produce of agricultural land. Known as *ushr*, meaning "tithe" or "tenth," the tax applied primarily to cereals and fruits. Governments collected one-tenth of farm produce grown using rainwater or natural springs and one-twentieth of the output if the landowner used irrigation or any other artificial means to raise the crops.

Renewed Interest. During the 1800s, European powers established political control over much of the Islamic world. Colonial governments introduced income taxes. Most Muslims evaded these payments, which generally undermined traditional Islamic methods of tax collection. As a result of the institution of secular* tax systems, *zakat* became a voluntary process.

In recent years, governments in some Muslim states—such as Jordan, Saudi Arabia, Pakistan, Libya, and Sudan—have taken steps to restore Islamic taxation. In Saudi Arabia, for example, *zakat* is the main form of taxation, and although contributions are voluntary, most Muslims willingly pay.

The nature and range of economic activity has changed significantly since the time of the Prophet. These developments have generated much debate among Islamic economists and lawyers regarding the types of assets that are subject to *zakat*. The type of tax structure that was appropriate for agricultural economies with only simple trading businesses clearly differs from one that is suitable for industrialized economies with businesses organized on a corporate basis. Islamic scholars have only recently begun to address these issues. (*See also* **Economics; Justice; Pillars of Islam.**)

Paying Islamic Taxes in Cyberspace

Some new players in the business world have taken on the task of aligning the Qur'an with the world of modern finance. In 2000 a company called IslamiQ.com began to offer various online investing services, including the payment of *zakat* to charitable organizations. A board of experienced Islamic scholars headed by Muhammad Taqi Osmani, a justice of Pakistan's Supreme Court, ensures that the company's activities correspond with Islamic principles. IslamiQ.com initially planned to offer its services in the United Kingdom and Asia but hopes to expand to the Middle East and the Americas.

* **secular** separate from religion in human life and society; connected to everyday life

Ta'ziyah

The *ta'ziyah* is a passion play (religious drama) that reenacts the death of Husayn ibn Ali, the grandson of Muhammad and the third Shi'i* imam*. In 680 Husayn traveled from Medina to Iraq to advance his claim to the caliphate*, which was under control of the Umayyad dynasty*. Forces loyal to the Umayyad rulers massacred Husayn's small band at Karbala. This martyrdom* became a defining event of Shi'i Islam.

Since Husayn's death, Shi'is have commemorated the Karbala tragedy. In the 1700s, they combined certain rituals into a drama. Performers staged *ta'ziyah* plays at crossroads, town squares, and marketplaces, and then in the courtyards of inns and private houses. Patrons later built special stages for performances, ranging from small temporary structures to large theaters that could hold several thousand spectators. Until recent times, the *ta'ziyah* was the only major form of drama performed in the Islamic world.

Ta'ziyah theaters consist of a central platform surrounded by a space for the audience and a circular strip of sand. The play's main events occur on the stage. Battles, subplots, and actions indicating journeys or the passage of time take place on the sand behind the spectators. The play thus surrounds the audience members, increasing their emotional involvement. Spectators often weep and beat themselves during critical moments. The stage

* **Shi'i** refers to Muslims who believe that Muhammad chose Ali ibn Abi Talib and his descendants as the spiritual-political leaders of the Muslim community

* **imam** spiritual-political leader in Shi'i Islam, one who is regarded as directly descended from Muhammad; also, one who leads prayers

* **caliphate** office and government of the caliph, the religious and political leader of an Islamic state

* **dynasty** succession of rulers from the same family or group

* **martyrdom** act of dying for one's religious beliefs

rotates between scenes, during which times the performers jump off and announce that they are going to a certain location. When they climb back on the stage, they may declare that they have arrived.

Ta'ziyah plays have a minimum of scenery in order to evoke the desolate, bleak desert of Karbala. Most props are symbolic. A water basin, for example, represents the Euphrates River, and a tree branch signifies a palm grove. Costumes also have symbolic value. Actors portraying heroes wear green, and villains are dressed in red. Green symbolizes paradise, the family of the Prophet, and Islam; red represents blood, suffering, and cruelty. Actors playing women wear baggy black garments and veils, so that even bearded men can perform these roles. A character who places a white cloth on his shoulders indicates that he is ready to sacrifice his life and will be killed shortly. This action provokes a highly emotional response from the audience.

The *ta'ziyah* drama consists of ten separate plays, each representing a specific event in the Karbala tragedy. *Ta'ziyah* troupes usually remain in a location for ten days to two weeks, performing a different play each day. A single performance lasts from two to five hours. Plays typically revolve around one hero fighting an entire army while the other characters reflect on their condition and make philosophical and religious remarks.

Shi'i monarchs in Iran have traditionally supported *ta'ziyah* productions. In the 1870s, they established the Royal Theater in Tehran, which surpassed many Western opera houses in splendor. In the 1930s, however, Reza Shah Pahlavi's secular* government restricted performances to rural areas. The *ta'ziyah* was revived in the 1970s to stir support for the Islamic revolution. The drama remains extremely popular in Iran today and its influence has spread. In 1991 the Avignon Arts Festival in southern France hosted a *ta'ziyah*, which received a rousing reception. (*See also* **Husayn ibn Ali; Karbala and Najaf; Martyrdom.**)

* **secular** separated from religion in human life and society; connected to everyday life

Technology

Between 900 and 1300, science and technology thrived in the Islamic world. Arab and other Muslim scholars made major advances in fields such as mathematics, engineering, and optics, and various states carried out large-scale irrigation and water supply projects. After 1300, however, a number of factors combined to stifle scientific progress, shifting the balance of technological power to Europe. In recent years, Islamic countries have made efforts to expand scientific research and instruction. However, many obstacles continue to block the spread of Western-style science in the Muslim world.

The Decline of Muslim Science. A major blow to Muslim science occurred when the Mongols, a tribal people from Central Asia, invaded the Middle East in the 1200s and 1300s. The invasions destroyed Muslim cities in present-day Iran and Iraq, posing a severe setback to learning. Around the same time, religious and intellectual conservatism* within Muslim society restrained scholarship in the sciences.

* **conservatism** general opposition to change, especially in existing political and social institutions

Use of computers and the Internet is growing rapidly in Muslim nations. Here students learn computer skills at a school run by Hizbullah in southern Lebanon.

Over the next few centuries, science and scholarship advanced in Europe. At the same time, they stagnated in the Ottoman Empire*. A lack of knowledge of European languages blocked the flow of new ideas between Europe and the Arab world. When the French general Napoleon Bonaparte invaded Egypt in 1798, bringing with him a group of scholars seeking knowledge about the region, it became clear just how far behind Muslims had fallen in the areas of science and technology.

The Expansion of Technology. In the late 1800s, Western technologies—such as railroads, steamships, and telephones—spread rapidly throughout the Middle East. In 1868 Egypt became home to the Suez Canal, the greatest engineering feat of the time. However, much of this new technology came from European companies. Governments in the region were content to purchase foreign technology rather than develop their own. They made little effort to help their people learn how to design new machines, adapt existing ones, or even maintain the ones they imported.

The first Western-style technical college in the Middle East, the Syrian Protestant College, opened in Beirut in 1868. Similar schools soon appeared in other major cities in the Islamic world. Although some wealthy Muslim families sent their children to these schools, they catered mostly to Europeans living in the region and to members of minority groups. The new universities did, however, make progress in one major area: they led the way in translating major scientific works into Arabic. Scientific societies also sprang up in several Middle Eastern cities to support newly formed communities of scientists.

Throughout the 1800s and early 1900s, the Islamic world showed little resistance to the spread of Western science and technology. Middle Eastern schools were quick to accept and teach new discoveries, especially in the field of medicine. During the early 1900s, new universities with a focus on medicine and engineering were founded in Egypt, Turkey, Syria, and Sudan.

* **Ottoman Empire** large Turkish state existing from the early 1300s to the early 1900s

Islam on the Internet

In 1999 a group of Muslims in Doha, Qatar, began operating a Web site called Islam Online. The site aims to strengthen unity among Muslims and to present a positive view of Islam to others. It includes news articles, advice pages, and discussions of issues related to Islam. In one section, called the "fatwa corner," readers can look up opinions from legal scholars and pose their own questions about Islam. The main site is written in Arabic, but an English version also exists for non-Arab Muslims. With its wide variety of material, Islam Online is one of the most popular Web sites in the Muslim world.

However, most nations of the Middle East did not make mastery of science and technology a major goal at this time. The one exception was Turkey, where president Mustafa Kemal Atatürk launched an ambitious program to expand industry and engineering education.

In the mid-1900s, many new independent nations emerged in the Muslim world. The governments of these nations were expected to do far more than previous governing powers had done. World War II (1939–1945) had brought to light the importance of advances in such areas as communications, transportation, and public health. Islamic nations have had mixed results in their efforts to bring these advances to their people.

Barriers to Science. There are several barriers to scientific progress in the Islamic world. These obstacles do not stem from Islam itself, as most Muslim scientists see no conflict between their faith and modern science. Cultural practices, however, have limited progress, mainly by discouraging women from studying science and engineering. Concerns about Western influence pose another threat to technology. Governments in many Muslim nations have persecuted scientists because of their attempts to travel abroad or to maintain contacts with foreigners. Language can also be a barrier because much scientific literature has never been published in Arabic. Adapting computers to the Arabic language also poses a difficulty.

One major problem is the lack of support for research. Most universities focus on teaching rather than research, and many of them lack necessary funds and equipment. Many students who study science and engineering at these schools eventually leave their countries to pursue more advanced studies in other parts of the world. Some of them remain abroad, and others seek jobs in the oil-rich nations of the Middle East, leaving other Muslim nations—such as Egypt, Sudan, and Pakistan—with a shortage of qualified scientists.

Government offices in some countries conduct research in the areas of agriculture, health, and public works, but these facilities tend to have limited budgets. They also lack ties to universities or private companies that could aid them. State-owned firms in nations such as Algeria and Syria have a poor record of conducting research and spreading the discoveries they do make. Most such firms are poorly managed and the people in charge are rarely held responsible for their actions.

The record of private companies is not much better. Most local firms still prefer to import technology rather than do their own research or cooperate with other scientists in universities and governments. Multinational corporations operating in the region usually conduct research in Europe or North America. Oil companies in the Middle East are responsible for some research, but most of it has been on a small scale.

Opportunities for Progress. Most nations in the Muslim world agree on the most important areas for research. These include solar energy, farming techniques suited to desert lands, desalination (removing salt from seawater), and creating chemicals from oil. A few countries have made efforts to cooperate on research in these areas, but such efforts have been slow to spread. Instead, most work in the field of technology continues to take place within individual nations. Pakistan, for example, has invested government resources into various forms of research, including a nuclear energy program. Indonesia has developed an aerospace industry, and Turkey has made advances in agriculture, textiles, and the study of water resources.

One major area in which progress has occurred throughout the Islamic world is communications technology. Cell phones have grown in popularity, expanding telephone access to rural areas. Cell phones have an advantage over traditional phones because they require much less effort and expense to install. Use of the Internet is also growing rapidly in major cities and population centers. Internet cafes give Muslims access to news and viewpoints other than those provided by local media, which are often controlled by the government. However, in some nations the government itself is the sole Internet provider, with the power to censor information it does not wish its citizens to see. Satellite television stations such as Al-Jazeera also provide Muslims in the Middle East with alternative sources of information. (*See also* **Jazeera, al-; Radio and Television; Science.**)

Terrorism

Terrorism is the deliberate and random use of violence against civilians for political goals. Since ancient times, various groups throughout the world have used terror for a wide range of purposes. Today many people associate terrorism with Islam because of the activities of high-profile militant* Islamic groups, such as Hamas and al-Qaeda. Although Muslim extremists generally appeal to religion to justify their violent actions, their message of hate and intolerance does not correspond to the teachings of the Qur'an*.

* **militant** aggressively active in a cause

* **Qur'an** book of the holy scriptures of Islam

A Framework. Terrorist groups represent a wide range of views and have different objectives, membership, and resources. One popular theory divides terrorism into three classes: revolutionary, subrevolutionary, and establishment terrorism. Revolutionary terrorism, the most common form, is practiced by groups who want to topple an existing regime* and replace it with a new one. Some radical* Muslims aim to overthrow oppressive governments that they consider un-Islamic or corrupted by Western influence. Subrevolutionary terrorist groups seek to change, but not entirely replace, existing political systems.

* **regime** government in power

* **radical** favoring extreme change or reform, especially in existing political and social institutions

Establishment, or state-sponsored, terrorism consists of acts carried out by or with the help of a nation's government. The targets may be the state's own citizens, certain groups within the government, or a foreign government or its citizens. Authoritarian* regimes often use terrorism against people in the country whom they regard as a political threat. During the late 1980s, the Iraqi government killed between 50,000 and 100,000 Kurds, many of them women and children, because of their desire to form an independent state.

* **authoritarian** relating to a strong government with unrestricted powers

Some nations provide organizational assistance, supplies, and funding to terrorists operating elsewhere. In the Muslim world, weak countries sometimes use terrorism to strike at powerful foreign enemies, such as Israel. Because of the difficulty of tracing the attacks to a particular government, the responsible parties often escape punishment. By supporting Hizbullah guerrillas* in southern Lebanon, for example, Iran and Syria can attack Israel without having to confront its well-equipped army.

* **guerrilla** member of a group of fighters, outside the regular army, who engages in unconventional warfare

Terrorism

A Growing Phenomenon. Terrorist groups have existed within the Islamic community from its early days. The Kharijis were a devout, but militant extremist group. In 656 they split from caliph* Ali ibn Abi Talib, believing that his actions constituted a rejection of the Qur'an. They later assassinated him. The Assassins, a splinter Shi'i* group headquartered in northern Iran, waged war against the Seljuk dynasty* (1038–1194), terrorizing princes, generals, and religious scholars.

Terrorism in the modern Muslim world began with Zionist* groups fighting British control of Palestine in the 1940s. After the Arab-Israeli conflict of 1967, known as the Six Day War, Israel occupied the West Bank, Gaza Strip, and Golan Heights. Palestinian guerrillas began to use terrorist tactics with the aim of eliminating Israeli authority in Palestine and destroying the state of Israel. They condemned the Israeli occupation as terrorism and argued that their own acts constituted legitimate resistance. These acts included hijackings, kidnappings, bombings, and the murder of Israeli athletes at the Munich Olympics in 1972.

Significantly, the Palestinian groups—which included factions within the Palestine Liberation Organization (PLO)—were inspired by secular* beliefs, not religion. At the same time, however, extremist Islamic movements were also gaining strength. The Islamic revolution in Iran in 1979, which overthrew the American-backed government of Muhammad Reza Shah Pahlavi, marked a major turning point in the history of militant Islam. Iran's new leaders called for a worldwide revolution that justified violence against pro-Western, secular governments. The ten-year war between the former Soviet Union and the mujahidin* in Afghanistan also stimulated the rise and expansion of Muslim terrorist groups. Among the radical religious groups that emerged during the late 1970s and 1980s were Hizbullah (Lebanon), Hamas (West Bank and Gaza Strip), Egyptian Islamic Jihad, and Al-Gamaat Al-Islamiyya (Egypt).

Since the end of the Cold War (the nonmilitary struggle between the United States and the former Soviet Union) in the early 1990s, terrorism has acquired an increasingly global nature. Instability in areas such as the Balkans, Afghanistan, and certain African countries has opened the way for terrorist training. The ease of travel and communication in the modern world has also contributed to the growth of terrorist activities. Al-Qaeda, an Islamic extremist organization established by Saudi Arabian militant Osama bin Laden around 1990, has been linked to a series of attacks on Western targets. These attacks include the bombings of two U.S. embassies in Africa in 1998, the attack on the USS Cole in Yemen in 2000, and the attacks on the World Trade Center and the Pentagon on September 11, 2001.

Identifying Motives. In general, Muslim militant movements have focused their activities on authoritarian governments, which they characterize as unjust, corrupt, or un-Islamic. Some groups aim to replace existing secular laws with religious law and to eliminate Western influence on Muslim society. Many base their ideas on the writings of the Egyptian revolutionary Sayyid Qutb, who was executed by the Egyptian government in 1966. Qutb argued that the faithful had a duty to overthrow rulers who ignored God's law.

Islamic militants blame not only their own governments for the problems of Muslim society, but also the United States. They accuse the United States of supporting repressive governments in the Islamic world. Many militants believe that the only way to bring about lasting change in the Middle East is to eliminate all traces of American influence there. For this reason they target not only local government figures, but also U.S. soldiers, military bases, embassies, and even tourists. Anger toward the United States is a major motivation behind the actions of groups such as al-Qaeda.

Returning to the Source. Islamic militants often use the term *jihad* (literally "striving") to describe their activities. The Qur'an outlines two broad meanings of the word. Acknowledging the difficulty of living a good life, the holy book commands Muslims to struggle against immorality, to seek virtue, and to spend time engaged in good works for the benefit of society. But the Qur'an also uses the term *jihad* to refer to armed conflict in defense of Islam. The mainstream Islamic community contends that militants have abused the concept of jihad, using it to justify their actions. Indeed, the Qur'an says, "And fight in the way of God with those who fight you, but aggress not: God loves not the aggressors."

Some militant Muslim groups justify violence by referring to the "sword verses" in the Qur'an, which call for the killing of unbelievers. These verses instruct Muslims to "slay the idolaters wherever you find them" and to "lie in wait for them at every place of ambush." However, the subsequent verses clearly indicate that violence against unbelievers is a last resort and should be used only if they fail to pay a special tax to Muslim authorities.

Most passages in the Qur'an emphasize peace. The text states that Muslims should honor an enemy's desire for reconciliation. It also says that God does not sanction a war against those who have not initiated an attack. Some terrorist groups explain the killing of innocent people as an unfortunate side effect of their struggle, even in situations where warfare is legitimate. However, the Qur'an clearly outlines permissible and forbidden actions. Civilians, women, children, and religious figures such as monks or rabbis should never be attacked unless they take up arms to fight. (*See also* **Arab-Israeli Conflict; Assassins; Bin Laden, Osama; Hamas; Hizbullah; Hostages; Intifadah; Jihad; Khariji; Martyrdom; Palestine Liberation Organization; Qutb, Sayyid; September 11, 2001; Suicide.**)

Funding Terrorism

Islamic terrorist groups use diverse methods to finance their recruitment, training, and operations. Criminal activities, such as the drug trade, smuggling, and counterfeiting, generate a sizeable portion of the funding for these organizations. Hamas, which operates in the Israeli-occupied territories of the West Bank and Gaza Strip, reportedly has South American agents who obtain money from drug cartels. The Philippine radicals who make up the Abu Sayyaf organization fund their activities through frequent kidnapping and extortion. Contributions to Islamic charities, which raise billions of dollars each year for humanitarian causes, sometimes flow to terrorist groups.

Textiles

Textiles serve many functions in the Islamic world. In the Middle Ages*, weavers in nomadic communities made woolen fabrics and animal-hair bags for personal use and for trade. In cities and royal courts, artisans* who specialized in spinning, weaving, and embroidery created luxurious fabrics of silk, velvet, and even gold. These fabrics adorned palaces and became valuable trading goods. In the 1800s, when Europeans began colonizing the Middle East, Western demand for Islamic textiles exploded.

Local Production and Function. In traditional farming and nomadic societies, the needs of the family determined textile production. In nomadic communities, which were often based on raising sheep or goats, weavers made woolen cloth for dresses and robes, tents, bedding, pillow covers, wall coverings, sacks, and animal trappings. They wove items that they could

* **Middle Ages** period roughly between 500 and 1500

* **artisan** skilled craftsperson

See color plate 4, vol. 1.

Textiles

Textiles have occupied an important place in Muslim societies. At imperial courts, luxurious fabrics were used for splendid clothing and for elaborate display. Starting in the 1800s, high quality textiles from Muslim lands attracted buyers around the world. In modern times, a worker in a silk factory in India unravels filaments from silkworm cocoons.

* **dynasty** succession of rulers from the same family or group

* **mystic** one who seeks to experience spiritual enlightenment and truth through various physical and spiritual disciplines

* **Sufi** follower of Sufism, which seeks to develop spirituality through discipline of the mind and body

easily pack and move from place to place. In farming communities, weavers had access to cotton. They created bags and draperies out of coarser material, reserving the softer weaves for robes and other garments. Nomadic groups often traded woolen goods for cotton clothing. Traditional communities rarely had access to materials such as silk or metallic threads.

In all Muslim societies, textiles had important functions in everyday life. Different styles of clothing distinguished rich from poor, nomads from urban peoples, and Muslims from Jews, Christians, or members of other groups. Clothing could also indicate family lineage or a certain affiliation. Descendants of Muhammad, for example, wore green and white turbans, and members of the Iranian Safavid dynasty* wrapped their turbans around a red baton. Mystics* wore scratchy woolen garments to signify rejection of worldly comforts, earning the name Sufi*, meaning "one who wears wool". Textiles also played a large part in meals, gatherings, and home life. Muslims sat on mats, slept on rugs, ate from trays spread on a cloth on the floor, and reclined against cushions. Tents made of woven cloth housed nomads and traveling rulers.

Royal Uses. Textile makers at imperial courts created luxurious fabrics for display as well as cloth for daily use. Muslim rulers established the tradition of the *khilah*, or "robe of honor," giving courtiers and visiting dignitaries gifts of splendid clothing. The *khilah* featured outfits made from elaborate silks with gold and silver threads, along with belts, sashes, and bands embellished with rich embroidery. *Khilah* rituals varied from region to region. At the courts of the Abbasid dynasty, black was the official color, and rulers gave judges finely woven black wool garments. In courts of the Fatimid dynasty, state officials received white garments. Provincial governors often sent tributes of clothing to the imperial court. The governor of Bengal, for example, provided the Mughal emperor Aurangzeb with yearly gifts of clothing and textiles in the 1700s.

Fabrics were used to drape the court's reception rooms and to decorate the routes of official processions. During the Fatimid rule in the 1000s and 1100s, white textiles were hung along a route in the royal city of Cairo for the ritual procession of the caliph* during the holy month of Ramadan. Likewise, elaborate multicolored silks festooned routes in Andalusia (Muslim Spain), India, and Turkey. Textile objects were used for brilliant displays. Fatimid ceremonial parades included bright yellow and red kites shaped like lions. Wind puffed out the skillfully designed kites and made the animal shapes three-dimensional. The colors, too, indicated wealth: the yellow came from saffron, an expensive dye made from the crocus flower. Ceremonial tents also featured ornate decorations, sometimes with gold and precious jewels. The tent of the Fatimid caliph al-Mustansir displayed a world map on its inside walls stitched with emeralds, rubies, diamonds, and sapphires.

Certain religious practices required textiles as well. A ritual developed around the *kiswah*, the cloth used to cover the Kaaba* in Mecca during the annual pilgrimage. In medieval* times, the government of the city of Mecca supplied the *kiswah* each year. Various rulers also placed covers on the Kaaba, each made of a cloth representing a different part of the Muslim empire. Some covers had stripes, others were patterned or plain, but most displayed Qur'anic* verses lettered in gold. In modern times, the government of Saudi Arabia provides the *kiswah*, which is embroidered in Egypt.

Clothmaking After Colonization. The growth of colonization in the 1800s and 1900s gave rise to a flourishing international trade. Europeans began to demand large quantities of textiles from the Muslim world. Made in Iran, Afghanistan, and India, chintzes—high-quality cotton fabrics patterned with flowers or birds—became popular in England and the United States. Weavers and other textile artisans had to learn more efficient manufacturing techniques to boost production. At the same time, cheap fabrics from Western nations flooded markets in Islamic countries. This competition threatened traditional textile industries, which almost died out in some areas.

By the late 1900s, however, textile artists had begun to revive traditional designs and techniques, although they sometimes worked with materials produced overseas. Traditional textiles continue to attract a large market both internationally and within the Muslim world. In Morocco, for example, tea drinkers often use embroidered cloths to cover their tea trays. Muslim women in Bangladesh continue to create richly embroidered fabrics to use as wraps, cushions, and Qur'an holders. In Cairo, weavers make tents with raised designs for the funerals of Muslim leaders. (*See also* **Art; Trade.**)

* **caliph** religious and political leader of an Islamic state

* **Kaaba** literally "House of God"; Islamic shrine in Mecca

* **medieval** refers to the Middle Ages, a period roughly between 500 and 1500

* **Qur'an** book of the holy scriptures of Islam

See color plate 7, vol. 1.

Theology

Theology focuses on questions that concern God, divine will, and other articles of faith. Referred to in Arabic as *kalam* (speech), theology developed in the Islamic world when early Muslim scholars defended their ideas against Christians, Jews, and other Muslims. Islamic theologians developed a sys-

Qom, a major Shi'i theological center, has played an influential role in the politics of Iran. In the 1960s, Qom was in the forefront of resistance to the westernization policies of Muhammad Reza Shah Pahlavi, and in the late 1970s it became a focal point of the Iranian Revolution.

* **Qur'an** book of the holy scriptures of Islam

* **predestination** doctrine that God alone determines whether a Muslim goes to paradise or to hell

* **Hindu** refers to the beliefs and practices of Hinduism, an ancient religion that originated in India

* **Buddhist** refers to the beliefs and practices of Buddhism, a religion of eastern and central Asia based on the teaching of Gautama Buddha

* **monotheism** belief that there is only one God

* **caliph** religious and political leader of an Islamic state

* **arbitration** settlement of a dispute by a person whose decision the conflicting parties agree to accept

* **Sunni** refers to the largest branch of the Muslim community; the name derives from sunnah, the exemplary behavior of the Prophet Muhammad

* **Shi'i** refers to Muslims who believe that Muhammad chose Ali ibn Abi Talib and his descendants as the spiritual-political leaders of the Muslim community

* **jihad** literally "striving"; war in defense of Islam

tem of reasoned arguments that inspired later scholars of all religions. Key issues include the relationship between faith and action, the nature of God and the Qur'an*, predestination*, free will, and the role of reason in interpreting scripture.

Origins of Religious Thought

Islamic theology has its roots in ancient religious traditions of the Middle East and South Asia. Jews, Christians, Hindus*, Buddhists*, Sabian star-worshippers, and members of other groups discussed various aspects of faith with early Muslims. Zoroastrians promoted the idea of a cosmic struggle between good and evil. Jews and Christians emphasized monotheism* and obedience to God. Greek philosophy contributed thoughts on the role of human beings in the universe. Muslim theologians often engaged in formal debates with other scholars and used these debates to spread their ideas. Most Islamic theological writings take the form of a conversation, and several schools developed from these discussions.

Khariji and Rightful Rule. The Kharijis (the seceders) applied the principles of Islam to politics. Originally supporters of the fourth caliph* Ali ibn Abi Talib, they denounced him when he failed to crush his opponents in battle and agreed to arbitration* instead. The Kharijis held that an individual who commits a major sin without repenting—as they believed Ali did—could not be a Muslim. Unlike the Sunnis* and Shi'is*, the Kharijis rejected the idea that an Islamic ruler must come from a certain lineage. They cited right action and faith as the only conditions of leadership. Devotion to Islam would cause a Muslim to practice virtuous behavior and would prevent him or her from committing an error. The race, sex, or color of a leader did not matter as long as that person practiced a pure form of Islam. The Kharijis envisioned their caliph as a religious authority who would wage jihad* against all non-Muslims. They did not accept any of the existing leaders and constantly rebelled against them. The most severe Khariji sects failed to survive the first two centuries of Islam.

Tolerance of the Murji'i. Jahm ibn Safwan (died 745), Abu Hanifah (died 767), and other scholars founded the Murji'i school in reaction to the extreme views of the Kharijis. Most Muslims felt little sympathy for the earlier group and followed the new one. The Murji'is avoided condemning Muslims who had committed grave sins. They believed that God served as the ultimate judge and that humans should not presume to take his place. They also maintained that God would deal with his subjects in a just, merciful manner. The Murji'is emphasized God's goodness and charity instead of his anger, rejecting the idea that God punished sinners eternally.

The Murji'is further stated that faith mattered far more than deeds and that a person's intentions should serve as the only basis for punishment. This idea influenced Muslim jurists and contributed to the Hanafi school of law, which became the most influential Muslim school. The Murji'is also rejected the Khariji position that Muslims should rebel against rulers who seemed unfit. They held that Muslims should support their rulers even if they disagreed with their policies or questioned their characters. They accepted the caliphs' assertion that they ruled by virtue of God's will.

Qadari and Free Will. The Qadari school of theology, founded by Ma'bad al-Juhani (died 699), Abu Marwan al-Dimashqi (died 730), and others focused on the issue of free will. Most Muslims believed that God controlled all events and that human choices for good or evil were predestined by God. The Qadaris stated that a power exists within each individual that makes him or her responsible for acts performed. This force distinguishes human behavior from all other events, over which God has full sway. The Qadaris stated that the existence of human freedom could alone justify God's power to punish and reward individuals. Their arguments led to the idea that caliphs were responsible for their actions and should be held accountable. The Qadaris charged the caliphs of the Umayyad dynasty* with emphasizing material gain over spirituality, and they joined opposition groups. The Umayyads executed the Qadari leaders al-Juhani and al-Dimashqi.

Mu'tazili Ideas on Reason. Founded by Wasil ibn Ata (died 748), the Mu'tazilis also concentrated on the question of free will. Like the Qadaris, they believed in human responsibility and taught that people could distinguish between good and evil without divine guidance. They cautioned Muslims to use reason when following the words of the prophets* in order to avoid making harmful decisions. They described the Qur'an as providing two valuable services—guiding humans along the path to correct behavior and informing believers of the obligations of their faith, such as praying and fasting.

The Mu'tazilis maintained a belief in the oneness of God. They opposed the prevailing view of the Qur'an as a part of the divine essence, holding that the book had been created in time and space for a specific community. They claimed that God had no attributes, such as body parts, will, and anger, and that Muslims must not take any Qur'anic descriptions of such characteristics literally. On the matter of punishment, the Mu'tazilis held that God is perfectly just and that he could no more pardon sinners than he could refuse to reward the righteous.

Andalusian Legacy

Córdoba, the capital of Muslim Spain, produced several leading philosophers and theologians. The scholar Ali ibn Hazm (died 1064) cited divine revelation, not logic, as the only source of truth. He argued for a literal interpretation of the Qur'an and attacked all others with such vigor that a popular saying likened his tongue to a sword. Moses Maimonides (died 1204), a Jewish philosopher, drew inspiration from Ibn Sina and Abu Hamid al-Ghazali. He incorporated their ideas into the *Guide of the Perplexed*, a text that attempts to formulate a rational philosophy of Judaism. Maimonides particularly revered the works of Ibn Rushd (died 1198), a Muslim theologian also from Córdoba. Educated in law, medicine, and poetry, Ibn Rushd maintained that philosophy and religion had the same goal—to help people live virtuously so that they could achieve salvation after death.

* **dynasty** succession of rulers from the same family or group

* **prophet** one who announces divinely inspired revelations

The Umayyad caliph al-Ma'mun (ruled 813–833) supported Mu'tazili ideas and demanded that his legal scholars accept them. The Mu'tazilis did not attract large numbers of followers, however. Their association with the harsh policies of al-Mam'un and their emphasis on the use of reason alienated many Muslims. Mu'tazili ideas, however, remain influential among the Shi'i community.

Ash'ari Debates. One of the greatest Mu'tazili thinkers, Abu al-Hasan al-Ash'ari (died 935) went on to found the Ash'ari school of theology, which became the leading school of Sunni Islam. Al-Ash'ari used reasoned analysis to expose what he considered the weaknesses in the Mu'tazili school and to defend the elements of Islam that lay beyond the powers of human understanding. He did, however, believe that reason and logic could help support belief. Regarding human responsibility, al-Ash'ari maintained that individuals acquire the power to act only at the moment of action, when God creates this power. Al-Ash'ari also taught that God alone can judge behavior as good or evil.

Another Sunni theologian, Abu Mansur Muhammad al-Maturidi (died 956) challenged al-Ash'ari's views. Maturidi believed that human beings are fully responsible for their actions, although their power to commit a certain act occurs only during the performance of the act. He also argued that human reason can distinguish between good and evil. Maturidi taught that people learn to control their passions by following the Qur'an and that any confusion about the meaning of the text lies within the reader and not within the holy book.

Philosophical, Mystical, and Political Influence

As Islamic theology developed, it became almost indistinguishable from Islamic philosophy. Many Muslim scholars, such as Ibn Sina (died 1035), Shihab al-Din Suhrawardi (died 1191), and Nasir al-Din al-Tusi (died 1274) devoted themselves to both areas, exploring the topics of God, free will, and the role of humans in the universe. They also wrote on a variety of other subjects, including mathematics, music, linguistics, and medicine. Other scholars rejected worldly matters to focus entirely on the mystical* aspects of theology. Modern reformers used theological ideas to promote the creation of a Pan-Islamic* state.

* **mysticism** belief that spiritual enlightenment and truth can be attained through various physical and spiritual disciplines

* **Pan-Islamic** refers to the movement to unify all Islamic peoples

Contributions of Philosophers. The author of over 200 books, Ibn Sina developed a sweeping philosophical theology that influenced such European thinkers as Saint Thomas Aquinas and René Descartes. He defined God as the only necessary being, stating that he brings forth all other entities through the act of self-contemplation. Ibn Sina maintained that prophets have the most perfect understanding of God, surpassing rational thinkers. He described union with God as providing the greatest happiness because, unlike physical pleasure, it has no limit. It enables individuals to come into contact not only with the infinite, but also with their own origins and essence. All people have an inborn love of absolute good that inspires them to perfect themselves and seek out the divine.

Al-Tusi revived Ibn Sina's ideas about 200 years after his death and popularized them. One of the most versatile of all Muslim thinkers, al-Tusi wrote almost 100 books, including commentaries on geometry, logic, astronomy, ethics, and mysticism. Al-Tusi did not believe in either absolute predestination or free will. He stated that the universe is the best of all possible worlds and that every entity has an assigned role and a destiny. Free will serves as one factor among many that causes events to occur. Individuals often remain ignorant of the mechanisms that determine their own will and the other forces that cause change.

Combining mysticism and philosophy, Suhrawardi also modified Ibn Sina's teachings. He expressed Ibn Sina's cosmological* system in terms of light and darkness. God is the light of lights, and baser entities give off less illumination. After death, purified souls enter a world of light, while darker spirits travel to a realm inhabited by images that they create. Suhrawardi's school became known as the School of Illumination.

Sufi Mysticism. The writings of Sufi* philosophers and poets added a new dimension to Islamic theology. Abu Hamid al-Ghazali (died 1111), Ibn al-Arabi (died 1240), and Jalal al-Din Rumi (died 1273) all contributed to the discipline. Sufi tradition emphasizes the oneness of God and the practice of self-denial to achieve a union with the divine.

One of the most prominent mystical philosophers, al-Ghazali taught that God and the soul both operate according to will—God in creating the world, and the soul in seeking personal salvation. The noblest states of mind are transforming experiences such as exuberance, urgency, and intimacy. Al-Ghazali held that traditional scholars wasted their time in pointless discussions and that only Sufis walked the right path, combining knowledge with action and striving to experience God directly. Al-Ghazali believed that good Muslims did not need to understand complex matters that interested theologians. They had only to believe in the teachings of God and to try to bring him into their lives.

Ibn al-Arabi agreed with al-Ghazali that every person has the ability to experience God. Ibn al-Arabi took this idea further, however, stating that each individual serves as a reflection of one of God's qualities. Because each person has a direct relationship with the divine, all faiths are valid. The only true reality is God, and God is the source of all love and beauty. Men's appreciation for women, in particular, can serve as a vehicle for divine contemplation. In his writings, Jalal al-Din Rumi also transformed the longing he felt for specific individuals into a yearning for God. The most famous poet in the Islamic world, Rumi wrote thousands of verses detailing every dimension of the human union with God. Rumi often read his poems while performing a whirling dance, inspiring the creation of the Mawlawiyah (Mevlevis), known in English as Whirling Dervishes*.

Modern Theological Movements. Recent theological movements reflect the impact of Western colonialism, modern technology, and changes in family and social structures on the Islamic world. Jamal al-Din al-Afghani (died 1897) blended Islamic theology with politics. He offered religious grounds for a Pan-Islamic movement that would revive the caliphate* and establish Islam as a world power. He declared that Muslims needed to strive for political and economic independence, recognize the superiority of Islam over other religions, and cultivate inner qualities such as modesty and honesty while following the Qur'an. Al-Afghani helped to inspire reform movements such as the Muslim Brotherhood and the Salafi movement in Egypt.

* **cosmology** study of the nature of the universe

* **Sufi** refers to Sufism, which seeks to develop spirituality through the discipline of the mind and body

See color plate 11, vol. 3.

* **dervish** Sufi mystic; member of an order that uses music and dance to enter a trancelike state

* **caliphate** office and government of the caliph, the religious and political leader of an Islamic state

One of al-Afghani's many followers, Muhammad Abduh (died 1905) also advocated large-scale social reforms. Like the Mu'tazilis, Abduh believed that both reason and revelation* should guide individuals. He invited Muslims to participate in activist movements and follow Islamic principles in their lives. Another reformer, Muhammad Iqbal (died 1938) believed that modernization held the key to Islamic advancement. He encouraged Muslims to embrace science and technology, calling for a reinterpretation of the Qur'an that would lead to the creation of a modern Islamic state. His efforts helped to bring about the founding of Pakistan in 1947.

Muhammad Husayn Tabataba'i (died 1989) was a prominent Shi'i theologian who also pushed for social reform. He acknowledged that objects can give pleasure, but taught that the mission of every human is to reflect on the true meaning of Islam and to submit completely to God. Tabataba'i's ideas contributed to the Iranian Revolution of 1979 and continue to exert significant influence in Iran and other Muslim nations. (*See also* **Abduh, Muhammad; Abu Hanifah; Afghani, Jamal al-Din al-; Ashari, Abu al-Hasan al-; Ghazali, Abu Hamid al-; Ibn al-Arabi; Ibn Sina; Iqbal, Muhammad; Mu'tazili; Philosophy; Rumi; Sufism.**)

* **revelation** message from God to humans transmitted through a prophet

Tijaniyah

* **Sufi** refers to Sufism, which seeks to develop spirituality through discipline of the mind and body

* **mystic** one who seeks to experience spiritual enlightenment and truth through various physical and spiritual disciplines

* **Sunni** refers to the largest branch of the Muslim community; the name derives from sunnah, the exemplary behavior of the Prophet Muhammad

* **sultan** political and military ruler of a Muslim dynasty or state

* *ulama* religious scholars

The Tijani Sufi* order takes its name from Algerian-born mystic* Ahmad al-Tijani (1737–1815), who founded the religious movement around 1782. As a young adult, al-Tijani traveled throughout northwestern Africa, seeking spiritual truth and experimenting with several Sufi orders. In 1782 he claimed that he had received a vision of the Prophet Muhammad, who authorized him to launch a new religious movement. Muhammad also instructed al-Tijani to sever relations with other Sufi orders.

Challenging the practices of traditional Sufi brotherhoods, the Tijaniyah observed Islamic law strictly but rejected the notions of poverty and seclusion from the world. In contrast to their rivals, they adopted a simplified set of rituals and system of organization. Although the Tijanis identified themselves as devoted Sunnis*, they greatly reduced the required number of devotional prayers and streamlined the pattern of recitation.

Al-Tijani claimed the title of *khatam al-awliyah* (seal of the saints), which implied that he was a link between the Prophet and all past and future saints. As such, his followers enjoyed a high spiritual rank and were promised access to paradise without having to give up their worldly possessions. This positive view of material wealth made the Tijaniyah attractive to rich merchants and government officials, as well as some prominent scholars. The reformist Moroccan sultan* Mawlay Sulayman (1792–1822), who sought to eliminate popular Sufism, also embraced the Tijani brotherhood.

Critics of the Tijaniyah objected to the movement's emphasis on worldly matters and simplicity of belief and practice. They felt that the Tijanis had abandoned the mystical elements of Sufi devotion. Rival orders and some members of the Moroccan *ulama* also resented al-Tijani's claim that he was the "seal of the saints," which gave him prestige over more traditional Sufi orders. Additional criticism came from the Tijani brotherhood's refusal to associate with other orders and to visit the tombs of their saints.

Although earlier Sufi movements had preached radical* activity against governments in northwestern Africa, the Tijaniyah emerged as a force for stability. Al-Tijani encouraged his followers to support established authority. This practical approach enabled the order to spread and prosper under the protection of the government. After al-Tijani's death, however, the Tijanis became less cohesive. During the 1800s and early 1900s, they generally supported the French colonial government in northern Africa but became the basis for a renewal movement in West Africa under al-Hajj Umar al-Tal. The order recruited new followers, even among the Berbers*, who usually opposed established authority.

The independence movement in northwestern Africa, which reached a peak in the years after World War II (1939–1945), forced the Tijaniyah and other Sufi orders to operate in secret. Tijani activities since then have been on a fairly small scale. (*See also* **Sufism.**)

* **radical** favoring extreme change or reform, especially in existing political and social institutions

* **Berber** refers to a North African ethnic group that consists primarily of Muslims

Titles, Honorific

Over the centuries, Muslims have used numerous titles to confer honor on individuals or to designate their rank in society. Five of the most important are *khan*, *sayyid*, *sharif*, *shaykh*, and *sultan*.

The honorific title *khan* traditionally referred to the leaders of nomadic tribes in an area extending from Central Asia to northern India, Iran, Turkey, and southern Russia. After Mongol tribes from Central Asia conquered much of the Islamic world in the 1200s, several Muslim societies adopted the title. The Safavids, who ruled Iran from 1501 to 1722, used it to designate the governor of a province. Today among Muslims in Afghanistan, Bangladesh, India, and Pakistan the word *khan* often appears as a surname or as a way to indicate a property owner.

Muslims who claim descent from Muhammad, especially through his second grandson, Husayn ibn Ali, take the title *sayyid*, meaning "lord, master, or prince." Sayyids have a high spiritual and social status and command great respect, particularly in Iran and on the Indian subcontinent. An important sayyid is revered as a saint, especially after his death, when his tomb is likely to become a place of pilgrimage. The founders of many Sufi* orders and most Sufi masters claimed the title of sayyid.

The Arabic word *sharif*, meaning "noble" or "high-born," is associated with honor and distinction. A sharif is a man who claims descent from prominent ancestors, usually the Prophet Muhammad through his grandson Hasan. (The feminine form is *sharifa*.) Throughout the Muslim world, men with this title often wear green and white turbans to distinguish themselves from others. Sharifs are not subject to the same religious requirements as other Muslims, and some believe that God will forgive their sins because of their special status. The title *sharif* is particularly important to Shi'is, who hold Muhammad's descendants in high regard. However, the Sunni rulers of Jordan and Morocco also claim the status of sharif.

* **Sufi** refers to Sufism, which seeks to develop spirituality through discipline of the mind and body

* **pre-Islamic** refers to the Arabian Peninsula or to the Arabic language before the founding of Islam in the early 600s

* **scripture** sacred writings that contain revelations from God

* **mosque** Muslim place of worship

* **dynasty** succession of rulers from the same family or group

In pre-Islamic* Arabia, the term *shaykh* was a title of honor given to men of distinction. (The feminine form is *shaykha*.) Muslims apply the term *shaykh al-din* (leader of the faith) to men who possess knowledge of scripture*. Heads of religious orders, Qur'anic scholars, legal scholars, and those who preach and lead prayers in mosques* are called *shaykhs*. However, the majority of *shaykhs*—today and in the past—have not been religious leaders. Rather, they have included clan elders and village and tribal chiefs. In the modern era, powerful *shaykhs* gained positions in several national governments. The control of vast oil reserves has additionally brought wealth and power to certain Arab *shaykhs*.

The Arabic word *sultan* means power, might, and authority. In Islam, it applies to the political and military ruler of a Muslim dynasty* or state. The Seljuk rulers of Baghdad were the first to adopt the title. Several other Islamic states later followed suit. Today only Brunei, Malaysia, and Oman continue to use the title *sultan*. (*See also* **Names and Naming; Sufism; Sultan.**)

Trade

* **Middle Ages** period roughly between 500 and 1500

* **Byzantine** refers to the Eastern Christian Empire that was based in Constantinople

* **caliphate** office and government of the caliph, the religious and political leader of an Islamic state

Trade has always played a significant role in the Muslim world. A well-organized trade system existed in the Middle East and Central and South Asia long before the founding of Islam. During the early Middle Ages*, merchant caravans carried spices from southern Arabia to markets in the Byzantine* Empire. As a young adult, Muhammad participated in this trade.

Captains of Industry. The establishment of Islam greatly expanded commerce in the Muslim world. The growth of the Muslim empire led to a corresponding increase in trade in the 600s and 700s. The Islamic caliphate* ruled a vast area from Spain and Morocco to India and Central Asia. Uniting so many regions under one government stretched overland trade links to unprecedented distances. Arab armies, moreover, gathered large quantities of gold and silver during their conquests. The acquisition of precious metals further stimulated commerce in the Muslim world.

Baghdad became the capital of an extensive trade empire in the 800s. An intricate network of caravan routes arose across the Middle East. Muslims imported paper, silk, rubies, ebony, and coconuts from China and India, and papyrus, cloth, donkeys, and hawks from Egypt and North Africa. They exported such goods as carpets, glassware, dates, and grains. Urban marketplaces across the empire boomed with activity, and Muslim merchants helped spread the faith.

Muslims adopted several measures to boost commerce. Merchants developed loan procedures by which a borrower wrote a note promising to pay back money owed within a set period of time. They also formed partnerships that allowed individuals to combine their resources to fund large business ventures. Each partner shared the risks and rewards. Muslim traders introduced many banking practices used today, including modern checking.

After 1000, warfare and European economic development led to a shift in trading activity. The eastern Mediterranean became the focal point of commerce, and Egypt emerged as the leading center of trade. Egyptian merchants

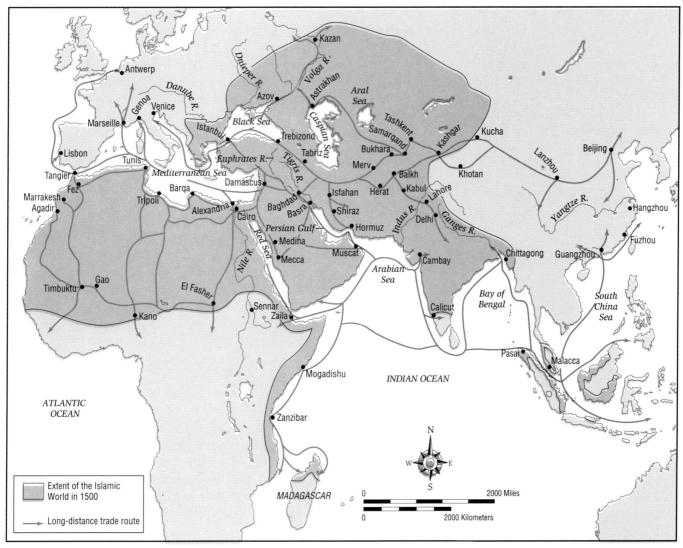

Extent of the Islamic
World in 1500

Long-distance trade route

sold flax and linen in the West and bought silk and metals from Europe. They continued to profit from their role as link between Asia and the West in the spice trade.

Muslim traders thrived during the Middle Ages. The following centuries, however, were a period of decline for Muslim commerce. European merchants established sea routes to Asia that allowed them to avoid Islamic markets. Muslim merchant income dropped in the 1500s, and the military defeats of the Ottoman Empire* in the 1600s and 1700s brought further economic decline. In the 1800s, Western nations assumed control over much of Africa, Asia, and the Middle East. Colonial powers dominated Islamic economies. Europeans forced the leaders of Muslim countries to sign trade agreements that favored the West.

Western Influence and Beyond. Colonialism continued to shape Islamic commercial patterns in the 1900s. Each Muslim country traded primarily with the European power that occupied it. India, for example, traded with Great Britain, and Algeria did business with France. For the most part,

Muslim traders thrived during the Middle Ages. Egypt was the center of Mediterranean trade. Egyptian merchants had a lively trade with Europe and served as the link between Asia and the West in the spice trade. However, as Europeans established their own sea routes to Asia in the 1500s, Muslim commerce declined.

* **Ottoman Empire** large Turkish state existing from the early 1300s to the early 1900s

* **postcolonial** refers to the condition of a state after the departure of conquering powers

Muslim countries exported natural products and raw materials, including wheat, barley, silks, animal skins, and fruits. The Islamic world bought machinery and manufactured items from the West. These trade patterns continued in the postcolonial* era, with Muslim countries exporting crude oil and importing European and American technology. Decades of European dominance left many Muslim countries economically underdeveloped, and the dominance of the oil industry hindered growth in other areas. Some Islamic leaders continue to import manufactured goods rather than encouraging scientific development and industry within their states.

Following independence, Islamic governments made efforts to improve their trade situation. In 1969 Muslim nations created the Organization of the Islamic Conference (OIC) to promote economic cooperation among member nations. The OIC established other agencies, such as the Islamic Development Bank, to boost development. Several Muslim nations joined the Organization of Petroleum Exporting Countries (OPEC) to increase oil revenue.

Muslim efforts at cooperation had only a modest impact on commerce, however. OPEC increased oil income in the 1970s and 1980s, but prices and production fell in the 1990s. The OIC has had little success in increasing trade among Islamic nations. Its members concerned themselves more with political unity than with economic cooperation. Moreover, Muslim leaders were reluctant to halt trade with former colonial powers because of the economic costs.

Several Islamic nations have taken steps sought to boost trade. Turkey, for example, enacted a series of reforms to increase commerce and industrial output. Initially, the program succeeded in both goals. Turkey's volume of foreign trade increased threefold in the 1980s. By 1993, however, political and economic problems created a trade imbalance. Recent commercial agreements with Europe led to slight improvements. Elsewhere in the Middle East, free trade agreements in Jordan and other areas offer the hope of increasing economic activity. (*See also* **Economics; International Meetings and Organizations.**)

Tribe

* **polytheistic** refers to believing in more than one god

Tribes—networks of extended families or clans—have always played a significant role in the Islamic world. In the 600s, warring clans dominated social, economic, and political life in Arabia. Muhammad challenged tribal leaders with his claim of prophetic authority and spoke out against the inequalities of life in tribal society. He promoted the rights of widows and orphans, encouraged fair business practices, and organized systems of charity. Muhammad also denounced tribal members for their polytheistic* beliefs. Not surprisingly, many Arabs rejected his teachings.

In 622 persecution by the Umayyads (a clan in the powerful Quraysh tribe) forced Muhammad to move from Mecca to Medina, where he helped resolve a dispute between rival tribes. With the help of his supporters, Muhammad launched several battles against the Umayyads. His victories inspired many clans to declare their loyalty to Islam. By 630 Islam had become the dominant power in Arabia. Although Islam created a sense of a common identity that transcended tribal loyalties, tribes continued to play a significant role as the religion spread beyond Arabia.

Tribes and Muslim Empires. Several Muslim empires emerged from tribal dynasties* or confederations. The Umayyads ruled the caliphate* from 661 to 750 and greatly expanded the Islamic state. The Oghuz, a confederation* of Turks, created the Ottoman Empire* in the 1300s. By the 1500s, the Ottomans had become the most powerful force in the Islamic world. The Ottomans' rival, the Shi'i* Safavid dynasty, owed its rise to the support of strong warrior tribes. In the 1900s, several Arabian groups backed the Saud family in creating the Kingdom of Saudi Arabia.

Certain tribes have played large roles in the Islamic world. The North African Berbers* helped the Muslims conquer Spain in the 700s, and they founded the Almoravid and Almohad empires in the 1000s and the 1100s. Although the Berbers readily adopted Islam, they retained tribal organization and clan loyalties. Bedouin* herders inhabited Middle Eastern countries such as Arabia and Syria. Those who herded camels had the most prestige, followed by sheep or goat herders, and then cattle herders. In medieval* times, Bedouin tribes frequently warred among themselves and raided nearby villages. After World War I (1914–1918), they had to submit to the rule of local governments. Some became integrated in urban society, taking jobs in construction or in the army. However, many still maintain a tribal lifestyle.

Tribal Composition. Tribal groups range from nomad societies to settled agricultural communities. They often organize around a certain resource, such as land, water, or trade routes. These groups encourage a sense of identity by promoting unique customs and rituals. Members establish local ties through marriages or political arrangements.

Tribal organization varies. Some are small, decentralized, and loosely organized. Local elders head these groups. Other tribes have a strong centralized hierarchy* and extend across many regions. The leaders of these groups are usually wealthy elites who have ties to the national government. Small tribes sometimes merge with larger groups when threatened by hostile forces. Conversely, large tribes may split into smaller groups to escape state regulation.

Tribal leaders, often called *shaykhs*, fulfill many important roles. They represent the tribe to government authorities and convey state regulations to tribal members. *Shaykhs* have four specific functions: resolving disputes, offering hospitality and giving gifts to important individuals, leading the tribe in times of war, and dealing with state governments. Before the establishment of modern states, *shaykhs* had a great deal of political power. They imposed taxes on peasants, charged escort fees to caravans passing through their territories, and owned large tracts of land. They also gained revenue from regional governments seeking their loyalty. In many tribes, the title of *shaykh* has continued down the same family line for centuries.

Tribal and State Relations. Tribes in the Islamic world serve many functions. They enable members to defend themselves from foreign armies and government oppression, and they provide members with political influence and economic opportunities. Many tribes play significant roles within

* **dynasty** succession of rulers from the same family or group

* **caliphate** office and government of the caliph, the religious and political leader of an Islamic state

* **confederation** group of states joined together for a particular purpose; an alliance

* **Ottoman Empire** large Turkish state existing from the early 1300s to the early 1900s

* **Shi'i** refers to Muslims who believe that Muhammad chose Ali ibn Abi Talib and his descendants as the spiritual-political leaders of the Muslim community

* **Berber** refers to a North African ethnic group that consists primarily of Muslims

* **Bedouin** nomad of the desert, especially in North Africa, Syria, and Arabia

* **medieval** refers to the Middle Ages, a period roughly between 500 and 1500

* **hierarchy** system of rank within an organization

the state. Before the mid-1900s, Muslim leaders often needed tribal support for tax collection and national defense. At times, a strong tribe ensured the survival of a state. Governments rewarded loyal tribal elites with authority and wealth. Rulers sometimes even shared power with tribal leaders.

Several modern Muslim governments have incorporated tribal leaders into their administrations. In Jordan, for example, tribal leaders hold positions in the legislature, serve as government ministers, and dominate the upper ranks of the military. In the Arabian Peninsula, they control vast oil reserves, and in Yemen, they rival government leaders in controlling foreign and domestic affairs.

Certain tribes, however, attract opposition from state governments. For example, Kurdish tribes have met with much resistance in trying to form a homeland. Living in parts of Iran, Syria, Turkey, and Iraq, Kurds have repeatedly tried to gain their independence. Military campaigns in Iraq in 1988 and 1991 led to the deaths of tens of thousands of Kurds and caused millions to flee from their homes. The Turkish government also killed thousands of Kurds after terrorist* attacks in 1992. Clashes between Turks and Kurds continue in the southeastern part of the country. (*See also* **Iraq; Jordan; Muhammad; Ottoman Empire; Safavid Dynasty; Saudi Arabia; Titles, Honorific; Turkey; Umayyad Caliphate; Yemen.**)

* **terrorism** use of violence against people, property, or states as a means of intimidation for political purposes

Tunisia

A nation slightly larger than the state of Georgia, Tunisia lies on the coast of North Africa between Libya and Algeria. Of its 9.8 million people, nearly all are Arab and Muslim. Christians, Jews, and others make up about 2 percent of the population. Sunni* Islam is the official state religion. Shi'is have no presence in Tunisia.

Early Islamic Period. Tunisia is the site of ancient Carthage, which became part of the Roman Empire and then of the Byzantine* Empire. Muslim Arab armies conquered Tunisia in 647. Islam spread quickly under Arab rule. As Tunisians adopted Islam, they blended it with many local customs such as saint veneration. In the 900s, a Shi'i* dynasty*, the Fatimids, came to power in Tunisia. Even at that time, however, the Shi'is made up only a small minority of the population.

In about 1229, the governor of a group of Berber* tribes known as the Almohads founded a dynasty in Tunisia and eastern Algeria. Tunisia eventually became home to many Spanish Muslims who were driven out of Spain in 1492. The country became part of the Ottoman Empire* in 1574 and remained under Ottoman rule for over 300 years. During this period, Tunisia's Zaytunah Mosque* in the capital city of Tunis became a major center of Islamic studies. By the early 1800s, Tunisia was essentially an independent state, although it officially remained under Ottoman rule. The nation called itself a *beylik*, ruled by a leader called the bey.

French Protectorate. In 1830 the French invaded Tunisia's neighbor, Algeria. Five years later, the Ottomans deposed the ruler of neighboring Libya

* **Sunni** refers to the largest branch of the Muslim community; the name derives from sunnah, the exemplary behavior of the Prophet Muhammad

* **Byzantine** refers to the Eastern Christian Empire that was based in Constantinople

* **Shi'i** refers to Muslims who believe that Muhammad chose Ali ibn Abi Talib and his descendants as the rulers and spiritual leaders of the Muslim community

* **dynasty** succession of rulers from the same family or group

* **Berber** refers to a North African ethnic group that consists primarily of Muslims

* **Ottoman Empire** large Turkish state existing from the early 1300s to the early 1900s

* **mosque** Muslim place of worship

Tunisia gained its independence from France in 1956. Habib Bourguiba, who became the new country's first president, waves to the crowds on his way to an independence celebration.

and reclaimed direct control over the nation. This move threatened Tunisia's ability to continue governing itself. Tunisian rulers tried to follow policies that would strengthen their country without angering the French or the Ottomans.

Ahmad Bey (ruled 1837–1855) modernized the nation's armed forces, abolished slavery, and made other reforms. His changes, however, weakened Tunisia's economy. Taxes increased and the nation's debt rose, causing unrest in the countryside. A revolt broke out in 1864, when the government attempted to raise taxes on the already hard-pressed peasants. The peasants nearly overthrew the government before the uprising was crushed. In 1869 the nation finally went bankrupt. An international financial commission, with members from Great Britain, France, and Italy, took control of Tunisia's economy. Nine years later at the Congress of Berlin, Britain agreed to let France take over the country.

France invaded Tunisia in 1881, claiming that the country had attacked its territory in Algeria. Several popular revolts broke out in the south in response to the French attack, but the French crushed them and assumed power over the nation. In 1883 the Treaty of La Marsa declared Tunisia to be a protectorate* of France. Officially, the bey remained in control of the nation, but in practice the French held supreme authority.

* **protectorate** country under the protection and control of a stronger nation

159

Tunisia

* **shari'ah** Islamic law as established in the Qur'an and sunnah, the exemplary behavior of the Prophet Muhammad

* **nationalist** one who advocates loyalty and devotion to his or her country and its independence

* **parliament** representative national body having supreme legislative power within the state

* **assassinate** to murder a politically important person

Restricting Ramadan

President Bourguiba angered many Tunisians in 1960 with his attack on the core Muslim practice of fasting during the month of Ramadan. Bourguiba claimed that fasting lowered workers' productivity and that economic development was a jihad, or holy struggle, that permitted the suspension of fasting. He openly rejected the fast and called on other Tunisians to follow his example. Most Tunisians, however, defied the president's order. In the next few years Bourguiba made further attempts to suspend the fast, which only increased public unrest. Eventually he gave up, but he had already lost the trust of many Muslims. In 1987 he was declared unfit to govern and placed under house arrest, where he remained until his death in 2000 at age 96.

At first the French allowed the *shari'ah** courts to handle matters of personal status, such as marriage, divorce, and inheritance. Gradually, however, they imposed French legal principles on Islamic law. A split arose between traditional Tunisian culture and French-influenced culture. This division affected all aspects of life, from law to education. Under the French administration, it became difficult for traditional Muslims to enjoy the full benefits of the French sector of society. They often had to choose between their religious practice and social or economic advancement. As a result, the moral and cultural symbols of Islam came to play a central role in the movement for independence from France.

Independence Movements. In the 1890s, a group of French-educated Muslim reformers known as the Young Tunisians began calling for greater rights for their people. Although their demands were moderate, the French took steps to suppress them. The first large-scale political movement was the Destour (Constitution) Party, which arose around 1920. This group demanded a constitution that would give Tunisians the same rights as Europeans. The elderly bey supported the Destour Party's demands, but French military action forced him to withdraw his support. The French then passed some minor reforms that quieted the nationalist* movement for a time.

In 1934 Habib Bourguiba and some colleagues broke with the Destour Party to form the Neo-Destour Party. The new organization soon gained popularity and began pushing for reforms. In 1938 severe unrest led the French to dissolve the party. They arrested Neo-Destour leaders, including Bourguiba, and deported them to France. However, the following year World War II broke out in Europe, pitting the Allied powers of Great Britain, France, and the Soviet Union against the Axis powers of Germany, Italy, and Japan. German forces took control of France and handed the Neo-Destour leaders over to the Italian government, which hoped to secure support from the leaders for the Axis.

At first, Bourguiba refused to cooperate with the Italians. In 1943 he finally agreed to make a vague statement that could be interpreted as supporting the Axis. The Italians then allowed him and the other Neo-Destour leaders to return to Tunisia, where the ruling bey had formed a government sympathetic to their cause. When World War II ended in 1945, the French reassumed power over Tunisia. They deposed the bey and accused Bourguiba of aiding the Axis in the war. He escaped prison by fleeing to Egypt in disguise.

Still, the movement for Tunisian independence continued, forcing the French to allow some reforms. In 1951 they permitted Salah ibn Yusuf, a leader with nationalist leanings, to take office. However, when the new government leader sought to establish a Tunisian parliament*, the French arrested most of its ministers. These events led to outbreaks of terrorist activity in the mountains. Finally, in 1954, the French promised Tunisia complete independence and allowed Bourguiba to return to the country. Ibn Yusuf, however, criticized the French plan, saying it placed too many restrictions on the Tunisian government. He organized armed resistance, but it was quickly crushed. Ibn Yusuf later fled the country to avoid imprisonment. In 1961 he was assassinated*.

An Independent Tunisia. On March 20, 1956, France formally recognized Tunisia's independence. Bourguiba assumed power, first as prime minister and later as president. He quickly took steps to bring Islamic institutions under state control. Instead of openly promoting a secular* society, however, Bourguiba tried to identify himself as a great Muslim reformer. He claimed that his goal was to restore Islam by placing religious activities under state control and by ending practices that were not in keeping with religious sources.

Bourguiba reestablished Islam as Tunisia's state religion. His government increased the number of mosques in Tunisia from 810 in 1960 to 2,500 in 1987. It also established spaces for prayer in universities and government offices. At the same time, however, Bourguiba began a program of reforms that challenged traditional Muslim practices. He replaced many areas of Islamic law with the Tunisian Code of Personal Status, which governed marriage, divorce, and child custody. Under this code, Tunisia became the first Arab country to outlaw polygyny*. Bourguiba also abolished *shari'ah* courts and brought religiously funded lands under government control. He banned some types of ritual practice and denied permission for festivals in honor of saints. Authorities even destroyed several shrines*.

In one case, however, Bourguiba's attempts to take control of Islamic practice backfired. In 1971 the government supported the creation of an Islamic group at the University of Tunis, believing it would serve to counter the influence of radical* student groups. Instead, the organization became a major revolutionary force in its own right. In 1981 it took the name Movement of the Islamic Way, known more popularly as the Islamic Tendency Movement (MTI). It remained the largest and most active Islamist* movement in Tunisia until 1987, when General Zine el Abidine Ben Ali seized control of the government and took steps to suppress the group. In 1988 the organization changed its name to Hizb al-Nahdah (Renaissance Party).

Ben Ali portrayed himself as a protector of Islam. His government adopted several policies that gave Islam a more prominent role in public life. Prayers were broadcast on television, and the Zaytunah Mosque gained the status of a university. Ben Ali also increased the size and budget of the Higher Islamic Council. These policies, however, failed to draw support away from the Islamist opposition. As a result, Ben Ali began to take a harsher stance against Islamist activity. By 1993 the government had effectively crushed the Renaissance Party.

Tunisia has prospered under Ben Ali's rule. The nation's economy grew by about 5 percent per year between 1995 and 2000. At the same time, Tunisians have faced political oppression. The government reads their private messages and bans any open criticism. Groups that monitor human rights claim that Ben Ali's regime* is holding 1,000 political prisoners. (*See also* **Colonialism; Ottoman Empire.**)

* **secular** separate from religion in human life and society; connected to everyday life

* **polygyny** practice of having more than one wife at the same time

* **shrine** place that is considered sacred because of its history or the relics contained there

* **radical** favoring extreme change or reform, especially in existing political and social institutions

* **Islamist** referring to movement advocating reintegration of religion and politics; also one who advocates reintegration of religion and politics

* **regime** government in power

Turabi, Hasan al-

1932–
Sudanese Islamist and political leader

Hasan al-Turabi has been a key figure in political and religious life in Sudan since 1964. Born in central Sudan to a devout Muslim family, al-Turabi studied law at Khartoum University, where he became a member of Sudan's Muslim Brotherhood. Al-Turabi later studied overseas at the University of London and at the Sorbonne in Paris. In 1964 he returned to Sudan and became a leading figure in the brotherhood. The group founded the Islamic Charter

Front (ICF), a small but vocal political party that called for an Islamic constitution in Sudan.

In 1969 Jafar Nimeiri seized power in a military coup*. The new leader dissolved the ICF and arrested several of its members, including al-Turabi. Eight years later, however, Nimeiri reversed course and joined forces with the Muslim Brotherhood. He made al-Turabi his attorney general and several other members of the brotherhood gained important government posts. In 1983 Nimeiri made the *shari'ah** the supreme law of Sudan. Many believe that al-Turabi influenced this decision.

A popular revolt ended Nimeiri's regime* in 1985, and Sudan held elections the following year. Al-Turabi's party, which had changed its name to the National Islamic Front (NIF), finished third. Nevertheless, it was clearly a rising force in Sudanese politics. In 1989 the NIF backed a successful coup by General Umar al-Bashir, who reinforced Islamic rule in Sudan. Al-Turabi became a major force in the al-Bashir regime. NIF and Muslim Brotherhood members dominated the government, civil service, and economy. Beginning in 1999, however, al-Bashir removed al-Turabi from his government posts. In 2001 he imprisoned al-Turabi, charging him with undermining the state.

In his writings, al-Turabi advanced certain liberal* ideas, such as democracy and pluralism*. In practice, however, he enforced harsh rule in Sudan. To build Islamist* power, he created an NIF police state that committed many abuses of human rights. He repressed political opponents through torture, execution, and imprisonment. Al-Turabi has also encouraged the rise of militant* Islam in neighboring countries. (*See also* **Muslim Brotherhood; Sudan.**)

* **coup** sudden, and often violent, overthrow of a ruler or government

* *shari'ah* Islamic law as established in the Qur'an and sunnah, the exemplary behavior of the Prophet Muhammad

* **regime** government in power

* **liberal** supporting greater participation in government for individuals; not bound by tradition

* **pluralism** condition in society in which diverse groups maintain and develop their traditional cultures or special interests

* **Islamist** referring to movement advocating reintegration of religion and politics; also one who advocates reintegration of religion and politics

* **militant** aggressively active in a cause

Turkey

Turkey emerged from the collapse of the Ottoman Empire* after World War I (1914–1918). Unlike most Middle Eastern countries, Turkey won its independence soon after the war and quickly developed into a modernized state based on Western political models. However, tensions between the secular* government and citizens calling for a stronger Islamic presence in the nation continue to the present day.

Slightly larger than Texas, Turkey bridges the continents of Europe and Asia. It lies along three major bodies of water—the Black Sea, the Aegean Sea, and the Mediterranean Sea—and has the strategic Bosporus Strait running through it. Turkey shares borders with Greece, Bulgaria, Georgia, Armenia, Iran, Iraq, and Syria. The country's mountainous terrain includes Mount Ararat, the supposed landing place of Noah's Ark. Its population consists of members of the Turkish ethnic* group (80 percent) and Kurds (20 percent). Nearly all Turks practice Islam, with fewer than one half of one percent following Judaism or Christianity.

* **Ottoman Empire** large Turkish state existing from the early 1300s to the early 1900s

* **secular** separate from religion in human life and society; connected to everyday life

* **ethnic** relating to groups of people who share a common racial, national, tribal, religious, linguistic, or cultural background

From the Ottomans to Atatürk

Asia Minor (modern Turkey) became part of the Islamic world in 1071, when Seljuk Turks conquered the Byzantines*. The Ottomans succeeded the Seljuks

* **Byzantine** refers to the Eastern Christian Empire that was based in Constantinople

Turkey bridges the continents of Europe and Asia. Antalya, a resort on the Mediterranean coast of Turkey, reflects a mixture of European and Middle Eastern cultures. Visitors find that the local cuisine resembles that of Italy, but they also encounter many reminders of the Seljuk dynasty and the Ottoman Empire.

See color plate 7, vol. 2.

in the early 1300s and slowly assumed control of most of the Middle East. Although the Ottoman Empire included significant numbers of Christians and Jews, Muslims dominated the government and the military.

Waning of Ottoman Power. The Ottoman Empire reached its peak in the mid-1500s but was hampered by severe economic problems and corruption. It had a weak central government, and local officials concerned themselves more with making a profit than with governing effectively. Crippling local taxes drove farmers from the land, sending them to the cities, where they suffered from food shortages and overcrowding. Guilds* and lo-

* **guild** association of craftspeople and tradespeople that set standards for and represented the interests of its members

* **parliament** representative national body having supreme legislative power within the state

* **regime** government in power

* **sultan** political and military ruler of a Muslim dynasty or state

* **nationalist** one who advocates loyalty and devotion to his or her country and its independence

* **caliphate** office and government of the caliph, the religious and political leader of an Islamic state

* **Sunni** refers to the largest branch of the Muslim community; the name derives from sunnah, the exemplary behavior of the Prophet Muhammad

* **Sufi** refers to Sufism, which seeks to develop spirituality through discipline of the mind and body

* **mystic** one who seeks to experience spiritual enlightenment and truth through various physical and spiritual disciplines

* *ulama* religious scholars

* **mosque** Muslim place of worship

* **caliph** religious and political leader of an Islamic state

cal religious associations were forced to assume many of the responsibilities ignored by the government.

In the 1700s, European powers recognized and took advantage of the Ottoman Empire's relative weakness. The Ottomans lost much of their territory in southeastern Europe. In the late 1700s, disastrous wars against Russia and other powers brought the empire close to collapse. This crisis led to a series of major government reforms called the Tanzimat (Reorganization). Aimed at increasing efficiency and reducing corruption, the Tanzimat introduced Western-style governmental institutions, such as a parliament*, that increased the power of the central government. It also opened the way to legal equality of non-Muslims and Muslims.

Ottoman Collapse and Independence. The years following the Tanzimat saw increasing Western influence and modernization in the empire. This angered many Turks, who called for a return to Islamic values. In 1878 Sultan Abdulhamid II disbanded the parliament and established a repressive regime* that relied on secret police and censorship. In the early 1900s, a group called the Young Turks rose up, overthrew the sultan*, and restored the constitutional government. They held their power only briefly, however, as they joined the group of countries that lost in World War I. With the defeat of the Central Powers in 1918, the Ottoman Empire collapsed.

Over the next five years, Turkish nationalists* led by Mustafa Kemal fought the victorious Allied forces and the Greeks to establish an independent Turkish state. By 1923 Mustafa Kemal, who became known as Atatürk (Father of Turkey), had driven out all foreign forces and established the Turkish Republic. Atatürk believed that the new state could only prosper with the adoption of secular and modern reforms. He abolished the caliphate* and sultanate in favor of an elected president and legislature.

Changing Role of Islam

During the Ottoman Empire, Sunni* Islam served as the faith of the ruling classes. Sufi* orders attracted popular support as mystical* nomads spread Islam throughout the countryside. Sufis bestowed magical protection on the army and adorned new sultans with swords. However, the Sunni *ulama* surpassed the Sufi teachers in influence, especially during the 1800s when Western influence in the empire increased. Because the Sufis opposed European customs, the sultans viewed them as an obstacle to modernization. Sultan Mahmud II (ruled 1808–1835) appointed the leading members of the Sunni clergy to government offices. He also took control of mosque* funding and Sufi orders to halt opposition to his policies.

Although the sultans took steps to secularize the nation, they continued to promote Islam, portraying themselves as the caliphs* of all Muslims. Atatürk cited the Muslim heritage of the region as a reason for fighting for Turkey's independence. When the Turkish Republic came into existence in 1923, he continued to support the private expression of faith, although he also worked to remove religious control over state policies.

Sweeping Reforms. Had his political rivals not used Islam to challenge his leadership, Atatürk might not have moved so swiftly to secularize Turkish society. However, the attempt of Caliph Abdulmecid to take power jolted

Atatürk into action. In 1924 Atatürk eliminated the position of caliph, placed all schools under state control, and created a ministry to oversee matters of religious dogma* and ritual.

> * **dogma** system of established principles

The following year, Turkey's Kurdish minority rebelled. The government launched an intense period of reforms that lasted four years. During this time, Atatürk removed religion completely from political life. He outlawed dervish* orders and public mystical devotional meetings. A new civil code based on Swiss law replaced Islamic law (*shari'ah*), and Islam lost its place as the official state religion.

> * **dervish** Sufi mystic; member of an order that uses music and dance to enter a trancelike state

Atatürk also worked to secularize Islamic society. To make Turkish men look more European, he banned the fez, a head covering introduced by Mahmud II in 1826 as an improvement on the turban. The Hat Law (1925) made the wearing of the fez a criminal offense and led to widespread rioting. Atatürk also exhorted women to remove their veils. He supported education for women and held dances to integrate the sexes. By 1935 Turkish women had gained the vote, and 17 women had entered the Turkish parliament. Concerned with high illiteracy rates, Atatürk replaced the elaborate Arabic script used by the Ottomans with Latin letters. He referred to this action as an effort to free Turkey "from these incomprehensible signs that for centuries have held our minds in an iron vice."

Atatürk did not seek to stamp out religion, but merely to remove it from national politics. In fact, the state sponsored and promoted religious groups and activities. It encouraged Friday prayer at mosques to build a sense of community. The government wrote the sermons to inform the public that their religious obligations included such duties as military service, paying taxes, and serving the government obediently. Atatürk also introduced religious instruction into military training to stimulate a sense of loyalty and discipline.

Growing Influence of the Military. The Turkish leaders who came to power after Atatürk's death in 1938 displayed more sympathy for Islam. In the 1940s, religious education returned to schools, and the tombs of saints were reopened. Islamists* sought a voice in government, along with Sufi orders that had remained influential despite years of secular policies. Although Atatürk had made great changes within the government and cities, his reforms had barely touched the countryside. When the Sufis tried to demand more power, however, the government punished them and jailed their leaders. The orders then joined various political parties, which used the orders to spread their messages.

> * **Islamist** Muslim who advocates reintegration of religion and politics

In 1960 conflicts between the Democrat Party and their rivals led to a political crisis. With the civilian leaders unable to agree on a government, the military took control. This was the first of several military coups* in modern Turkish history. The military regime created a new constitution that granted the Turks more rights, such as freedom of speech and the right to hold strikes. It quickly returned power to civilians, but remained ready to step in if religious tensions again threatened political chaos.

> * **coup** sudden, and often violent, overthrow of a ruler or government

The National Order Party (MNP), Turkey's first openly Islamic party, came into existence in the late 1960s. Banned by a military regime that seized power in 1970, it reappeared under a different name only to be abolished again in 1980. The MNP's leader, Necmettin Erbakan, bounced back to form

a new party called the Welfare Party (RP). In 1996 the RP joined with secular parties to form a coalition government with Erbakan as prime minister. Once again, the military intervened. Worried about the party's Islamic roots, the army pressured Erbakan's main political ally to abandon him. This forced the creation of a new government. Many Turks grew concerned that the military had gained too much control over the country.

Current Issues. Despite the hardships facing Islamic political parties, the Islamist Justice and Development Party (AKP) won a parliamentary majority in 2002, gaining control over the government. Party leader Recep Tayyip Erdogan assured Turkish citizens that the AKP would fight for human rights and freedoms. To further this goal, he pushed for Turkey's membership in the European Union (EU). The EU, however, denied the nation membership in part because of the large role the military plays in state decisions.

Despite this humiliation, Turkey generally enjoys a strong relationship with the West. Unlike other Middle Eastern states, it maintains friendly relations with Israel. It serves as a member of the North Atlantic Treaty Organization (NATO) and has provided a base for Western military troops during several wars. Turkey has, however, attracted criticism from the West for its treatment of its Kurdish minority. When Turkey became a state, it refused to give up territory to the Kurds despite an earlier agreement that promised the Kurds a homeland. The Kurdish people revolted against Turkey three times between 1925 and 1938, but the Turks retaliated with aerial bombardments and poison gas. In response to Kurdish terrorist* attacks in 1992, the Turks killed more than 20,000 Kurds, sending millions into exile.

Turkey faces complaints of human rights abuses among its Turkish population, as well. Prisoners have frequently complained about the use of torture in the justice system. Many Muslims also feel that they lack freedom of religion. In 1998 the National Board of Higher Education banned head scarves for female students, keeping women in veils from attending classes, taking exams, and graduating. This move angered many Muslims and symbolizes the ongoing tension between orthodox* Muslims and the secular government in Turkey. (*See also* **Atatürk, Mustafa Kemal; Istanbul; Ottoman Empire; Secularism; Seljuk Dynasty.**)

* **terrorism** use of violence against people, property, or states as a means of intimidation for political purposes

* **orthodox** conforming to accepted beliefs and practices

Twelvers   See *Ithna Ashari.*

Ulama   See *Religious Scholars.*

Umayyad Caliphate

* **caliphate** office and government of the caliph, the religious and political leader of an Islamic state

The Umayyad caliphate* ruled the Islamic world from 661 to 750. A clan in the powerful Quraysh tribe, the Umayyads dominated economic and political life in Mecca in the early 600s. Although they opposed Muhammad early in his career, the Umayyads converted to and became a strong force within Islam.

After Muhammad's death in 632, the Umayyads became embroiled in disputes over leadership. Uthman, a leading Umayyad, became caliph in 644. He caused resentment by appointing many of his clan to positions of power. An assassin ended Uthman's reign in 656, and Muhammad's cousin Ali ibn Abi Talib became caliph. Mu'awiyah, the Umayyad governor of Syria, opposed Ali's rule, as did many others. After Ali's murder in 661, Mu'awiyah seized control of the caliphate and began the Umayyad dynasty*.

* **dynasty** succession of rulers from the same family or group

The early Umayyad caliphs faced serious unrest. Several Muslim factions rejected their leadership. One group invited Ali's son Husayn ibn Ali from Medina to fight the Umayyad rulers. When Umayyad troops massacred Husayn and his family at Karbala in Iraq, outraged followers of this group turned the Shi'i* branch of Islam into an important movement. Civil wars divided the empire. Even within the Umayyad clan, rival groups battled each other for power.

* **Shi'i** refers to Muslims who believe that Muhammad chose Ali ibn Abi Talib and his descendants as the spiritual-political leaders of the Muslim community

The Umayyads, however, maintained their dominant position in the Islamic world. They embarked upon an ambitious campaign of Muslim expansion. Prior to Mu'awiyah's reign, Islamic armies had occupied Syria, Egypt, Iraq, Libya, and most of Iran. During the early 700s, Umayyad forces added North Africa, Spain, and Portugal to the empire. Muslim armies even threatened France before their defeat at the Battle of Tours in 732. The Umayyads retained the southern French city of Narbonne until 759. In the east, Umayyad troops marched through Iran and entered Central Asia and northwest India. Muslim advances in the north brought Umayyad troops to the Byzantine* capital of Constantinople. These armies besieged the city, suffering devastating losses before the defenders pushed them back.

* **Byzantine** refers to the Eastern Christian Empire that was based in Constantinople

The Umayyads ruled their vast empire from Syria. They combined Arab and local political ideas to create effective government. A trusted amir* ruled each province and reported directly to the caliph. Syrian warriors formed the core of Umayyad military strength. The Umayyads established Arabic as the official language of government and religion, and Arabs settled throughout the empire.

* **amir** military commander, governor, or prince

Islam served as the unifying force of the caliphate. Umayyad rulers claimed legitimacy as the defenders and promoters of the faith. They developed the concept of succession sanctioned by God and not subject to questioning. Many non-Arabs converted to Islam. The Umayyads contributed to the development of a uniquely Islamic culture. Scholarship, poetry, and art thrived under their rule. They built mosques*, lavish palaces, roads, and canals. They supported charities for the poor and disabled. Trade flourished as caravan routes spread across the empire.

* **mosque** Muslim place of worship

Despite the Umayyad successes, divisions continued to plague the empire. The members of the small ruling class enjoyed special privileges, paying fewer taxes than the rest of the population and sharing in the prizes of war. Non-Arab Muslims, however, suffered discrimination. Christians and Jews had a lower social status and faced a higher tax burden. For a short period, leaders even discouraged conversion of non-Muslims to Islam in order to maintain a large tax base. The resentment of minority groups boiled over into open rebellion. The Abbasids, descendants of Muhammad's uncle al-Abbas, raised an army of non-Arabs in northern Iran. In the 740s, they defeated the Umayyads in several battles. After killing Umayyad leaders, the Abbasids gained control of the caliphate and established their capital in Baghdad.

One prominent Umayyad family member, however, survived the carnage. Abd al-Rahman fled to Spain and set up an independent Islamic state. The Abbasids remained unable to conquer this last Umayyad stronghold. The Umayyads retained their power there for nearly three centuries, battling the Christian kingdoms in the northern part of the country. Internal disorder finally brought down their government in 1031, but they left a lasting legacy in southern Spain with mosques, gardens, palaces, and libraries. (*See also* **Abbasid Caliphate; Andalusia; Caliphate; Husayn ibn Ali; Shadow of God; Ta'ziyah.**)

Ummah

The term *ummah*, often translated as "Muslim community," is a fundamental concept in Islam. It represents the essential unity of believers worldwide, regardless of their geographical or cultural settings.

* **Qur'an** book of the holy scriptures of Islam

* **prophet** one who announces divinely inspired revelations

Scholars who study the Qur'an* maintain that the word *ummah* refers to a people to whom God sends a prophet*, or a people who are the objects of a divine plan of salvation. According to these studies, the *ummah* is a single group that shares common religious beliefs. In actual usage, however, the term has many different meanings, and at times, the Qur'an refers to the community in a civil, rather than religious, sense.

Aside from the Qur'an, the earliest existing Islamic source on the word *ummah* is a set of documents dictated by Muhammad shortly after his arrival at Medina. Commonly referred to as the Constitution of Medina, these documents were designed to regulate social and political life in the city. The constitution indicates that the different groups living in Medina and the surrounding area—the Muslim tribes of Medina, Muslims who emigrated from Mecca, and Jews—form "one distinct community (*ummah*) apart from other people." In this context, the term *ummah* refers to a social unit that includes believers of different forms of monotheism*.

* **monotheism** belief that there is only one God

* **hadith** reports of the words and deeds of Muhammad (not in the Qur'an, but accepted as guides for Muslim behavior)

The hadith* literature helped narrow the concept. Although the hadith also vary somewhat in usage, the reports generally define the *ummah* as a spiritual community of Muslims united in their shared beliefs. As members of a worldwide *ummah*, Muslims have a religious identity that transcends tribal and ethnic* loyalties. Islamic doctrine further teaches that all believers are equal and should defend and protect one another.

* **ethnic** relating to groups of people who share a common racial, national, tribal, religious, linguistic, or cultural background

The concept of *ummah* evolved in the decades following Muhammad's death. Early Muslims accepted the idea that the *ummah* needed a single leader to preserve its unity. During the Middle Ages*, Muslim scholars asserted that the preservation of Islam itself depended on protecting the unity of the *ummah*.

* **Middle Ages** period roughly between 500 and 1500

The *ummah* also acquired legal status within Islamic societies. Islamic law classified Muslims as believers and others—including Jews and Christians—as nonbelievers. The nonbelievers had rights, but they were subordinate to Muslims. No formal requirements existed for joining the *ummah*, aside from being born to Muslim parents or freely choosing to become a Muslim. Community membership became a form of citizenship that guar-

anteed, at least in theory, equality for all Muslims. In the 800s, some legal scholars declared the consensus of the community to be a valid source of Islamic law. Supporters of this position cited Muhammad's statement that his *ummah* "would never agree on an error." Only the Qur'an and the traditions of Muhammad had more legal authority.

During the 1800s and 1900s, European powers colonized much of the Islamic world. Nationalists* urged the members of the *ummah* to defend Islamic lands against foreign invasion. They also called for religious solidarity to revive the *ummah*. Loyalties clashed, however, with the rise of independent Muslim nation-states in the mid-1900s. Certain nationalist groups began calling for the separation of religious and national identities, emphasizing political rather than religious loyalty.

> * **nationalist** one who advocates loyalty and devotion to his or her country and its independence

The increase of secular* influences in the late 1900s further weakened the bonds of religious identity. Nonetheless, the *ummah* remains a powerful concept in the Islamic world today. Many Muslims regard the worldwide *ummah* as their primary social identity. This solidarity is displayed in the support provided to believers in other lands who are victims of political or religious persecution or natural disasters. (*See also* **Islamic State; Nationalism.**)

> * **secular** separate from religion in human life and society; connected to everyday life

United States

Islam is the second largest religion in the world, with about 1.2 billion people in a variety of countries around the world. Islam is also the fastest growing religion in the United States, with around 6 million Muslims and 1,500 mosques. There are 400 Islamic schools in the states, 3 colleges, 400 associations, 200,000 Muslim-owned businesses, and 9,000 Muslim Americans on active duty in the U.S. military. Around 62 percent of American Muslims are registered voters. By the year 2010, Islam will be the second largest religion in the United States, next to Christianity.

Yet before the bombing of the World Trade Center in 1993 and the events of September 11, 2001, which were perpetrated by Muslim terrorists, Americans knew little about Islam. Since 9/11 Muslims and non-Muslims have made special efforts to familiarize Americans with the beliefs of traditional Islam and the historical development of Islam in the United States.

Immigration Begins

Muslims in America assert that there is no inherent contradiction between being a good Muslim and being a good American. If there is an ongoing challenge for American Muslims, especially among young people, it is the same challenge that other religions face—how to reconcile moral and spiritual values with the materialistic orientation of modern life.

> See color plate 8, vol. 3.

Beyond Arabia. Islam originated in Arabia in the 600s. Its founder, Muhammad, is revered by Muslims as the final prophet in the long line of prophets that include Adam, Abraham, Isaac, Ismail, John the Baptist, and Jesus. Muhammad brought the knowledge of God (Allah) to humankind. The revelations of God's will to Muhammad took place over a 20-year period,

In August 2002, the largest annual convention of American Muslims met in Washington, D.C., to discuss the impact of the terrorist attacks of September 11, 2001.

*hadith reports of the words and deeds of Muhammad (not in the Qur'an, but accepted as guides for Muslim behavior)

from 610 to 632, and were compiled in the Qur'an, the sacred text of Islam. The Qur'an and the hadith* constitute the foundation on which traditional Islamic beliefs and practices are based.

The people of Mecca rejected Muhammad's teachings at first. The Qur'anic message threatened the economic and religious structures of their society. Nevertheless, his teachings spread rapidly and by 750, Islam had become a major political and religious power in the Middle East and beyond—India, Pakistan, Sri Lanka, China, Malaysia, Indonesia, Spain, Africa, and Central Asia.

Patterns of Immigration. Islam has had quiet but steady growth in the United States. The earliest Muslims to arrive in the United States were West Africans who were brought as slaves between 1530 and 1851. Forced to give up their religion, many of them passed their traditional practices to their descendants in secret.

The largest group of Muslims in the United States consists of immigrants who came from the Middle East and other Muslim-populated regions in a succession of waves beginning in the late 1800s. The first wave of Muslim immigrants arrived in the United States between 1875 and 1912. They came from the Arab countries of Syria, Lebanon, Jordan, and Palestine.

Communities formed in the manufacturing centers of the midwestern United States—Cedar Rapids, Iowa; Toledo, Ohio; Detroit, Michigan; and Chicago, Illinois. Most were uneducated and unskilled workers seeking economic opportunities in America. These immigrant families founded the first mosques in the United States. They tended to focus on social issues and placed little emphasis on traditional mosque functions. Finding difficulty integrating into American society, most of these immigrants maintained social bonds with fellow Muslims and Arabs exclusively. During this period, the primary function of the mosques was to keep families close, offer solidarity in a new land, and provide fellowship for various rites of passage, such as marriage, birth, and burial. Some of the early mosque communities even adapted to some American church patterns, such as religious education classes and community events on Saturdays.

Another wave of immigrants arrived between 1947 and 1960 and included Muslims not only from the Middle East, but also from India, Pakistan, Eastern Europe, the Soviet Union, and other parts of the Islamic world. Some were the children of wealthy ruling families, and some simply came for higher education opportunities.

The last major wave of immigrants began in the late 1960s and continues. Many in this last wave, especially Pakistanis and Arabs, are educated professionals. Some immigrated because of revolution or political upheaval in their homelands. Many are from Egypt, Jordan, Turkey, Kuwait, Iraq, Iran, and Afghanistan, but more recently from the Sudan, Uganda, Guyana, Bermuda, and the former Yugoslavia.

Reviving Traditional Islam

Muslim immigrants who arrived in the United States after the 1970s tended to bring a heightened level of religious and political self-consciousness, reflecting developments in Islam in other regions. The second half of the 20th century was a time of religious revival in Islamic countries, as Muslims reflected on their loss of land, power, and prestige as a result of colonialism and the economic and political domination of the West. Muslims questioned whether the losses they experienced were the result of adopting Western values and lifestyles. Many saw the answer in a return to traditional Islam.

Tradition and Society. One symbol of Islamic revivalism is the increasing number of women who have adopted the *hijab* (the traditional dress for Muslim women, generally referring to the veil and long dress). *Hijab*, especially among the urban, educated women, had been in decline in Muslim countries. The question of how to reconcile tradition and modernity is an ongoing issue, not only in Muslim countries, but also in the Muslim community in the United States.

Most Muslims in America who were raised in traditional Islamic cultures speak of the tension that arises as they attempt to remain close to their linguistic, cultural, and religious roots while trying to find a sense of belonging in their adopted home. American lifestyles sometimes seem incompatible with Muslim family life. Work schedules do not easily accommodate the five-times-daily prayers or the Friday congregational prayers. Institutional eating facilities are not set up to accommodate Islamic dietary restrictions (such as the prohibition of pork). The pervasiveness of alcohol, sexual permissiveness, and immodesty are seen as negative influences on the Muslim community. Nevertheless, American Muslim individuals and families continue to find ways to follow *shari'ah*, traditional Islamic law, in the midst of modern American society.

Changes in Mosque Function. The mosque is the center for congregational Friday prayers in communities throughout the Islamic world. In the United States various types of mosque communities have evolved. Some mosques function in the same way as America's ethnic churches, where cultural identity is emphasized and preserved and where immigrants learn as much about American life as about their religion. Some mosques become outreach centers, educating Americans about Islam, utilizing the Islamic tradition of hospitality to establish communication and goodwill with the surrounding community. Such activities have been especially important in the aftermath of 9/11 as Muslim communities engage with local groups to reduce misunderstanding and intolerance between Muslims and non-Muslims.

Another positive new trend is emerging in Muslim American mosques—the so-called mega-mosque, which serves the needs of large racially and ethnically diverse communities, such as in Los Angeles.

Unlike the Catholic Church, which is headed by the pope, Islam has no central authority. Both major theological* divisions in Islam—Sunni and Shi'I—have mosques in the United States. Mosque governance in the United States is similar to some Protestant denominations in which each community decides on its local leadership, and that leadership determines how conservative or progressive the mosque community is in its interpretation of the Qur'an, its approach to gender issues, and its participation in the American political system. The imam in the American mosque has the role of spiritual leader, administrator, and counselor—going beyond the traditional function in Islamic countries.

*theological refers to the study, qualities, and will of God

Helping New Immigrants. Several Islamic organizations have emerged to provide services to American Muslims. The need for a unifying force led second-generation Muslim immigrants to create an association of mosques to pool resources and facilitate communication among mosques. Originally called the Federation of Islamic Organizations, it is now known in the United States and Canada as the Federation of Islamic Associations. Student organizations on college campuses, most notably the Muslim Student Association, support the growing and diverse Muslim student population in their efforts to create a Muslim community and to serve Islam.

Many professional organizations developed, such as the American Association of Islamic Social Scientists, Islamic Medical Association, the Islamic Teaching Center, the Malaysian Islamic Study Group, the International Institute of Islamic Thought, and the American Muslim Mission. These and other groups have their own governing boards and committees but are under the umbrella of the Islamic Society of North America (ISNA). Since the 1980s, ISNA has encouraged active participation in the American political system through voting, forming political action committees, lobbying, supporting candidates, and becoming candidates themselves.

African Americans and Islam

African Americans form the largest group of converts to Islam in the United States. The growth of Islam among African Americans—as well as the use of Islamic terminology in black popular culture—reflects the importance that Islam holds for black Americans, namely a religious faith that respects their African heritage and one that symbolizes racial inclusiveness.

Black Muslim Leaders. The roots of a black Muslim perspective can be traced to Timothy Drew (later called Noble Drew Ali), a poor North Carolina black who saw Islam as a means of uniting Americans of African heritage and giving them a sense of pride. He founded the Moorish American Science

Temple in 1913 and the organization soon spread to several cities. After his death in 1929, Wallace Fard Muhammad started another movement in Detroit. He preached some Islamic teachings, such as submission to Allah and the avoidance of alcohol, gambling, eating pork, and sex outside of marriage. His organization, The Lost-Found Nation of Islam in the Wilderness of North America, came under the leadership of Elijah Muhammad. Although he advocated hard work, self-respect, and economic independence, Elijah Muhammad's other teachings countered traditional Islamic teachings, particularly his preaching of white society as evil.

Perhaps the most famous convert to the Nation of Islam was Malcolm X, whose fiery speeches during the 1960s were the major reason for the growth of membership in the organization. Malcolm X's pilgrimage to Mecca and his experience of a universal brotherhood in submission to Allah, without regard to color, led him to break with Elijah Muhammad in favor of what he saw as true Islam.

Elijah Muhammad's son, Warith Deen Muhammad, took over the leadership of the Nation of Islam, rejected the preaching of racial hatred, and instituted traditional Islamic beliefs and rituals. In 1985 Warith Deen Muhammad decentralized the organization, making it more mainstream, a move that disappointed some members. One of those was Louis Farrakhan, the well-known spokesman for Elijah Muhammad's original teachings. Farrakhan retained the organization's name of Nation of Islam. Although he does not represent mainstream Islam, Farrakhan's preaching has served as an outlet for the frustration of poor inner city residents. The intertwined histories of these various organizations have contributed to confusion in the public's mind as to what Islam is.

Promoting Education. A major contribution of the American Muslim mission has been its nationwide system of schools—the Sister Clara Muhammad schools, named for the wife of Elijah Muhammad. The schools not only raise the quality of life and education in trouble-ridden urban neighborhoods, but also draw children of recent immigrants into already established African-American communities, fostering a sense of community across ethnic lines. Teachers are sometimes immigrants themselves, often with advanced degrees in their native countries. Islamic studies are interwoven with history and English, and Arabic is taught as early as kindergarten. The schools maintain a philosophy that is racially inclusive and preach tolerance of other faiths.

Prison Converts. Another major constituency of African American Muslims consists of black Americans who convert to Islam while in prison. For many of these people (mostly men), Islam becomes an important means of identity formation. Because many mosques are involved in prison ministries, incarcerated converts are able to build important links to stable communities on the outside. Legal questions arise, however, regarding religious liberties of Muslims in prison, such as the granting of considerations of religious expression, such as dietary requirements and a time and place for worship.

Sufi Islam in America

Sufism, the mystical branch of Islam, offers the faithful a means of deeper devotion and religious knowledge. Beginning in the 800s, Sufi brotherhoods organized around popular teachers, who taught prayers and rituals of re-

Latino Muslims

Latinos represent an ethnic group that is experiencing growing numbers of converts to Islam. It is estimated that the Latino Muslim population in the United States is currently around 40,000. Along with rising numbers of Latino converts, several Latino Muslim organizations have emerged, including the Alianza Islamica and Propagación Islamica para la Educación e la Devoción a Ala' el Divino (PIEDAD). Latinos often cite as their reasons for conversion the desire for an immediate relationship with God without intermediaries or wanting to reclaim the heritage of Spain when Muslims, Christians, and Jews lived together in peace under Muslim rule.

membrance of God (such as night vigils or the recitation of the Beautiful Names of God), which Muslims practiced in addition to their required daily prayers. These orders, such as the Qadiriyah, Naqshbandiyah, Tijaniyah, and Mawlawiyah, usually bear the name of the founder of the order. Just as traditional Sufi orders were instrumental in the transmission of Islam to many diverse geographic regions of the world, Sufi groups have been significant in their transmission of Islamic spirituality to a modern American audience. Sufi groups tend to focus on spiritual development rather than on political issues and have attracted Christians and Jews to Islam, as well as recent immigrants from Muslim countries.

Challenges for American Muslims

American Muslims currently face several key issues. First and foremost is finding ways to present Islam to the public in a manner that does not deny the reality of extremist factions in Islam, such as al-Qaeda and the Taliban, but offers an understanding of Islam as it is lived by most Muslims. Organizations, such as the Arab Anti-Defamation League, the American Muslim Council, and the Council on American-Islamic Relations are engaged in these efforts.

Another issue for American Muslims is seeking support to resolve injustices done to Muslims and Arabs, such as the treatment of Palestinians in Israel, without becoming linked to terrorist groups. A related issue concerns the impact of the Homeland Security Act, enacted by the U.S. Congress in the aftermath of 9/11, on the civil liberties of Muslims and Arabs in America.

Finally, America has become the melting pot of young, culturally diverse Islamic scholars and activists. In the United States, these people have the political and academic freedom to reinterpret the Qur'an and *shari'ah* in addressing the social injustices that occur in the name of Islamic tradition— gender inequality, suppression of religious dissent, and mistreatment of religious minorities in some Muslim countries. Working through academic institutions, grassroots organizations, and community study groups, today's Islamic scholars are working to create a modern, progressive Islam that remains true to its spiritual roots and to contemporary democratic ideals.

Universities

See color plate 13, vol. 1.

Higher education has been a part of Islamic culture for centuries. The first colleges appeared in the Muslim world in the 600s and 700s. Islamic universities were established in the following centuries, long before such institutions emerged in Europe. After a period of preeminence, however, Islamic universities fell into decline. When European powers colonized much of the Muslim world in the 1800s, they set up Western-style schools in place of Islamic ones. In the years since Muslim nations gained their independence, many of them have made efforts to restore Islamic learning.

Development of Higher Education. The main educational institution in the early Islamic world was the *madrasah*. The vizier* Nizam al-Mulk

*vizier Muslim minister of state

(died 1092) created the first network of these schools, which usually focused on Islamic law. Other subjects included theology*, Arabic grammar, and study of the Qu'ran*. The Qarawiyin Mosque, founded in Fez, Morocco, in 859, was the location of one of the world's great early universities. Al-Azhar in Cairo, established in 970, became the most famous mosque-university in the world. Other universities arose throughout the Middle East, and the Umayyads in Spain developed an extensive university system. Universities were similar to *madrasahs*, but they taught a wider range of subjects. Islamic rulers provided funds for them, constructing libraries and beautifully designed building complexes.

Meanwhile, western European scholars had begun to take an interest in Islamic education. Impressed with al-Mulk's *madrasah* system, Christian crusaders* brought reports of it back to their native countries. European students began to attend universities in the Middle East and to study Islamic culture. Western intellectuals learned Arabic, read Islamic literature, and engaged in Muslim-style oral debates. In France, Italy, and Spain, educators adopted Muslim teaching methods, basing their first institutions of higher learning on Islamic models.

Religious Debates. As the Muslim empire expanded, Muslim schooling also changed. Islamic scholars began to encounter the "Greek sciences" of mathematics, philosophy, and medicine. Because they believed that all forms of knowledge were God's gift to humankind, Muslim scholars adopted these new branches of learning and taught them in universities.

The combination of Greek and Muslim thought created a new school of theology that blossomed between the 800s and the 1100s, posing a challenge to orthodox* views of religion. Conservative religious leaders responded by drawing clear lines between what they termed "transmitted" and "intellectual" science. Transmitted science consisted of knowledge given directly to humans by God through the Prophet Muhammad. Intellectual science was any form of knowledge gained through the use of human reason. Some scholars believed that both transmitted and intellectual science had a place in Islamic education. For example, Abu Hamid al-Ghazali (1058–1111) claimed that all Muslims had a duty to acquire at least a basic understanding of Islamic sacred law, or *shari'ah*. All other forms of knowledge were optional for individuals, but necessary for society as a whole. However, many orthodox leaders took a more hostile attitude to secular* learning. They succeeded in excluding intellectual science from the *madrasahs*. This decision proved to be a serious setback for Islamic education.

East Meets West. European universities, meanwhile, were developing a secular approach to learning. The Western educational system stressed reason as the means of gaining knowledge and truth. This approach made its way into the Muslim world in the 1800s, when European powers began colonizing Muslim nations. Colonial governments established Western-style schools and universities. They planned to use these schools to educate a new ruling class that would control, guide, and modernize society in the Islamic world.

Colonial governments followed a strict policy of keeping religion out of the public schools. At the same time, they allowed the traditional *madrasahs* to continue to operate. Thus, a dual education system existed, forcing Muslims to choose one type of school or the other. Only those who attended sec-

* **theology** study of the nature and qualities of God and the understanding of His will

* **Qur'an** book of the holy scriptures of Islam

* **crusader** person who participated in the holy wars against the Muslims during the Middle Ages

* **orthodox** conforming to accepted beliefs and practices

* **secular** separate from religion in human life and society; connected to everyday life

Universities

One of the oldest universities in the world, al-Azhar in Cairo, Egypt, has adapted to changing times in the Muslim world. In the 1960s, the university added secular subjects such as engineering, medicine, and commerce to its curriculum and opened a separate female college.

* **missionary** person who works to convert nonbelievers to a particular faith

* **nationalist** one who advocates loyalty and devotion to his or her country and its independence

ular schools received a modern education, while only those in the *madrasahs* had a thorough knowledge of Islam.

Ironically, the Western-style universities in the Muslim world eventually became centers of resistance to colonial rule. Schools founded by foreign missionaries* in Syria, Palestine, Lebanon, and Jordan helped revive interest in Arab culture. Over time, the nationalist* ideas born in the universities grew into larger movements throughout the region. In Lebanon, for example, both the Jesuit University of St. Joseph in Ghazir and the American University of Beirut played a large role in modernization and in the spread of Arab nationalism.

Secularization and Independence. As Muslim nations began to gain their independence from colonial powers, many of them sought to reform their educational systems. Beginning around 1900, countries such as Egypt, Turkey, and Iran established several new universities. Reform-minded leaders also undertook changes to existing schools. For example, Mustafa Kemal Atatürk, who came to power in Turkey in 1923, placed all schools under state control.

These efforts to remove religious education from the schools did not succeed for long. In the 1940s and 1950s, after Atatürk's death, Turkish universities began teaching Islamic studies. Religious study also made its way into the primary schools. Elsewhere, by contrast, religious institutions, such as al-Azhar University, adopted more secular subjects. In the 1960s, al-Azhar added engineering, medicine, and commerce to its curriculum. It also opened a separate college for female students.

In Iran, a revolution in 1979 brought an Islamic government to power. Textbooks and courses took on a more Islamic slant, and a division arose between religious and secular universities. This split between secular and Islamic learning persists throughout the Muslim world today. Muslim nations have addressed the issue in a variety of ways. Malaysia and Indonesia, for instance, have a long-standing system of Islamic schools known as the *pesantrens*, which exist alongside secular universities. Over time, many of the Muslim schools in Indonesia have evolved into full-fledged Islamic universities. Saudi Arabia has replaced nearly all its *madrasahs* with more modern schools, but the subjects taught at these schools, as well as the texts used, reflect the Muslim faith. The nation is also home to the Islamic University of Medina, which uses modern methods to teach the same subjects taught in the old *madrasahs*. Many nations, including Jordan, Morocco, and Algeria, have introduced courses on Islamic culture in their universities. (*See also* **Azhar, al-; Education; Madrasah; Science; Secularism.**)

Urdu

Urdu is an Indo-European language used by Muslims that originated in northern India. It serves as the official language of Pakistan and one of several officially recognized languages of India. About 50 million people speak Urdu, and another 50 million can understand the language.

Urdu is a variation of Hindustani, the most common language of northern India. Indian Muslims created it from elements of the Persian language and the Arabic alphabet. Urdu differs from Hindi, another form of Hindustani that was developed by Hindus using a modified form of Sanskrit*. Urdu and Hindi have a similar grammar and pronunciation, and the two languages share much vocabulary. Their written forms are quite different, however, because of the influence of Sanskrit on Hindi and of Persian and Arabic on Urdu.

Muslims have produced a large body of literature in Urdu. They composed histories and religious writings as early as the 1300s. Urdu poetry flourished in the 1500s, and prose fiction developed in the 1800s. Around this time, Urdu authors replaced the ornate, classical form of Urdu with a more informal version of the language based on local speech. Beginning in the 1800s and con-

* **Sanskrit** ancient classical language of India and Hinduism

*Pan-Islamic refers to the movement to unify all Islamic peoples

*nationalism feelings of loyalty and devotion to one's country and a commitment to its independence

tinuing throughout the 1900s, Urdu literature concentrated on themes such as Pan-Islamic* unity and nationalism*. Both poetry and prose dealt with the role of Islam and the duties of Muslims in modern society. Urdu authors such as Muhammad Iqbal (1877–1938) influenced social reformers, and Iqbal's ideas led to the creation of Pakistan in 1947. (*See also* **Arabic Language and Literature; India; Iqbal, Muhammad; Literature; Pakistan.**)

Veiling

See *Hijab.*

Virtue

See *Taqwa.*

Vizier

*caliphate office and government of the caliph, the religious and political leader of an Islamic state

*dynasty succession of rulers from the same family or group

*bureaucracy agencies and officials that comprise a government

*sultan political and military ruler of a Muslim dynasty or state

*Ottoman Empire large Turkish state existing from the early 1300s to the early 1900s

In the late 700s, Muslims adopted the term *vizier* (*wazir* in Arabic) to refer to the position of chief minister or deputy of a caliphate*. Initially, the vizier served as the financial officer of the Islamic state. Under the Abbasid caliphate (750–1258), the position of vizier took on a broader role. The vizier acted on behalf of the ruler in military and civil matters. During the early years of the caliphate, the position of vizier passed among the Barmakids, a family of Iranian origin that served in the administration.

During the later Islamic dynasties* of the Seljuk and Mamluk families, the role of the vizier varied. Sometimes the position was simply a reward given to a royal supporter. At other times, the vizier occupied a prominent place in the bureaucracy*.

The sultans* of the vast Ottoman Empire* bestowed the rank and title of vizier on several officials at once. The most senior of the viziers was called the grand vizier. In addition to his traditional functions, he supervised the lesser viziers as well as other state officers. As the empire grew, so did the responsibilities of the grand vizier, and in effect, he became the ruler of this large state. During the 1800s, Ottoman sultans wanted to reform their government along Western lines. They modified the duties of the grand vizier to those of a prime minister. Although the grand vizier retained considerable power as the chief of a council of ministers, he could use his power only to the degree that the sultan allowed. (*See also* **Abbasid Caliphate; Mamluk State; Ottoman Empire; Seljuk Dynasty.**)

Wahhabi

*conservative generally opposed to change, especially in existing political and social institutions

Wahhabi is the name of a movement in Islam that began in Arabia in the 1700s. Of the many movements in Islam, Wahhabi Islam, or Wahhabism, is one of the most conservative*. In the region that is now Saudi Arabia, the Wahhabi movement has played a central role in politics, law, and society since the mid-1700s. Today, Wahhabi principles guide every aspect of Saudi legal and social life.

History. The Wahhabi movement takes its name from its founder, Muhammad ibn Abd al-Wahhab. He was an Islamic scholar who lived in the Najd region of the Arabian Peninsula in the 1700s. Ibn Abd al-Wahhab believed that Muslims in Arabia had fallen into moral and political decline. He proposed a return to what he regarded as the ideal form of Islam. Ibn Abd al-Wahhab placed a strong emphasis on monotheism*. He also argued for a strict reliance on the Qur'an*, sunnah*, and hadith* as the only sources of Islamic belief and practice. Ibn Abd al-Wahhab taught that Muslims had a duty to fight nonbelievers and to establish a Muslim society based solely on Islamic law.

Around 1750 Ibn Abd al-Wahhab joined forces with Muhammad ibn Saud, a local tribal chief. Together, they launched a major effort to conquer and unite the various tribes of Arabia and convert them to Wahhabism. By the early 1800s, the Saudi-Wahhabi alliance had brought all of Najd under its control. Their forces had also occupied the Islamic holy cities of Mecca and Medina in western Arabia. They had even attacked Karbala, a holy city of the Shi'i* Muslims in Iraq. Together, Ibn Abd al-Wahhab and Ibn Saud established the first Saudi state and made Wahhabism the strongest religious movement in the Arabian Peninsula.

Shortly after it began, the first Saudi empire fell to the more powerful Ottoman Empire*. Within a few years, however, the Saudi ruler, Faysal I had partly restored Saudi-Wahhabi rule. At the end of the 1800s, the empire was destroyed again, this time by tribes from northern Arabia. In the early 1900s, another Saudi leader, Abd al-Aziz ibn Saud, reunited the tribes of Arabia and revived Wahhabism throughout the peninsula. In 1932 he formally established the Kingdom of Saudi Arabia, ensuring that Wahhabism would continue to dominate the Arabian Peninsula.

The new kingdom inspired renewal movements in other parts of the Muslim world. Starting in the 1950s, the Saudis gave money and built mosques* and other institutions in poor Muslim communities around the world. Some wealthy Saudis also provided money and support to extremist groups.

Wahhabi Principles. Muhammad ibn Abd al-Wahhab wrote about a variety of Islamic subjects, including law, theology*, and the life of the Prophet Muhammad. Several issues dominated his writings, and his views on these issues are the basis of Wahhabism. The central principle of the movement is *tawhid*, which refers to the unity or oneness of God. According to *tawhid*, God alone created the universe, provides for it, and determines what happens within it. The belief in the unity of God is so central to Wahhabism that its followers refer to themselves as Muwahhidun, or "Unitarians."

A related Wahhabi principle limits worship to God alone. Ibn Abd al-Wahhab even criticized the practice of visiting tombs to pray for dead ancestors because he believed it could lead to worshipping these ancestors. For this reason, he insisted that grave markers should be level with the ground and free of any decoration. Followers of Wahhabi Islam considered it their duty to destroy existing tombs in order to help prevent the possible development of ancestor worship. Even the tomb of Muhammad was not spared.

Another Wahhabi principle prohibits intercession. This word refers to the practice of calling on someone, such as a saint or the Prophet Muham-

* **monotheism** belief that there is only one God

* **Qur'an** book of the holy scriptures of Islam

* **sunnah** literally "the trodden path"; Islamic customs based on the exemplary behavior of Muhammad

* **hadith** reports of the words and deeds of Muhammad (not in the Qur'an, but accepted as guides for Muslim behavior)

* **Shi'i** refers to Muslims who believe that Muhammad chose Ali ibn Abi Talib and his descendants as the spiritual-political leaders of the Muslim community

* **Ottoman Empire** large Turkish state existing from the early 1300s to the early 1900s

* **mosque** Muslim place of worship

* **theology** study of the nature and qualities of God and the understanding of His will

Repeat Performance

In 1802 Wahhabis destroyed sacred Shi'i sites in Karbala, Iraq. The destruction included the tomb of the Prophet Muhammad's grandson, Husayn ibn Ali, who is one of the holiest figures in Shi'i Muslim history. Shi'i Muslims never forgot or forgave the destruction of Husayn's tomb and the other holy sites of Karbala. Centuries later, Shi'is are still hostile toward followers of Wahhabi Islam. In 2001 some of them recalled the events at Karbala when the Taliban, a conservative Islamic group in power in Afghanistan, destroyed several ancient Buddhist statues in that country. Although the members of the Taliban were not Wahhabis, some believed that their actions reflected the ideals of the Wahhabi movement.

mad, to approach God on the speaker's behalf. Ibn Abd al-Wahhab believed that intercession violated the principle of worshipping God alone. He also opposed innovation, the adoption of new ideas or practices. He defined innovation as any doctrine* or action not based on a strict interpretation of the Qur'an, sunnah, and hadith. Ibn Abd al-Wahhab rejected all additions to the practice of Islam that had been adopted after the Prophet's lifetime, such as the celebration of Muhammad's birthday. (*See also* **Hadith; Saudi Arabia; Sunnah; Tawhid.**)

* **doctrine** principle, theory, or belief that is taught or presented for acceptance

Warith Deen Muhammad

1933–
African American Muslim leader

Warith Deen Muhammad (originally named Wallace Delaney Muhammad) is an internationally recognized leader in the African American Muslim community. His father, Elijah Muhammad, headed the Nation of Islam from 1934 until his death in 1975. This African American religious and political organization flourished under the leadership of Elijah Muhammad and spokesman Malcolm X. Elijah Muhammad called on African Americans to convert to Islam as he envisioned it. This included the belief that white people were evil and that black Americans should form a separate nation, teachings alien to mainstream Islam.

Warith Deen Muhammad joined the Nation of Islam after completing high school in the late 1950s. Sent to jail for resisting the draft, he studied Islam in prison and realized that some of the principles of the Nation of Islam contradicted those of the traditional faith. After being released from prison, Warith challenged his father's teachings. Elijah Muhammad suspended him from the Nation of Islam twice for his views.

When Elijah Muhammad died, Warith took over as leader of the Nation of Islam. He made major changes in the organization, moving it away from the militant* black nationalism* of his father and toward mainstream Sunni* Islam. Warith opened up membership to people of all races. He became involved in American politics and placed more women in positions of power. He also changed the name of the organization to the World Community of Islam in the West, and later to the American Muslim Mission.

* **militant** aggressively active in a cause

* **nationalism** feelings of loyalty and devotion to one's country and a commitment to its independence

* **Sunni** refers to the largest branch of the Muslim community; the name derives from sunnah, the exemplary behavior of the Prophet Muhammad

* **imam** spiritual-political leader in Shi'i Islam, one who is regarded as directly descended from Muhammad; also, one who leads prayers

* **mosque** Muslim place of worship

In 1977 a group of black Muslims led by Louis Farrakhan split off from the organization. These people strove to uphold the spirit of Elijah Muhammad, which they thought Warith had corrupted. The following year, Warith transferred leadership of the American Muslim Mission to an elected council of six imams*. In 1985 he replaced the organization with a coalition of mosques* called the Muslim American Society. Although Warith Deen Muhammad no longer heads a national organization, he remains a leader of African American Muslims. In 1992 he became the first imam to offer morning prayers in the U.S. Senate. In 1996 Pope John Paul II invited him to the Vatican. (*See also* **Elijah Muhammad; Farrakhan, Louis; Malcolm X; Nation of Islam.**)

Washing

See *Ablution.*

West Africa

West Africa extends from the Sahara in the north to the Gulf of Guinea in the south. It includes such countries as Nigeria, Mauritania, and the Ivory Coast. Berber* traders first arrived in West Africa in the 800s and 900s. Islam spread slowly throughout the region. Some West African states acquired large Muslim majorities. Others resisted Islam and never developed more than a Muslim minority.

Some West African countries, such as Mali, Mauritania, and Senegal, are overwhelmingly Muslim. The nations of Burkina Faso, Nigeria, and Sierra Leone are about 50 percent Muslim. Cameroon, Ghana, and Liberia have 20 percent or fewer Muslims in their populations. The non-Muslim people in these countries typically follow Christianity or African traditional religions.

* **Berber** refers to a North African ethnic group that consists primarily of Muslims

Islam in West Africa

Muhammad established Islam in the mid-600s, unifying Arabian tribes for the first time. During the following centuries, Islamic empires came to dominate the Middle East. Muslims also gained control of regions as far apart as India and Spain. Some settled in parts of North Africa, and traders spread Islam throughout the continent. Muslim empires and centers of learning thrived in West Africa. In the 21st century, Islam continues to have a strong presence in the region. However, Muslims sometimes experience conflicts with one another and with other groups. Sufis* and Islamic reformers often clash in their views of the role of Islam in the modern state.

* **Sufi** follower of Sufism, which seeks to develop spirituality through discipline of the mind and body

Spread by Trade. West Africans first encountered Islam when Berber merchants traveled south in the 800s. From North Africa, they developed trade routes across the Sahara that connected many towns and villages. As they traveled along these paths, they slowly spread Muslim culture and philosophy. Nomadic tribes and local traders adopted the religion and aided in its expansion.

During the Middle Ages*, Islam gained widespread acceptance in West Africa. Several Muslim empires and states arose, including the Mali Empire (1200s–1400s), the Songhay Empire in present-day Niger (1300s–1500s), and the Kanem-Bornu Empire in present-day Chad (1200s–1800s). Cities such as Timbuktu (in Mali) and Kano (in Nigeria) flourished as centers of Islamic learning. As Islam spread throughout West Africa, it united tribal peoples with a common faith and rituals. When the celebrated Muslim travel writer Ibn Battutah visited West Africa in the mid-1300s, he noted the strong Muslim influence on the region.

* **Middle Ages** period roughly between 500 and 1500

In the early 1800s, Usuman Dan Fodio, a member of the Muslim Fulani tribe, declared jihad* against rulers who had not truly accepted Islam. He became head of the Sokoto caliphate*, which brought together many West African states for the first time. By the mid-1800s, the caliphate had assumed control over most of the northern region of Nigeria as well as parts of present-day Niger and Cameroon. The Fulani converted many West Africans to Islam.

Sufi orders also spread throughout West Africa during this period, including the Qadiriyah and Tijaniyah. Sufi leaders established Islamic schools

* **jihad** literally "striving"; war in defense of Islam

* **caliphate** office and government of the caliph, the religious and political leader of an Islamic state

Muslims make up about 90 percent of the population of the West African country of Mali. Here children attend class at a Qur'anic school in the ancient city of Timbuktu.

* **mosque** Muslim place of worship

* **protectorate** country under the protection and control of a stronger nation

* **missionary** person who works to convert nonbelievers to a particular faith

and mosques*, which became the chief Islamic social organizations. Disciples referred to their leaders as marabouts, a term derived from an Arabic word for a religious member of the military. The marabouts gained many followers, and Sufism became a popular and influential form of Islam in West Africa.

Colonial Period. Virtually all the countries of West Africa became European colonies or protectorates* in the late 1800s and early 1900s. Along with the colonizers came Christian missionaries* who competed with Islamic religious leaders for the devotion of their people. While Western rulers promoted Christianity, however, they generally approved of Islam and took few steps to halt its progress. Islam grew in popularity during this time. Roads built by the Europeans allowed Muslim teachers and traders to travel into the interior of West Africa. Several Muslim scholars embarked on missions to spread Islam. They established Muslim communities, building mosques and religious schools.

Some colonial rulers regarded Muslims as more civilized than non-Muslim Africans. Because Muslims tended to have a better education as well as political experience, colonial powers recruited them to help administer certain regions. However, they also feared Muslim leaders as political rivals and usually monitored their activities.

Some Muslim groups played a significant role in stirring resistance to European control. Sufi marabouts raised large forces and declared a holy war against the Westerners. Eventually, however, they realized that they could not defeat the Europeans. To protect their economic and religious interests, the Sufis decided to collaborate with the colonial powers.

Islamic Reform. To help strengthen Islam against colonial rule, some Muslim scholars initiated reform movements. Muslims who had attended universities in the Middle East or who had made the pilgrimage* to Mecca promoted a return to the lifestyle of Muhammad and his early followers. One of the most popular and influential reform movements was the Wahhabi

* **pilgrimage** journey to a shrine or sacred place

movement. It had no connection with the Wahhabi movement that arose in Saudi Arabia in the 1700s, but it was given that name by the Europeans, who saw similarities between the two. Wahhabi reformers encouraged Muslims to study the Qur'an* and the hadith*, to end the practice of saint worship, and to rid their rituals of animist* elements.

Reform movements spread rapidly along trade routes, succeeding especially in areas where Sufism lacked a strong presence. The increasing popularity of the reform movements led to conflicts between Muslims of different groups. For example, Muslims disputed among themselves over the control of local mosques. These arguments often led to the formation of separate mosques in each town.

Most West African countries gained their independence in the mid-1900s. During this time, Islamic reform movements became even more popular. Young Muslims often rejected Sufi practices and criticized the marabouts for their cooperation with colonial powers. They also opposed national governments that tried to restrict Islam. These Muslims turned increasingly to Wahhabism and movements to promote social reform.

Beginning in the 1970s, Islamic organizations in North Africa and the Middle East began to support Arabic instruction and the development of Islamic culture in West Africa and other Muslim regions. Money for mosques, Islamic schools, health clinics, and cultural centers poured into West Africa from Saudi Arabia, Libya, and Egypt. These countries also provided scholarships for students who wanted to attend universities in the Middle East. Such contributions encouraged more Muslims to push for the creation of an Islamic state.

Islam in Selected West African Countries

Mauritania, Senegal, and Mali are all good examples of West African nations with Muslim majority populations. They illustrate the overall trends that have characterized West African Islam since its development. They also reveal key differences in the history and role of Islam in West African countries.

Mauritania. Mauritania is a republic with Islam as the official state religion. Islam became well established in the northern part of Mauritania by the 1500s and spread slowly throughout the south. The people who live in the north speak the Arabic language and claim Arab ancestry. In the south, tribal peoples speak local languages and have little in common with their northern peers. Sufi orders, especially the Qadiriyah and Fadiliyah, helped to spread Islam throughout both areas. In the 1800s, the French colonized Mauritania. Marabouts organized repeated rebellions against them. They remained largely unsuccessful, however, and most leaders decided to cooperate with the French.

Mauritania gained its independence in 1960. Its first president, Moktar Ould Daddah, came from the northern part of the country and denied the southern Mauritanians prominent positions in government. The dominance of the northerners created tensions that the common bond of Islam could not dissolve. Starting in 1978, one military regime* after another took control of the country. In the 21st century, the military still holds power in Mauritania, and deep rifts continue to divide the north and south. The govern-

* **Qur'an** book of the holy scriptures of Islam

* **hadith** reports of the words and deeds of Muhammad (not in the Qur'an, but accepted as guides for Muslim behavior)

* **animist** refers to the belief that natural phenomena and objects have souls

Pilgrimage of Mansa Musa

A milestone in the history of West African architecture occurred after the legendary pilgrimage to Mecca of Mansa Musa, emperor of Mali (ruled 1312–1337). According to medieval accounts, Musa traveled in splendor through Cairo to the holy cities of Islam. He returned to his native region with an Arab architect named al-Sahil and commissioned him to organize the construction of new mosques in Timbuktu. Adorned with impressive minarets and domes, these structures were made of a revolutionary new material, brick, rather than the pounded clay that Africans had always used. Al-Sahil's work left a lasting impact on West African architecture. Islamic-style mosques cropped up all over the region, serving as places of worship and centers of learning.

* **regime** government in power

* *shari'ah* Islamic law as established in the Qur'an and sunnah, the exemplary behavior of the Prophet Muhammad

* *secular* separate from religion in human life and society; connected to everyday life

ment of Mauritania keeps Islam under tight state control, forbidding Islamic political parties and running mosques and Islamic schools. The legal system follows *shari'ah** and French civil law.

Senegal. Like Mauritania, Senegal is an overwhelmingly Muslim nation, with 94 percent of its population following Islam. However, it has a secular* government. In the late 1800s, internal wars and French colonialism shattered traditional tribal structures. The Senegalese people turned to Sufi marabouts for leadership. Sufi orders came to dominate society. Members did not strictly observe Islamic rituals such as daily prayer, however, and often lacked knowledge of Islamic law. Many believed in charms and magic, looking to the Sufi leaders for supernatural guidance.

Some Sufi orders became prominent in peanut farming, which flourished in the Wolof region. Founded by Amadu Bamba in the late 1800s, the Muridi order organized a vast peanut export industry during the colonial period. Because the brotherhood was so well organized and had such strong economic power, the French grew fearful of Bamba. To reduce his influence, the government sent him into exile three times. The French ultimately recognized his peaceful intentions, however, and accepted him as a spiritual and economic leader in the early 1900s.

Senegal gained its independence in 1960. Unlike Mauritania, it is a relatively unified country. Most Senegalese speak the Wolof language, and Islamic leaders generally cooperate with government officials. Sufi orders play a large role in organizing society and providing social welfare. Nonetheless, tensions exist within Senegal. Some Muslims reject the authority of the marabouts and look to Mauritania as a model of a strong Islamic state.

Mali. The population of Mali is about 90 percent Muslim. Like Senegal, the country has a secular government. In the Middle Ages, several northern Mali cities became major centers of Islamic education. Sufi orders such as the Qadiriyah took root in northern Mali in the early 1800s. However, the southern part of the country resisted Islam until a series of movements and revivals in the late 1800s expanded it into tribal regions. When the French colonized Mali, Islam grew in strength and popularity.

Mali became an independent nation in 1960. Since that time, the government has either broken up or taken control of many Islamic organizations. The government also regulates Islamic education. As in other West African countries, Muslims increasingly speak out against the Sufis for their unorthodox* rituals and their reliance on magic. (*See also* **Colonialism; Nigeria; Qadiriyah; Sokoto Caliphate; Sufism; Tijaniyah.**)

* *unorthodox* contrary to accepted beliefs and practices

West Bank and Gaza

See *Palestine.*

Whirling Dervishes

See *Mawlawiyah.*

Women

The role of women in Muslim society has changed significantly in the centuries since Islam began in Arabia in the early 600s. Their position has varied with shifting social, economic, and political circumstances. Although Islam regards men and women as moral equals in the sight of God, women have not had equal access to many areas of Islamic life.

Women in Islamic Society

Historically, Muslim women have not been treated as men's equals. Certain rulers and administrators and most legal scholars imposed a system of inequality, which they justified by their interpretations of the Qur'an* and the traditions of the Prophet. Colonial authorities challenged these views, and their Western notions of the rightful position of women in society took hold among some segments of the Muslim population. Since much of the Islamic world became independent in the mid-1900s, however, women have been caught between traditionalists and reformers as they compete for dominance in Islamic society.

Making Some Gains. Before the rise of Islam in the early 600s, Arabs lived in a traditional, patriarchal (male-dominated) society. Men regarded women as their property, to be married or divorced at will. No limitations on polygyny* existed. Women generally did not have a say in the choice of a husband. Once married, they lacked financial security, as the groom's dowry* was paid directly to the bride's male relatives. Female infanticide (the killing of baby girls at birth) was common.

With Islam, the status of women improved considerably. The Qur'an and the sunnah* emphasized the spiritual equality of all Muslims. Islamic law

* **Qur'an** book of the holy scriptures of Islam

* **polygyny** practice of having more than one wife at the same time

* **dowry** money or property that a bride or groom brings to the marriage

* **sunnah** literally "the trodden path"; Islamic customs based on the exemplary behavior of Muhammad

Female athletes from Afghanistan take part in the opening ceremony of the Third Muslim Women Games in Tehran, Iran, in 2001.

See color plate 15, vol. 1.

* **scripture** sacred writings that contain revelations from God

* **revelation** message from God to humans transmitted through a prophet

* **rhetoric** art of speaking and writing effectively

* **caliph** religious and political leader of an Islamic state

* **Byzantine** refers to the Eastern Christian Empire that was based in Constantinople

recognized a woman's right to choose her own marriage partner, and it set limits on the practice of polygyny. A man could have as many as four wives, if he could provide for and treat them equally. Islamic regulations also defined marriage as a contract between a man and a woman or a man and a woman's legal guardian (*wali*). They also required the groom to pay the dowry directly to the bride. In addition, the Qur'an and sunnah specified that women are entitled to inherit wealth and that married women should be able to control their own money and property. These sources further stated that husbands must support their wives financially during marriage and for a certain period after a divorce.

Although Islamic law extended some rights to women and limited the privileges of men, it did not change the dominant position of men in Muslim society. For example, the Qur'an requires women to be obedient to their husbands, and it describes men as a degree higher than women in rights and responsibilities. The scriptures* also permit men to divorce their wives without cause and deny women custody rights over children who have reached a certain age.

Experiencing Some Losses. Historical evidence indicates that women contributed significantly to the early development of the Muslim community. Women were the first to learn of Muhammad's initial revelation*. They later played an important role in the process of collecting all the revelations from both written and oral sources into a single, authoritative text. Women were entrusted with vital secrets, including the location of Muhammad's hiding place when he was being persecuted and his plans to attack Mecca. The Prophet often consulted women and considered their opinions seriously. His first wife, Khadija, was his chief adviser as well as his first and foremost supporter. His third and youngest wife, A'ishah, was a well-known authority in medicine, history, and rhetoric*. At Muhammad's death, the distinguished women of the community were consulted about the choice of his successor. Caliph* Umar ibn al-Khattab (ruled 634–644) appointed women to serve as officials in the market of Medina.

Islam spread well beyond the Arabian Peninsula in the years after the Prophet's death. In the 600s, Arab-Muslim armies captured territory that had been part of the Byzantine* and Persian Empires. The Muslim community gradually incorporated the values and customs of the conquered peoples, including the practice of veiling and secluding women. Veiling referred to the use of garments to cover the head, face, and body. Seclusion involved limiting women to the company of other women and close male relatives in their home or confining them in separate female living quarters. Although Islamic sources do not specifically require veiling and seclusion, some Muslims have used passages from the Qur'an and sunnah to justify these practices.

Men and women had distinct, complementary roles in Muslim societies. The husband's primary responsibility was to support and protect the family. The wife cared for and disciplined the children and maintained the home. Although Islamic law taught that the husband and wife were equal before God, women were subordinate to men. Nonetheless, women exercised considerable influence in family and social life.

Breaking With Tradition. During the 1800s, most Islamic societies came under the control of European powers. Colonial rule brought Western ideas and values about women, marriage, and the family to the Muslim world. Intellectuals, professionals, and civil servants began to question legal and social restrictions on women, especially those related to education, seclusion, heavy veiling, polygyny, and slavery. These developments created a sense of insecurity among the general population. Muslim men tended to react by observing traditional customs and rituals more strictly.

Demands for reform led to the establishment of primary and secondary schools for girls, and in such places as the Ottoman Empire*, Egypt, and Iran, universities were opened to women. Women founded newspapers and educational and charitable organizations. They also joined student and nationalist* movements.

In the early 1900s, the governments of newly independent Muslim states such as Turkey took steps to modernize the role of women. The Turkish government adopted a new family law that discouraged polygyny and gave women the right to obtain divorces. Turkish women gained the right to vote in municipal and national elections in the 1930s. Iranian leader Reza Shah Pahlavi outlawed the practice of veiling. In general, the tradition of female seclusion declined dramatically. During the 1950s, Egyptian women entered politics and were elected to public office. Women also began to earn advanced academic degrees and to work in professions previously closed to them. In most countries, however, new freedoms and opportunities in education and employment benefited only upper and middle classes in urban areas.

Several factors limited these developments. More traditional Muslims regarded the social and political changes as anti-Islamic and a threat to the cultural value of male superiority. Concerns about a lack of employment opportunities among men fueled arguments that women should stay at home in their traditional roles of wives and mothers. Islamic states tried to balance the conflicting demands of women and traditional Muslims by making cautious reforms.

Debate continues over the appropriate role of women in the community. Muslim societies regard women as key to social continuity and the preservation of the family and culture. They see the status of women as directly connected to maintaining or reforming tradition. The role of women may also be a means of defining national identity. For example, some of the Gulf states and other conservative* rural societies follow the practice of secluding women from unrelated men. Although Muslim governments have promoted education for both boys and girls as a way of achieving economic growth, the percentage of girls enrolled in schools in developing countries remains relatively low.

Poor economic and political conditions in some Muslim countries have forced women to become more involved in the outside world. Factors such as war and labor migration have increased the number of households headed by females. Economic necessity has led women to seek work outside the home, usually in low-paid, unskilled jobs.

Many Muslim women have become active in grassroots organizations, development projects, charitable associations, and social services. During the 1990s, women achieved positions of leadership in some parts of the Muslim world. Benazir Bhutto of Pakistan, Tansu Ciller of Turkey, and Shaykh Hasina and Khaleda Zia of Bangladesh served as prime ministers in their respective countries.

* **Ottoman Empire** large Turkish state existing from the early 1300s to the early 1900s

* **nationalist** one who advocates loyalty and devotion to his or her country and its independence

The Spirit World

Muslim women in many parts of Africa participate in spirit cults. Such cults are based on the belief that angry spirits cause both physical and emotional illness. Cult followers host feasts and perform special dances in an attempt to calm the spirit in question and to obtain a cure. Women may serve as officers of the cults or as members of their musical troupes. Although spirit cults are not Islamic in origin, the Qur'an describes the existence of spirits and their effects on humans. As a result of such teachings, these cults have spread in some parts of the Islamic world.

* **conservative** generally opposed to change, especially in existing political and social institutions

Women and Islamic Religious Life

The Qur'an requires the same religious duties of men and women and promises them the same spiritual rewards. Nevertheless, certain factors have tended to restrict women's involvement in Islamic religious life. These include social customs, lack of education, and ideas about ritual purity. The specific limitations on the participation of Muslim women in religious matters and the ways that they have responded to these restrictions have varied across the Islamic world. Furthermore, during the 1900s, the changing role of women in society created new opportunities for women in the religious sphere as well.

Different Standards. Muslim women must observe the Pillars of Islam, including praying five times each day, fasting during the holy month of Ramadan, and—like every Muslim who is physically and financially able—making at least one pilgrimage* to the holy city of Mecca. However, women may not pray, fast, or touch the Qur'an during menstruation or for a period following childbirth. During these times, they are considered to be ritually impure. In addition, women who are pregnant or nursing are exempt from fasting during Ramadan. Nonetheless, they must make up the days that they have missed at a later time.

Ideas about whether women should pray in mosques* or in their homes have changed over time. According to the hadith*, the Prophet commanded men not to bar women from public worship. In the days of Muhammad, women performed the morning prayer at the mosque, although they were required to line up in rows behind the men. They left the mosque before the men, preventing, at least in theory, any contact between the sexes. During the caliphate* of Umar ibn al-Khattab, women had to pray in a separate room of the mosque with their own imam*. By about 700, Muslim religious authorities completely banned women from mosques. They justified their reversal of the Prophet's order by claiming that public spaces were unsafe for women.

Studies from a number of different Islamic countries indicate that the presence of women in public is considered to be a source of temptation and conflict. Therefore, keeping them out of mosques is regarded as necessary to preserve the holiness and dignity of religious ceremonies. For centuries, mosques were primarily male spaces. The Islamic resurgence that has swept the Muslim world since the 1970s has modified these attitudes. Recently, Muslims have constructed mosques that provide a separate space for women. However, the women often remain isolated in areas where they cannot see the preacher, which reinforces their marginal role in mosques.

Although almost always separated during Muslim religious observances, men and women interact on the pilgrimage to Mecca. Moreover, while performing the hajj*, women do not have to cover their faces. Males and females may also interact during celebrations at the shrines* of saints.

Education. Muslim women have always played a role in the spread of religious knowledge. Muhammad's wife A'ishah was an important source of the hadith. In fact, he reportedly told his followers they would receive half their religion from her. Muhammad himself taught religious lessons to women.

See color plate 9, vol. 1.

* **pilgrimage** journey to a shrine or sacred place

* **mosque** Muslim place of worship

* **hadith** reports of the words and deeds of Muhammad (not in the Qur'an, but accepted as guides for Muslim behavior)

* **caliphate** office and government of the caliph, the religious and political leader of an Islamic state

* **imam** spiritual-political leader in Shi'i Islam, one who is regarded as directly descended from Muhammad; also, one who leads prayers

* **hajj** pilgrimage to Mecca that Muslims are required to make once in their lifetime

* **shrine** place that is considered sacred because of its history or the relics contained there

Throughout Islamic history, some daughters of wealthy families received private education in the home. More often, however, women were excluded from formal education, and illiteracy was common. During the 1800s, schools for girls opened in many Muslim countries. They received instruction in such subjects as crafts and housekeeping. Since the independence of the Muslim world in the mid-1900s, both girls and boys have had access to secular education. Nonetheless, religious instruction for girls and women has lagged behind that of boys and men. Occasionally, women have gained recognition as Islamic scholars for their writings, not for obtaining a degree in Islamic studies. Because many Muslims do not believe that women have the capacity to teach men, even women who have religious training may only serve the needs of other females.

Sufism and Shrines. Unlike the legal and scholarly dimensions of Islamic religious life, which depend on literacy and formal education, Sufism* involves various physical and spiritual disciplines. Traditionally, Sufi *shaykhs** were effective religious teachers in Muslim society as well as popular counselors and healers. Not surprisingly, therefore, women have been relatively more involved in the Sufi movement than other areas of Islam. The most famous Sufi woman, Rabiah al-Adawiyah (died 801), wrote poems of love for God that have continued to inspire mystics* to the present day. She is not unique in the Sufi tradition. Javad Nurbakhsh has translated into English the biographies of some 124 Sufi women.

Some Sufi *shaykhs* in the Mamluk dynasty* (1250–1517) and Ottoman Empire admitted women into their orders. Despite the general acceptance of women within Sufism, however, their participation in the orders and in *dhikr*, the distinctive Sufi ritual chanting of the names of God, has been controversial. Moreover, some Sufi men have regarded women as obstacles to their spiritual life. Today Moroccan and Algerian orders frequently have separate women's groups with female leadership. Despite an official ban on female membership in Egyptian Sufi brotherhoods, women continue to participate in many of its orders.

Unlike mosques, which are usually regarded as male spaces, shrines dedicated to Muslim saints have traditionally been open to women. Some Muslims, mostly Sufis, believe that saints are individuals who can intercede with God on behalf of the faithful and perform miracles. After their deaths, their tombs often become places of worship and refuge for their followers and others. Muslim women frequently visit these shrines, some of which address women's concerns, such as fertility. Visiting the shrines of saints has been an essential part of the religious lives of Muslim women all over the world.

Religious reformers have criticized saint veneration as un-Islamic. They argue that women need formal religious education so they can become part of orthodox* Islam once again. Throughout the 1900s, independently founded voluntary associations assumed the task of providing such instruction. These organizations also offered courses in literacy and crafts. Many government-operated mosques also provided religious lessons to women. (*See also* **A'ishah; Clothing; Divorce; Education; Family; Hijab; Khadija; Law; Marriage; Muhammad; Saints and Sainthood; Sexuality; Shrine; Sufism; Women and Reform; Women in the Qur'an.**)

* **Sufism** Islamic mysticism, which seeks to develop spirituality through discipline of the mind and body

* **shaykh** tribal elder; also, title of honor given to those who are considered especially learned and pious

* **mystic** one who seeks to experience spiritual enlightenment and truth through various physical and spiritual disciplines

* **dynasty** succession of rulers from the same family or group

* **orthodox** conforming to accepted beliefs and practices

Women and Reform

The role and status of women is one of the most controversial topics in the Islamic world. Many Muslims consider women the culture bearers of their societies and view their status as a reflection and source of national identity. As a result, they tend to emphasize the traditional roles of women as wives and mothers. However, women in the Islamic world play other roles in public life and in a variety of professions, including business, medicine, education, government, law, and politics. Women have even served as prime ministers in Pakistan, Bangladesh, Turkey, and Indonesia. Efforts to improve the status of women in the Muslim world and to expand their rights and opportunities began in the 1800s.

Women's Role in Islamic Society

Although Islam proclaims that all human beings are equal morally and have the same religious duties, men and women have not always been placed on equal legal footing. The introduction of Islam brought important reforms that improved the status of women, such as prohibiting female infanticide and recognizing women as property owners and legal partners entitled to engage in contractual agreements. Islam also guaranteed women certain financial and inheritance rights in marriage and offered special protection to widows and orphans. However, despite these improvements, Muslim societies remained largely patriarchal*, and women tended to be subordinate to male family members who did not always respect their legal rights.

Pre-Colonial Status of Women. Women have played an active role in public life in Islamic societies since the beginning of Islam. During Muhammad's lifetime, women prayed next to men in the mosque, provided sanctuary to men, owned and sold property, engaged in commercial transactions,

* **patriarchal** referring to a society in which men hold the dominant positions

In 1999 Muslim women in Jakarta, Indonesia, demanded more rights in the upcoming elections. The poster at right calls for officials to take action against election violators.

pursued education, and worked as teachers. Under the early caliphs*, women served as officials and legal experts.

Still, the legal enforcement of women's rights varied in different times and places in the Islamic world. By the 1700s, a number of Muslim scholars began reform movements to revive early Islamic practices and values. For example, Muhammad ibn Abd al-Wahhab of Arabia (died 1791) included the revival of women's rights in such areas as marriage, divorce, and inheritance in his reform program. The court records of the Ottoman Empire* show that women were aware of their marriage, divorce, and inheritance rights under Islamic law and used the courts to enforce them. Finally, throughout Islamic history, the practices of veiling, seclusion, and polygyny*—often considered hallmarks of the lives of Muslim women—were neither uniformly required nor observed.

Changes After Colonization. Starting in the mid-1800s, European colonialism brought far-ranging change to the legal systems of the Muslim world. Secular* courts were established to handle criminal and civil cases. Only family law came under the jurisdiction of the *shari'ah** courts, where Islamic law remained in force.

Islamic reformers called for expanded rights for women within Islam, focusing on education and employment for women as the best means of bringing the Islamic world into the modern era. In Egypt, Muhammad Abduh (1849–1905) and other modernists worked for legal and theological* reforms, such as outlawing polygyny. Others, such as Qasim Amin, addressed social issues. Amin identified the oppression of Muslim women as the major cause for the decline and deterioration of Muslim families and societies. He pointed to social practices like arranged marriages, the wife's practical inability to initiate divorce, and the husband's unlimited right to divorce as sources of bondage for women. Some activists, such as Egypt's Huda Sharawi (1879–1947), pressed for reforms and expansion of women's rights along Western models.

Egypt led the Muslim world in introducing legal reforms related to marriage, divorce, and inheritance. The Egyptian Code of Organization and Procedure for Shari'ah Courts of 1897 required written documentation in marriage, divorce, and certain inheritance claims. In 1923 Egypt also addressed the issue of child marriages by prohibiting marriage certificates for brides under the age of 16 and grooms under the age of 18. Although these reforms protected women's rights through documentation, they remained Islamic in orientation.

A more secular approach can be found in Turkey and Iran. Turkey abolished Islamic law altogether and introduced secular, Western-style law in 1924. Turkey also outlawed the veil and insisted that all Turkish citizens wear Western dress. In Iran, the shah* outlawed the veil and encouraged giving women access to schools, the workplace, and other public areas.

Following independence in the mid-1900s, most Muslim countries introduced plans for modernization and development, including the expansion of education and employment for both men and women. Even such traditional countries as Saudi Arabia routinely sent both male and female students to the West to study engineering, medicine, computer technology, and business in order to develop their home countries and provide services.

* **caliph** religious and political leader of an Islamic state

* **Ottoman Empire** large Turkish state existing from the early 1300s to the early 1900s

* **polygyny** practice of having more than one wife at the same time

* **secular** separate from religion in human life and society; connected to everyday life

* **shari'ah** Islamic law as established in the Qur'an and sunnah, the exemplary behavior of the Prophet Muhammad

* **theological** refers to the study of the nature, qualities, and will of God

* **shah** king (Persian); ruler of Iran

* **conservative** person generally opposed to change, especially in existing political and social institutions

When the economic boom of the modernization era ended, however, many conservatives* called for women to return to their traditional roles at home and leave the jobs for men. Although many professional women have continued to work by choice, economic necessity has often kept less skilled women at work. In some cases, the income of both husband and wife is needed to provide for the family. In other cases, women serve as heads of household in the absence of a male provider due to divorce, widowhood, the husband's work abroad, or active military service. The importance of the wife's income for family survival has led some women to argue that their rights in marriage should be expanded to reflect their increased family responsibilities. They have also maintained that, in cases of divorce, the length of the marriage and the wife's contribution to the household and the husband's career should be taken into account in the divorce settlement.

Reform in the Muslim World

In recent years, most Muslim countries have passed some legislation reforming the application of Islamic law to such issues as marriage, divorce, and inheritance. Although Islamic law remains largely in force, it reflects a modern understanding of the important role women play in the family.

The Middle East. In the Middle East, reforms related to women's issues have focused largely on family law. All countries have set minimum ages for marriage. Legislation has granted a woman the right to establish certain conditions in her marriage contract—including restriction of her husband's right to take other wives—and has required documentation of marriage and divorce. In most countries, the husband can no longer simply tell his wife that she is divorced or divorce her in secret. Safeguards have been put in place to assure that the wife is aware of her status as either a wife or a divorced woman.

* **dowry** money or property that a bride or groom brings to the marriage

Reforms have also bolstered the woman's right to her dowry* and maintenance. Most countries regard the husband's failure to pay maintenance as legal grounds for divorce. The grounds for divorcing a husband have been expanded to include desertion, the presence of an incurable or contagious disease, moral impropriety, and domestic violence—although maltreatment is sometimes difficult to prove in court. Reforms have also affirmed the woman's status as a property holder, and they have supported the Qur'anic* rule that a woman's dowry and maintenance belong to her and should not be under the control of her husband.

* **Qur'an** book of the holy scriptures of Islam

Concerns have been raised about the apparent loss of women's rights in Iran since the 1979 Islamic revolution. Although women have been required to wear Islamic dress, they enjoy relatively free access to education, employment, and politics. Furthermore, Iran has been willing to consider modern medical advice in addressing matters of Islamic law, such as the minimum age for marriage. Thus, although classical Islamic law set the minimum age for marriage for girls at 9, Iran raised the age to 15. The nation also passed legislation in 1982 requiring the inclusion of 12 conditions favorable to women in every marriage contract. The most important conditions are those granting the wife the right to divorce under certain circumstances and entitling the wife to half of the wealth accumulated during the marriage.

Muslim reformers in Iran also won the right of women to compensation in the event of divorce for their labor during marriage, including housework.

North Africa. In North Africa, women played an important role in the wars for independence in the mid-1900s. They expected that their support and work in liberating their countries would be rewarded in the new states. However, though women gained greater access to education and work following the wars of independence, family matters remained largely under the jurisdiction of Islamic law.

Tunisia, the most secular of the North African countries, was the only one to outlaw polygyny. Tunisia also allows both men and women complete freedom in contracting their own marriage. In other countries, polygyny is restricted, rather than outlawed, and marriage contracts must be drawn up by marriage guardians. However, Algeria forbids the marriage of any woman against her will and does not allow the guardian to block a marriage desired by the woman as long as it is beneficial to her. Morocco and Algeria allow women who claim to have suffered harm from their husbands' marrying an additional wife to seek divorce. All North African countries grant the wife the right to establish favorable conditions in her marriage contract.

South Asia. Women's participation in nationalist movements in India and Pakistan led to greater access to public life for women, particularly in education. Women also gained the right to inherit all forms of property. Although many were concerned that Pakistan's implementation of Islamic law during the 1970s and 1980s would restrict the rights and roles of women, women remain active in the public realm. In recent years, President Pervez Musharraf sought to increase women's participation and representation in the legislative system by reserving one-third of the seats in local elections for women. However, literacy levels in Pakistan remain low and a traditional patriarchal culture remains intact. As a result, it is often difficult for women to act independently of male family members, who see themselves as guardians of the family's honor.

The most important legislation passed in Pakistan was the Muslim Family Laws Ordinance of 1961, which prohibited the right of the man to divorce his wife by declaring a triple divorce at one time. The law also restricted the man's right to polygyny, required the registration of marriages, and discouraged quick divorces. In addition, reforms in inheritance laws gave orphaned grandchildren inheritance rights.

Legal reforms and advances in women's rights in Pakistan have often not trickled down to the rural poor, who make up the majority of the population. Rape remains unrecognized as a crime. A woman who brings a case of rape to the court system is likely to be accused of adultery, which has led to an underreporting of rape cases. Honor killings remain a serious social problem in the country. Furthermore, although the law requires official registration of marriages, failure to register does not make the marriage invalid. Although a small fine or short prison sentence may be imposed, the marriage itself remains legal.

Southeast Asia. Women in Southeast Asia have traditionally enjoyed broader involvement in social and political affairs than Muslim women in other regions. Malaysia, for example, is a matriarchal society that traces lineage through women, and women there have traditionally been the heads of household and major property holders. As in other colonized regions, the women of Southeast Asia participated in the struggle for independence and supported women's education as critical to progress. Post-independence, women were strongly represented in politics, both in forming parties and in government positions. Women also play an important role in social services, running orphanages, maternity clinics, hospitals, and daycare centers.

Family law reforms in Malaysia, as in other regions, have required the registration and documentation of marriages and divorces. Dowry amounts are fixed. A man must promise to provide his wife with maintenance, and the court can have the maintenance deducted directly from a man's paycheck. An arbitration process in which women counselors play a prominent role is required prior to divorce. Malaysia has also restricted the practice of polygyny by requiring the man to obtain the written permission of both his current wife and the appropriate religious office to seek an additional marriage. Nevertheless, cultural issues, like domestic violence, remain widespread in the country and are the focus of women's organizations.

Current Issues in Women's Rights

The issues of veiling and gender segregation remain controversial in Islamic societies today. While some view Islamic dress as a limitation on personal freedom—as in the extreme case of Afghan women under the Taliban—others believe that secular societies that require Western dress also limit a woman's personal freedom. The 1998 case of a female member of parliament in Turkey who was banned from her seat in parliament because she insisted on wearing a headscarf raised serious questions about freedom of dress.

Furthermore, in many countries, women are deciding to wear Islamic dress because they find that it brings respect and access to public space while preserving their modesty. Many educated professionals are choosing to wear the *hijab** to identify themselves as Muslims and to show that they are religious, moral women.

*hijab** refers to the traditional head, face, or body covering worn by Muslim women

Domestic violence, honor killings, and rape remain major social problems. Reforms in these matters are supported by a variety of women's organizations, from the grassroots level to government ministries. Recognition that these issues are as much cultural as religious has led to calls for basic reeducation of men and women on these issues, as well as legal reforms affecting family law. (*See also* **Divorce; Education; Family; Hijab; Inheritance; Law; Marriage; Women.**)

Women in the Qur'an

Qur'an book of the holy scriptures of Islam

Muhammad allegedly stated that "Of worldly things, women and perfume are dearest to me. . . . " The Qur'an* is the only world scripture that has an entire chapter entitled "Women." Concern for the welfare of women is a distinctive feature of the Qur'an, and the book refers to prominent figures such as the Queen of Sheba, the wife of an Egyptian Pharaoh, and Mary, who has a whole chapter named after her. The Qur'an also recognizes the spiritual equality of men and women. A verse in surah* 33 states:

* **surah** chapter of the Qur'an

> For Muslim men and women, for believing men and women,
> For devout men and women, for truthful men and women
> For men and women who are patient and constant, for men
> and women who humble themselves, for men and women
> who give in charity, for men and women who fast
> (and restrain themselves), for men and women who guard
> their chastity, and for men and women,
> who engage much in God's praise,
> For them has God prepared forgiveness and a great reward.

Unlike the Hebrew Bible, the Qur'an does not single out Eve as the cause of humankind's fall. In one version of the Qur'an, Adam receives blame for giving in to temptation, and in another, he and his wife are both held accountable. The Qur'an depicts both sexes as pure at birth, equally capable of achieving moral perfection.

The Qur'an grants specific legal and civil rights to women, many of them unprecedented in both Eastern and Western societies of the time. In pre-Islamic societies in the Near East, men treated women largely as their property. Most women had no say in choosing their marriage partners. They had to give all their belongings to their husbands, and they lacked financial security, unless they had inherited wealth. Female infanticide (the killing of baby girls at birth) was common. The Qur'an abolished these practices, requiring that women inherit property from their male relatives, have a say in their marriage, and have the right to initiate divorce in specific circumstances.

The Qur'an requires that wives obey their husbands and stipulates that men have more rights than women because they are financially responsible for them. In Islamic law, however, women are treated as social inferiors in some ways. For example, a woman's testimony in court has half the value of a man's, men may divorce their wives at any time by making a simple statement, women do not have custody rights over their children after a certain age, and men may have up to four wives if they provide for them equally. Nevertheless, marriage relationships are supposed to be mutually supportive.

Most controversial, however, is a passage in surah 4 stating that men with disobedient wives should "admonish them, then banish them to beds apart and strike them." Scholars suggest that this striking refers only to a single blow, as the word takes the singular form. They argue that the verse actually intends to restrict violence against women, which occurred freely in pre-Islamic times. Various hadith* caution against causing wives pain or harm when striking them, and the Qur'an commands men to live with their wives on a "footing of kindness and quality." Some Muslims, however, have cited the verse on striking to justify domestic violence.

* **hadith** reports of the words and deeds of Muhammad

The Qur'an specifically requires women to "lower their gaze and be modest . . . and to draw veils over their bosoms, and not to reveal their adornment save to their own husbands and [male relatives and servants]." Of the seven Qur'anic verses in which the word *hijab* appears, only one refers specifically to women, describing the need for Muhammad's wives to cover themselves while the Prophet converses with male guests. Some modern

* **hijab** traditional head, face, or body covering for Muslim women

scholars maintain that this verse does not concern Muslim women in general. Others, however, argue that the rules that apply to the Prophet's wives apply to all Muslim women.

The Qur'an does not prescribe seclusion for women, and many women played prominent roles in the early Muslim society. Muhammad's wife A'ishah, for example, was a scholar of many subjects and an influential teacher. Historical evidence seems to indicate that veiling and seclusion became common in the Muslim world after the Islamic conquests of Iran and Byzantium, where high-born women wore veils and lived in harems*. Muslim men began to hide and cover their women as a sign of status and wealth. Islamic scholars argued that Qur'anic requirements of modesty supported these practices.

* **harem** place where the women of a Muslim household lived; female members of a Muslim household

Cultural practices in conquered areas have often influenced the ways in which Muslims interpret Qur'anic writings on women. Although the Qur'an requires the consent of women in marriage transactions, local customs override this requirement in some Muslim societies, allowing the male guardian exclusive authority in this matter. Many scholars have interpreted the Qur'an in ways that limit the rights promised to women. Some researchers even suggest that later Muslim authorities made up hadith denouncing women as incapable of leadership.

Female Muslim scholars and activists increasingly rely on egalitarian interpretations of the Qur'an to empower themselves politically and socially and to promote gender equality in their societies. Islamic women participate in such organizations as the Sisters in Islam (Malaysia) and the Muslim Women's League (United States). Some write for feminist journals such as the Iranian *Zanan*. Muslim feminist scholars in the West include Azizah al-Hibri, Amina Wadud, and Asma Barlas. (*See also* **A'ishah; Divorce; Harem; Hijab; Marriage; Women; Women and Reform.**)

Wudu

See *Ablution*.

Yemen

* **Sunni** refers to the largest branch of the Muslim community; the name derives from sunnah, the exemplary behavior of the Prophet Muhammad

* **Shi'i** refers to Muslims who believe that Muhammad chose Ali ibn Abi Talib and his descendants as the spiritual-political leaders of the Muslim community

* **dynasty** succession of rulers from the same family or line

* **Ottoman Empire** large Turkish state existing from the early 1300s to the early 1900s

Yemen is a country on the southwestern tip of the Arabian Peninsula, where the Red Sea meets the Gulf of Aden and the Indian Ocean. Sharing borders with Saudi Arabia and Oman, it occupies a key position on the route between the Mediterranean Sea and Asia. For thousands of years, local tribes have fought among themselves and with vast empires for control over Yemen. Struggles continue between the Sunni* Muslims and the locally dominant division of Shi'i* Islam called Zaydi. One of Yemen's islands, Socotra, contains sweet-smelling trees that led to its reputation in ancient times as "island abode of bliss."

History and Government

Yemen has a long history of internal conflict and invasions by outside forces. Various Muslim dynasties* occupied the region, and the Ottoman Empire* and Great Britain struggled for control of Yemen's ports. Since the independence of North Yemen in 1918, Yemenis have experienced revolutions, a civil war, and the reunification of their country.

Power Struggle. As early as 1200 B.C.E.*, Yemeni kingdoms ran a highly profitable spice trade between India and Egypt and the Mediterranean Sea. A series of local kings ruled Yemen before the Abyssinians, a Christian group from Ethiopia, conquered the region in 525 C.E.* Fifty years later, the Persians overthrew the Ethiopians, dominating Yemen until the rise of Islam in the early 600s. Islam spread quickly among the Yemenis. By 628 Arab-Muslim armies had gained control over Yemen, which was ruled by Sunni Muslim caliphs* for the next 250 years.

The caliphs' rule did not go unchallenged. Tribes in western Yemen (San'a) rebelled against the caliph in 632. In eastern Yemen (called Aden after its main port), local warlords still held some power in the countryside. In the late 800s, the Zaydis established a dynasty in San'a that played a leading role in government for the next thousand years. A Shi'i group from Iraq, the Zaydis accept Muhammad's great-grandson Zayd ibn Ali as the fifth imam* and successor to the Prophet. Yemen experienced its golden age from the mid-1200s to the mid-1400s. Led by the local Rasulid dynasty, Yemen saw great achievements in science, literature, and architecture.

In the early 1500s, Yemen fell to the expanding power of the Ottoman Empire. However, the Ottomans had no more success than the earlier caliphs in ruling Yemen, and by 1635 the Zaydis had driven them from the country. But Zaydi leaders were unable to hold Aden, which came under the control of local tribes. In 1839 the British seized hold of the port of Aden and the surrounding countryside, and shortly afterwards, the Ottomans reoccupied San'a.

Independence and Reunification. The defeat of the Ottomans in World War I (1914–1918) led to the breakup of their empire. San'a gained independence as North Yemen—one of the only Ottoman territories granted autonomy* immediately after the war. Zaydi imams ruled North Yemen until 1962, when they were overthrown in a coup* by members of the military. Soon after, the country fell into a civil war between supporters of the new government and those who wanted the Zaydis returned to power. Egypt and the former Soviet Union aided the new government, and Saudi Arabia and Jordan backed the Zaydis. The war flared on and off until Saudi Arabia and Egypt pulled back after the Arab defeat in the 1967 war with Israel. The two sides signed a truce in 1970, establishing a democratic constitution. However, the military staged a coup four years later and suspended the constitution. Ali Abdullah Saleh, who became president in 1978, gained the trust of the North Yemenis with improvements in the economy and government.

Aden, meanwhile, remained under British control as the Aden Protectorate*. The British finally withdrew their forces in 1967 under pressure from local nationalist* groups. The South Yemenis formed the People's Republic of South Yemen later that year. However, a coup in 1969 brought a Marxist* government to power and the country formed an alliance with the Soviet Union. Under the new regime*, hundreds of thousands of South Yemenis fled to the north. This led to increased tensions between the two states. During the 1970s, North and South Yemen fought two border wars. They established more peaceful relations in the 1980s, however, after cooperating on key political matters.

* **B.C.E.** before the Common Era, which refers to the same time period as B.C.

* **C.E.** Common Era, which refers to the same time period as A.D.

* **caliph** religious and political leader of an Islamic state

* **imam** spiritual leader in Shi'i Islam, one who claims to be descended directly from Muhammad; also, one who leads prayers

See map in Gulf States (vol. 1).

* **autonomy** self-government

* **coup** sudden, and often violent, overthrow of a ruler or government

* **protectorate** country under the protection and control of a stronger nation

* **nationalist** one who advocates loyalty and devotion to his or her country and its independence

* **Marxist** refers to a political philosophy that rejects capitalism and advocates a classless society

* **regime** government in power

Yemen

Happy Arabia

The three main pre-Islamic kingdoms in Yemen were the Minaean, the Sabaean (followers of the Queen of Sheba), and the Himyarite. These powers prospered through the trade of spices, especially frankincense and myrrh, which the ancients prized for their medicinal and aromatic qualities. The states of ancient Yemen became known as *Arabia Felix*, or "Happy Arabia," because of their prosperity. The sandy, barren land north of Yemen, on the other hand, was termed *Arabia Deserta*. When the Romans redirected their trade routes around 100 B.C.E., "Happy Arabia" lost much of its wealth and influence.

* **Ismaili** refers to a major branch of Shi'i Islam

* **shari'ah** Islamic law as established in the Qur'an and sunnah, the exemplary behavior of the Prophet Muhammad

* **assassination** murder of a politically important person

A brief civil war in South Yemen forced the president to flee the country in 1986. Three years later, North and South Yemen agreed to merge into a single country to consolidate their oil resources and to avoid further conflict. The Republic of Yemen emerged in 1990, and a constitution was drafted. However, the new country suffered from economic problems and poor relations with its powerful neighbor, Saudi Arabia. Civil war broke out in 1994, a year after Yemen's first multiparty elections. The elected president Saleh quickly crushed the conflict, and new elections were held. Saleh won again, and in 1999, he was reelected for a second five-year term.

Culture and Religion

Zaydi Islam has played a central role in Yemeni culture and politics since the late 800s. It rapidly became the most popular faith in the highlands of San'a, where tribes accepted its laws on morals, justice, family matters, and taxation. However, the tribes continued to use their own laws to settle criminal affairs. Zaydi ideas gained followers in some parts of Aden, although most southern Yemenis never accepted Zaydi rule. Over half of all Yemenis are Zaydi, with the other half consisting of Jews, Ismailis*, and Sunni Muslims.

This nearly equal division between Zaydis and other groups has led to many conflicts. Zaydi beliefs anger many Yemenis. For example, the Zaydis argue that only members of their group can serve as legitimate Islamic rulers. Even among this group, only a tiny fraction meets the 14 requirements that allow a Zaydi to become imam. Moreover, during their rule, many Zaydi leaders sought to suppress other forms of Islam. The Zaydis' domination of political power and their intolerance toward other religious groups contributed significantly to the overthrow of the last imam in 1962.

The Zaydis' battles were not limited to rival groups within Yemen, but extended to the larger Sunni Islamic world. The Zaydis refused to acknowledge the legitimacy of the caliphate and clashed with Muslim rulers from a succession of dynasties. The Ottomans met fierce resistance when they tried to establish Sunni civil and criminal law in the highlands. One imam who made a deal allowing the Ottomans to control San'a in the mid-1800s was overthrown by his own people and killed by his successor. Despite their hatred of the Ottomans, however, Zaydi imams refused to aid the British in toppling the empire.

After the independence of North Yemen in the early 1900s, Imam Yahya worked to limit the power of Yemeni Muslim groups, including some influential Zaydi families. He also imposed *shari'ah** over the country. This move offended tribal leaders who had always used their own laws to settle disputes. These policies led to Imam Yahya's assassination* in 1948. His son Ahmad took over the imamate, and Ahmad's son, Muhammad al-Badr, replaced him when he died in 1962. Al-Badr reigned for a week before rebel factions deposed him. The last of the Zaydi imams, he agreed to go into exile in 1962. Yemen became a republic, with some prominent Zaydis integrated into the government.

Since 1962 Zaydi Muslims have faced a dilemma. In theory, the Zaydi community must have an imam to be considered legitimate. However, Muhammad al-Badr now lives in a London suburb and has not had any authority for more than 40 years. Nevertheless, many Zaydis are not ready to declare their community dead. Some support the creation of a constitutional imamate. However, even if some form of imamate returns to Yemen, it will likely bear little resemblance to the traditional office. (*See also* **Communism and Islam; Imam; Shi'i Islam; Zaydi.**)

Youth Organizations

Youth organizations have played a key role in the cultural and political revival* of Islam since the 1960s. They have provided leaders for Islamic political parties and have had a significant influence on the return to traditional values and beliefs in Muslim societies. The most prominent Islamic youth organizations are student movements and revival movements that draw support and members mainly from young people. Population trends in Muslim countries have caused some forms of Islamic revivalism to become closely associated with youth.

Islamic Student Movements. Student movements typically emerge in societies where Islamic revival has already become an important political force. Some groups, such as Pakistan's Islamic Society of Students, are directly connected to a specific political party. Others, including Egypt's Islamic Societies, maintain ties to various Islamic political parties and groups. Still others, such as the Indiana-based Muslim Student Association of North America, operate independently.

Despite organizational differences, Islamic student movements share some similar characteristics. All of them have developed partly as a reaction to the activities of radical* organizations on various campuses. For example, at times the Pakistani regime* has encouraged the Islamic Society of Students to suppress leftist activity at universities. Islamic student movements have also produced reformist leaders and activists. Some of the leaders of Iran's 1979 revolution were former members of the Muslim Student Association of North America.

Islamic student movements have spread the ideals of revival on campuses through speeches, meetings, and publications. Some also try to enforce a strict code of ethics. They have been very successful at winning campus elections, and this has led other political forces—both Islamic and secular*—to increase their efforts to gain student support. Consequently, the level of political awareness and activity among students as a whole has increased.

The power of Islamic student movements stems from the sense of community that they provide. On campus, such organizations act as aid societies for students from small towns and rural areas. By offering the services of tutors and help with academic and administrative problems, they win supporters. These efforts have helped youth organizations plant the seeds of Islamic revival among people who are not usually reached by political parties.

A Broader Base. Several prominent Islamic revivalist movements began as youth movements and later developed into political parties. This was especially true during the early years of contemporary Islamic revivalism, when political and religious protest tended to originate among the youth. Although the focus of these groups has shifted from the campus to the larger society, they continue to draw much support from young people. For example, the

* **revival** return to traditional values or beliefs

* **radical** favoring extreme change or reform, especially in existing political and social institutions

* **regime** government in power

* **secular** separate from religion in human life and society; connected to everyday life

Iranian Mujahidin and Iran's Charitable Society of the Hidden Imam both recruited heavily among high school and university students during the 1960s and 1970s. After the Iranian Revolution of 1979, the latter group joined the new government. The Mujahidin, however, became a major voice of dissent.

Unlike Islamic student movements, these revivalist movements have always functioned primarily as antigovernment protest organizations. They also have a broader base of support than student movements. The Charitable Society of the Hidden Imam, for example, is popular among government officials, the *ulama**, the armed forces, merchants, and artisans*, as well among students. Unlike student movements, revivalist groups generally enjoy consistency in leadership and membership because their leaders and members do not leave the organization upon completion of their studies.

Changing Population. The emergence of Islamic revival movements has occurred at the same time as a population shift in the Muslim world. In recent years, the percentage of young people in Muslim nations has grown dramatically, and in many regions their numbers continue to rise. This development has put pressure on the economies of those countries, which cannot create enough jobs to employ all the job seekers. With fewer adults contributing to the economy, the governments in many Islamic countries cannot provide adequate public services. This situation has led to great frustration and anger among the youth, who see little hope of a better life.

Such conditions have caused many young people to turn to opposition political groups to cure their social ills. The most important of these groups have been Islamic revivalist organizations. Thus, the politics of these movements have come to reflect the frustrations and demands of the young. But even though youth organizations have had a significant political role in the Islamic world, their main contribution is not political. Instead, it is in the important part they have played in spreading Islamic thought and practice among new generations who will lead future Muslim societies. (*See also* **Islam: An Overview; Mujahidin; Universities.**)

* *ulama* religious scholars

* **artisan** skilled craftsperson

Zakat

See *Charity.*

Zawiyah

* **Sufi** refers to Sufism, which seeks to discipline the mind and body in order to experience directly the presence of God

A *zawiyah* is a Sufi* institution that serves as a center for worship and social and charitable activity. At one time, *zawiyah*s played a central role in the Sufi community, and they could be found even in remote villages in the Muslim world. However, the influence of the *zawiyah* has declined considerably since the 1800s.

Place of Worship. *Zawiyah*s grew out of a Sufi tradition of religious leaders guiding young believers along a path (*tariqah*) to spiritual enlightenment. As Sufism spread, various *tariqah*s emerged, each developed by a different Sufi leader. The term *tariqah* came to refer to the group of followers itself and took on the meaning of religious order or brotherhood. Sufi leaders eventually established centers called *zawiyah*s where each taught his particular *tariqah*.

In joining a *zawiyah*, Sufi disciples seek to achieve union with God and to discover the hidden reality behind all experiences. They work to attain the two highest spiritual states—*tarbiyah* and *khalwah*. Both require the follower to isolate himself, eat and sleep little, and recite ritual prayers (*dhikr*). A Sufi master oversees this process and gives the disciple guidance as necessary. During *tarbiyah*, the Sufi loses himself in God and utters ecstatic phrases. Although he ultimately returns to a normal condition, he is strengthened by the experience. *Khalwah* leads to a similar state but also serves a social function. Repeated practice enables spiritual leaders to reinforce their reputations and raises disciples to positions of leadership.

Social and Political Institution. *Zawiyahs* function not only as places of learning but also as mosques* in which Sufis recite prayers and conduct ceremonies, such as funerals and celebrations of the birthdays of saints. *Zawiyahs* also provide relief to poor and disabled members of the local community. With charitable donations, Sufis offer food, shelter, and other necessities to struggling Muslims. During times of poor harvest, *zawiyahs* feed the hungry and provide farmers with seeds. In North Africa, *zawiyahs* historically served as places where fugitives could seek refuge from the law. Authorities often blocked access to these institutions while chasing a criminal suspect.

* **mosque** Muslim place of worship

During the early 1800s, the *zawiyahs* of North Africa became a base for political power after Sayyid Muhammad ibn Ali al-Sanusi founded one in Cyrenaica (in present-day Libya). He eventually built a network of *zawiyahs* on the sites of ancient Roman fortresses and used them to control trade throughout northeast Africa. In the late 1800s, however, colonial governments in the region took control of the charitable funds that supported the *zawiyahs*. Orthodox* Muslims attacked the Sufis as heretics*, further weakening their influence. Similar events occurred in other parts of the Islamic world, and the *zawiyahs* lost much of their social and political power.

* **orthodox** conforming to accepted beliefs and practices

* **heretic** person whose belief or practice is contrary to established religious doctrine

Zawiyahs continue to thrive in rural communities, and they perform a spiritual function in urban areas. In American and European cities, *zawiyahs* have cropped up in private homes and small mosques. State institutions, however, have taken over most of the educational and charitable functions performed by *zawiyahs*. (*See also* **Sanusiyah; Sufism.**)

Zaydi

The Zaydis are a moderate sect* of Shi'i* Muslims founded after the death of the fourth imam* in 713. They are sometimes known as Fivers because they broke with the other Shi'is over support for the fifth imam, Muhammad al-Baqir. The Zaydis chose to follow Zayd ibn Ali, who was a grandson of the martyr* Husayn ibn Ali, the grandson of the Prophet Muhammad.

The Zaydis chose to follow Zayd ibn Ali because he was the first of Husayn's descendants to rebel against the Umayyad dynasty*, which persecuted the Shi'is. Zayd ibn Ali died in 740 while leading an uprising against the Umayyads, and Zaydis took part in several more uprisings after his death. In 864 al-Hasan ibn Zayd founded the first Zaydi state in Iran, which lasted until 1126. Another Zaydi state arose in northern Yemen

* **sect** religious group adhering to distinctive beliefs

* **Shi'i** refers to Muslims who believe that Muhammad chose Ali ibn Abi Talib and his descendants as the spiritual-political leaders of the Muslim community

* **imam** spiritual leader in Shi'i Islam, one who claims to be descended directly from Muhammad; also one who leads prayers

* **martyr** one who dies for his or her religious beliefs

* **dynasty** succession of rulers from the same family or group

in 893 and survived over 1,000 years until a coup* in 1962 removed the last imam from power.

Zaydi religious beliefs differ from those of other Shi'i sects in several ways. For example, Zaydis do not believe that the imam is God's representative on earth or has special God-given powers. For them anyone descended from Muhammad's daughter Fatimah and her husband Ali ibn Abi Talib may become imam as long as that person is a faithful Muslim and has no physical imperfections. Zaydi belief thus allows for the possibility of several imams at once or no imam at any given time.

Zaydis maintain that an imam must be able to take up arms to defend Islam. Thus, an infant cannot be imam. Zaydis also reject the idea of the "hidden imam" popular among Twelver Shi'is, which holds that a descendant of Ali ibn Abi Talib and Fatimah is waiting in some otherworldly realm to reclaim the title of imam and bring about a golden age on earth. The Zaydis also tend to follow a strict moral code and to disapprove of Sufi* teachings. (*See also* **Shi'i Islam; Umayyad Caliphate; Yemen.**)

Zaynab

about 627–684
Granddaughter of the
Prophet Muhammad

Zaynab was the child of Muhammad's daughter Fatimah and the fourth Sunni* caliph* (first Shi'i* imam*), Ali ibn Abi Talib. Muslims look to her life as an example of bravery in the defense of faith and submission to the will of Allah.

Muhammad died when Zaynab was a young child, and Fatimah's death followed shortly thereafter. According to tradition, Zaynab foresaw their deaths in a dream. In it, she was caught in a huge tree that was uprooted by a strong wind. As she grabbed at its branches, they broke off, and she woke up just as she began to fall. Muhammad told her the dream meant that her parents and brothers would all die before her.

Zaynab's father, Ali, died in 661, and her brother Hasan became caliph. However, Hasan was pressured into yielding his power to a political rival, Mu'awiyah, the founder of the Umayyad caliphate. Zaynab's other brother, Husayn, disapproved of Mu'awiyah's rule. When Mu'awiyah died in 680, leaving the caliphate to his son Yazid, Husayn refused to accept his rule. In 680 Husayn traveled to the town of Kufa to lead an armed uprising against Yazid. Zaynab and two of her sons joined him.

Supporters of Yazid learned of Husayn's plan and ambushed him before he could raise a large force. At the Battle of Karbala, Yazid's troops slaughtered Husayn and his few men, including Zaynab's sons. The only man to survive the battle was Husayn's young son Ali Zayn al-Abidin, who had been too ill to fight. Yazid's men tried to kill him as well, but Zaynab persuaded them to spare his life.

Yazid's forces marched Zaynab and the other survivors to Damascus and paraded them through the streets to the palace. When Yazid began boasting to the crowd about his victory, Zaynab interrupted him. She condemned him and his actions and challenged him when he tried to give one of the prisoners away as a slave. News of Karbala and of Zaynab's speech spread rapidly. People were unhappy that Yazid would treat a member of the Prophet's family so poorly. Worried about the growing unrest in his realm, Yazid released Zaynab and the other captives. They returned to Medina, where Zaynab died less than one year later. (*See also* **Ali ibn Abi Talib; Fatimah; Husayn ibn Ali; Karbala and Najaf.**)

Books and Online Sources

1. OVERVIEW

Arberry, Arthur John. *Aspects of Islamic Civilization.* Westport, CT: Greenwood Press, 1977.

Belt, Don. *World of Islam.* Washington, DC: National Geographic, 2001.

Denny, Frederick. *An Introduction to Islam.* New York: Macmillan Publishing Company, 1994.

Esposito, John L., ed. *The Oxford Encyclopedia of the Modern Islamic World.* New York: Oxford University Press, 1995.

———, ed. *The Oxford Dictionary of Islam.* New York: Oxford University Press, 2003.

Fārūqi, Isma'il R. al-, and Lois Lamya al-Fārūqii. *The Cultural Atlas of Islam.* New York: Macmillan Publishing Company, 1986.

Glassé, Cyril, and Huston Smith. *New Encyclopedia of Islam: The Concise Encyclopedia of Islam.* Walnut Creek, CA: AltaMira Press, 2003.

*Haneef, Suzanne. *What Everyone Should Know about Islam and Muslims.* Des Plaines, IL: Library of Islam, 1995.

Laurance, Robin. *Portrait of Islam: A Journey through the Muslim World.* New York: Thames & Hudson, 2002.

Nasr, Seyyed Hossein. *Islam: Religion, History, and Civilization.* San Francisco: HarperSanFrancisco, 2003.

*Netton, Ian Richard. *A Popular Dictionary of Islam.* Lincolnwood, IL: NTC Publishing Group, 1997.

Ruthven, Malise. *Islam: A Very Short Introduction.* New York: Oxford University Press, 2000.

Shaikh, Farzana, ed. *Islam and Islamic Groups: A Worldwide Reference Guide.* Detroit, MI: Gale Research, 1992.

Weekes, Richard V., ed. *Muslim Peoples: A World Ethnographic Survey.* Westport, CT: Greenwood Press, 1984.

*Wilkinson, Philip. *Islam.* New York: Dorling Kindersley, 2002.

van Donzel, E. *Islamic Desk Reference.* New York: E.J. Brill, 1994.

* Appropriate for younger readers.

2. HISTORY

Armstrong, Karen. *Islam: A Short History.* New York: Modern Library, 2002.

Esposito, John L., ed. *The Oxford History of Islam.* New York: Oxford University Press, 1999.

Fromkin, David. *A Peace to End All Peace: Creating the Modern Middle East, 1914-1922.* New York: Henry Holt and Company, 1989.

Goodwin, Jason. *Lords of the Horizons: A History of the Ottoman Empire.* New York: Henry Holt and Company, 1999.

Hazard, Harry W. *Atlas of Islamic History.* Princeton, NJ: Princeton University Press, 1954.

Hitti, Philip Khuri. *History of the Arabs: From the Earliest Times to the Present.* New York: Palgrave Macmillan, 2002.

Holt, P.M., Ann K.S. Lambton, and Bernard Lewis, eds. *The Cambridge History of Islam.* Cambridge: Cambridge University Press, 1970.

Hourani, Albert Habib. *A History of the Arab Peoples.* Cambridge, MA: Belknap Press of Harvard University Press, 2002.

Jenkins, Everett. *The Muslim Diaspora: A Comprehensive Reference to the Spread of Islam in Asia, Africa, Europe & the Americas.* Jefferson, NC: McFarland, 1999.

Lapidus, Ira M. *A History of Islamic Societies.* New York: Cambridge University Press, 2002.

Levtzion, Nehemia, and Randall L. Pouwels, eds. *The History of Islam in Africa.* Athens: Ohio University Press, 2000.

Lewis, Bernard. *The Middle East: A Brief History of the Last 2,000 Years.* New York: Scribner, 1995.

Mantin, Peter, and Ruth Mantin. *The Islamic World: Beliefs and Civilisations, 600-1600.* New York: Cambridge University Press, 1993.

*Moktefi, Mokhtar. *The Arabs in the Golden Age.* Brookfield, CT: Millbrook Press, 1992.

*Robinson, Francis. *Cambridge Illustrated History of the Islamic World.* New York: Cambridge University Press, 1996.

Sonn, Tamara. *A Brief History of Islam.* Oxford: Blackwell, 2000.

3. POLITICS AND GOVERNMENT

Choueiri, Youssef M. *Islamic Fundamentalism.* Washington, DC: Pinter, 1997.

Denny, Frederick. *An Introduction to Islam.* New York: Macmillan, 1994.

Eickelman, Dale F., and James Piscatori. *Muslim Politics.* Princeton, NJ: Princeton University Press, 2003.

Esposito, John L. *Islam and Politics.* Syracuse, NY: Syracuse University Press, 1998.

Voll, John O. *Islam: Continuity and Change in the Modern World.* 2nd ed. Syracuse, NY: Syracuse University Press, 1994.

MIDDLE EAST AND AFRICA

Callaway, Barbara. *The Heritage of Islam: Women, Religion and Politics in West Africa.* Boulder, CO: Lynn Rienner, 1994.

Hourani, Albert, with Philip S. Khoury and Mary C. Wilson, eds. *The Modern Middle East: A Reader.* Berkeley: University of California Press, 1993.

Keddie, Nikki R. *Iran and the Muslim World: Resistance and Revolution.* New York: New York University Press, 1995.

Levtzion, Nehemia, and Humphrey J. Fisher, eds. *Rural and Urban Islam in West Africa.* Boulder, CO: Lynne Rienner Publishers, 1997.

Mottahedeh, Roy. *The Mantle of the Prophet: Religion and Politics in Iran.* New York: Pantheon Books, 1986.

Murphy, Caryle. *Passion for Islam: Shaping the Modern Middle East: The Egyptian Experience.* New York: Scribner, 2002.

Roy, Olivier. *Islam and Resistance in Afghanistan.* New York: Cambridge University Press, 1990.

Saad-Ghorayeb, Amal. *Hizbu'llah: Politics and Religion.* Sterling, VA: Pluto Press, 2002.

Sonn, Tamara. *Between Qur'an and Crown: The Challenge of Political Legitimacy in the Arab World.* Boulder, CO: Westview Press, 1990.

ASIA

Esposito, John L., ed. *Islam in Asia: Religion, Politics, and Society.* New York: Oxford University Press, 1987.

Haghayeghi, Mehrdad. *Islam and Politics in Central Asia.* New York: St. Martin's Press, 1996.

Hefner, Robert W. *Civil Islam: Muslims and Democratization in Indonesia.* Princeton, NJ: Princeton University Press, 2000.

* Appropriate for younger readers.

Hefner, Robert W., and Patricia Horvatich, eds. *Islam in an Era of Nation-States: Politics and Religious Renewal in Muslim Southeast Asia.* Honolulu: University of Hawaii Press, 1997.

Rashid, Ahmed. *Taliban: Militant Islam, Oil and Fundamentalism in Central Asia.* Waterville, ME: Thorndike Press, 2002.

———. *Jihad: The Rise of Militant Islam in Central Asia.* New Haven, CT: Yale University Press, 2002.

THE WESTERN WORLD

Ahmed, Akbar. *Islam under Siege.* London: Polity Press, 2003.

Daniel, Norman. *Islam and the West: The Making of an Image.* Oxford: OneWorld Press, 1997.

*Denny, Frederick. *Muslims in America.* New York: Oxford University Press, 2002.

Esposito, John L. *The Islamic Threat: Myth or Reality?* New York: Oxford University Press, 1999.

Haddad, Yvonne Yazbeck. *Islamic Values in the United States: A Comparative Study.* New York: Oxford University Press, 1987.

———, ed. *Muslims in the West: From Sojourners to Citizens.* New York: Oxford University Press, 2002.

Haddad, Yvonne Yazbeck, and John L. Esposito, eds. *Religion and Immigration: Christian, Jewish, and Muslim Experiences in the United States.* Walnut Creek, CA: AltaMira Press, 2003.

———, eds. *Muslims on the Americanization Path.* Atlanta, GA: Scholars Press, 1997.

Hunter, Shireen T. *The Future of Islam and the West.* Westport, CT: Praeger, 1998.

———. *Islam, Europe's Second Religion.* Westport, CT: Praeger, 2002.

Lewis, Bernard. *What Went Wrong? Western Impact & Middle Eastern Response.* New York: Oxford University Press, 2002.

Sachedina, Abdulaziz, and Joseph Montville. *The Islamic Roots of Democratic Pluralism.* New York: Oxford University Press, 2001.

Said, Edward. *Covering Islam: How the Media and the Experts Determine How We See the Rest of the World.* New York: Vintage Books, 1997.

Sick, Gary. *All Fall Down: America's Fateful Encounter with Iran.* New York: Random House, 1985.

Smith, Jane I. *Islam in America.* New York: Columbia University Press, 1999.

4. RELIGION AND PHILOSOPHY

Al-Qur'an. A contemporary translation by Ahmed Ali. Princeton, NJ: Princeton University Press, 2001.

Abu-Hamdiyyah, Mohammad. *The Qur'an: An Introduction*. New York: Routledge, 2000.

Armstrong, Karen. *History of God: The 4000-Year Quest of Judaism, Christianity, and Islam*. New York: Random House, 1993.

————. *Muhammad: A Biography of the Prophet*. San Francisco: Harper San Francisco, 1992.

Asad, Muhammad. *The Message of the Quran*. Gibraltar: Dar al-Andalus, 1980.

Barlas, Asma. *"Believing Women" in Islam*. Austin: University of Texas Press, 2002.

Bloom, Jonathan, and Sheila Blair. *Islam: A Thousand Years of Faith and Power*. New Haven, CT: Yale University Press, 2001.

Esposito, John L. *The Straight Path*. New York: Oxford University Press, 1998.

Fakhry, Majid. *A History of Islamic Philosophy*. New York: Columbia University Press, 1970.

————, trans. *The Qur'an: A Modern English Version*. Berkshire: Garnet Publishing, 1996.

Haykal, Muhammad Husayn. *The Life of Muhammad*. Trans. by Ismail R. al-Faruqi. Indianapolis: American Trust Publications, 1976.

*Islam, Yusuf. *A is for Allah*. Chicago: Mountain of Light, 2000.

Nasr, Seyyed Hossein. *Ideals and Realities of Islam*. Chicago: Kazi Publications, 2000.

————, ed. *Islamic Spirituality: Foundations*. New York: Crossroad, 1987.

Peters, F.E. *The Children of Abraham: Judaism/Christianity/Islam*. Princeton, NJ: Princeton University Press, 1984.

Schimmel, Annemarie. *Islam: An Introduction*. Albany: State University of New York Press, 1992.

*Schuon, Frithjof. *Understanding Islam*. Bloomington, IN: World Wisdom Books, 1998.

Sharif, Mian Mohammad. *A History of Muslim Philosophy: With Short Accounts of Other Disciplines and the Modern Renaissance in Muslim Lands*. Karachi, Pakistan: Royal Book Company, 1983.

Stowasser, Barbara Freyer. *Women in the Qur'an, Traditions and Interpretation*. New York: Oxford University Press, 1994.

Wadud, Amina. *Qur'an and Woman: Re-Reading the Sacred Text from a Woman's Perspective*. Oxford: Oxford University Press, 1999.

Wolff, Michael. *The Hadj: An American's Pilgrimage to Mecca*. New York: Grove Press, 1998.

5. SOCIETY AND CULTURE

Ahmed, Leila. *Women and Gender in Islam: Historical Roots of a Modern Debate*. New Haven, CT: Yale University Press, 1992.

*Ansary, Tamim. *West of Kabul, East of New York: An Afghan American Reflects on Islam and the West*. New York: Farrar Straus & Giroux, 2002.

Athar, Shahid. *Reflections of an American Muslim*. Chicago: Distributed by Kazi Publications, 1994.

Cardini, Franco. *Europe and Islam*. Oxford: Blackwell, 2000.

Göle, Nilüfa. *The Forbidden Modern: Civilization and Veiling*. Ann Arbor: University of Michigan Press, 1996.

Haddad, Yvonne Yazbeck, and John L. Esposito, eds. *Islam, Gender, and Social Change*. New York: Oxford University Press, 1997.

Khan, Shahnaz. *Muslim Women: Crafting a North American Identity*. Gainesville: University Press of Florida, 2000.

Keddie, Nikki R., and Beth Baron, eds. *Women in Middle Eastern History: Shifting Boundaries in Sex and Gender*. New Haven, CT: Yale University Press, 1991.

Lewis, Bernard, ed. *The World of Islam: Faith, People, Culture*. New York: Thames and Hudson, 1992.

*Mallon, Elias. *Neighbors: Muslims in North America*. New York: Friendship Press, 1989.

Nanji, Azim A., ed. *The Muslim Almanac: A Reference Work on the History, Faith, Culture, and Peoples of Islam*. Detroit, MI: Gale Research, 1996.

ART AND ARCHITECTURE

Blair, Sheila, and Jonathan Bloom. *The Art and Architecture of Islam, 1250-1800*. New Haven, CT: Yale University Press, 1994.

*Brend, Barbara. *Islamic Art*. Cambridge, MA: Harvard University Press, 1991.

Clévenot, Dominique. *Splendors of Islam: Architecture, Decoration and Design*. New York: Vendome Press, 2000.

Ettinghausen, Richard, and Oleg Grabar. *The Art and Architecture of Islam, 650-1250*. New York: Penguin Books, 1987.

* Appropriate for younger readers.

Fathy, Hassan. *Architecture for the Poor.* Chicago: University of Chicago, 1973.

Grube, Ernst J. *The World of Islam.* New York: McGraw-Hill, 1967.

Hillenbrand, Robert. I*slamic Art and Architecture.* London: Thames and Hudson, 1999.

Nasr, Seyyed Hossein. *Islamic Art and Spirituality.* New York: Oxford University Press, 1990.

Stierlin, Henri. *Islamic Art and Architecture: From Isfahan to the Taj Mahal.* London: Thames and Hudson, 2002.

LITERATURE

Asani, Ali Sultaan Ali. *Celebrating Muhammad: Images of the Prophet in Popular Muslim Poetry.* Columbia: University of South Carolina Press, 1995.

Burton, Sir Richard Frances. *The Arabian Nights: Tales from a Thousand and One Nights.* New York: Modern Library, 2001.

*Carrick, Carol. *Aladdin and the Wonderful Lamp.* New York: Scholastic Reprint Edition, 1992.

Gibran, Kahlil. *The Eye of the Prophet.* Berkeley, CA: Frog, 1995.

Khayyam, Omar. *Rubaiyat of Omar Khayyam.* Broomall, PA: Chelsea House Publishers, 2003.

*Nourallah, Riad. *Loving Letters: An Islamic Alphabet.* Beltsville, MD: Amana Publishers, 1996.

*Nye, Naomi Shihab. *The Space Between Our Footsteps: Poems and Paintings from the Middle East.* New York: Simon & Schuster Books for Young Readers, 1994.

Peters, F.F. *Mecca: A Literary History of the Muslim Holy Land.* Princeton, NJ: Princeton University Press, 1994.

Shackle, Christopher. *Hali's Musaddas: The Flow and Ebb of Islam.* New York: Oxford University Press, 1999.

Sperl, Stefan, and Christopher Shackle, ed. *Qasida Poetry in Islamic Asia and Africa.* New York: E.J. Brill, 1996.

SCIENCE

*Beshore, George. *Science in Early Islamic Culture.* New York: Franklin Watts, 1988.

Hassan, Ahmad Y. al-, and Donald R. Hill. *Islamic Technology: An Illustrated History.* Cambridge: Cambridge University Press, 1992.

Hoyt, Edwin. *Arab Science: Discoveries and Contributions.* New York: Nelson, 1975.

Nasr, Seyyed Hossein. *Islamic Science: An Illustrated Study.* London: World of Islam Festival Publishing Company, 1976.

Sayili, Aydin. *The Observatory in Islam.* Ankara, Turkey: Turk Tarih Kurumu Basimevi, 1960.

FILMS

Inside Islam. A & E Home Video, 2002.
Islam: A Closer Look. Tapeworm, 1995.
Islam—Empire of Faith. PBS Home Video, 2001.
Living Islam Series. BBC/Ambrose, 1993.
Pillars of Faith: Religions Around the World. Kultur Video, 1998.
The Story of Islam: A History of the Misunderstood Faith. Mpi Home Video, 1983.

6. ONLINE RESOURCES

About Islam and Muslims. http://www.unn.ac.uk/societies/islamic

Ahlul Bayt Digital Islam Library Project. http://www.al-islam.org/

The Arab-American Online Community Center. http://www.cafearabica.com/

Dictionary of Islamic Philosophical Terms. http://www.muslimphilosophy.com/pd/default.htm

Quraan.com Authentic Islamic Literature. http://www.quraan.com/

Islam & The Global Muslim eCommunity. http://www.islam.org/

Islam.com. http://www.islam.com

Islamic Assembly of North America. http://www.iananet.org

The Muslim Community Online. http://www.muslimsonline.com/

The Muslim Directory Online. http://www.ummah.net

The Muslim Student Association of the US and Canada. http://www.msa-natl.org/

The World of Islam @ nationalgeographic.com. http://magma.nationalgeographic.com/ngm/data/2002/01/01/html/ft_20020101.5.html

* Appropriate for younger readers.

Glossary

ablution ritual washing that Muslims must perform before prayer

adhan Muslim call to prayer that occurs five times daily

Allah God

Allahu akbar "God is most great," beginning of Muslim call to prayer

amir military commander, governor, or prince; **amirate** office or realm of authority of an amir

aqidah Islamic creed, which consists of the five articles of faith: belief in God, angels, prophets, scriptures, and the Last Day (or Day of Judgment)

arabesque artistic style that uses foliage, fruit, or figural outlines to produce an intricate pattern of interlaced lines

ayatollah highest-ranking legal scholar among some Shi'i Muslims

burqa traditional garment worn by some Muslim women that covers the whole body, leaving only the eyes visible

caliph religious and political leader of an Islamic state; caliphate office and government of the caliph

chador veil worn by Muslim women in public that covers the whole body except the face, hands, and feet

Crusades during the Middle Ages, the holy wars declared by the pope against non-Christians, mostly Muslims

dar al-harb "Land of War;" place where inhabitants do not practice Islam

dar al-Islam "Land of Islam;" place where Islamic law is observed

da'wah call to Islam; refers to efforts to convert people to Islam or to draw Muslim individuals and communities back to God

dawlah Arabic for "state"

dhikr Sufi chant for the remembrance of God

dhimmi non-Muslims under the protection of Muslim law; typically applied to People of the Book, particularly Christians and Jews

Dhu al-Hijjah last month of the Islamic calendar and month of pilgrimage to Mecca

Eid al-Adha Feast of the Sacrifice, celebration commemorating Abraham's willingness to sacrifice his son to God; comes at the end of the pilgrimage to Mecca

Eid al-Fitr Feast of the Breaking of the Fast of Ramadan; celebration that ends the holy month of Ramadan

fatwa opinion issued by an Islamic legal scholar in response to a question posed by an individual or a court of law

fiqh human efforts to understand and codify divine law

Five Pillars of Islam five acts required of all Muslims: pledging one's faith, praying five times daily, putting aside a portion of one's wealth for the poor, fasting during the month of Ramadan, and making a pilgrimage to the holy city of Mecca

hadith reports of the words and deeds of Muhammad (not in the Qur'an, but accepted as guides for Muslim behavior)

hajj pilgrimage to Mecca that Muslims who are physically and financially able are required to make once in their lifetime

halal permissible; acceptable under Islamic law

haram illegal; prohibited by Islamic law

harem room in a Muslim household where the women live; also, female members of a Muslim household

heresy belief that is contrary to established religious doctrine or practice

hijab refers to the traditional head, face, or body covering worn by Muslim women

Hijrah celebrated emigration of Muhammad from Mecca in 622, which marks the first year of the Islamic calendar

hudud punishments prescribed by the Qur'an for specific crimes

ijma consensus of scholars on issues of law

ijtihad use of independent reasoning, rather than precedent, to interpret Islamic law

imam spiritual-political leader in Shi'i Islam, one who is regarded as directly descended from Muhammad; also, one who leads prayers

iman in Arabic, "faith"

Glossary

insha'a Allah Arabic phrase meaning "if God wills"

intifadah Arabic word for "uprising"

jami congregational mosque used specifically for Friday prayers

jihad literally "striving"; war in defense of Islam

jinn spirit beings

jizyah tax imposed by Muslims on non-Muslims

kaffiyah head cloth worn by some Muslim men

kalam in Arabic, "speech"; refers to the field of theology

kalam Allah in Arabic, "God's speech"; refers to the Qur'an

khan honorific title used for leaders in certain Islamic societies

khutbah sermon delivered at Friday prayers

kohl black powder applied to the edge of the eyelids

Kufic angular style of Arabic calligraphy

kuttab Islamic elementary school

loya jirga tribal council in Afghanistan

madhhab school of legal thought

madrasah religious college or university; also religious school for young students

Mahdi "divinely guided" imam who Muslims believe will return to earth to restore the faith and establish a just government

marabout African term for Sufi leader

mashhad gravesite of a martyr

masjid mosque; place for Muslim communal affairs

Mawlid an-Nabi Muhammad's birthday

mihrab niche, or recess, in a mosque indicating the direction of Mecca

minaret tall, slender tower of a Muslim mosque from which the faithful are called to prayer

minbar mosque platform used for the Friday sermon

monotheism belief that there is only one God

mosque Muslim place of worship

muezzin person who calls the faithful to prayer

mufti scholar who interprets Islamic law and issues fatwas

Muharram first month of the Islamic calendar

mujahidin literally "warriors of God"; refers to Muslim fighters in proclaimed jihads, such as the war against the Soviet invasion of Afghanistan

mujtahid legal scholar who interprets law according to independent reasoning (ijtihad)

mullah Muslim cleric or learned man

musalla informal areas and open air spaces for prayer

mutah a type of marriage contract allowing temporary marriage; prohibited in Sunni Islam.

mystic one who seeks to experience spiritual enlightenment and truth through various physical and spiritual disciplines

nabi "one who announces"; Arabic term for prophet

Pan-Islamic refers to the movement to unify all Islamic peoples

People of the Book for Muslims, religious group with written scriptures, mainly Christians and Jews

polygyny practice of having more than one wife at the same time

polytheism belief in more than one god

pre-Islamic refers to the Arabian Peninsula or to the Arabic language before the founding of Islam in the early 600s

prophet one who announces divinely inspired revelations

qadi judge who administers Islamic law

qibla direction of prayer indicated by the mihrab (niche) in the wall of a mosque

qiyas type of reasoning that involves the use of analogy, or comparison based on resemblance

Qur'an book of the holy scriptures of Islam

Ramadan ninth month of the Islamic calendar and holy month during which Muslim adults fast and abstain from sex from sunrise to sunset

revelation message from God to humans transmitted through a prophet

sadaqah voluntary charitable offering of an amount beyond what is required; may enable a Muslim to atone for sins or other offenses

salat prayer; one of the five Pillars of Islam

sawm fasting; one of the five Pillars of Islam

sayyid honorific title equivalent to lord or sir; descendant of Muhammad

scripture sacred writings believed to contain revelations from God

shah king (Persian); ruler of Iran

shahadah profession of faith: "There is no God but God (Allah), and Muhammad is the messenger of God"

shahid martyr, or one who dies for his or her religious beliefs

shari'ah Islamic law as established in the Qur'an and sunnah, the exemplary behavior of the prophet Muhammad

sharif nobleman; descendant of Muhammad

shaykh tribal elder; also, title of honor given to those who are considered especially learned and pious

Shi'ism branch of Islam that believes that Muhammad chose Ali ibn Abi Talib and his descendants as the spiritual-political leaders of the Muslim community

shura consultation; advisory council to the head of state

Sufism Islamic mysticism, which seeks to develop spirituality through discipline of the mind and body

sultan political and military ruler of a Muslim dynasty or state

sunnah literally "the trodden path"; Islamic customs based on the exemplary behavior of Muhammad

Sunni refers to the largest branch of the Muslim community; the name derives from sunnah, the exemplary behavior of the prophet Muhammad

surah chapter of the Qur'an

talaq type of divorce in which a husband repeats the words "I divorce you" three times

taqiyah act of concealing one's true religious beliefs in order to prevent death or injury to oneself or other Muslims

taqwa piety, virtue, and awareness or reverence of God

tariqah path followed by Sufis to attain oneness with God; Sufi brotherhood

tawhid refers to the oneness or unity of God; monotheism

tazir punishments not required in the Qur'an but administered by an Islamic judge

ta'ziyah Shi'i religious drama about the martyrdom of Husayn ibn Ali, Muhammad's grandson

ulama religious scholars

ummah Muslim community

vizier Muslim minister of state

waqf donation of property for charitable causes

zakat charity; one of the five Pillars of Islam

zawiyah Sufi center that serves as a place of worship and a welfare institution

ziyadah in a mosque, the wall that holds the facilities for ablution, or ritual cleansing

People and Places

Abbas I (ruled 1588–1629) Shah of Safavid empire of Iran

Abbasids (750–1258) Dynasty that controlled the caliphate after the Umayyads; established capital in Baghdad in 762

Abd al-Qadir (1808–1883) Sufi poet; led uprising in Algeria against French 1832–1847

Abduh, Muhammad (1849–1905) Egyptian scholar and architect of Islamic modernism

Abraham Patriarch of Judaism, Christianity, and Islam; father of Ismail

Abu Bakr (ca. 573–634) Companion and follower of Muhammad; served as the first caliph from 632 to 634

Abu Hanifah (699–767) Legal scholar who founded the Hanafi, one of the four Sunni schools of law

Afghani, Jamal al-Din al- (1838–1897) Political activist and writer, best known for his role in the Pan-Islamic movement

Ahmad Khan, Sayyid (1817–1898) Islamic writer and reformer in British India who sought to modernize the interpretation of Islam

A'ishah (614–678) Muhammad's third and youngest wife; daughter of Abu Bakr, one of the Prophet's most important supporters

Akbar, Jalaludin Muhammad (1542–1605) Mughal emperor who expanded the realm and improved the efficiency of government

Alawi Minority Shi'i sect in Syria and Turkey

Ali ibn Abi Talib (ca. 597–661) Cousin and son-in-law of Muhammad who became the fourth caliph; conflicts over succession and Ali's assassination ultimately led to the division of Muslims into Shi'is and Sunnis

Andalusia Southernmost region of Spain controlled by Muslims from 711 to 1492

Arafat, Yasir (1929–) Founder and leader of Palestinian Liberation Organization

Ash'ari, Abu al-Hasan al- (ca. 873–935) Theologian who founded the Ash'ari school of Islamic thought

Assad, Hafiz al- (1928–2000) President of Syria from 1971 to 2000

Atatürk, Mustafa Kemal (1881–1938) Revolutionary leader and founder of modern Turkish state

Banna, Hasan al- (1906–1949) Founder of Muslim Brotherhood and Egyptian reformer

Bedouins Desert nomads, especially in North Africa, Syria, and Arabia

Beg, Toghril (died 1063) Early Seljuk leader who conquered Iran and Iraq

Berbers North-African ethnic group, primarily Muslim

Bin Laden, Osama (1957–) Islamic militant from Saudi Arabia; head of the al-Qaeda network

Byzantine Empire (330–1453) Eastern Christian Empire based in Constantinople

Caucacus Region of southern Europe between Black and Caspian Seas

Córdoba Caliphate in Muslim Spain from 756 to 1016; also important city and cultural center

Dan Fodio, Usuman (ca. 1754–1817) Founder and ruler of Sokoto caliphate in Nigeria

Druze Offshoot of Shi'i Islam, found mainly in Lebanon and Syria

Elijah Muhammad (1897–1975) Longtime leader of the Nation of Islam, militant religious group promoting the development of African American society

Farabi, Abu Nasr al- (870–950) Arab scholar, regarded as father of Islamic political science

Farrakhan, Louis (1933–) Leader of Nation of Islam, militant religious group promoting the development of African American society

Fatimah (ca. 605–633) Daughter of Muhammad and wife of Ali ibn Abi Talib

Fatimid Dynasty (909–1171) Family claiming descent from Fatimah that established caliphate that controlled North Africa; extended rule as far as Syria

Gasprinskii, Ismail Bey (1851–1914) Reformer who worked to help Turkish Muslims living under Russian rule in Crimea

Ghazali, Abu Hamid al- (1058–1111) Influential Muslim thinker who studied many areas of religion and science

People and Places

Ghazali, Zaynab al- (1917–) Founder of Muslim Women's Association

Gulf States Refers to four nations on the Persian Gulf-Bahrain, Kuwait, Qatar, and the United Arab Emirates

Hagar In Bible, wife of Abraham and mother of Ismail; revered by Muslims

Harun al-Rashid (764–809) Fifth and most famous Abbasid caliph; ruled from 786 to 809

Holy Land Refers to ancient Palestine, land containing sacred sites of Muslims, Jews, and Christians

Husayn ibn Ali (626–680) Grandson of Muhammad and third Shi'i imam; led unsuccessful revolt against caliphs and died in battle; revered as a martyr by Shi'is

Hussein, Saddam (1937–) President of Iraq from 1979 to 2003

Ibn Abd al-Wahhab, Muhammad (1703–1791) Saudi Arabian reformer who founded Wahhabi movement

Ibn al-Arabi (1165–1240) Sufi mystic and poet in Muslim Spain

Ibn Battutah (died ca. 1368) Arab who traveled widely throughout the Muslim world, including West Africa and Southeast Asia

Ibn Hanbal (died 855) Muslim jurist and theologian; founded the Hanbali school, one of the major Sunni schools of law

Ibn Khaldun (1332–1406) Scholar who wrote on society and politics in the Arab world; regarded by some as the founder of sociology

Ibn Rushd (1126–1198) Philosopher and physician in Muslim Spain, known as Averroës in West; gained recognition for his writings on Aristotle

Ibn Sina (980–1037) Philosopher and physician, known as Avicenna in West; wrote the influential *Canon of Medicine*

Ibn Taymiyah (1263–1328) Hanbali jurist and reformer who advocated *ijtihad*; still influential among Islamic reformers

Iqbal, Muhammad (1876–1938) Poet and philosopher from India who advocated the creation of a separate state for Muslims

Ismail Son of Abraham and Hagar, called Ishmael in the Bible; considered the father of the Arab nation

Jafar al-Sadiq (died ca. 756) Shi'i imam who founded the Jafari school of Islamic law

Jinnah, Mohammad Ali (1876–1948) Indian who led Muslim League at time of partition; revered as a founder of Pakistan

Kaaba Shrine in Mecca considered the most sacred place in the Muslim world

Karbala Iraqi city containing the tomb of Husayn ibn Ali; important shrine and pilgrimage site for Shi'i Muslims

Kashmir Contested territory between India and Pakistan

Khadija (565–ca. 623) Muhammad's first wife and supporter

Khayyam, Umar (1038–1131) Persian mathematician and poet

Khomeini, Ruhollah al-Musavi (1902–1989) Leader of Iran's Islamic Revolution in 1979 and the country's political and religious leader during the 1980s

Maghrib, al- coastal region of North African countries of Tunisia, Algeria, Morocco, and Libya

Malcolm X (1925–1965) Controversial African American leader, assassinated by opponents in the Nation of Islam

Malik ibn Anas (ca. 713–795) Scholar who founded the Maliki school, one of the main Sunni schools of Islamic law

Mamluk State (1250–1517) Islamic state based in Egypt, ruled by slave soldiers; controlled Syria and parts of Asia Minor and Arabia

Maryam Jameelah (1934–) American convert to Islam who became a prominent critic of Western society

Mawdudi, Sayyid Abu al-Ala (1903–1979) Founder of Jamaat-i Islami revivalist movement calling for return to traditional Islamic values

Mecca Birthplace of Muhammad and site of Kaaba; most important pilgrimage destination for Muslims

Mehmed II (1432–1461) Ottoman sultan who conquered Byzantine Constantinople in 1453

Mongols Nomadic people from Central Asia who established an empire in the early 1200s that lasted about 200 years; at its peak the empire included much of Asia, Russia, eastern Europe and Middle East

Mughal Empire (1520s–1857) Muslim empire on subcontinent of India founded by Babur; British deposed the last emperor

Moors North African Muslims who conquered Spain

Muhammad (ca. 570–632) The Prophet of Islam, viewed by Muslims as God's messenger

Mulla Sadra (1571–ca. 1640) Influential Persian philosopher

Nasser, Gamal Abdel(1918–1970) Nationalist leader who seized control of Egypt in 1952 and became its president in 1956

Ottoman Empire Large Turkish empire established in the early 1300s that eventually controlled much of the Balkans and the Middle East; disintegrated after World War I (1914–1918)

Pahlavi, Muhammad Reza Shah (1919–1980) Last monarch of Iran, overthrown by Islamic Revolution in 1979

Palestine Historic region on the eastern Mediterranean that includes modern Israel and western Jordan, as well as the city of Jerusalem

Persia name foreigners used for Iran until 1935

Qaddafi, Mu'ammar al- (1942–) Ruler of Libya since 1969

Qom Site of the tomb of Fatimah and major Shi'i pilgrimage site in Iran

Qutb, Sayyid (1906–1966) Influential thinker associated with Muslim Brotherhood; regarded by many as founder of militant Islamic politics

Rashid Rida, Muhammad (1865–1935) Syrian reformer who advocated the establishment of a modern Islamic state based on a reinterpretation of Islamic law

Rumi (died 1273) Persian religious poet; his followers founded the Sufi order known as Mawlawiyah (also known as Mevlevis and Whirling Dervishes) that incorporates dance in its rituals

Rushdie, Salman (1947–) British-Indian author who wrote The Satanic Verses (1988), considered by many Muslims to be blasphemous

Sadat, Anwar el- (1918–1981) President of Egypt 1970–1981; assassinated by Islamic extremists

Sadr, Musa al- (1928–ca. 1978) Iranian cleric who led Shi'i movement in Lebanon; disappeared in 1978

Safavid Dynasty (1501–1722) Ruled Iran and parts of present-day Iraq; converted country to Shi'ism and founded the city of Isfahan

Saladin (1137–1193) Muslim leader who defeated the Fatimids in Egypt in 1171 and founded the Ayyubid dynasty; defeated the Crusaders, ending Christian occupation of Jerusalem

Seljuks (1038–1193) Turkic dynasty that ruled Iran and Iraq and parts of Central Asia; established a sultanate in Turkey that lasted until the Mongols invaded in 1243

Shafi'i, Muhammad (767–820) Jurist who founded the Shafi'i school, one of the major Sunni schools of Islamic law

Sokoto Caliphate Islamic state in Nigeria, founded in the 1800s by Usuman Dan Fodio

Suleyman (1520–1566) Sultan during the peak of the Ottoman Empire; called the Lawgiver in the East and the Magnificent in the West

Tamerlane (Timur Lang) (1336–1405) Mongol chieftain who came to power in Iran and conquered large areas of the Islamic world, including Anatolia and parts of Syria and India

Turabi, Hasan al- (1932–) Sudanese political leader who led efforts to form an Islamic state in Sudan

Umar ibn al-Khattab (ruled 634–644) Close friend of Muhammad and the second caliph; began expansion of Islamic empire

Umayyad Dynasty (661–750) Ruled Islamic caliphate; expanded the empire westward through North Africa and into Spain

Warith Deen Muhammad (1933–) Son of Nation of Islam leader Elijah Muhammad; assumed leadership of the organization in 1975

Zaynab (627–684) Granddaughter of Muhammad and daughter of Ali and Fatimah

Photo Credits

VOLUME 1

COLOR PLATES

for *Daily Life* between pages 104 and 105:
1: Reuters NewMedia Inc./Corbis; 2: Bojan Brecelj/Corbis; 3: Paul Almasy/Corbis; 4: Michael S. Yamashita/Corbis; 5: AFP/Corbis; 6: Reuters NewMedia Inc./Corbis; 7: Lawrence Manning/Corbis; 8: Nik Wheeler/Corbis; 9: Michael S. Yamashita/Corbis; 10: AFP/Corbis; 11: Moshe Shai/Corbis; 12: AFP/Corbis; 13: Lindsay Hebberd/Corbis; 14: Harry Gruyaert/Magnum Photos; 15: Reza/Webistan/Corbis.

BLACK-AND-WHITE PHOTOGRAPHS

1: Roger Wood/Corbis; 5: Reuters NewMedia Inc./Corbis; 11: Reuters NewMedia Inc./Corbis; 20: V Riviere/Corbis Sygma; 23: Eric Wessman/Stock Boston Inc./PictureQuest; 29: Fernando Alda/Corbis; 32: Werner Forman/Art Resource, NY; 37: Peter Turnley/Corbis; 42: J. Messerschmidt/eStock Photography/PictureQuest; 47: Victoria and Albert Museum, London/Bridgeman Art Library; 57: Time Inc./Getty Images; 67: Ron Johnson/Index Stock Imagery/PictureQuest; 69: AFP/Corbis; 72: Chris Rainier/Corbis; 76: Khaled Zigari/AP Photo; 87: Christel Gerstenberg/Corbis; 91: Ric Ergenbright/Corbis; 97: British Museum, London/Bridgeman Art Library; 100: Mohammad al Sehety/AP Photo; 105: Owen Franken/Corbis; 107: Chester Beatty Library/Bridgeman Art Library; 109: Hulton-Deutsch Collection/Corbis; 119: Archives Charmet/Bridgeman Art Library; 127: Julia Waterlow; Eye Ubiquitous/Corbis; 132: Wendy Stone/Corbis; 139: Antoine Gyori/Corbis Sygma; 145: Hulton-Deutsch Collection/Corbis; 153: Jassim Mohammed/AP Photo; 156: Jacques M. Chenet/Corbis; 162: AFP/Corbis; 166: Getty Images; 171: Liba Taylor/Corbis; 188: Underwood & Underwood/Corbis; 190: Mohammad El-Dakhakhny/AP Photo.

VOLUME 2

COLOR PLATES

for *Art and Architecture* between pages 110 and 111:
1: Angelo Hornak/Corbis; 2: Musée des Arts d'Afrique et d'Oceanie, Paris/Bridgeman Art Library; 3: Bridgeman Art Library; 4: The Stapleton Collection/Bridgeman Art Library; 5: Tibor Bognar/Corbis; 6: Charles & Josette Lenars/Corbis; 7: Chris Hellier/Corbis; 8: Bridgeman Art Library; 9: Jeremy Horner/Corbis; 10: Brian A. Vikander/Corbis; 11: Fernando Alda/Corbis; 12: John and Lisa Merrill/Corbis; 13: Adam Woolfitt/Corbis; 14: Eric and David Hosking/Corbis; 15: Victoria & Albert Museum, London/Bridgeman Art Library.

BLACK-AND-WHITE PHOTOGRAPHS

1: AFP/Corbis; 5: Bettmann/Corbis; 6: Reuters NewMedia Inc./Corbis; 12: Index/Bridgeman Art Library; 23: Sergio Dorantes/Corbis; 31: Hasan Sarbakhshian/AP Photo; 35: Helen King/Corbis; 40: Lefteris Pitarakis/AP Photo; 64: Royalty-Free/Corbis; 68: Reuters NewMedia Inc./Corbis; 79: Reuters NewMedia Inc./Corbis; 85: Hulton-Deutsch Collection/Corbis; 88: AFP/Corbis; 100: Roger Wood/Corbis; 104: Lindsay Hebberd/Corbis; 106: Jim Holland/Stock Boston Inc./PictureQuest; 109: Royal Asiatic Society, London/Bridgeman Art Gallery; 116: Sergio Dorantes/Corbis; 124: Bettmann/Corbis; 127: Kate Brooks/Corbis; 130: Maher Attar/Corbis Sygma; 134: SEF/Art Resource, NY; 141: Christie's Images/Corbis; 162: Bibliotheque Nationale, Paris/Bridgeman Art Library; 167: Danny Lehman/Corbis; 174: Hulton-Deutsch Collection/Corbis; 181: Reza/Webistan/Corbis; 184: AP Photo; 196: James Nubile/Image Works/Time Life Pictures/Getty Images; 204: Nik Wheeler/Corbis.

Photo Credits

VOLUME 3

COLOR PLATES

for *Culture* between pages 110 and 111:

1: Historical Picture Archive/Corbis; **2:** Erich Lessing/Art Resource, NY; **3:** Giraudon/Bridgeman Art Library; **4:** Giraudon/Art Resource, NY; **5:** Giraudon/Art Resource, NY; **6:** Bernard Bisson/Corbis Sygma; **7:** British Library, London/Bridgeman Art Library; **8:** Daniel Laine/Corbis; **9:** Stapleton Collection/Corbis; **10:** Reuters NewMedia Inc./Corbis; **11:** Werner Forman/Art Resource, NY; **12:** Patrick Ward/Corbis; **13:** Archives Charmet/Bridgeman Art Library; **14:** Aijaz Rahi/AP Photo; **15:** AFP/Corbis.

BLACK-AND-WHITE PHOTOGRAPHS

2: Charles Crowell/Black Star Publishing/PictureQuest; **8:** Ronald Sachs/Archive Photos/PictureQuest; **18:** David Butow/Corbis Sygma; **20:** Art Resource, NY; **28:** Giraudon/Art Resource, NY; **34:** AFP/Corbis; **38:** AFP/ Corbis; **46:** Chris Rainier/Corbis; **52:** Royal Asiatic Society, London/Bridgeman Art Library; **61:** David Austen/ Stock Boston Inc./PictureQuest; **65:** Hulton-Deutsch Collection/Corbis; **75:** Bob Krist/Corbis; **82:** SEF/Art Resource, NY; **88:** AFP/Corbis; **91:** Stapleton Collection/ Bridgeman Art Library; **97:** Peter Ward/Bruce Coleman Inc./PictureQuest; **103:** Charles & Josette Lenars/Corbis; **110:** RAOUF/AP Photo; **114:** The Pierpont Morgan Library/Art Resource, NY; **123:** Los Angeles County Museum of Art/The Nasli M. Heeramaneck Collection, gift of Joan Palevsky; **129:** Christine Osbourne/Corbis; **141:** AFP/Corbis; **146:** Hulton-Deutsch Collection/Corbis; **148:** Attar Maher/Corbis Sygma; **159:** Bettman/Corbis; **163:** Nik Wheeler/Corbis; **170:** Susan Walsh/AP Photo; **176:** Yann Arthus-Bertrand/Corbis; **182:** Nik Wheeler/Corbis; **185:** Vahid Salemi/AP Photo; **190:** Bullit Marquez/AP Photo.

Index

Note: Volume numbers precede page numbers.
Boldfaced page numbers refer to main discussions of a topic.

Index

Index

Index

Index

Index

Index

Index

Index

Index